Performance
Marketing
with
Google™ Analytics

Strategies and Techniques for
Maximizing Online ROI

Performance Marketing
with
Google™ Analytics

Strategies and Techniques for Maximizing Online ROI

Sebastian Tonkin
Caleb Whitmore
Justin Cutroni

Wiley Publishing, Inc.

Performance Marketing with Google™ Analytics

Published by
Wiley Publishing, Inc.
111 River Street
Hoboken, N.J. 07030
www.wiley.com

Copyright © 2010 by Wiley Publishing.

Published by Wiley Publishing, Inc., Indianapolis, Indiana

Published simultaneously in Canada

ISBN: 978-0-470-57831-5

Manufactured in the United States of America

10 9 8 7 6 5 4 3 2 1

For general information on our other products and services or to obtain technical support, please contact our Customer Care Department within the U.S. at (800) 762-2974, outside the U.S. at (317) 572-3993 or fax (317) 572-4002.

Wiley also publishes its books in a variety of electronic formats. Some content that appears in print may not be available in electronic books.

Library of Congress Control Number: 2009943642

Credits

Acquisitions Editor
Stephanie McComb

Editorial Manager
Robyn B. Siesky

**Vice President and
Executive Group Publisher**
Richard Swadley

**Vice President and
Executive Publisher**
Barry Pruett

Business Manager
Amy Knies

Marketing Manager
Sandy Smith

Technical Editors
David A. Booth
Corey Koberg

Cover Design
Michael Trent

Copy Editor
Steven Hiatt

About the Authors

Sebastian Tonkin joined product marketing at Google in 2007, driving metrics and acquisition strategy for iGoogle before joining the Google Analytics marketing team in 2008. On the Google Analytics team, Sebastian continued to shape acquisition strategy and also served as managing editor of the official Google Analytics blog. Prior to joining Google, Sebastian led an independent Web consultancy, developing and promoting Web sites for clients in industries including insurance, consulting, manufacturing, education, and film. Sebastian graduated *summa cum laude* from the University of Pennsylvania with a B.A. in history.

Caleb Whitmore is a veteran user of Google Analytics and a frequent speaker and contributor to blogs on the subject of performance marketing. He is best known for helping clients solve business and marketing challenges using Google Analytics. Caleb is founder of Analytics Pros, a Google Analytics authorized consultancy providing specialized products, consulting, training, and support to agencies, startups, and enterprise-level clients worldwide. Prior to this, Caleb built the Search & Analytics team at POP, a leading independent interactive agency and one of the first Google Analytics authorized consultancies. Caleb lives in Seattle with his wife and children, and in his spare time enjoys skiing and fly fishing.

Justin Cutroni is a respected leader in the Web analytics industry who helps organizations integrate Google Analytics and Web analytics into their decision-making processes. Working with marketers, senior management, and IT teams, Justin helps teams develop implementation plans and processes needed to generate actionable data and business insights. Justin is also an active participant in the Web analytics community, with a strong passion for sharing knowledge and advancing the industry. Justin is the author of the popular blog Analytics Talk and frequently speaks at conferences and trade shows.

Acknowledgments

We'd like to start by thanking the Google Analytics team for making such a great product. Over the years numerous people have listened to our feedback, shared technical details, and given us support to share Google Analytics with the world. Thanks Alex, Phil, Nick, Amy, Eva, Brett, and Avinash for sharing everything you know.

Also, thank you to the community of Google Analytics authorized consultants, with whom we have had the privilege to interact, sharing ideas and knowledge, and who have built some of the fantastic tools and community additions we cover in this book.

A special thank you to Dave and Corey from Webshare for all their help in pulling together this project and to all the individuals and organizations who took the time to contribute case studies.

We'd also like to thank the great team at Wiley that helped pull this book together! Thanks to Stephanie for the guidance, support, and — most important — patience!

Contents

Part III: Controlling Costs and Planning Profits   195

Chapter 8: Maximizing Web Site Performance   197

Chapter 9: Search Engine Marketing (SEM)   227

Chapter 10: Measuring and Optimizing Display Advertising   257

Part IV: Growing Organic Search and Conversions   279

Chapter 11: Search Engine Optimization (SEO) and Google Analytics   281

Chapter 12: Social Media Marketing   319

Chapter 13: Measuring E-mail Marketing   343

Part V: Extending Google Analytics   359

Chapter 14: Tracking Offline Marketing   361

Chapter 15: Using the Data Export API, Community Additions, and Other Tools   375

Part VI: Appendixes   389

Appendix A: Other Resources   391

—

Foreword

There are many wonderful books on Web analytics. So why should you buy this one? One simple reason: It tries, really hard, to teach you how to think.

We live in a world where data is plentiful and often free. The key to real and magnificent success is not the ability to purchase a tool (Web analytics or otherwise) but rather the ability to ensure a clean implementation and bring to it a mental model that will rock this world. This book is focused, page after detailed page, on doing just that.

Among them, Justin, Sebastian, and Caleb have a thousand years of experience with Google Analytics (okay, so maybe that is a minor exaggeration, but they do have more experience than you or I will ever have!). You'll feel that experience whispering sweet wisdom to you as you read the thoroughness of the implementation instructions in Part II to ensure you get off to a flying start or the amazing ways in which you can extend Google Analytics explained in Part V. It will be a rare experience that you'll have a question that is not answered in this book.

At the end of the day, your success will come not from the tool. Instead, it will come from doing something with the data. Taking action. Taking calculated risks. Measuring success. The concepts you'll learn in Parts III and IV are really geared toward that. Helping you figure out how to best analyze data that you get from search engines or from e-mail campaigns you are running or even trade show booths you might have or — if you indulge in the last bastion of faith-based initiatives — TV. I encourage you to re-read and truly internalize, these parts of the book.

I am very very passionate about the Web, and a large part of that passion is sourced from the fact that the Web, and everything action we take on the Web, is measurable. But what I love beyond belief is the fact that the Web makes it easier for me to fail faster. I can try new things (never done video ads? why not? never tried a dancing baby on the home page? why not?), I can do that at a low cost and, if I fail miserably, I can discover that quickly and move on. Amazingly, this strategy of failing faster empowers me to discover new strategies and become better at a pace that is almost unreal.

That is the real power of being good at this data thing. Failing faster.

One last thought: The problem is no longer budget; there are many affordable options now. The problem is no longer access to tools; regardless of your size, you have access to world-class tools. The problem is the will to get good.

With this book you have demonstrated that the will exists. The rest is going to be easy. I wish you all the very best.

—*Avinash Kaushik, author,* Web Analytics 2.0

Introduction

> *"Everybody gets so much information all day long that they lose their common sense."*
>
> —Gertrude Stein

The Web has done a remarkable job connecting users with a staggering amount of raw information. In many ways, it's done the same thing for marketers. The problem is there's now so much data out there that it is becoming harder and harder for businesses and consumers alike to sort out what's important from what's not.

This book provides strategies and techniques for getting past data overload to extract real business value from Google Analytics. Instead of being written from the perspective of a Web developer trying to collect more or different types of data, it's written from the perspective of a marketer trying to make sense of the data that's there. If you're trying to build a better Web site, maximize ROI on your advertising spend, drive repeat purchases, and get your message out to the world as efficiently as possible, this book has been written with you in mind. If you have ever glanced at your Google Analytics reports and wondered how to make them more useful and actionable, this is the book for you.

Staying competitive in online space demands an entirely new approach to marketing, one that puts empirical data about customer behavior at the center of strategy and decision-making.

We call this *performance marketing* — a philosophy of continuous improvement that challenges marketers to prove their contribution, to experiment with new approaches using testing and optimization, and to listen to what customers are saying through each click, pageview, and point of interaction. This book is about just that: performance marketing with Google Analytics.

Why You Should Read This Book

The Web is changing the competitive landscape for businesses across-the-board. It is the most measurable marketing channel ever created, meaning that online marketers who want to stay competitive must learn to work with data and online feedback on a daily basis. Mastering Google Analytics can be a bit like learning a foreign language at first, but once you've aligned your analysis with your marketing activities and your business objectives, you will begin to see your business and your customers in a completely different light. Our goal is to help you succeed in that journey without adding to the problem of data overload or drowning you in technical jargon. We want to see every reader of this book gain confidence and credibility as an analyst and have fun in the process.

Reading through to the conclusion of this book will help you do the following:

- Adopt an analytical, ROI-focused mindset to marketing.
- Build a strong team to support Google Analytics inside your organization.
- Understand key ingredients in a data-driven culture.
- Combine voice-of-the-customer and competitive research with Google Analytics to give you a complete picture of online performance.
- Maximize the efficiency and effectiveness of your Web site and online marketing efforts.
- Create customer loyalty through efficient online experiences.
- Learn to harness a cycle of continuous improvement to outstrip competitors.
- Uncover new opportunities to succeed online.

What's in This Book

This book is divided into five parts. We've also included lots of additional detail on the companion Web site for the book, www.analyticsformarketers.com.

- **Part I: Competing for Customers on the Web.** Understand the effect the Web is having on marketing and business and master basic strategies for effective online marketing. Learn how to combine qualitative and competitive research with Google Analytics to understand customers and online performance. Explore what it means to create a data-driven culture, how to structure your organization to make use of Google Analytics, and how other organizations have overcome data overload to meet and exceed their online business goals.
- **Part II: Google Analytics Essentials.** See how Google Analytics collects data, how to configure and validate your Google Analytics installation, and how to add additional capabilities to Google Analytics to allow you to track e-commerce transactions, inbound marketing, and complex visitor actions. Learn the terminology and best practices you need to communicate tracking requirements to your developer or Web team for implementation and keep your Google Analytics data accurate and accessible to key decision makers. Master basic and advanced features of the Google Analytics interface from the Date Selector tool to advanced segments and custom reports.
- **Part III: Increasing ROI on Online Advertising.** Get a 360-degree view of your Web site's performance and learn to put your insights into practice with Web site testing and conversion optimization. Use multidimensional analysis and advanced research techniques to maximize ROI on your search, rich media, and display advertising budgets. Identify common online advertising pitfalls and how to avoid them.
- **Part IV: Growing Organic Traffic and Conversions:** Understand how your SEO, e-mail, and social media campaigns are performing and what you can do to improve them. Define reliable conventions you can use to easily track different marketing activities. Learn to track down and make sense of online conversations about your brand or products and how to stay one step ahead of competitors online.

- **Part V: Extending Google Analytics.** Bridge the gap between online and offline marketing using simple techniques such as vanity URLs and prebuilt integrations for phone tracking and CRM integration. Understand the capabilities for integrating Google Analytics data with customer records or financial data using the Google Analytics API.

How to Use This Book

We present lots of foundational concepts in the first half of the book, so we strongly recommend reading through at least Chapter 5 before jumping to Parts III and IV. If you are not a Web developer, we strongly recommend teaming up with one to tackle the steps laid out in Part II. It is important to build confidence in your Google Analytics data before reporting on findings, and this starts with a sound implementation.

In many cases, we introduce concepts that we can't hope to cover in full detail. In these instances, we've done our best to refer you to quality resources. We also invite you to join the conversation on the companion site `www.analyticsformarketers.com` if you have questions or concerns. Our hope is to respond to every comment or question that doesn't get an answer from another user, so drop us a line! We'd love to hear your feedback.

A note on conventions used in this book: This is not a hands-on guide to going through Google Analytics' menus and other options, so you won't see a lot of computer instruction. But there are some conventions relating to Google Analytics "driving" that you should note:

- We use `code font` to indicate code, settings, URLs, and other literal text that you would enter in Google Analytics, a Web browser, or another application.
- We capitalize as if they were proper names labels in Google Analytics, whether for report names, pop-up menu options, check boxes, or field names. Some of these labels are also used as generic terms; in these cases, we show them in lowercase like any generic term. You'll know we mean a specific element if we treat it as a proper name by capitalizing it.
- If we instruct you to choose a menu option, you'll see the ▶ symbol used between steps. For example, Edit ▶ Paste means to click the Edit menu and then click the Paste option in its drop-down or pop-up menu.

That's it! As we've said, this book is about how to use Google Analytics as part of your performance marketing strategy, so you'll mainly see explanatory text in plain English.

—

Competing for Customers on the Web

Swimming in the Digital Sea

The Web is a powerful platform. Consumers can now seek advice from other consumers, search, sort, and filter product options, find the lowest prices, and navigate past sales and marketing hype. The Web is therefore unfamiliar territory for marketers trying to understand customer behavior. It was easier to interact with customers in a store environment than on the Web where it's harder to measure customer satisfaction. How do you know if you're satisfying customers when you don't see or talk to them? What does it mean when someone comes to your Web site and leaves in 20 seconds?

This chapter addresses the basic realities that define the competitive landscape on the Web, where attributes such as transparency, clarity, and ease of use can drive more sales than a prized location or an elaborate pitch. We also explore seven principles of effective online marketing, including the importance of using empirical observation to drive your online strategy and decisions.

This chapter explains why it's worth going through the time and effort to make your online marketing measurable and accountable with Google Analytics. If you don't take this necessary step, your competitors will.

Understanding the Impact of Data Democracy

In 1983, a young college administrator left her comfortable life in the city and moved to a tiny university town in upstate New York.

Unfortunately, she would be far from any decent place to shop, the closest being a rundown department store near the Canadian border. Cringing at the thought that she might never escape the monotony of Foxy Roxy's diner and the Super Duper grocery, she decided it was time to buy a car. At least that way she could visit Ottawa or Albany from time to time if small-town life got too tough.

With a reputation for hard dealings on the New England crafts fair circuit, she was no sucker when it came to comparison shopping. She always knew how to hunt for deals at outlets, time trips to the store to catch the best sales, trade intel with friends, and blend inexpensive purchases with expensive ones to create an overall image of taste and sophistication. She's never loved cars, though, and dreaded the thought of visiting a dealership, being condescended to for being a woman (it was 1983), and listening to a sleazy sales pitch. Her one experience with car buying had been easy because that little blue lemon she chose was the only secondhand car for sale.

She started her research by telephone. She called a contact in the new town to ask what kind of cars people drove. The lady replied that only a Chrysler would do, since there were no other dealers in the area. This turned out to be false, but without other contacts or the Internet, there was no way to check. Upon her arrival, she found the Chrysler dealer in the phone book. It looked to be the only dealership accessible by public transportation (also false). At the dealership, she was greeted by a friendly salesman with an aggressive 1980s power suit and a serious comb-over. He successfully hid the fact that 1983 was one of the "wilderness years" for Chrysler, with serious quality issues plaguing most models. He even more skillfully disguised serious defects in his recommended car choice, particularly the fact that it was not designed for cold weather and had a tendency to lose mufflers. After haggling for a price and driving off with a strong feeling she'd been ripped off, she drove off and did her best to forget the whole experience. As she recalls, none of the resources she used regularly, including *Consumer Reports* and her immediate friends, had anything to say about this car model. For this reason, she had a hard time negotiating with the dealer. Sure enough, over the next five years the paint on the hatchback began to chip, the heating system failed, and the car famously shed three mufflers.

Fast-forward to 2009: When she made her most recent car purchase, her experience couldn't have been more different. She used Google Maps to track down more than 20 dealerships within easy driving distance. Before making the trek to the dealer, she visited the Web site of each major brand to find models that caught her eye, zeroing in on a Toyota Prius. On Cars.com, she compared the Prius with a half-dozen other models based on resale value, safety ratings, and detailed feature analysis. On the J.D. Power site, she read expert reviews alongside direct feedback from verified owners. She even used Autotrader.com to find dozens of dealers in the area, and tons more options for a used model.

By combining this exhaustive search with casual conversations with friends, she was able to walk into a dealership knowing almost exactly what she wanted and what a good price would be. When she encountered dealers who bent the truth, she simply raised an eyebrow and stared them into submission. She can't imagine making a big purchase without such information any more.

The Internet has made it possible to research facts, stats, personal reviews, and expert analysis. You can build your own car model online and see what it will cost; you can check buyer satisfaction rates and repair histories. Your friends can recommend dealers and you can check their Web sites, and then see whether they're halfway-decent salespeople. They can't lie about their product because you can pull out your laptop and say, "Not so fast!"

In the end, she settled on a Lexus IS, whose performance has been near perfect except for some annoying bugs brought on by overzealous use of technology (the dark side of rapid change).

Looking at this simple anecdote, it is clear the Internet is influencing more and more stages of the buying process, empowering customers with tools for comparison shopping, confidence about price, flexibility about who to buy from, peer reviews, and options for circumventing marketers.

This story is meant to show two things. First, the Web has empowered shoppers and brought about profound consequences for anyone selling an idea, a product, or a service online *or* offline. Second, if you have a marketing role, you need to take concrete steps to acknowledge the new climate and market accordingly, or your organization is going to get left behind.

Our goal in this book is to show you which concrete steps you need to take, what realities about the online environment you need to aware of, and how to define an online strategy based on performance, not hype.

Having helped scores of businesses — from Google to Morgan Stanley to the NHL — attract and retain customers and advertisers online, we believe that adopting this empirical mindset to online marketing is the *most important first step* you can take in defining a successful online strategy. The Web is perfectly suited to a methodology of continuous improvement and iteration. The key to making the process work for your organization is to guide your efforts based on direct feedback from your customers and well-defined measures of business value, both of which are modern-day hallmarks of Web analytics.

Recognizing Customer Empowerment and Why It Matters

In case you're not convinced of the impact the Web is having on business, here are some stats. According to ComScore, 1.4 billion Internet users spent more than 300 billion hours online in 2009, forking over hundreds of billions of dollars in e-commerce in the process. A recent report by Forrester Research showed that Americans now spend as much time online each week as they spend watching TV. Apple recently sold its 250 millionth iPod, and almost 20 percent of the U.S. population can now connect to the Web wherever using a smartphone.

The pace of technological change that created these statistics is unprecedented since ... well ... ever. In a little over a decade, we've gone from dial-up Internet and America Online to premium on-demand television, social networks with hundreds of millions of users, massive virtual worlds, and hundreds of thousands of mobile apps from mortgage calculators to Find the Nearest Starbucks. You can take a room full of vinyl records with you on a device that fits in your pocket. You can have the newspaper delivered to you over a cellular network. No matter how you look at it, the Internet revolution is a pretty big deal.

As fun as it is to marvel at all this change, however, there's writing on the wall when it comes to the impact the Web is having on businesses. For example, if you're a stockbroker, you may find it harder and harder to explain why clients should pay you instead of trading themselves. If you're a retailer, you may wonder when customers got so savvy about discounting. Most dramatically, if you're a professional journalist, you may be out of work entirely. This may not seem relevant just yet, but the disruptive forces making waves in media, publishing, and a host of other areas may be coming to your industry next. So how do you prepare yourself?

A good starting place is to break down the impact of the Web into meaningful pieces. In all the hype surrounding the Web, marketers often overlook basic realities about Internet surfers. Here are a few realities we believe are relevant to Google Analytics.

Reality 1: Users lead, businesses follow

It's important to note that unlike TV, print, and radio, the Web is a self-service medium. Instead of following a linear broadcast model where one source broadcasts to many individuals, the Web is decentralized, with lots of asynchronous conversations going on among many individual contributors.

Web surfers take full control over what they look at, when they look at it, and how they want to voice their opinions. On the Web, surfers are in charge. Google has turned the idea of putting the user first into a mantra that can be heard everywhere in the company, from discussions over where to place ads to policy debates over censorship in China. Google was one of the first companies to realize that Web surfers don't like to be pushed around. Online, it's just too easy for them to find alternatives.

In this environment, the challenge for the marketer goes from serving customers directly to serving them indirectly by refining the content you offer and the choice of online channels you use to deliver it. Companies can still chat with users or respond via e-mail, but potential buyers can't be interrupted or herded the way they can be in a physical store or through TV ads.

Moving messaging and customer-facing business processes online is almost like converting a team of friendly, personable bank tellers into ATMs. How do you keep customers loyal and happy without relying on personal interactions? How do you make them love your brand if half their interactions with your content happen on a lifeless computer screen?

It turns out there's lots you can do, but no matter what you do, you must accept that online visitors are *unbelievably flighty and impatient*. They demand intuitive, fast-loading, efficient Web experiences above all else. If your Web site doesn't comply, it will drive customers away and damage your brand. Think of the disastrous trend of Flash introductions that slowed down Web surfers on the entrance to every Web site.

In some ways, the trend toward self-service is a double-whammy for marketers. Just as the Web demands that marketers pay extra attention to usability, it also forces them to learn a whole new set of techniques for understanding what works and what doesn't. These demands can be tough — but then again, nobody said becoming an online marketing superstar was going to be easy!

Reality 2: The almighty algorithm decides

On the Web, there's so much information that the only way searchers can sort out what's relevant and important is to use computers or crowd-sourcing, usually in the form of a fancy equation called an algorithm.

The most famous algorithm is the one that powers Google's search results. It makes or breaks businesses every day by determining which Web sites are the most authoritative and relevant for a given search term. Another powerful relevancy engine is the voting system powering social bookmarking sites such as Digg and Reddit, where users vote to surface the most valuable and interesting content.

In this dynamic environment, a brand's position at the top of the heap is never secure. It's not possible to get a 100-year lease to stay at the top of search rankings the way it is with a real-world location.

The engineers refining these algorithms are constantly seeking better performance according to well-defined performance measures. This means that back-scratching and expensive dinners can't keep a brand visible, either. If customers decide to start trashing a business, word can spread incredibly quickly, turning up on the first page of search results when users search for that brand. This is akin to installing a giant billboard advertising a company's failings right outside the front door. Your online presence demands supreme vigilance.

Reality 3: No product is safe from comparison shopping

Before the Web, if you wanted to buy a pair of sneakers, you could either drive to a store or request a catalog and page through images and descriptions designed explicitly to get you to buy. With several

---

FIGURE 1.1

Google's search results for the keyword "sneakers."

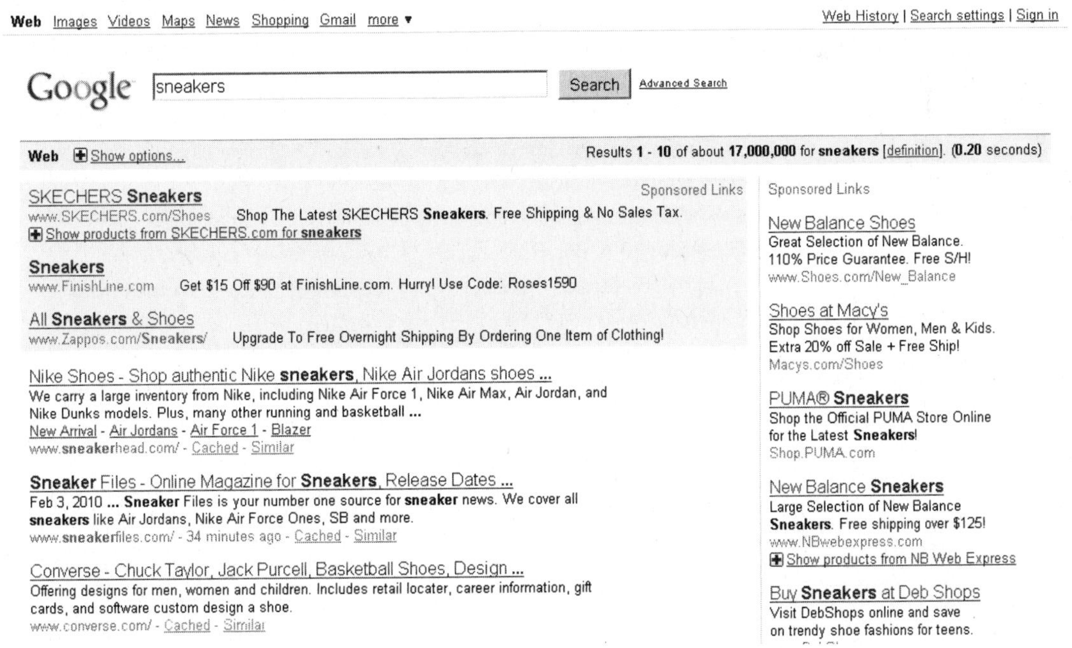

hours of effort, you might be able to uncover a few hundred options to choose from. These days, you can access 17 million search results on Google in a few seconds, as shown in Figure 1.1.

Navigating from Google to Zappos, one of the many online retailers, you can immediately browse a catalog of 1,214 brands, 129,829 styles, and 3,549,906 products. You can filter the results to show only gray sneakers by New Balance under $80 with free shipping.

By searching, filtering, sorting, and comparing side by side, Web surfers can conduct organized analysis with a fraction of the hassle involved with paper and pencil. We've already seen this trend at work with the earlier example of buying a car. In the past, marketers could count on customers not checking out the competition, but those days are numbered, particularly for big ticket items.

Reality 4: Web surfers listen to one another first and marketers second

A hotel owner in Belize traced over half his business directly back to the positive reviews his hotel had received on TripAdvisor, a social networking site that allows travelers to share their travel experience. When a disgruntled couple saw a monkey in a cage that looked inhumane by their standards, they railed against the hotel online and crippled bookings almost overnight.

The Web is littered with stories of how small PR gaffes can grow into social media firestorms and appear on the top 10 search results of a brand name. These comments can never be erased from the Web. From a marketing perspective, it is imperative to ensure that customer expectations match closely with what's delivered. If not, it can lead to an army of detractors trashing your product or service at every turn.

For many years sales people counted on having a leg up on their customers when it came to providing information. This *information advantage* was a big part of sales strategy. By attending conferences, talking with clients, reading trade publications, and so on, marketers and salespeople were able to provide their customers with information that wasn't available elsewhere. They knew what their competitors were charging. They knew where the holes were in their offerings and how to cover them up. They knew which critics to impress in order to get the best review.

The democratization of information on the Web is eroding this advantage and pushing businesses to look for new ways to get a leg up. Just as the Web is making it more important to set customer expectations, it's making it equally important to create a value proposition that will resonate with customers without the exaggerated claims that often dominate traditional media.

Reality 5: Online competitors spring up at a moment's notice

If you ran a flower store a decade ago, you might have competed with the supermarket and other small shops nearby. The same store today competes with hundreds of Web sites located across the country. Even after you've caught a customer's attention, he may use the Web to find a better price elsewhere, particularly since the comparison tools get more and more sophisticated every year. The barriers to entry for online merchants are incredibly low compared to opening a brick-and-mortar store. The Web has had the effect of enlarging the competitive set in all types of industries, from banking to video games. Depending on your industry, this trend can be the most disturbing, because it means you'll need to step up efforts across the board to stay competitive.

Building an Online Strategy Based on Evidence instead of Hype

Looking across the trends identified in the previous section, it's clear that most of them boil down to a common theme of *customer empowerment*. In other words, the Web's primary effect on commerce has been to present consumers with more choices, information, leverage, and tools they can use to seize control of their buying process.

This empowerment raises pressure on businesses to evolve or to be stamped out forever by negative customer reviews, poor visibility in search engines, and poor conversion rates. That said, it's more important than ever to dedicate your efforts to satisfying customers online.

Here's the silver lining: It turns out that just as the Web has given consumers access to a wealth of new information about businesses, it has also given businesses a wealth of new information about consumers. We're talking about a quantity of data that could wrap around the sun. What could it be but *Web analytics*?

Web analytics involve closely monitoring and measuring visitor behavior, customer feedback, desired outcomes, and competitive context in order to make smarter decisions about your online strategy. Google Analytics is just one Web analytics tool, but it's an important one. It can form the backbone of your online measurement strategy and serve as the most important means for understanding your Web site's performance.

The argument for Web analytics follows a common vein in business thought dating back to Henry Ford (if not further) that states that businesses must exist in a state of continuous improvement, never ceasing to innovate and improve processes and performance. This is the same philosophy advocated by management gurus such as Peter Drucker, J.M. Juran, Peter Crosby, and Tom Peters. In the words of W. Edwards Deming, one of the fathers of modern efficiency theory and a primary contributor to the postwar Japanese industrial revival, businesses must "improve constantly and forever the system of production and service, to improve quality and productivity, and thus constantly decrease costs."

Web analytics are tools and methods you can use to measure quality and productivity online, thus allowing you to put Deming's philosophy of continuous improvement into practice to increase the impact and ROI of your marketing efforts. Web analytics is based on quantitative measures of real-world behavior, making it one of the most effective tools for guiding strategy ever devised.

John Wanamaker, an entrepreneur from Philadelphia who built a department store empire in the late 19th and early 20th centuries, remarked, "Half the money I spend on advertising is wasted; the trouble is I don't know which half." This quote embodies the core of what has changed in marketing over recent years as a result of Web analytics: You no longer need to wonder which half of your marketing is working and which isn't.

As more and more customer interactions happen online, businesses have the opportunity to gather more and more quantitative information about customer behavior. Each click, each pageview, each point of interaction becomes a point of feedback. When combined with qualitative information taken from surveys and online conversations, as well as new forms of competitive data, everyone from Macy's to Murray's Dry Cleaners suddenly has access to a staggering wealth of information about their customers and their markets.

Our basic argument is that companies that invest in the people and tools needed to draw insights from this data and apply those insights to daily operations will gain a sustainable competitive advantage over companies that do not.

It's important to note that in Wanamaker's day, everyone wasted 50 percent of their advertising, so the playing field was more or less equal. Today, even if you are not taking an empirical approach to marketing, there's a good chance your competitors are. Merchants competing for the most valuable search terms are already involved in a constant race to extract as much value as possible from their search advertising spend.

As frightening as it might sound, this type of data-driven advertising strategy is growing faster than any other segment in advertising.

Moreover, if your company is not creating satisfied customers online, it will be harder and harder to get found in the first place. Google already measures how many searchers return immediately from a Web site's landing pages in order to weed out poor-performing sites. Social media platforms require participants to vote up content in order for it to gain visibility.

To get found online, it's important not to ignore the specific actions that influence ranking in these dynamic systems. On the other hand, no brand can escape the long-term imperative the Web has created to refine your positioning, your products, your checkout process, your advertising, and the rest of your marketing to *actually become the best*.

Even though around 75 percent of the U.S. population is now online and spends more than $225 billion annually on online retail products, consider also that 25 percent of the population is still not online and more than $3.7 trillion in consumer spending still happens in the brick-and-mortar environment. The potential the Web has to revolutionize marketing and commerce has barely begun to materialize.

Seven Basic Principles of Effective Online Marketing

We hope we've convinced you of the real value in Web analytics if you haven't been convinced already. There's been an interesting trend in the analytics space for the last few years: Companies have begun talking about the value of measurement, but only a tiny percent of companies have actually executed on this belief. Why?

Becoming truly data-driven takes an investment in time, expertise, and technology. It also takes an attitude adjustment both at the individual and the organizational levels. These facts explain why most businesses have not yet executed on measurements-based analytics.

On the other hand, many organizations have successfully navigated this transition. We've developed seven principles that all companies should master to stay competitive and satisfy customers online. Our hope is that you will see areas where your organization is strong, and find areas where you can improve as you embark down the road of continuous improvement through Web analytics.

Principle 1: Be real about putting customers first

Focusing on the customer is one of the biggest clichés in business. Everyone claims they're doing it, but few really are.

Putting yourself in your customers' shoes in an authentic way is hard. Dan and Chip Heath do a particularly good job illustrating this difficulty in their book *Made to Stick* with an idea they call the Curse of Knowledge, stating, "When we know something, it becomes hard for us to imagine not knowing it. As a result, we become lousy communicators. Think of a lawyer who can't give you a straight, comprehensible answer to a legal question. His vast knowledge and experience renders him unable to fathom how little you know." The Heath brothers offer another great example of the Curse of Knowledge: Sit down with someone and tap out a simple tune on a tabletop. Ask the person to guess the name of the song you're tapping. The tune will seem painfully obvious to you, but the person listening will likely have no clue what the song is. To you, the tune seems obvious, because you have information the listener doesn't have. Recognizing this discrepancy and making the effort to get beyond your own assumptions is what we mean by developing a real understanding of your customers.

There are several ways to focus on your customers. In the past, you might have spent time with actual customers in a retail branch, conducted a focus group, mailed a survey, or paid for a research report. Today, you still need to do many of these things, but increasingly you can build your understanding of customers more efficiently by collecting and analyzing feedback online.

List the data sources you regularly consult to understand your customers and your market — whether it be face-to-face meetings, e-mail correspondence, or reports such as those generated by Google Analytics. Think about the content of these interactions. What things seem obvious to you about your customers? Have you ever validated these assumptions? What questions have you struggled with? You may be surprised by what you find, particularly if you're a manager and you realize you haven't actually talked to a customer in months.

Take ownership of customer understanding and make it part of your daily routine to get inside the minds of users.

Don't settle for "best practices" and secondhand knowledge. Be curious. In the next chapter, we explore the tools you have at your disposal for understanding customers online; in Chapter 3, we describe the organizational steps you can take to integrate your findings into everyday business decisions. For a marketer, there are few things more integral to success than customer understanding. We'll come back to this point again and again as we explore the ins and outs of Google Analytics.

Principle 2: Know your desired outcomes

With analytical marketing, everything ultimately comes back to value — whether that value is profit or another measure that relates to the fiscal reality of your organization. For a nonprofit organization, "value" may simply be engaging with a particular community of users. A for-profit corporation may have fiscal profits and social responsibility as its bottom lines.

Whatever shape it takes, value rules. Defining value provides a reference point for everything. Just like a compass in the backcountry, a defined business goal becomes the bearing by which you can judge when you're getting lost in data or staying on the right track.

For example, Google Analytics contains an unbelievable quantity of information. It is easy to look at all this information and not know to what to do with it.

The trick is to stay focused on your business objectives by asking questions about your data that tie back to specific business goals. Instead of asking how many visitors your Web site had yesterday, ask how many leads it generated for your sales team. Instead of asking how many visitors arrive at your site through search engines, ask how much revenue those visitors generated.

If you're wondering whether your research question is a good one, put it through the "why" test. Keep asking why you want to know something until you get back to a specific bottom-line business objective, such as revenue, cost-savings, or customer satisfaction. If you don't lose sight of these bottom-line objectives, you'll avoid the analysis paralysis that has so many companies stuck.

One final word: If you haven't defined a coherent online strategy with measurable objectives yet, make that your first priority. You can't do analytical marketing without business objectives. It's like trying to optimize the postal system when you don't know how to send a letter. For more tips on goal-setting, read Chapter 3.

Principle 3: Keep it simple

The Web provides users with an unprecedented amount of choice and information. At the same time, because there's so much information available online, users need to be careful how they spend their mental energy. If they give too much attention to any one source without being sure they're going to get what they came for, they risk failing in their search.

Smart companies have learned to thrive online by keeping functionality, design, and content straightforward and fast-loading.

Keep content easy to scan, use visuals, and avoid jargon and self-promotion. Be as open and direct as possible and focus on a two-way relationship with your customers rather than bluntly telling them what to think. We provide more specific recommendations for doing this in Chapter 8.

Principle 4: Embrace change

We explained earlier in this chapter how you can use a basic cycle of continuous improvement to increase the impact of your online marketing.

A key point, however, is that innovating and experimenting means that sometimes you will fail. To excel at Web analytics, you need to expect failures and setbacks and thus create an environment that makes setbacks okay. If you work inside a rigid culture, failure can be extremely difficult at first. Your company may refuse to compromise on style guides. Your company may have committees that need to sign off on changes, or a boss who always likes to play it safe.

The bottom line is that *the Web rewards experimentation in a way the offline world does not.* Instant feedback on the results of a change, the ability to easily provide different experiences to different customers, and the ability to roll back changes at a moment's notice are all game-changers.

Figure 1.2 summarizes the basic cycle of experimentation you can harness to improve the customer experience and pull ahead of your competition online.

Instead of trying to hit a home run with every campaign, you'll get better results in the online world by launching quickly and making incremental improvements until you've reach that big audacious goal.

Principle 5: Treat data as a strategic asset

The Web can provide a wealth of data on visitor behavior. This data is a valuable tool for understanding customers, but it takes work to realize its value. Companies need to invest not only in a strong foundation for measurement, but also in the expertise and organizational elements needed to analyze data and socialize findings. In Chapter 3, we present a framework called GETUP to help you focus your effort. GETUP is a mnemonic for five areas you'll need to address as part of your measurement strategy:

- **Goals and strategy**: You can't do analytical marketing without measurable business goals. If you don't have goals in place, start here.
- **Expertise**: Tools alone will not do Web analytics for you. You need smart people and time. You also need an analytics champion and a permanent home for analytics in your organization.

FIGURE 1.2

The basic cycle of continuous improvement through analytics

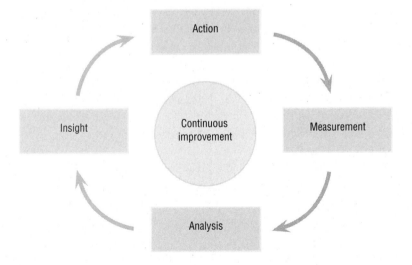

- **Tools**: Installing and validating Google Analytics is a great start but you need to make sure Google Analytics is installed and configured appropriately for your business.
- **Unified data**: Web analytics alone isn't enough to realize data as a strategic asset. You also need qualitative and competitive data. No matter what tools you have available, it's crucial that you integrate data sources to answer complex questions and maintain integrity in the information you collect and share.
- **Process integration**: Integration is where the rubber meets the road. Web analytics is a means to understanding your customers and providing a more efficient online experience. But you will only begin to realize value from analytics data when it is applied to actual decisions.

It is a mistake when companies focus only on tools and forget the other four areas. True analytical marketing pervades every area of practice, from the broadest strategic questions to the most mundane tactical issues.

Principle 6: Use the right tool for the right job

We want you to get the most value possible from your Google Analytics data, but at the same time, we want to make sure you understand the other options available. Most important, Google Analytics is geared toward *quantitative* data about visitors on your Web site. There are specialized tools to obtain *qualitative* insight into your visitors' intentions and satisfaction, as well as tools that can give you quantitative metrics about your market and competitors. These tools provide context on your performance while helping you understand why your data looks as it does. Without competitive and qualitative data, it's extremely difficult to make heads or tails of your analytics.

In Chapter 2, we present frameworks you can use to understand the array of options as well as specific recommendations on tools you can use.

Principle 7: Expect and accept accountability

With this new world of measurement comes an opportunity to drive change, to optimize through making constant advances. The catalyst to making change, to taking action in marketing, can best be summed up by the word accountability. Accountability in marketing can be defined simply as "using data to prove the value of marketing rather than relying on subjectivities alone."

Businesses must hold marketers more accountable, and do so in real or near real time. Other fields readily accept accountability, and are even dependent on it — think finance or manufacturing, for example — and so must marketing. Why *must*? Because companies that make marketing accountable will grow stronger, gaining an advantage over companies who don't, leaving simple market theory to do the rest.

Accountability shouldn't become a dark shadow following you around the office (take note, directors, VPs, and CEOs) but rather a means by which you can identify success and failure and learn from what went well and what went badly.

—

Data-Driven Marketing Basics

This chapter presents a framework you can use to organize marketing into logical categories called channels and orient your activities toward measurable conversion goals. It also explores the concepts and methods behind voice-of-the-customer and competitive research, two complementary areas of analysis required to get the most from your Google Analytics data. The goal of this chapter is get you in the mindset of an analytical marketer and help you understand the immediate steps you can take to get a handle on your organization's online performance.

Making Online Marketing Measurable and Goal-Driven

In the early days of the Web, an army of Web designers convinced businesses to build an "online presence." This design usually involved converting the company brochure into a Web page. Text was often long and difficult to scan (since it had been created for print media), stock photography was everywhere, navigation was confusing, and most sites included little interactivity beyond a contact form. The worst offenders even put 90-second Flash introductions on their home pages. Once a Web site was published, the design sat idle instead of being continuously improved. This was the world of Web 1.0.

The Web 1.0 approach worked well to get businesses online quickly, but it failed in fundamental ways. Most important, it considered the Web site in isolation, when in fact a Web site represents a tiny node in a system of over *1 trillion* pages that exist on the Web today. An individual user session crosses dozens or hundreds of pages, flowing in and out of different domains, and sometimes from one language to another or from a laptop to a mobile phone. The complexity of these sessions is beautiful in its own way and amazing when you think about it: so many users flowing over so much information at such a rate.

Your Web presence as a living, breathing system

However, to escape the Web 1.0 mindset, it's important to acknowledge that your online presence *doesn't* exist in isolation. It's part of a system of information your visitors use each time they open a browser. It's also a key part of the financial and operational systems of your business (or at least it has that potential). By viewing your online marketing efforts as a *system for advancing your business goals* instead of as a series of isolated pages filled with text, you will adopt the analytical mindset you need to benefit from Web analytics.

Committing to measurable marketing demands is a shift in mindset from the free-flowing, soft cliché of traditional marketing. Doing so allows you to take the emphasis off fuzzy factors and place it on desired outcomes, accountability, and overall business value. *This doesn't mean you need to stop being creative!* Even as you deploy compelling, emotionally driven collateral and brilliant messaging to attract customers, you're doing so with an eye toward results and clarity of vision that's never before been available to marketers.

Figure 2.1 shows the major components of a typical online marketing system.

You can use Web analytics to address strategic questions such as where to allocate budget and where to hire more skilled team members. You can also analyze what's going on inside each area of your system at a tactical level. The technology behind Google Analytics is so precise that, for example, you can use it to analyze how a specific ad creative performs on a specific Web site in a specific city. This incredible granularity is one of the reasons many businesses are overwhelmed by the data they see in Google Analytics.

The left column of Figure 2.1 shows marketing activity you can use to drive traffic into your site. We refer to these categories as *inbound marketing channels*, *acquisition channels,* or simply *channels*. At the center of the system is your Web site, which in most cases is a brand's online presence.

The right side of the illustration shows the two most important processes for analytical marketing: the *conversion process* (a.k.a. the *checkout process*, *lead-generation process*, and *transaction process*) and the *post-sales process* (that is, the activities you undertake to maximize repeat business and lifetime value*)*.

We call the virtuous cycle of acquiring new customers and converting them to repeat buyers the *customer ecosystem*. Strengthening this ecosystem by raising the percentage of repeat buyers, increasing the percentage of Web site visitors that buy, and shortening the time between purchases is a key value proposition of Google Analytics.

At this stage, you may wonder how this systemic view applies if your organization doesn't sell products. No matter what your goal — whether raising awareness of a social issue, providing basic information to stakeholders, or just sharing your thoughts with the world — you can apply this view. Maybe you just want people to spend a couple of minutes on your site each time they visit. If so, that's okay. You can use Google Analytics to help understand how well you're succeeding, and what to focus on to do even better.

FIGURE 2.1

The major components of an online marketing system

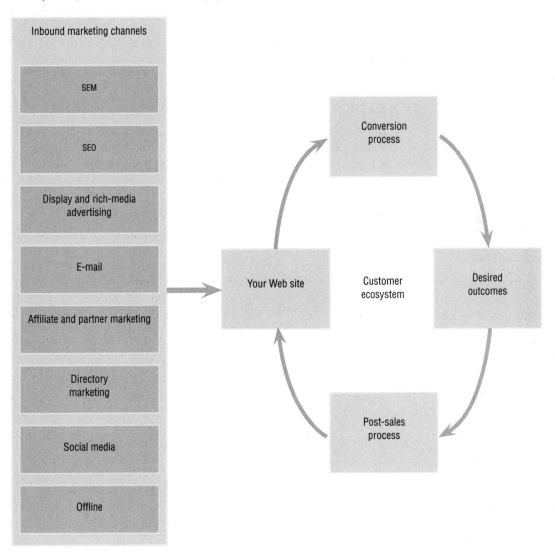

Planning your online strategy by channel

Looking at Figure 2.1, each channel represents one avenue for driving awareness, engaging with potential customers, and attracting new visitors to your site. You can use many of the same channels (such as e-mail) to drive repeat purchases, but for now we're emphasizing acquisition. Think of channels as a way to group and organize your activities to allocate budget, divide your efforts, and analyze your performance in workable chunks. Each channel groups a variety of activities. For example, the Display and Rich Media Advertising channel group includes running banner ads, audio ads, and in-video ads, all of which require different tools and expertise. Table 2.1 includes a definition of each channel we've identified so far.

The channels in Table 2.1 continue to evolve with the Web, and each has its own tools, tactics, strengths, weaknesses, and best practices. To develop a strong online marketing strategy, you'll need to be familiar with each channel. In this book, we focus on how you can use Google Analytics to analyze and improve performance in these areas. To get an in-depth view of tactics and tools for a given channel, refer to Appendix B for recommended additional reading.

For now, be aware that if you configure Google Analytics correctly, you can quantify the exact ROI you receive from each channel in near real time. This is hugely powerful. For the first time in the history of marketing, you can determine with amazing accuracy which marketing efforts are advancing your business goals and which are a waste of time and money. Optimizing your activities and spend across channels is one of the most basic, high-level applications of Google Analytics.

TABLE 2.1

Online Marketing Channels

Channel	Purpose
Search engine marketing (SEM)	Increase visibility in search engine result pages through paid advertising or paid inclusion.
Search engine optimization (SEO)	Increase visibility in search engine result pages through modifications to your Web site or direct efforts to get others to link to your site.
Display and rich media advertising	Attract users' attention and clicks with image-based video, online audio, widget, in-game, or animated online advertisements.
E-mail	Attract new visitors through opt-in e-mail advertising (but not spam!), encourage repeat purchases, and increase engagement among existing customers; develop leads from other channels.
Affiliate and partner marketing	Provide financial incentives to others to close transactions on your behalf or drive traffic to your site in exchange for a commission on completed sales, branding, or other non-monetary rewards.
Directory marketing	Increase visibility in niche directories, local search engines, price comparison engines, booking engines, and other vertical-specific directories and aggregators.
Social media	Publish content and solicit user-generated content via blogs, tweets, feeds, profile pages, contests, managed communities, and other social media platforms.
Offline	All traditional offline media including print, direct mail, television, events, out-of-home, and radio advertising.

Marketing for conversions

In Figure 2.1, each channel serves as an entry point to drive traffic to your Web site, which exists at the center of your online presence. There are exceptions to this model, however. For example, many hotels receive most of their bookings through online travel agents (rather than their own Web sites) and many restaurants receive most of their referrals through local directories such as Yelp.

We think of these aggregators in the same way you think of distributors, resellers, and channel partners. If your business receives most of your sales through an aggregator, it will be more difficult to deploy Google Analytics, since many important visitor interactions happen outside the sphere of your Web site. In these cases, you may have access to a set of metrics provided by the aggregator, or you may be able to place your own tracking code on the third-party site (this is an advanced topic, and your approach will vary by industry). For now, we'll assume that most of your key customer interactions (such as the actual point of purchase) occurs on your Web site.

Orienting your Web site toward a conversion process

From the perspective of an analytical marketer, your Web site's main function is to entice new and repeat visitors to move through the conversion process toward your desired outcomes (again see Figure 2.1). *Desired outcomes* are measurable actions taken by site visitors that generate business value and align with your business objectives. For example, if you run an ecommerce site, your desired outcome is for a visitor to buy something. These visitor actions are also referred to as *conversion goals* or *conversion actions.* Visitors who complete a conversion action are said to have *converted,* and each instance of a visitor converting is called a *conversion.* The ratio of visits that include a conversion action to total visits is called a *conversion rate.*

You can divide Google Analytics Conversion Goals into two main categories: *Transactional Goals* and *Engagement Goals.* Transactional Goals relate to a specific outcome that has a direct monetary value — buying something, becoming a lead, registering for an account, and so on. Engagement Goals relate to reaching a point or threshold of interaction that doesn't have a direct monetary value, such as reaching a certain class of content within the site, viewing a certain number or set of pages, or spending a certain amount of time on the site. While engagement goals don't provide immediate or direct monetary value, deeper engagement most often builds deeper brand equity and a propensity to convert at the transactional level later in the visit or on a future visit.

Think of your Conversion Goals as the output from your factory or the crops you harvest each season. They're the reason the whole marketing system exists, and they're what each technician (copywriter, SEM specialist, e-mail marketer) should be ultimately striving to impact. They're also the key measure you can use to analyze overall performance. It is crucially important that the Conversion Goals you define for your Web site align perfectly or near-perfectly with thought-out business objectives. To quote Peter Drucker, "There is nothing so useless as doing efficiently that which should not be done at all."

The specific metrics you use to track your Conversion Goals (such as transaction count) are often referred to as *key performance indicators* (KPIS). This term is used in a wider organizational context to signal that a particular metric is a strong indicator of business success and deserves lots of attention. For the remainder of the book, we rely on the term *Conversion Goal* more than KPI to reflect the terminology used in Google Analytics, but both terms are important to recognize.

Defining good Conversion Goals

To use Google Analytics to evaluate each component of your marketing system, it's important that you track as much of the system as possible. It's great to be able to say that 300 people arrived at your Web site through an e-mail you sent, but it's more powerful to be able to say that the e-mail generated $768 in incremental revenue. To perform this type of attribution, you need to be able to measure what's going on at each stage of the visitor session, starting with the e-mail and ending with your Conversion Goals.

To translate business objectives into a Google Analytics Conversion Goal, you must be able to tie that objective to a specific action taken by a Web site visitor, specifically one that Google Analytics can track. Good Conversion Goals have the following in common:

- **They're measurable.** A Conversion Goal that can be measured through Google Analytics is better than one that has to be pieced together from your financial data, CRM data, and sales records each week. If the Conversion Goal happens on your Web site and corresponds to a unique pageview, length of session, or number of pages viewed, then thanks to Google Analytics you're in good shape. If not, we have suggestions for you later on.
- **They correspond to bottom-line business objective.** If you're optimizing against a Conversion Goal that isn't tied to revenue or other business success factors, how can you be sure you're moving your organization forward? For example, directing your efforts toward increasing "traffic," instead of focusing on traffic that provides value, can lead to wasted effort. It doesn't matter that an advertisement sends you lots of visitors. Those visitors need to do something on your site that generates value, such as complete a purchase; otherwise, there's a high probability your money was wasted. Value is key.
- **They can be connected to your marketing efforts.** You may have an easily measurable and relevant Conversion Goal, but if it can't be connected to your advertising spend and other activities, its utility is significantly reduced.

There's nothing new about the concept of a Conversion Goal. In the past, a business owner might measure the success of a promotion by combing through receipts or inventory at the end of the day. The difference for the Web is that Conversion Goals are now easier to measure, they're easier to connect with earlier phases of the buying process, and they're easier to optimize against.

If you're still struggling to identify what the Conversion Goals might be for your Web site, take a look at Table 2.2, which provides examples of both types of Conversion Goals (Engagement Goals and Transactional Goals), as well as the business objectives and measurable actions they correspond to in Google Analytics.

What if your Web site includes only Engagement Goals and no Transactional Goals? Perhaps your Web site simply includes information about your product or service, but no way to buy. Perhaps your

TABLE 2.2

Sample Conversion Actions

Bottom-line Business Goal	Desired Action	Classification	Measurement Action
Direct sales/e-commerce			
Grow revenue	Add item to shopping cart	Transactional	Pageview on `cart-contents.aspx`
Grow revenue	Place a telephone order	Transactional	Hit on unique phone number (tracked using an integration between a phone tracking tool and Google Analytics).
Control costs	Use e-mail form, FAQ, or chat to contact support	Transactional	Visit to `e-mail-submitted.html`, visit to an FAQ, or click on Chat Now link
Indirect sales/lead generation			
Drive interest	Download a white paper or coupon	Engagement	Click on Download or Print link
Generate leads	Request an estimate, brochure, newsletter, or callback	Transactional	Visit to `request-received.html`
Advertising-serving			
Grow revenue	View page with four ad slots	Engagement	Pageview on `article1.html`
Grow revenue	Click a text link	Engagement	New click in AdSense
Subscription-based			
Grow subscribers	Complete registration	Transactional	Visit to `welcome.html`
Increase usage	Personalize preferences	Engagement	Visit to `settings-change.html`
Branding/awareness			
Raise awareness	Watch a video	Engagement	`video-complete` event fired
Raise engagement	View more than five pages or complete a two-minute session	Engagement	Threshold goal complete

sales cycle takes months and there's no way to connect revenue with visitor activity. If you're struggling with these issues you have three main options.

- **Bring your desired action online, where it can be tracked**. Maybe you create a streamlined estimate form to generate leads instead of just showing an e-mail address. Maybe you make a coupon available that customers can bring into a store and you can track. It may seem absurd to alter your sales process just to make it measurable, but often a small tweak is all you need. For example, Twiddy, the vacation rental business we look at in Chapter 3, put its standard lease online, allowing Twiddy to track ROI from its advertising through the entire sales process using an advanced technique called *custom variables*. Customers were actually happier they no longer had to use a scanner or send a fax to complete their transaction.

- **Expand your tracking capabilities beyond your Web site.** Another option is to expand your tracking capabilities to cover a wider variety of user actions. This usually involves advanced implementation, or the purchase of add-ons such as phone tracking solutions, and requires either budget or time from IT. This option often comes down to connecting two data sources, such as integrating your CRM system with Google Analytics.
- **Develop a model**. Your last option is to use math and statistics to fill gaps in your tracking. This option is more common in the enterprise sector (an example is a lifetime value model) and is generally resource-intensive. A common risk to this approach is that an analyst will go to great lengths to produce a model that few in the company understand and thus have a hard time trusting when it comes to making hard decisions.

For some organizations, none of these options work well. This is one of the hard realities about Web analytics. Without a measurable Conversion Goal connected to a bottom-line objective, it is difficult to use data to drive your activities because you will have to fall back on an indirect measure or a mathematical model to orient your activities and judge your success.

For example, no one buys a Prius on Toyota.com, so Toyota must try to infer the impact of the Web site from Engagement Goals, such as how many people completed the Build Your Own Prius application. Toyota can also assign a value to a visitor signing up for a test on the site because it knows how many test-drives lead to a sale.

As more transactions move online and tracking technology evolves, indirect situations will become less common.

Tools for Understanding Visitors and Performance

So far, we've covered many of the basic components of an online marketing system, including channels, the buying cycle, the customer ecosystem, and Conversion Goals. Now it's time for a more in-depth look at the tools and techniques you can use to make your system run more efficiently. These can be divided into the three categories shown in Figure 2.2. These groupings are based on an earlier model pioneered by Avinash Kaushik, one of the most important advocates of Web analytics to date.

Together, these three areas of research form a powerful lens for understanding your organization's customers, market, and performance, supporting Peter Drucker's claim that "the aim of marketing is to know and understand the customer so well the product or service fits him and sells itself."

Google Analytics tells you *what* your visitors are doing, *when*, and *how much*. Voice-of-the-customer research tells you *why* they're doing what they're doing, *how they perceive* your brand and your Web site, what *problems* they have completing tasks, and how *satisfied* they are with your site.

FIGURE 2.2

The major categories of online customer insight tools

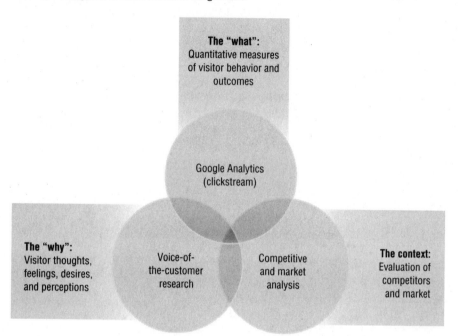

Competitive and market analysis tells you *how you're doing in your market*, what techniques your competitors are using, and what your visitors are experiencing before and after they come to your site.

By combining these three classes of intelligence, you can gain competitive advantage in everything from the broadest strategic questions to the most finite tactical and operational decisions. When we say that the Web offers businesses a wealth of options for understanding customers, this is what we're talking about.

Understanding the "what" with Google Analytics

As visitors navigate a Web site that's been *tagged* with a Web analytics tool such as Google Analytics, each page they load and, in some cases, each action they take is recorded in a database. We explain more about this process in Chapter 4. For now, be aware that the data set assembled through tracking visitor activity on a Web site is called *clickstream* data. Google Analytics is geared primarily toward clickstream analysis.

What Google Analytics does for you

You can use Google Analytics to help you do the following:

- **Make better decisions about online strategy and tactics**. Google Analytics gives you the general understanding of what's happening with your online presence to raise the overall quality of your decisions as a marketer and a manager.
- **Be more goal-driven**. By setting measurable goals that correspond with real business value, Google Analytics can help drive specific actions and measure success against those actions.
- **Eliminate waste.** Google Analytics can show you when advertising dollars or other initiatives fail to impact objectives so you can shift budget and attention elsewhere.
- **Reward success.** Once you can define and measure success, you can also take steps to reward the people and the campaign that have the most positive impact. This allows you to reinforce positive trends in your activities.
- **Plan for the future**. Once you build a base of analytics data, you can use past performance to predict future trends and evaluate the potential of future campaigns.

In line with these goals, Google Analytics is a great tool for answering the following kinds of questions:

- What kinds of visitors purchased something?
- Which marketing channels generate the highest ROI?
- Where do I lose the most potential customers in my checkout process?
- Which marketing campaign generated the most conversions?
- Which campaigns and team members are having the biggest impact?
- What's the overall contribution of my marketing efforts to the bottom line?
- Which type of content gets the most attention?
- How often do visitors return after buying something?
- What keywords do people use to find my site?
- What areas of the world send me the most visitors?
- What language do my visitors speak?

Think of Google Analytics as your radar for the Web. It's the medium you use to quantify and report on visitor activity on your site. If you're not using Google Analytics or another clickstream analysis tool to evaluate your online activities, you're basically flying blind.

To get back to our framework of the marketing system, Google Analytics gives you a reading on what's happening at every stage in the system. It tells you where your site is attracting traffic from, where your site is generating business value, and which efforts are making a dent in your objectives. You can even use existing integrations of the Google Analytics API to connect these capabilities to other areas of your business.

What Google Analytics does not do for you

On the other hand, as you look through your Google Analytics reports, ultimately you will reach a stage when you need to know *why* visitors are behaving in a certain way to formulate a plan to improve. This is where Google Analytics leaves off and voice-of-the-customer research begins. It's a common tendency when you're looking at Google Analytics reports to ascribe meaning to the data that is simply not there. You may notice a drop-off in a checkout process and jump to the conclusion that the drop-off is due to a particular form field, even if users are leaving for completely different reasons. Clickstream data alone rarely tells the whole story, especially when it comes to the thoughts, feelings, and motivations of your visitors. This is a crucial point to understand, and if you can internalize this now, it will spare you frustration down the road.

How Google Analytics compares to other Web analytics tools

If you're reading this book, there's a high probability you've already made a commitment to using Google Analytics. In case you're still shopping, the other leading tools are Adobe Omniture, WebTrends, Unica, Coremetrics, and Yahoo Web Analytics.

Each of these analytics tools has different strengths and weaknesses, but in our experience, there is an increasing amount of overlap in their capabilities. We'll stop short of providing a buying guide, but we want to address some of the myths about Google Analytics before you research alternatives.

Top 10 myths about Google Analytics

When considering the use of Google Analytics, beware these top myths:

1. **You get what you pay for. Google Analytics is free, which means it's not powerful.** False. Google Analytics uses the same underlying technology to collect data as all the most popular alternatives, it runs on some of the world's best infrastructure, and now boasts many of the capabilities as the most expensive tools on the market.

2. **Google Analytics is basic and doesn't have "advanced" features or metrics.** This may have been true once upon a time, but Google Analytics now includes Advanced Segmentation, Custom Reports, Multiple Custom Variables, and a number of other fancy and powerful features that place it well outside the label *basic*.

3. **Google Analytics uses third-party cookies.** False! Google Analytics has always used first-party, not third-party, cookies.

4. **Google Analytics is not accurate.** Google Analytics uses JavaScript tags to collect data. This industry-standard method yields reliable trends and a high degree of precision, but it's not perfect. Most of the time, if you are noticing data discrepancies greater than 10 percent, it's due to an installation issue. Common problems include JavaScript errors, redirects, untagged pages, and slow client-side load times. All Web analytics tools face the same technical limitations posed by JavaScript tags, so if a vendor claims their tool is more accurate, ask for evidence.

5. **It's not possible to export your data from Google Analytics.** Not true! You have two options for exporting data. Use the Export button at the top of each report to export the current view in PDF or XML, or use the Google Analytics Data Export API to extract large amounts of data in any format you like.

6. **With Google Analytics, you can't control how your data is used.** You have three options for data sharing in Google Analytics. You can change these options at any time from inside your Analytics account. Your three options are to not share your data, share your data with Google to

improve its products, and share your data anonymously for benchmarking. If you opt out of data sharing, your data remains in Google Analytics and is not shared with other products or services. If you decide to share your data with Google, it is used to improve those products and services. If you decide to share your data anonymously, it remains anonymous and is aggregated with other data to support the Google Analytics benchmarking feature.

7. **There is no professional support for Google Analytics.** Google Analytics maintains a network of authorized consultants who can manage all aspects of Google Analytics implementation, reporting, and analysis (full disclosure: we participate in this program).

8. **Google Analytics isn't well integrated with other tools.** Google offers a full range of marketing products including Google AdWords and Google Website Optimizer. Google Analytics integrates more readily with these tools, which actually give it a leg up in terms of integrations. Many other companies also offer their own integrations, which we cover in Part V.

9. **You can't easily segment data in Google Analytics.** This one has not been true since 2008, when Google released Advanced Segmentation.

10. **You have to spend a lot of money to get "real" Web analytics.** Getting a return from your Google Analytics data does take an investment, but not necessarily in tools. The most important investment to start with is making sure you or someone in your organization has the expertise and time to put your data to use. Avinash Kaushik framed this in terms of what he calls the 90/10 rule, where 90 percent of your budget should be advocated to expertise and 10 percent to tools.

Understanding the "why" with voice-of-the-customer research

Now that you know Google Analytics can help you understand *what* is going on with your Web site, it's time to look at how you can understand *why* it's happening. *Voice-of-the-customer research* is also called *user experience research* or *usability research* and includes more branches then we can cover in this book. The most important components of voice-of-the-customer research are:

- **Ethnographic research:** This is a holistic form of customer research geared toward understanding customers in a real-world setting (that is, at home or at work). Its emphasis is on obtaining the fullest possible context through observation, field studies, and in-depth interviews.

- **Focus group research:** This is a moderated discussion of your product, service, or Web site using a representative panel of customers. It is conducted in a controlled environment, and now occasionally online.

- **Surveys:** This is done through questionnaires administered to Web site visitors or customers via a panel, e-mail, a link, or an overlay on your Web site.

- **Cognitive exercises:** These are sorting, walkthroughs, or other conceptual exercises designed to understand the optimal way to structure information, workflow, and Web site navigation to match visitor perceptions.

- **Expert evaluations:** This is a heuristic analysis of your Web site by a professional usability expert, who applies best practices and techniques to identify and correct common problems.
- **Usability testing:** This involves testing your Web site on real customers to see how well they can accomplish basic tasks.

These options range in price dramatically, but — not surprisingly — the Web is making it more economical to collect and organize feedback from customers and visitors.

What voice-of-the-customer research does for you

From an online marketing perspective, voice-of-the-customer research is the best tool for getting past your assumptions and taking on the mindset of your customers. It will help you do the following:

- **Write more compelling copy.** By interacting with customers directly or indirectly, you get a better sense for the terminology they know and don't know, and you can uncover the clearest ways to explain your product or service. By learning to speak the same language as your visitors, you can minimize confusion, improve site navigation, and increase the clarity of your message.
- **Learn what makes your visitors' blood boil.** It's always nice to hear positive reviews from Web site visitors, but since you're focused on improving the site, it's generally more valuable to hear complaints and criticism to help you correct the most pressing problems.
- **Understand visitor intent.** If you survey enough visitors, you can learn the most important reasons they come to your site. This understanding puts all your design choices in clear context and lets you make better decisions about how to structure information and present your offerings.
- **Understand where you're losing people.** Looking at quantitative data, you may notice which page visitors exit from, but it can be difficult to identify the missing piece of information, specific error, or point of confusion that's driving people away. Uncovering these missing pieces is a key value proposition of usability testing.
- **Gather suggestions for new functionality and features.** Starbucks used an online community to come up with the idea for a spill stick, a small piece of plastic designed to prevent coffee from spilling out of the top of a to-go cup. When you begin requesting feedback from your visitors, you may get some great ideas for product enhancements or new site functionality.
- **Understand how to improve layout or design.** Sometimes users have valuable suggestions about how to make your site cleaner and more intuitive. Are there too many fields in your form? Would you be better off presenting your copy in bullet format rather than paragraphs? Your users can often help.

What voice-of-the-customer research does not do for you

Perceptions and motivations can be notoriously difficult to pin down; it takes a lot of time and effort to get a deep understanding of customers. Like Google Analytics, voice-of-the-customer research is an iterative process whereby you form a hypothesis about why your customers behave a certain way and then continuously refine that hypothesis by actual customer testing. Because every customer is different, you may find that after a usability test or survey, you actually have more questions about your site than when you started. If you begin to feel lost, remember that you don't need a perfect understanding of customers to improve things; you just need to know enough to plan your next move.

Top five methods for understanding your visitor experience

Voice-of-the-customer research is a wide field, with many books written on each branch we mentioned. Our recommendation of the top five methods to build a better qualitative understanding of your Web site are:

1. **Do simple usability testing, with an emphasis on simple.** Take a look at Steve Krug's *Don't Make Me Think* for a fantastic guide to testing crucial aspects of your Web site quickly and inexpensively. You begin by examining what it is visitors are trying to accomplish on your site, and then watch as they try to accomplish it. The results can be astonishing. If you don't have time to collect any other qualitative feedback, follow the steps in Krug's guide. If you don't have time to do this yourself, consider hiring an expert or using an inexpensive online service such as UserTesting.com (www.usertesting.com).

2. **Interview your sales people and customer service reps**: Find the people in your company who interact directly with your target audience and interview them at length. If your organization keeps records about why customers call, ask to see them. Even better, encourage these folks to let you know when people call in complaints or questions about the Web site and sit in on the customer service calls yourself, or respond to customers directly.

3. **Ask for feedback on your site**: Implement a feedback tool such as Kampyle or OpinionLab on your site to allow customers to ask a question or lodge a complaint. These tools help organize feedback so you can use it quickly and efficiently, and they are less invasive than other feedback tools. If you don't want another tool, you can start by putting an e-mail link near a point of focus on your Web site that says, "Tell us what you think of this site." You may be surprised by what you hear.

4. **Do some semi-scripted phone interviews with customers**: There's no substitute for direct contact with customers, and it can often be easy to arrange phone interviews to bounce off ideas or ask them to look at materials you send. Our advice is to take a semi-structured approach, where you identify key areas and then let the conversation remain free-flowing within each area. If you have a local customer base, you can also invite these customers to lunch or an open house.

5. **Work your online presence into your other feedback tools**: If you're in a large organization, you may find that the company is already surveying customers. Incorporate specific questions about the Web site into your survey to find out the impact your site is having on buying decisions, the biggest problems with your site, or suggestions for new site functionality.

As you make progress in these areas, don't lose site of your business goals. Remember that you're looking for insights that will help you engage more users, drive more conversions, or deliver better customer service on your site. Use these goals as a way to filter the information that comes back.

Also, just because you hear suggestions from customers doesn't mean you need to accept every piece of feedback wholesale. Customers are great at telling you what they don't like, but they have a harder time expressing what they might want. As you collect suggestions from customers, make it clear that you want honest feedback.

Seeing the big picture with competitive and market analysis

The third component of the Web analytics trifecta involves looking at the *context* around visitor behavior. As we mentioned earlier in this chapter, your visitors often come to your site as one small piece of a much larger browsing session. They may visit your competitors' sites at the same time as yours, changing how they perceive your offering. They may have access to reviews about your products or other content before they even arrive. For these reasons, it's important that you spend a portion of your time looking at what's going on *off* your Web site as well as *on* it. We've grouped this type of analysis under the blanket term *competitive and market analysis.*

What competitive and market analysis does for you

Competitive and market analysis widens your understanding to include the broad context that surrounds your Web site. It's a powerful tool to help you do the following:

- **Manage perceptions around your brand.** By monitoring the conversations going on about your brand in the social media space, you can often uncover a wealth of free user-to-user commentary about your brand in the form of blog posts, tweets, comments, reviews, and ratings. You can use these conversations to identify your biggest strengths and weaknesses to better organize your site and strengthen your messaging. It's especially important to review these conversations because they're publicly visible and actively influencing your visitors before they reach your site.

- **Find inspiration for site improvements.** Imitation is the sincerest form of flattery. This is definitely true on the Web, where you can quickly see what your competitors are up to and use the information to develop ideas for more effective design elements, more efficient workflows, and better site organization.

- **Benchmark your reach.** There are several quantitative tools that can help you understand how many visitors you're reaching compared with competitors and where you fall in the hierarchy of sites in your market. This information can help you evaluate how well you're getting exposure online.

- **Monitor brand health.** You can use panels and other tools to survey the Internet population at large and benchmark your brand's awareness and strength against competitors. Monitoring can be a powerful way to measure the effectiveness of branding campaigns, for example.

- **Understand who you're reaching.** Many online services can help you understand which demographics visit your site as opposed to competitors' sites. This information can help you target your audience more precisely, address different segments with appropriate content, and more intelligently define your ideal customer.

What competitive research does not do for you

Competitive research is a great way to put your efforts into context, but it's not a substitute for innovation. You'll never become the best by copying others. Use competitive research as a way to set smarter goals and evaluate your performance, but don't become too complacent if you have a big lead or too disheartened if it looks like you're behind.

Top five methods for competitive and market analysis

Because competitive research extends to the entire Web, the tools at your disposal range from a simple Google Search to multimillion dollar annual services from Nielsen and others. Here are some ideas to get started:

- **Browse your competitors sites regularly:** Identify your top competitors, bookmark their sites, and surf them at least once a month to see what they're doing. If this is too low-tech for you, you can also subscribe to an inexpensive competitive monitoring tool such as Versionista (www.versionista.com) to notify you when a competitor's site has changed. Look for things your competitors do well, and make sure you're doing things to stand out from the crowd.

- **Monitor search behavior on Google Insights for Search**: Google Insights for Search lets you see what people are searching for on Google, including how many people are searching for your brand relative to competitors. You can even filter results by geographic area and visualize trends over time. It's a great tool to monitor the impact of a branding or awareness campaign, as is the similar Google Trends tool.

- **Search user-generated content for your site and your competitors:** Run regular searches and monitor mentions of your brand and products alongside competitors using some or all of the following free tools. If you search for "buzz monitoring" or "social media search," you'll find dozens more options. These are just a few of our favorites: BlogPulse (www.blogpulse.com), HowSociable (www.howsociable.com), Google Alerts (www.google.com/alerts), Technorati (www.technorati.com), and Twitter Search (search.twitter.com). Also be sure to subscribe to your competitors' RSS feeds if they have them.

- **Check your visitor count and demographics against competitors:** Services including Hitwise, Quantcast, Compete.com, AdCenter Labs, and Nielsen NetRatings can give you a quantitative understanding of how many people you are reaching compared to your competitors, as well as the demographics of the people you do reach.

- **Get creative in your industry:** In Chapter 3, we show how Twiddy, a vacation rental company, uses the Web to monitor the occupancy rates of competitors. Depending on your market, you may be able to uncover inexpensive options to keeping tabs on competitors.

Tying it all together

We've mentioned a lot of tools and methods for understanding customers in this chapter. For the rest of this book, we focus mainly on Google Analytics, which as you can see represents just one piece of the pie.

Our advice is to spend a few hours browsing through the resources we've listed for voice-of-the-customer and competitive research, but don't try to tackle everything at once. Start by getting a firm understanding of Google Analytics and gradually expand your knowledge in the other areas. Alternatively, team up with a colleague or department who can "own" one of the other areas for you. If you can work in tandem, you'll see results that are greater than the sum of your individual activities. These three areas give you the integrated understanding you need to make your online strategy more effective *and* more efficient.

—

Putting Google Analytics to Work in Your Organization

When you peer under the hood of most Web sites, you'll find Web analytics tags everywhere. It's also common knowledge that most organizations do little to apply the data to everyday decisions. Why is this the case?

This chapter outlines the key ingredients of a data-driven culture, not just for marketers but for all business functions. It also outlines how to assemble a strong team that can translate the data from Google Analytics into actionable insights that reach the right decision-makers at the right time. We also show you how three organizations are using Web analytics to drive marketing strategy today. We hope all this will provide inspiration for you to start applying the techniques we present in later chapters.

Leading the Charge for Analytics

In 1964 IBM released the System 360, a large mainframe that looks a bit like the robot from *Lost in Space* ("Danger, Will Robinson!"). Geeks loved the new system because it gave them a full 8MB of RAM to power their applications. It wasn't long before geeks and analysts teamed up to attack business problems, and within three years a researcher from MIT, John D.C. Little, launched MEDIAC, the first media planning application and one of the first programs in a branch of computer science called *decision support systems* (now called *business intelligence*). In a paper describing the system, Little wrote, "A great deal of data are available on who reads (or sees or hears) what. There are considerable data on what kinds of people are prospects for which types of product. … It would seem that there should be some organized way of combining judgments and data into a model, setting an objective, and then optimizing it to produce a good media plan."

Little was certainly on to something, but even after a revolution in computing power, most companies still struggle to apply data in the way Little describes.

Why? There is just too much data to deal with. There's a lack of trained analysts, and lots of expensive tools that are difficult to work with. More important, Little couldn't foresee back in the 1960s that math and tools were just the beginning. It's the human element in analytical decision-making that is the difficult part. Most organizations are stuck on the need to make data relevant and exciting, the need to educate staff and reward experimentation, and the need to put personal opinions aside and analyze impartially.

This chapter will help you prepare for the avalanche of data Google Analytics provides by explaining how to pull together the people and processes you need to turn that data into insights. Companies from every industry have made huge strides in using data to improve their decisions and processes. The key is to start small, build basic skills, and never forget that analytics is as much about politics and decision-making as it is about math and JavaScript.

Every organization that has made significant gains from Google Analytics has someone we call an *analytics champion*. This internal advocate makes a commitment to trust what can be measured and to convince others to adopt this same mindset.

The commitment begins with a basic skepticism about the way people portray ideas and describe their activities. Being data-driven means not doing things out of tradition, or out of respect for the boss's opinion. It means asking the hard questions. Some champions relish this role: "I answer to no one but the data, so take your nonsense elsewhere!" But if the analytics champion works too hard at being independent-minded, he or she is ignored when it is time to make decisions. So when you're working to get your organization to take analytics data seriously, play nice on the outside even while you're skeptical on the inside. Eventually, you'll be able to get measurable initiatives prioritized over initiatives that can't be measured, which is a great place to start.

These days there is so much data available, at so little cost, that there is just no excuse for doing things any other way.

You may be a bit nervous about the analytics champion role. Take heart: The truth is that no one individual can fill this role alone. Being an analytics champion is about showing your colleagues that it's possible to use numbers *and* be creative, to place media buys through evidence rather than expensive golf games, and to do it all without knowing a thing about JavaScript. In the end, you may find that popular initiatives within your team may have actually produced few returns and that there are opportunities where you would never have thought to look.

Moving toward analytical decision-making can be a bumpy ride, but companies that learn to compete using analytics stand a better chance of succeeding in the long term. If you get started now, the rewards can be spectacular.

So, where to begin? Table 3.1 defines four focus areas needed to make productive use of Google Analytics. Take a look at the figure and assess which task you're most suited to and which tasks you'll need help with. We go into more detail on these tasks later in the chapter.

TABLE 3.1

The Four Key Skill Sets Needed to Make Productive Use of Your Data

Code and Configuration		Business Insight	
Configure	**Administer**	**Analyze**	**Socialize**
• Expand capabilities • Deploy code • Customize code • Troubleshoot issues • Integrate data sources	• Control access • Control account settings • Log changes • Adjust account structure • Develop filters • Enforce standards	• Tie metrics to goals • Tie metrics to financials • Lead KPI development • Distribute reports • Respond to crises • Define best practices • Identify trends	• Secure resources • Train colleagues • Support colleagues • Engage executives • Promote accountability • Settle disputes • Clarify reports

The most important distinction in Table 3.1 is between the Code and Configuration tasks and the Business Insight tasks. The Code and Configuration tasks are about building your capabilities, and they exist only to enable the Business Insight tasks. The Business Insight tasks affect priorities and decisions.

From a marketer's standpoint, being successful with Google Analytics means being successful at Business Insight. It's a bit like driving a car: You can drive to work every day for 30 years without having a clue how your car actually works. By leaving the JavaScript and configuration to a teammate or a consultant, you can focus your talents on impacting your conversion goals.

But what if you don't have a developer or a budget for an outside consultant? If the following list describes your company, you should be able to proceed alone. If not, we give suggestions later in this chapter for getting technical help.

- The Web site you want to track is hosted on a single domain (such as yourwebsite.com).
- You don't sell products through a shopping cart, PayPal, or other type of online transaction.
- You don't need to track video, Flash, or other rich media.
- You don't use AJAX on your site.
- You can access and change your Web site's code.
- You know HTML well enough to paste code on every page on the site and tweak site elements.
- You understand where customer and sales data is stored and how to access that data.
- You can access and make changes to your company's AdWords account.
- Your Web site does not use redirects.
- Your company has less than 20 Google Analytics users.
- You understand URL parameters and your Web site doesn't use them.
- Your needs are not likely to change for one to two years.

If you answered "no" to any of these statements, we strongly suggest you get help. Even if you can master all the technical work yourself, every moment of your time that goes into development is a moment you're not analyzing, socializing, or acting on your data. Remember, as someone who recognizes the value of analytics, you are a valuable resource in your organization.

NOTE

This book is written with the analyst in mind. If you've decided you're more of a developer, consider a more technical volume to supplement this book or check the Google Analytics code site at `code.google.com`.

To illustrate the point a bit further, Table 3.2 shows the kinds of questions you should focus on as a marketer, rather than as a developer.

Separating Web analytics tasks into two functional areas helps the marketing and sales departments concentrate on improving their returns while the technical group concentrates on redirects, cookies, and the technical details. That way, marketers don't feel bad when they don't know what a 303 error message means, and developers don't get tasked reporting on unfamiliar campaigns.

On the other hand, for the whole system to function, *both* groups must learn to work closely together and use a common language, which is why it is so important to have a central home for analytics.

Assembling a Google Analytics Dream Team

By now you're aware of the tasks involved in drawing insight from Google Analytics within your organization. We've created four personas around the focus areas listed in Table 3.2 (Develop, Administer, Analyze, and Socialize) to describe the person who might fill each role. We've used one of the most successful dream teams ever, the Teenage Mutant Ninja Turtles, to describe the team. Not every organization can afford to devote four people to analytics, so our dream team is more an ideal than a necessity.

TABLE 3.2

Marketing versus Business Questions

Marketing Question	Business Question
How do people arrive at my Web site?	Why aren't the campaign variables in our campaign URLS registering properly?
What defines a valuable visitor to my site?	How can I configure custom variables to track individual groups of users over time?
Which marketing channel is driving the most valuable visitors at the lowest cost?	How can I set up e-commerce tracking to process product SKUS correctly?

Four essential skill sets for a successful team

Let's meet the analytics dream team.

Raphael, the developer

Raphael sometimes had a hard time getting along with the rest of the team, but he would often come to the rescue with a brilliant solution. In the Google Analytics world, Raphael is a developer: He works with the Web site code to make things happen. His role is to make changes to the company Web site that allow the analytics dream team to collect more comprehensive and accurate data about visitors, such as tracking specific items purchased or actions taken.

Raphael also helps the team merge data from Google Analytics and other data sources, such as the company's accounting system. Because he is familiar with the other systems at the company, he can help troubleshoot data discrepancies and mysterious changes the rest of the team can't access.

Raphael is proficient in JavaScript, HTML, relational database design, SQL, basic server administration, and the Google Analytics code base. He uses blogs, forums, and online documentation to stay on top of new features and developments.

Raphael enjoys explaining to users the ins and outs of how Google Analytics works, but he sometimes overwhelms them with details and technical jargon. Raphael dislikes meetings, and one of his biggest frustrations is when the marketing department gives him a vague request for an advanced analytics configuration and expects him to fill in the gaps in their reasoning. Raphael prides himself on attention to detail and can almost always return a workable solution as long as he's given a well-thought-out set of requirements.

Leonardo, the administrator

While fighting crime, Leonardo was great at keeping the team on course and making sure everyone played by the rules. On the analytics dream team, Leonardo manages access and settings for the company's Google Analytics installation, and he works with Raphael to make sure Google Analytics is configured correctly to meet the needs of individual users and departments.

As the organization has grown, Leonardo has had to adjust the Google Analytics account configuration several times to create segments and group Web properties into individual profiles. Leonardo uses the Annotations feature to track every change he makes to the account and helps teammates define links for their online campaigns that can be easily tracked.

Leonardo has a deep knowledge of the workings of Google Analytics, but he does not do much coding, and is instead more focused on maintaining the company's systems rather than building them. When the dream team needed to configure Google Analytics to work on a new microsite, it turned to Leonardo first. He used his technical knowledge of Google Analytics to translate what the team needed into detailed requirements for Raphael.

Leonardo is extremely good at helping users understand how to access Google Analytics and use its different features, but he does not know the business well enough to help the team make recommendations on specific business decisions.

Donatello, the analyst

Donatello was the genius behind the ninja turtles, the one who helped the team see a better way to rescue April and destroy their enemies. On the analytics dream team, Donatello's job is to work with the Google Analytics interface and other analytics tools to extract insight to share with the team. He coordinated an effort to develop key performance indicators for the marketing organization and designed custom reports to deliver the exact metrics colleagues needed. Donatello also runs ad hoc analysis around specific campaigns to pinpoint ROI and help the executive team prioritize. Donatello has documented his most successful techniques and runs monthly workshops with Michelangelo to train colleagues on how to use key metrics to make smarter decisions.

Donatello is comfortable letting his colleagues know when he thinks improvements could be made in certain areas. Some employees think he is too big for his britches, but in general they will listen to his advice when presented in a nonthreatening way (Michelangelo helps him do this). Donatello reads the official Google Analytics blog to keep up-to-date on current trends.

Donatello's biggest annoyance occurs when he discovers inconsistencies in the data that he thinks are related to technical problems. He performs regular audits, and if he encounters anything he can't explain, he meets with Raphael and Leonardo until the problem is solved. Donatello usually waits until he has strong evidence before communicating his findings to the team, but once he's convinced of his opinion, he's difficult to sway.

Michelangelo, the motivator

Michelangelo was a much-loved ninja turtle. He loved to party and keep the team feeling good. In the Analytics realm, Michelangelo is a close friend of Donatello, and his main role on the team is to take the insights Donatello has uncovered and present them to fellow marketers in a way that's fun and interesting. He also works closely with the executive team to make sure its members understand what the analytics dream team is doing and what it contributes to the rest of the organization. Michelangelo is a people person, and he loves chatting and collaborating rather than working solo.

Michelangelo has managed to carve out time in the marketing organization's weekly check-in to discuss the latest trends in analytics data. He has become a key figure in the quarterly budgeting meeting by highlighting the top five missed revenue opportunities uncovered through Donatello's work. Michelangelo designed an Analytics Attack workshop series where two teams face off on basic company's performance questions, and he works one on one with a variety of team members to show them how to analyze their campaigns.

At a recent a dinner party at the CMO's penthouse, Michelangelo persuaded the executive team to allocate additional headcount to the analytics group to help them expand their workshop series and kick off an optimization plan on the Web site. He also worked with Donatello to persuade the CMO to give a quarterly bonus to the marketing campaign with the most converted sales as measured in Google Analytics. Michelangelo hopes to design a two-hour training session for all new employees to help them understand how to use analytics in their daily work.

Tips for building your team

Looking over the dream team personas, you should have some idea of the skill sets needed on your analytics dream team, as shown in Table 3.1. So what do you do about the skills you personally don't have? Depending on your situation, you have a few options:

- **Get someone to help**: If you're a manager who controls headcount, this is an easy option. If you need to persuade your manager to assign a technical resource, here are three good arguments to use:
    1. We spend $X on advertising. For a fraction of that amount, I can increase our ROI by up to 50 percent. I just need help from IT to get started.
    2. Every day we don't optimize is costing us money. Let me start with our AdWords campaign. I just need help from IT to get started.
    3. I keep reading about companies that are doing amazing things with analytics (the Boston Red Sox, for example). I can actually get us going with just a few hours from IT.
- **Find a buddy**: Sometimes the best way to get help is to beg, borrow, or steal. Find a friend in IT, take him out to lunch, and explain your needs. Explain that Web analytics is a marketable skill set to develop and that with basic configuration assistance you won't need help querying data anymore. Schedule a weekly meeting with a rolling agenda, prioritize what you need, and try to get as much done as possible. Bring swag or a bottle of wine, and tell everyone you know how helpful that IT person is.
- **Hire an outsider**: A consultant can be a great resource for taking the strain off your Web master. She can walk you through everything you need to know, help you plan for the future, train your colleagues, and add legitimacy to your effort. The only thing she can't do is change the code on your Web site (at least without permission), so you'll still need help from an in-house developer. At some point, the consultant will have to hand over administration to your team; this can be a big responsibility, so you'll need to be prepared.
- **Learn to do everything yourself**: This is the option of last resort, and it is much more palatable if you have a simple Web site or a small organization. If you make too many mistakes early on, the company might lose faith in the data you provide and you might have difficulty regaining its trust. Look at the checklist earlier in this chapter to find out if your Web site would make it easier to do everything yourself.

After you've found the people you'd like to involve, schedule a kickoff meeting and include the following on the agenda:

- Create a name for the team and the project.
- Find a recurring time that works for everyone, weekly or biweekly.
- Identify any gatekeepers who will prevent you from proceeding and discuss how to approach them.
- Identify any potential executive sponsors who can help you secure resources and legitimacy.

- Define the first milestones in your measurement strategy (see the next section).

GETUP and Go: Defining Your Measurement Strategy

Once you have assembled your analytics dream team, your first priority is gathering requirements for your Google Analytics installation. We cover this in detail in Part II, but first examine the organizational elements that need to be considered. The five elements listed below consistently come up whenever we work with a new company eager to get started with analytics, and they make up a useful framework for assessing where your organization stands. Together they spell the acronym *GETUP*.

- **Goals and strategy.** Companies that define clear and attainable business goals, refine their priorities regularly, and use varied inputs to educate their decisions do best in this area. Clear goals and strategy success are tied to a culture of innovation and experimentation, which often includes managers who listen to their team and conduct research rather than dictate priorities.

- **Expertise.** Not surprisingly, companies that devote more brainpower to analytics do better. Often, successful companies hire a consultant to assist with initial implementation and help plan for growth. At the bare minimum, someone in the organization needs to "own" analytics.

- **Tools.** Most organizations have some Web analytics tool in place. Few have gone through the important step of validating the implementation of the tool. Similarly, few have explored voice-of-the-customer and competitive analysis tools that can be paired with Google Analytics.

- **Unified data.** Companies that generate direct revenue online are at an advantage in this area, since they can easily connect Web analytics data to direct revenue. Another key to success is building trust in the data, which can come only through clear measurement standards and regular audits of key metrics across data sources.

- **Process integration.** This is where the rubber meets the road. Organizations that succeed on this front have combined user training, ad hoc analysis, and formal reporting to continuously inject Web analytics data into strategic and tactical decision-making. They've created a culture that rewards performance based on measurable data, that promotes an attitude of *kaizen* (continuous improvement), and that uses standardized definitions and terminology to keep everyone on the same page.

We've put together the following list of questions to help you think critically about how well your company is suited to using analytics data. You can use these questions as the agenda for the first weekly meeting of your analytics team. Don't worry if you don't know the answer to every question. This list is meant to get you thinking about the organizational context of using Google Analytics at your company.

Goals and strategy

- What is the primary purpose of our Web site?
- What are the main marketing channels we use to attract visitors to our Web site?

- Who is involved in managing those channels?
- What percentage of our revenue, leads, or customer interactions comes from our Web site?
- What is our online marketing budget?
- What process is used to allocate the marketing budget? What is the timeline for this allocation?
- How often does our team get together to discuss priorities (weekly, monthly, never)?
- What inputs go into the priorities as they are currently set?
- How do we define success for an online campaign?
- What kinds of online marketing initiatives are we considering for the future?

Expertise

- Who is available to assist with this project?
- How much time are they prepared to give?
- Which of the skill sets listed previously do we have covered and where do we need help?
- Do we have a representative from the development or IT team to support the effort?
- How does management feel about analytics?
- Can any of our teammates make time for in-depth analytics training?
- Do we have budget available to hire outside help?
- Who has a background in analytics we could speak with?
- Who might be a good advocate to get headcount or resources for the project?

Tools

- Do we have Google Analytics installed?
- When was it installed?
- Has the installation ever been validated to make sure it works properly?
- Who manages access to the tool?
- Which Web sites does it cover?
- Does it have any advanced configurations setup such as ecommerce tracking or event tracking?
- What other tracking tools do we have set up?
- Are we using Google AdWords, DoubleClick, or another online advertising platform?
- Are we running usability or user experience testing?
- Have we ever run any A/B or multivariate testing on the Web site?
- What tools do we use to track competitors?

Unified data

- Have we ever combined analytics data with other data sources?
- Have we ever audited our conversion goals to make sure they are configured properly?
- What other systems do we use that we might want to connect to Google Analytics?

- Who administers these systems?
- Do these administrators have time to contribute to the project?
- Can we tie our sales back to the first customer touch point?

Process integration

- Who on the marketing team has working knowledge of Google Analytics?
- Do we have time to train the team to work with the tool?
- Who should have direct access, and whom do we want to support?
- What tactical decisions could be better informed by analytics?
- What forum can we use to report our findings?
- Are there existing reports we can incorporate into analytics data?

These questions should help you think holistically about how to incorporate your analytics data into your day-to day business decisions. As you dive into the details of Google Analytics, try to keep these five areas in mind and continuously ask yourself how the company could improve along every dimension. Too many organizations focus on tools alone when in reality the tools are often the least important area.

25 tips for putting data to work

We hope these questions will help you start thinking about the organizational elements that will impact your analytics effort. Now here are 25 tips for making progress in each of the five focus areas. Share these with your analytics team and keep them in mind as you move forward with your effort.

Goals and strategy

- **Don't lose sight of top-line objectives.** No matter what your company's business, it is important to tie all your activities back to the simple goals that keep you in business. If it's a for-profit company, the objective is increasing revenue, cutting costs, and raising customer satisfaction. If it's a not-for-profit, the goal is filling an unmet need or influencing perception. Your measurement strategy starts with these foundational goals.
- **Align the right goals with the right stakeholders.** Individual goals should align with team goals; team goals should align with division goals; division goals should align with corporate strategy. Working together effectively starts with everyone being on the same page. Advocate a formal process for goal-setting. Also, make sure that every goal has a clear owner and that the owner has the authority to execute on that goal, or assign the goal to someone who has the authority.
- **Create an inclusive forum for priorities.** The most efficient form of government might be a benevolent dictator, but dictators who want to make analytical decisions need to incorporate lots of different inputs when setting priorities. Do your team a favor and create a monthly

priorities meeting where team members can give their opinion on existing projects and add new projects for consideration. Find a specific time in this forum for Google Analytics data.

- **Reprioritize often.** Quarterly planning might have worked 20 years ago, but today you need to be nimble if you want to effectively capitalize on feedback. Look at your team priorities at least monthly and your individual priorities at least once a week to stay ahead of the curve. Be sure to consider Google Analytics data.
- **Reward performance and hold people accountable.** When you set measurable goals, hold people accountable to their measured results. If your goal-setting isn't tied to recognition, financial incentives, promotions, budget increases, or other rewards, people might set goals and forget about them. Give top performers recognition in a public forum. Trust us, it works! Don't give praise or blame blindly, though — there might be mitigating circumstances to consider for those who don't reach their targets.

Expertise

- **Create a central hub to support users.** An organizational structure without a dream team at the center will not work. Web analytics includes specialized terminology, skills, and processes that need a home. A central analytics group is more than the sum of its parts, so form your group as soon as possible or you risk problems such as poorly configured tools, miscommunication, and data overload.
- **Include diverse skill sets (technical, analytical, interpersonal).** The dream team example is a good starting place for assembling your team. You'll need at least one technical member who understands JavaScript and at least one businessperson who can analyze data and translate findings into understandable information for your colleagues. Hiring someone who has direct experience in analytics is a huge plus, but for now, these folks are hard to come by.
- **Consider outside help.** If this is your organization's first foray into serious Web analytics, consider hiring professional help, such as a Google Analytics authorized consultant. An analytics professional can help you validate your installation, train team members, identify key metrics, and launch a testing program. Once you have a strong collection system running, they can also help you take action on the data by implementing test variations and optimizing your advertising spend.
- **Plan for ongoing support.** Installing and validating Google Analytics will get you about 5 percent of the way toward making effective use of the data. If a vendor tells you otherwise, don't believe it! Your dream team will need to help colleagues gain access to data and make sense of the numbers they receive. Many of their questions will be straightforward and procedural, but they're often crucial and need answering.
- **Include an education component.** One of the mantras of your dream team should be "Teach people to fish." Build deep analytical knowledge in your central team, but document that knowledge and train colleagues to repeat the analysis. You can even include common analysis

techniques into custom reports or automated processes to reduce the need to reinvent the wheel. Keep these techniques simple and reserve the complex stuff for the experts.

Tools

- **Keep it simple.** For years Web analytics tools were sold based on the quantity of data they returned and their sophistication. *Complexity is a liability.* The limiting factor on how well you can apply your data is the ability of nontechnical personnel to quickly comprehend and use the data to prioritize activities and execute better. The more complex your tools, the more work it is to parse the information they need.
- **Don't pay for what you don't need.** Use free tools to their full capacity before you consider spending money on a more expensive solution. You may be surprised how long it takes to reach that point. It's tempting to think that buying a tool will take the work out of applying data, but that is just not the case. Usually it's the reverse, and data from expensive tools will be more difficult to apply.
- **Use the right tool for the right job.** Chapter 2 explains the tools you have at your disposal for understanding your customers. Be sure to apply the right tool to the right job. Use voice-of-the-customer research to understand what your users think instead of looking at clickstream data. Place your performance in context using competitive tools. Also, don't use a jackhammer when you need a chisel. How do you know which tool is right? When in doubt, start with the simplest option that is the fastest to get running and try it out.
- **Validate your installations.** Just because vendors claim their tools work "out of the box" doesn't mean they do. If you accidentally make mistakes during installation — which is common — you may undermine confidence in the data and make historical trending difficult. Validation means checking data sources against one another and against the ultimate benchmark of common sense.
- **Centralize administration.** It may be tempting, but don't give everyone the keys to the castle. Some administrative tasks — such as granting access, changing filters, and scheduling reports — are best managed centrally. Otherwise, you may wind up with a mess and nobody with a strong-enough incentive to clean it up.

Unified data

- **Monetize metrics.** The holy grail of analytics is the ability to connect every dollar you spend with every dollar you take in. Once you've achieved that goal, you can optimize your spend with certainty and get a complete picture of the visitor buying cycle. However, this is not always possible and you will need to be courageous and make decisions based on the information you have without suffering analysis paralysis.
- **Use prebuilt integrations.** Many CRM systems, e-mail platforms, call-tracking packages, shopping carts, and content management systems are already integrated with Google Analytics.

Look at the prebuilt solutions first for your integration needs, but be aware that they sometimes don't work as planned. If you have the budget, consider hiring an expert to make sure both systems talk to each other correctly.

- **Don't fall into the accuracy trap.** No Web analytics tool is 100 percent accurate! This reality will likely be with us for the long term, so your goal should be to have all your data sources produce results within 15 percent of expected values and then move on. For example, if your sales database records 650 sales in January and Google Analytics only shows 648, don't worry too much. Perfect accuracy is a mirage.

- **Do it manually before you automate.** If you're convinced that bringing two data sources together will solve a host of problems, try combining the data manually first and then take simple actions. For example, you may think that if you could combine your CRM system with Google Analytics, your salespeople would finally recognize the value in Google Analytics. In this case, try using the export feature to manually bring the data together into a single report, and then evaluate the result. If the combined data generates a great deal of excitement, then consider making the investment to automate the process.

- **Start small.** The idea of gaining a "360-degree view" of your customer base is highly seductive, but obtaining that view can also be overwhelming. Start small by connecting one or two data sources and prioritize your other activities. Once you're making full use of the data sources you have, consider adding new ones.

Process integration

- **Launch early and often.** Experimentation is one of the cornerstones of online marketing success. In the past, you only had one chance to develop the perfect television commercial or direct-mailing piece. Today you can put out a communication or promotional element, collect feedback as you go, and refine the element over time using the stream of feedback you get from Web analytics. Think of every launch as an ongoing activity where the bulk of your time will go into refinement, and where you can optimize against metrics that are directly tied to your bottom line.

- **Deliver the right metrics to the right people.** If you have a marketer who focuses purely on search engine marketing (SEM), give him or her a report that has only the metrics relevant to SEM. If you give open access to your teammates without advising them on what to look at, they might become overwhelmed and go back to making decisions based on instinct. Every irrelevant metric they have to look at saps a bit of mental energy. Keep it simple and put people at the center of your decisions regarding what data to track and report on — not the data.

- **Test and retest.** The Japanese term *kaizen* is used to describe a mindset of continuous improvement. Until you convert 100 percent of potential buyers into actual sales, there is always room to improve. Don't set ridiculous or unattainable goals, however. You should be ready to proceed in short bursts for a long period, rather than all in one big push.

- **Create a common language.** When the sales team says "conversion," it might mean something different from when the marketing team uses the same term. Use your dream team to document and communicate definitions so that when people quote terminology or metrics in meetings, they can tie what they say back to a source. Don't accept any data without a source, especially not in PowerPoint presentations. Accepting undocumented data is worse than no data at all.

- **Teach people to fish.** If your marketing group is using data in its day-to-day tactical activities, it needs to be able to access the data it needs, either through an automated report or through read-only access to your analytics data. The group also needs training to understand what analysis to do, and tech support to address problems as they arise. Supporting decision-makers should be the most important function of your central analytics team after providing clean data and insights. Only when decision-makers start acting on the data will your organization see real results.

Seeing GETUP in action

To bring this advice into context, we're providing the following real examples of companies that have made the shift to analytical marketing. We've chosen different-size companies to show you the types of challenges faced as more stakeholders are added.

Twiddy & Co.: The little guy

Off the coast of North Carolina, on a quiet island full of hammocks and picket fences, Twiddy & Co. sits in a sprawling Cape Cod–style office helping mainlanders find the perfect summer vacation home. On a good day, the office is buzzing with calls from potential renters asking questions about whether Duck township or the neighboring Corolla is better for keeping the kids entertained, and whether Twiddy has any homes with a pizza oven or a rotisserie for an extra-special family cookout.

Doug Twiddy and his management team discuss the outlook for the coming year's vacation season, a ritual they've been going through each spring since 1978, when Doug founded the company. "I think we need to play it safe this year on staffing," declares Jake Paulson, the vice president, waiving a tattered copy of the *Wall Street Journal*. "I just don't see how we're going to compete with these guys. This article says they've already cut deals for 1,600 properties in 12 weeks — 16 *hundred* — and I keep hearing chatter about the national ad campaign they've kicked off." Paulson is referring to a publicly traded company called Resort View that had recently set its sights on Twiddy's Outer Banks area as the next big vacation spot to bring under its corporate umbrella. "Hang on a sec, Jake," interjects Ross Twiddy, the company's marketing lead. "I've heard the chatter too, but I've got something here you should take a look at."

Ross leans over and drops a printed report from Google Analytics comparing this season's visitor activity on the Web site with the previous years. The report shows growth across the board in everything from engagement goals such as individual listings viewed to conversions from paid search advertising. "If I had to guess," Ross says with a twinge of his patented southern charm, "I think we're going to be just fine."

"I'm going to have to disagree with you Ross," Jake responded with his own broad smile. "I don't care what the numbers there say — you don't cozy up next to a huge company on a small island like this and not feel the squeeze. Let's just say that if your numbers are right, I'll be buying you a beer."

Since the company had closed its first reservation online in the late 1990s, Doug Twiddy had seen more and more information from cyberspace flowing into his planning meetings, mostly from Ross. He recalled the meetings he'd held in the early days of the company, before the Web, when he'd heard a lot of impassioned speeches from his team about unseasonably warm weather in New England and other distant factors that were "sure" to set the tone for the market that year. He also remembered the "missions" when he sent his young sons out to scout for vacancies on competitors' properties and help them benchmark the week's occupancy rate.

Things had changed so much since then, and he'd come to rely more and more on the insights Ross provided when deciding on everything from what types of photos to feature, which areas they should be looking at when acquiring properties, and what amenities they needed to invest in.

He could trace the genesis back to a casual conversation on the front porch of the office when Ross had asked for a few thousand dollars to hire a part-time programmer and online marketer to try to attract more rentals through the Web site. Doug Twiddy had said yes, on the condition that they start small and see if they could close 10 percent of weekly rentals through the Web site. Ross hit that target in less than a month, and he kept exceeding expectations straight through for five years, bringing on three new staff members and raising the percentage of rentals closed online to more than 75 percent. Over that time Ross and his programmer, Joe, learned the ins and outs of Google Analytics, managing issues ranging from installation to data discrepancies to new feature launches, and even a bout of analysis paralysis when the small team wasted a week trying to make sense of data that turned out to be incomplete.

After the staff meeting, Doug asked his son to join him for a beer at the inn down the street. "Ross, I have to say I'm pleased to see such a good set of numbers, given how much of a stir Resort View's been making. Still, I think Jake's point is a good one. Whatever you've been doing with the Web site is working, and we're going to need a lot more of it if we're going to survive this."

"Don't worry dad," Ross replied. "Evan and the guys know how serious this is, and we've already started on a new set of ideas I think are going to help us book a lot more rentals this summer."

The next morning, Ross sat down with Evan, the company's analyst and search marketer, and Joe, the programmer, to craft a plan of attack. They kicked off the meeting with a presentation from Evan, who had been up for half the night poring over two years of Google Analytics data, looking for areas to improve. After a short presentation and over an hour of Q&A, Ross started scrawling notes on a whiteboard on some initiatives to start on. The team accelerated its plans to deploy Google Website Optimizer, a free testing tool, to let it test new variations on the listing pages, and the team sent out a photographer to gather fresh shots for properties with low conversion rates.

The team wrote a detailed spec on three potential improvements to the Web site's search engine, which it could see was involved in more than 80 percent of converted sales, but performed poorly on a subset of keywords. Evan combed through hundreds of keywords on AdWords, raising bids on some and excluding others that didn't convert entirely. The team made a list of the top 10 entry points for the site, and created a detailed spec to test new variations on each one. Last, it called a Google

Analytics authorized consultant, who it hoped would help Twiddy & Co. complete an initiative that would link visitor data from the new online lease back to the first touch point a visitor had on the site, giving it an end-to-end view of the ROI for each marketing channel.

Over the next two years, Ross and his team burned the midnight oil time and time again, testing different variations on key Web site features and content almost daily. Each morning, Ross would wander downstairs for a session with the reservationists he called "interrogation," where he would interview each representative about customers calls and their inquiries, what they'd liked and disliked, and how many calls they had received. Ross paired this qualitative data with the numbers he looked at each day in Google Analytics to understand which issues on the Web site needed to be fixed right away and which could wait, and how well the team's expectations for each home matched the renters' actual experience.

"Interrogation" was something Doug had started early on in the business. The difference now was that Ross had an online proving ground where he could quickly test ideas for improvement that came out of the sessions. The team began to notice that as they launched new features on the site, Resort View would often copy them, but often months later and without the additional refinements that came from testing them in action.

To keep tabs on Resort View's performance and Twiddy & Co.'s other competitors, Ross dispatched an intern to manually check occupancy rates on their Web sites each day. Later, Ross automated the process. In the weekly management meetings, the team looked to Ross to let them know how they were doing in relation to their competitors for the week. Ross was also able to let them know that visitors were constantly searching for houses with pools, and Twiddy & Co. had only a single oceanfront home with a pool in their inventory. The team dispatched a sales rep to track down and win over additional homeowners who maintained properties with pools, and Twiddy & Co. saw the places snapped up almost immediately for the duration of the summer.

Additionally, when homeowners complained about being unable to rent properties through Twiddy, the sales team could now check Google Analytics to prove that the property had been seen hundreds or even thousands of times, which helped them convince even stubborn owners to alter pricing and amenities to meet demand. All the while, Doug marveled at how things had changed, thinking back to the company's lone brochure and fixed seasonal pricing that it had relied on as its sole marketing medium for almost two decades.

The seasons progressed, and one afternoon Jake walked in to a management meeting with a copy of the *Wall Street Journal*, just as he had five years earlier when the crisis over Resort View's entry into the market first became clear. This time he had a smile on his face. "It's official. They're finished. They've been absorbed into a new parent, and they're pulling out of the whole market." The team let out a loud holler and everyone headed out early to grab a celebratory drink.

The first toast was to Ross, for turning the company's online channel into the centerpiece of its growth and for giving everyone from housekeeping to finance ammunition in the battle to win over renters and homeowners from Resort View. Ross's face lit up in a grin and he turned to Jake and said, "All in a day's work, and you know you should really be getting your news online. I saw that story break three days ago on an industry blog. I was just waiting for you old-timers to catch up." Jake let out a loud hoot, "Fair enough, but there's something to be said for taking it a bit slower. We are in the vacation business after all."

The key takeaways:

- **Start small.** Twiddy & Co. began with the goal of closing 10 percent of its sales online and gradually expanded its efforts to keep pace with demand.
- **Gather the right expertise.** Ross knew he wasn't a developer when he began, so from day one, he made the wise step of finding a developer instead of trying to do everything himself.
- **Launch and iterate.** Twiddy & Co. never stopped optimizing its site after it was launched — a much better mindset than launching and walking away.
- **Combine analytics and qualitative data.** Through his regular "interrogation," Ross was able to find qualitative feedback from customers to combine with Google Analytics reports.
- **Pay attention to competitive context.** As an organization, Twiddy & Co. recognized that its business didn't exist in a vacuum, and it used the Web to monitor competitors' activities as well as drive its own sales.

PBS: Teaching people to fish

What works better, a centralized Web analytics team with deep technical knowledge, or nonexpert users spread throughout an organization? This was the question faced by Amy Sample when she joined PBS Interactive as Web analytics director in fall 2007. PBS Interactive helps individual PBS producers and local PBS stations create and promote microsites for programming such as *Nova*, *American Masters*, and *Sid the Science Kid*. Amy had the difficult task of helping these managers make educated decisions about how to improve the microsites they develop for each of their shows.

When Sample came on board, she learned that PBS had standardized on a single analytics tool. This was a good first step, but few at the company were familiar with the tool, and the reports it generated were not being used to take action. Producers wanted to know more about how people interacted with microsites for their programs, but they weren't sure what to focus on. At the same time, the analytics group had a hard time keeping up with demands from so many stakeholders. According to Sample, "The producers wanted to dig deeper into their site data than a monthly report could provide."

Her response was two-fold. First, after consulting with a pilot group of producers and members of the interactive group, she decided to deploy an installation of Google Analytics. In Sample's words, "We chose Google Analytics because we had a diverse group of needs and limited resources. We wanted a system where a user with little training could get insights right away." Second, Sample worked with LunaMetrics, a Google Analytics authorized consultant, to manage the complex issues PBS faced with cross-domain tracking and a complicated account structure. LunaMetrics also created training materials, hosted an on-site training for PBS staff, and conducted a series of training Webinars for producers and local stations.

As it turns out, despite the challenges of getting resources assigned to tag pages and working out the right account structure, deploying Google Analytics was the easy part. In Sample's experience, the more challenging problem came in spreading knowledge and awareness of analytics through the organization in a way that allowed people to take action on the data. "My approach has been to teach people how to fish," Sample explains. "It's been about doing training classes and one-on-one work with key practitioners, creating specific training decks by job function, and getting other groups to use analytics data in their daily activities."

Google Analytics has been a key facilitator in the transformation of PBS online. Stakeholders are no longer focused on monthly reports. Increasingly, they are using analytics to inform actual business decisions. Here are some examples highlighted by the PBS team:

- **Site search tracking:** The PBSkids.org site has implemented changes as a result of insights gleaned from site search tracking that have increased traffic to the site 30 percent in the last year (see Chapter 10).
- **Funnel optimization:** The PBSkids Island team used funnels to optimize their registration path resulting in a 3 × improvement in Conversion Rate (see Chapter 10).
- **Content optimization:** An analysis of users' video consumption behavior on PBS.org and PBSkids. org led to the development of the PBS Video and PBSkids Go broadband portals. PBS went even further, basing a full 2008 PBS.org redesign on data that indicated which content visitors access (see Chapter 10).
- **Advertising optimization**: PBS's marketing group also looks at what visitors do after they arrive from display ad campaigns in order to zero in on referring sites that send high-quality traffic. They use this information to optimize successive campaigns (see Chapter 10).

Sample's long-term vision is to extend analytics to measure engagement with PBS content both on-site and off-site. She also hopes to gauge the impact of online content on TV tune-in and to track online donations while expanding her training efforts to teach producer colleagues how to segment traffic and drill deeper into visitor behavior on their microsites.

The lesson learned is that no matter what analytics tool you're using, a well-planned deployment is only a first step. The hard part is "teaching people to fish," making analytics data a key component in your organization's everyday business decisions.

The key takeaways:

- **Find your analytics champion.** PBS put itself ahead of the game when it created the position of analytics director and gave analytics a permanent advocate.
- **Don't work in a vacuum.** From the moment she started, Sample made sure she was actively engaging with the decision-makers who would use the data. This ensured that Google Analytics didn't exist in a vacuum and that data made it into key decisions.
- **Socialize your successes.** The beauty of becoming a master of your analytics data is that is gives you hard numbers to share with team members that prove your impact. Don't be afraid to publish numbers that show your contribution.

Nokia: Enforcing standards in a big company

What do General Electric, Procter & Gamble, and Nokia all have in common? They are all conglomerates, and big ones at that — really big. If you can believe it, Nokia began its long history in 1865 as a paper mill on the banks of a river in southern Finland. From these humble origins, Nokia diversified into everything from rubber tires to telegraph cable, buying competitors, reinvesting profits, and rising eventually to become an industrial powerhouse and Finland's largest company. As the conglomerate crossed into its second century, it continued moving up the value chain, spinning off a variety of business units, and placing a growing emphasis on its consumer brand and telecom business. In many ways, this is where Nokia's analytics story begins. With the company's desire to place customers at the center of decisions came an immediate need to understand what they wanted.

Before the Web, the company used the same combination of surveys, focus groups, and panels favored by market researchers for decades. After the advent of the Web, however, the amount of data available on the preferences and activities of Nokia's customer base exploded beyond all measure. Unrefined metrics and data points streamed in daily from dozens of disparate systems, burying the management team under an avalanche of numbers. Each business unit was left to make sense of this avalanche in its own way, leading to a medley of homegrown dashboards and frustration over a lack of common standards and definitions. Unvalidated statistics circulated without a source, finding their way into important discussions over strategic and tactical issues.

After years of listening to vendors' promises of more and better data, the company realized it was time to devote resources to sorting the data that was already there. With a strong mandate from upper management to reinvent Nokia as a customer services company, the company formed the Consumer Data and Interaction Program to put the avalanche of data to productive use.

The CDIP team immediately got to work building a structure and team around data analysis and reporting. The team began by interviewing key stakeholders and gradually identified six key issues with Nokia's data management practices. From the perspective of GETUP, the framework laid out earlier in this chapter, the issues the CDIP team identified mirrored those of other companies large and small:

- Common language is missing (unified data).
- Consumer data is fragmented (unified data).
- Consumer data quality is poor (tools).
- Analytics competencies are missing (expertise).
- Consumer data and insights are not part of business processes (process integration).
- Marketing activities are not guided by common principles (goals and strategy).

The team's response was multipronged and began with the formation of the Services Intelligence and Analytics Business Unit. Unlike CDIP, this team would be a permanent fixture at Nokia and would not only coordinate the turnaround effort for Nokia's services but continue to support analytics long into the future.

The team positioned itself in a supporting role to Nokia's diverse business units, with a mandate to help managers and operational staff incorporate customer data into strategic and tactical decisions.

Nokia turned to outside recruiters to fill key positions. Executives from the team also attracted top talent by sharing wins and information from major conferences, while also announcing that the team was hiring. Greg Dowling, one of the earliest hires, describes the early days of the program as a "whirlwind" of activity, interviews, and tough choices. The team worked hard to staff a diverse team with strengths ranging from quantitative analysis to data management to interpersonal and presentation skills. It also conducted a rigorous vendor evaluation process early on to select technology partners it still relies on today.

With new recruits flowing in each month, the team set to work developing an organizational structure and business process around data and analytics. One of its first steps involved separating analysis and reporting into two separate teams. Analysts worked one on one with stakeholders to assess what needed to be measured, when it needed to be measured, and who needed to have access to the data. The measurement team worked with technology vendors to make this plan a reality, enforcing standards, and keeping information organized and current.

This approach mirrors the structure laid out in Table 3.2, which separates analysis from technical implementation and administration. The team placed strong emphasis on maintaining transparency, clarity in message, and predictability when dealing with the business units they supported. By starting small and sticking to this mantra, the team was gradually able to win the attention and support of a variety of operational teams. Analysts were paired directly with team leads to create strong relationships and ensure that findings made their way into key discussions. Some teams went a step further to create standing meetings to discuss the latest insights produced by analytics unit.

Dowling credits the decision to centralize analytics functions as a crucial element in the company's effort to build a data-driven culture. By centralizing processes like documentation, tool selection, data integration, and user support, the team was able to develop the common terminology and best practices that the company needed to make sense of data intelligently.

Every metric flowing in from the company's multitude of data sources was carefully audited and documented in a single spreadsheet, with clear indications of its technical origins, its meaning in plain English, and its purpose in relation to the company's business goals. Metrics that could not be tied back to short- or long-term business goals were downplayed or cut entirely to protect against data overload. Each business unit in turn received clear requirements and recommendations from the central analytics team on which metrics to use to benchmark their performance.

Metrics were grouped into three tiers, with Tier 1 comprising the most general metrics common to all units, Tier 2 consisting of metrics common to a specific business model (such as subscription payments), and Tier 3 being unique to a given unit. This gave upper management a common system for comparing the performance of one unit versus another and assigning budget and resources accordingly. It also retained the flexibility each business unit needed to define metrics associated with short-term tactical goals.

Some holes were identified in Nokia's understanding, leading to deployment of new tools and one of the largest qualitative segmentation studies ever conducted. On the other hand, the emphasis remained on first cleaning up the data the company already had and then deploying new collection techniques, rather than the reverse.

As Nokia expands into new areas and analytics technology matures, there is still plenty to keep Dowling's team busy. By creating a flexible and sturdy measurement standard and an analytics dream team to enforce it, Nokia is well positioned to handle new challenges as they arise. At the end of the day, Dowling cites the team's goal of making stakeholders' lives easier rather than harder as the most crucial element in their success.

When it comes to analytics, it's important to remember that the business needs to come first, and that the data is there to make it run smoother and more efficiently, not the other way around.

The key takeaways:

- **Give analytics a permanent home.** Nokia realized that, to capitalize on its avalanche of data, it needed a permanent base of organizational knowledge and legitimacy as well as specialized expertise and tools.
- **Validate your tools.** Nokia's first step was cleaning up definitions and data for analysis. This is a crucial step to ensure that you build trust in your data.
- **Pare analysts with stakeholders.** By putting analysts in direct contact with managers, Nokia helped build trust and understanding around findings.
- **Make life easier for managers.** The analytics group at Nokia made the wise decision to incorporate standards directly into tools whenever possible, and it worked hard to minimize unnecessary demands on decision-makers. This helped managers adopt a positive attitude toward analytics rather than viewing it as burdensome and difficult.

Overcoming common obstacles

Even with these stories in mind, you'll find that the trickiest stumbling points you encounter won't go away easily.

Long sales cycles and the "fuzzy factor"

When you can *monetize* your Conversion Goals (assign real dollar values to different measures of visitor behavior), they become instantly more relevant. Quite simply, it is easier to assign values if you are generating direct revenue online. If you run a subscription business, or a business with a long sales cycle, you will need more complex mathematical or technical configurations to "close the loop" and connect income all the way back to your first marketing touch points. Take a look at the following categories, and assess the *primary* focus of your company's Web site:

- **Ecommerce**: Direct, one-time revenue through product sales; this also includes online donations.
- **Subscription**: Subscription revenue generated through recurring payments; this includes SaaS (software as a service).
- **Lead generation**: Indirect revenue generation by capturing contact info to use in a sales process.
- **Advertising-driven**: Direct revenue generated through online advertising.

- **Branding**: Indirect revenue generated by positively influencing brand perception.
- **Other engagement**: These include educational sites, online communities, and knowledge exchange.

If your company Web site sounds like it falls closer to the bottom of this list, it will be more difficult to see immediate gains from Google Analytics than it would be for an ecommerce site. Be sure to set expectations accordingly.

No senior advocate

Some companies have managed to integrate analytics into multiple divisions in their organization, but without a senior advocate it can be difficult to orchestrate a large-scale cultural shift. The role of a senior advocate is also political, because you will encounter resistance as you try to shift focus to more measurable initiatives. Start small and try to show quick wins that will gradually gain you support. You will find many techniques in Part III.

Another tactic that works well involves tying metrics directly to top-line objectives such as revenue, which will let you make a financial case for a pilot optimization effort.

Last, instead of creating new reports for Web analytics data, you can get executives' attention by integrating key metrics into existing reports that they are used to receiving.

—

Google Analytics Essentials

Understanding How Google Analytics Works

Understanding how to use Google Analytics requires a solid understanding of how Google Analytics works. So first we'll describe how data is collected and processed to give you that grounding before we explain what each report means and show you how to analyze the data.

Don't worry if you're not a programmer or a nerd. This section, like most sections in this book, is geared toward marketing professionals. We're not going to overcomplicate this objective! If you still haven't created your Google Analytics Account or logged into your reports, don't worry. We'll show you how later on. Explaining how Google Analytics works is all about process. There are three fundamental processes that work together to create all the reports in Google Analytics.

The first process is data collection, or how Google collects data about your Web site traffic and sends it back to Google's Analytics servers. The second is data processing, which is how Google turns the raw data collected during data processing into reports. The third process is report generation. Reports are generated in real time, every time you view a report in your browser.

How Data Is Collected

Google Analytics, like many Web analytics tools today, uses a technology called a *page tag* to track Web site traffic. A page tag is a small piece of JavaScript code that is placed on all the pages of your Web site. In Google Analytics, we affectionately refer to the page tag as the Google Analytics Tracking Code, or GATC for short. This code collects data about the Web site visitor and sends it off to Google. It actually does a few more things, but we cover the rest later in this chapter.

For those of you who are not familiar with JavaScript, it is a programming language used to enhance Web sites by giving programmers the ability to interact with a Web browser's settings, thus allowing for more interactive Web sites.

The GATC is the foundation for all data in Google analytics. If you want data, which we all do, you must add the GATC to all the pages on your site. We explain how to add the GATC to your site later. For now, we describe how Google Analytics collects data using the diagram shown in Figure 4.1.

The data collection process starts when a person visits your Web site. It doesn't matter how he or she found your site — via a bookmark, a search engine results page, or other mechanism — what's key is that the person is visiting your site.

Opening a page in a browser generates a request to your Web server. Basically the browser is telling the Web server that it wants a specific page. Being the obedient computer that it is, your Web server

FIGURE 4.1

The Google Analytics data collection process

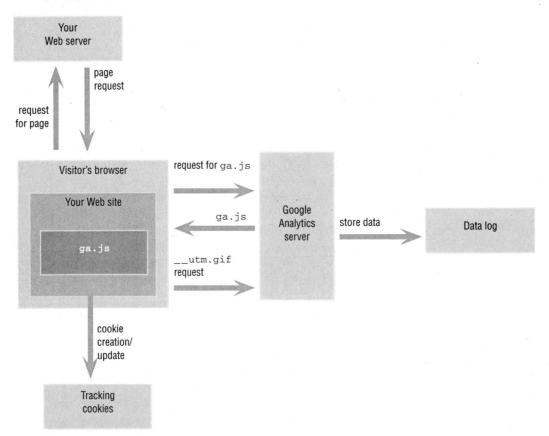

responds with the requested page. Within that page is the GATC. Remember, this code (shown below) must be on every page of the site so Google Analytics can track traffic correctly.

As your page loads in the visitor's browser, the code behind the page executes sequentially, starting at the top of the page and progressing to the bottom of the page. (If you've never seen the code behind a Web page, you can use the View Source feature of your browser. This feature is usually found by right-clicking on a page.) When the browser reaches the Google Analytics Tracking Code, which is normally at the bottom of the page, it springs into action.

First, the tracking code requests a file named ga.js from a Google server. This happens in the first section of the GATC, as shown in this code:

```
<script type="text/javascript">
var gaJsHost = (("https:" == document.location.protocol) ? "https://
    ssl." : "http://www.");
document.write(unescape("%3Cscript src='" + gaJsHost + "google-
    analytics.com/ga.js' type='text/javascript'%3E%3C/script%3E"));
</script>

<script type="text/javascript">
try {
    var pageTracker = _gat._getTracker("UA-XXXXX-1");
    pageTracker._trackPageview();
} catch(err) {}
</script>
```

This ga.js file is a set of instructions. It contains the logic that Google Analytics needs to track the visitor. The visitor's Web browser requests this file from www.google-analytics.com/ga.js, which is just another computer on the Internet. However, it is important to point out that this request automatically goes to the closest Google Analytics server to minimize any potential delays to your Web site.

For example, if the visitor is physically located in San Francisco, Google automatically detects that the visitor is located in San Francisco and retrieves the file from the data center closest to San Francisco.

When the Google Analytics server receives the request, it responds by sending the file back to the browser. Once the file has been retrieved by the browser, it is usually cached (or stored) by the browser to eliminate having to make the same request during the rest of the visitor's visit.

After the ga.js file has been delivered to the browser, the second section of the tracking code begins to execute and collects data about the visitor. This tracking code uses data stored in the visitor's browser to learn where the visitor came from, what type of operating system he or she has, what type of browser is being used, etc.

Once all this information has been collected, the tracking code sets (or updates, depending on how many times the visitor has been to the site) a number of cookies on the visitor's machine. A cookie is a small piece of text stored on a user's computer. Cookies are not programs; they are small text files that store information. This information can be almost anything from the visitor's login name to the date of his or her last visit. The important thing to know is that this data is specific to your Web site.

Cookies are critical to Google Analytics. If Google Analytics cannot set cookies on the visitor's computer, the visitor will not be tracked. It's that simple: No cookies, no tracking.

It's important to note that Google Analytics uses a type of cookie called a first-party cookie. There are two types of cookies, first-party cookies and third-party cookies. A first-party cookie is a cookie that is created by the Web site the visitor is viewing. For example, if you're looking at `www.wsj.com`, and the Web site sets a cookie, that cookie has the domain `www.wsj.com`.

A third-party cookie is a cookie that is set with a domain that is different from the domain of the Web site the visitor is viewing. For example, if I'm viewing `www.wsj.com`, and the Web site tries to set a cookie with a domain of `www.tracking.com`, that is a third-party cookie.

It is important to understand the difference between a first-party cookie and a third-party cookie. Many modern browsers are, by default, configured to block third-party cookies. And remember, Google Analytics will not work without cookies. First-party cookies are more reliable than third-party cookies.

Google Analytics uses four or five first-party cookies to track Web site visitors. The exact number depends on the complexity of the implementation. Table 4.1 lists the basic Google Analytics tracking cookies.

Using cookies to track Web site visitors is not 100 percent accurate. Any Web analytics tool that uses cookies is susceptible to data issues due to the very nature of cookies and a user's ability to manipulate (and delete) cookies using the browser's settings. For example, cookies are specific to each Web browser on your computer. So the cookies set when a visitor visits your site using

TABLE 4.1

Basic Google Analytics Tracking Cookies

Cookie Name	Purpose
__utma	**Visitor identification cookie.** Among other things, this cookie contains a unique numerical identifier. Google Analytics literally counts each __utma cookie to track the number of people, also known as Unique Visitors, to the site.
__utmb	**Session identifier.** Google Analytics uses this, and the __utmc cookie, to calculate time based metrics, like Time on Site and Time on Page.
__utmc	**Session identifier.** Google Analytics uses this, and the __utmb cookie, to calculate time based metrics, like Time on Site and Time on Page.
__utmz	**Visitor source.** Identifies where the visitor came from for this specific visit. It tracks things such as marketing campaigns, keywords, and referral traffic.
__utmv	**Custom variable.** This cookie is used with a feature called Custom Variables. It is used to store information that you the business owner choose to associate with your Web site visitors.

The Reliability of Tracking Visitors with Cookies

Several well-known industry professionals have conducted studies about the cookie habits of Web site visitors. A 2007 study by ComScore, showed that 30 percent of U.S. Internet users delete their cookies (http://www.comscore.com/press/release.asp?press=1389).

If you want to understand how your visitors block your cookies, you can run a test to measure the *block rate*. It's not a complicated test, but it does involve planning and IT support. You will need to create code that tries to set a cookie on the visitor's computer and then checks for the cookie. Identifying how many cookies you tried to set versus how many were actually set will provide insight into the percentage of visitors who are blocking cookies.

Microsoft's Internet Explorer are different from the cookies set when the visitor uses Firefox, Safari, Chrome, Opera, or another browser.

The result is that a visitor can have multiple occurrences of the Google Analytics cookies (one for each browser or computer that the person uses). And because Google Analytics identifies a unique visitor by counting the number of __utma cookies, a visitor who has multiple __utma cookies on his or her computer will be seen as multiple visitors (one for each browser used).

Cookies can also cause inaccuracies when counting new visitors and returning visitors. A new visitor is identified as someone who has not been to the site in the timeframe you're analyzing (whether or not the visitor's browser has a __utma cookie) or as someone who does not have a __utma cookie at all (and is thus presumed to have never visited the site before using that browser and computer). However, if a person regularly deletes cookies from the computer's browser, he or she will appear as a new visitor each time he or she visits the site, rather than be seen as a returning visitor.

Finally, all browsers provide a way for visitors to block cookies, even first-party cookies, thus breaking Google Analytics tracking and showing even repeat visitors as new visitors.

This process can help build confidence with those that use the data because it removes an unknown influence on the data, giving you better context for interpreting what the data means. Can you avoid some of these issues? In reality, no. There are too many variables that cannot be controlled. But you must consider the visitor's privacy. People should have a choice in how they are tracked on the Web. If they choose to delete their cookies, you need to deal with that choice. The best course of action is to understand how cookies can cause data issues and account for that issue during your analysis. One way we often address cookie issues is by looking at trends in the data rather than absolutes. When reviewing your data, look for trends in your data and investigate any anomalies

After the cookies have been set, the Google Analytics tracking code sends the data back to the Google Analytics servers by requesting an invisible image file named __utm.gif. All the data collected and stored in the cookies is sent as part of the request for the image; the GATC attaches the data in the form of query string parameters.

The query string is a series of name-value pairs in a URL (Uniform Resource Locator, or Web address) that appear after the question mark (?). These parameters are used for a number of reasons but usually to pass information back to the server. The server then uses this information to build the page that the visitor requested. The query string can contain multiple query string parameters separated by an ampersand (&) used for different purposes.

A sample __utm.gif request is shown here:

```
http://www.google-analytics.com/__utmgif?utmwv=4.3.1
    &utmn= 1683225979&utmhn=www.epikone.com&utmcs=UTF-8
    &utmsr=1920x1200&utmsc=24-bit&utmul=en-us
    &utmje=1&utmfl=10.0%20r22&utmdt=Analytics%20Talk
    &utmhid=490283110&utmr=-&utmp=/blog/&utmac=UA-30208-1
    &utmcc=__utma%3D100957269.1439956126833082000.1249748879.
    1249748879.1249748879.1%3B%2B__utmz%3D100957269.1249748879.
    1.1.utmcsr%3D(direct)%7Cutmccn%3D(direct)%7Cutmcmd%3D(none)
    %3B
```

When Google receives the data, it logs it into temporary storage. Once the data has been stored, the data collection is complete.

The data collection process is completely independent from the data processing. By keeping the data collection separate from the data processing, Google has added a failsafe to the system: If something should happen to the data processing engine, Google can continue to collect data because the two processes are not connected. This architecture also makes it possible for Google to update the data processing code without interrupting data collection.

Here are the important takeaways to remember about data collection:

- You must place the GATC on every page on your site that you want to track in Google Analytics.
- Every time a visitor opens a Web page that includes the GATC, a request is sent to Google and the information is stored. This process happens as long as the visitor's browser accepts the Google Analytics tracking cookies.
- Visitors who use multiple browsers, or delete their cookies between visits, are counted multiple times. Visitors who don't accept cookies aren't tracked at all. You can account for this by assuming that 30 percent of your visitors delete their cookies or by running a cookie-deletion test each month to get cookie-deletion percentage numbers more accurate for your site's actual visitors.
- Google Analytics is not 100 percent accurate, but then no Web analytics tool is. Google Analytics is more than accurate enough to detect trends and help you take action. It's also much more accurate than traditional marketing measurement approaches such as TV ratings.

How Data Is Processed

Now that we've explained how your Google Analytics data is collected, we need to cover how it is processed. One to three hours after the data has been collected, Google processes the data; Figure 4.2 shows the details of the data processing process.

During data processing, several things happen. First, Google Analytics creates fields. Fields, also called dimensions, are attributes of Web site visitors and the visits they create. Why two terms — *field* and *dimension* — to describe the data? *Field* is a term originally used when Google acquired Urchin Software, the precursor to Google Analytics. When Google started adding features like Advanced Custom Segments and Custom Reports to Google Analytics, it decided to use the term *dimension*. There are other differences between the two terms, which we describe later in this chapter.

Fields are created from the data sent to Google Analytics when the __utm.gif image is requested from the Google Analytics server. For example, one piece of visitor data collected by Google Analytics is the page title. This value is displayed at the top of the browser window, as shown in Figure 4.3.

The value for the page title is sent to Google as the utmdt query string parameter in the __utm. gif request. Below is the original request sent to Google for the page in Figure 4.3. The section highlighted below in boldface contains the utmdt parameter and thus the page title:

```
http://www.google-analytics.com/__utm.gif?utmwv=4.6.5
    &utmn= 48229232&utmhn=www.googlestore.com&utmcs=UTF-8
    &utmsr=1920x1200 &utmsc=24-bit&utmul=en-us&utmje=1
    &utmfl=10.0%20r42&utmdt=Google%20Online%20Store
    &utmhid=304333769&utmr=0&utmp=%2Fshop.axd%2FHome
    &utmac=UA-735212-16&utmcc=__utma%3D148589601.685288534.126=487604
    7.1264876047.1264876047.1%3B%2B__utmz
    %3D148589601.1264876047.1.1.utmcsr%3D(direct)
    %7Cutmccn%3D(direct)%7Cutmcmd%3D(none)%3B
```

FIGURE 4.2

Details of the Google Analytics data processing process

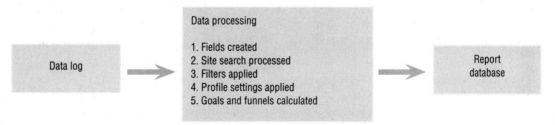

FIGURE 4.3

The page title, located at the top of a browser tab

Page title

During data processing, Google turns the utmdt value into the Page Title field and the Page Title dimension. This dimension is then used as the foundation for the Page Titles report, shown in Figure 4.4. The report is created by displaying all the values for the Page Title dimension as the rows of the report, and metrics that correspond to each value of the Page Titles field.

If you look at the __utm.gif request earlier, you can see other pieces of information about the visitor that are turned into fields, such as the monitor's screen size (for example, 2400x1920& is 1,920 by 1,200 pixels) and the default browser language (en-us, for example, means U.S. English). Each request is turned into a field and a dimension in Google Analytics.

A complete list of Google Analytics fields can be found in the Google Analytics Code section at http://code.google.com/apis/analytics/docs/tracking/gaTrackingTroubleshooting.html#gifParameters.

Although fields and dimensions are similar, there are some distinct differences. All fields are dimensions, but not all dimensions are fields. Fields are created only from the data in the __utm.gif request. Dimensions are created from all the fields as well as using information that is calculated during the data processing. We explain fields and how they are used in filters in Chapter 5, and we cover dimensions and their application in Chapter 7.

Once fields and dimension have been created, Google starts to apply the configuration settings to the data. Google Analytics begins by processing site search information. (See Chapter 5 for more information about configuring site search.) Next, Google applies filters to the data to modify the data. And finally, it applies profile settings to the data. All these settings work together to modify the data in a Google Analytics Profile; we explain each setting in Chapter 5.

After the configuration settings have been applied, Google Analytics stores the processed data in a report database. Once the data has been stored, it can never be changed. This is an important point that we want to reiterate: Once the data has been processed and stored in the reporting database, it can never

FIGURE 4.4

In the Content by Title report, each row of data in the report is a different value in the page title dimension.

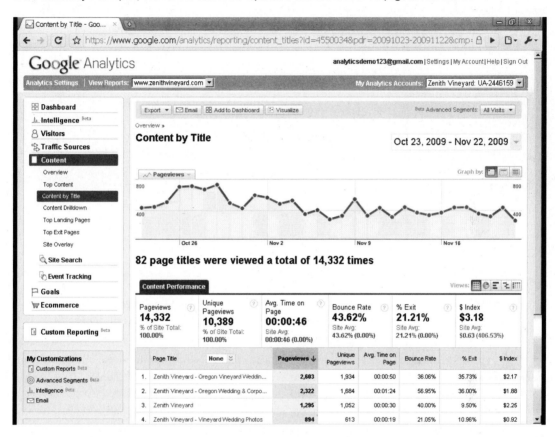

be changed! This means that any data issues caused by incorrect settings can never be resolved. Thus, it is critical to configure Google Analytics correctly and maintain a stable implementation in order to avoid any potential discrepancies in the data.

Accounts and Profiles: Data Organization

Google Analytics data is organized using a simple hierarchy involving accounts and profiles, as shown in Figure 4.5.

At the top of the hierarchy is a Google Account. A Google Account is a way for Google to identify you and attach you to the different services that Google provides. If you use Google AdWords, Gmail, or other Google service, you already have a Google Account. In the eyes of Google, Google Analytics is simply one more service that you can use. Your Google Account is identified by your personal login ID,

FIGURE 4.5

Left: Google Analytics is organized using accounts and profiles. Right: How to find the Google Analytics account number and profile number in the Google Analytics tracking code.

Account number

```
<script type="text/javascript">
try {
    var pageTracker = _gat._getTracker("UA-XXXXX-1");
    pageTracker._trackPageview();
} catch(err) {}
</script>
```

Profile number

which is an e-mail address. For example, john.doe@gmail.com could identify my Google Account. But it does not need to be a Gmail address; you can also create a Google Account using a non-Gmail e-mail address, like john@mysite.com.

The next part of the hierarchy is your Google Analytics Account. Like all Google services, your Google Analytics Account is attached to your Google Account. A Google Analytics Account is a way for Google to organize the data it collects for the Web sites you track. There are also several settings that are attached to your Google Analytics Account, such as data sharing (we explain these in Chapter 5).

Within your Google Analytics Account is a structure called a *profile*. You can have multiple profiles in your Google Analytics Account. Most people think of profiles as the data for a specific Web site. To some extent this is true. But profiles also contain configuration settings that alter the data. These settings are critical to ensuring that the data in Google Analytics is accurate and actionable.

Within the Google Analytics Tracking Code is a numeric identifier. This number identifies the Google Analytics Account and Profile where the data is sent. Figure 4.5 identifies how to find your Google Analytics Account number and the Google Analytics Profile number. Notice that both the account number and the profile are listed in the tracking code. The Google Analytics Account/Profile number combination is called the Web Property ID.

FIGURE 4.6

A single Google account can access profiles in multiple Google Analytics accounts.

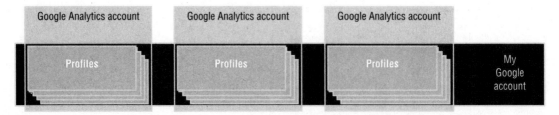

Using accounts and profiles, you can control access to data and create different sets of data in Google Analytics.

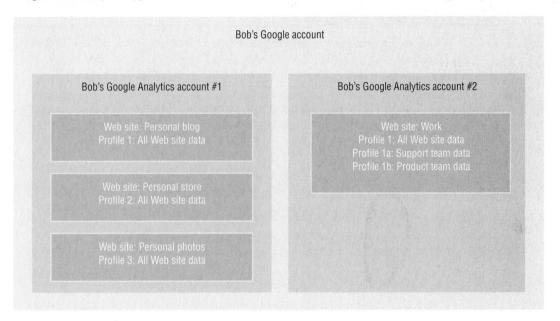

This structure of accounts and profiles makes many things possible. First, you can access other companies' Google Analytics Accounts and Profiles, if they grant you access. If you have administrative access to a Google Analytics Account, you can grant other users access to profiles in the account. In essence, your single Google Account can be used to access data in multiple Google Analytics Accounts. And because a single Google Analytics Account can have multiple Google Analytics Profiles, it is possible for you to have access to multiple profiles in multiple Google Analytics Accounts. A Google Account is a "one Google Account to many Google Analytics Accounts" relationship, as shown in Figure 4.6. (We explain how to add additional users to your account later in this chapter.)

Having profiles also adds flexibility to Google Analytics. Profiles have settings associated with them, and these settings can be used to change the data in the profile. Creating multiple profiles for a single Web site, each with its own settings, results in multiple profiles with very different data. Why is this important? You can change how the data looks and who has access to the data using various Profile Settings, as we explain in Chapter 5.

When you fully leverage the account and profile structure, you can create multiple sets of data for multiple Web sites or for the same Web site, and you can grant access to multiple users (see the example in Figure 4.7). At the top level is, for example, Bob's Google Analytics Account. This account has access to two Google Analytics Accounts: Bob's personal Analytics Account and his work Analytics Account. Within those accounts are several profiles. All the profiles in Bob's work account are for the same Web site, while each profile in Bob's personal Analytics Account are for different Web sites.

Chapter 5 describes the strategy behind setting up these accounts.

Generating Reports

The data reporting process is fairly straightforward. It is not as complicated as the data collection process or the data processing process. Once your Web site data has been processed (after a few hours), that data begins to appear in your reports.

Google Analytics reports are generated on-demand, which means that Google creates the report when you view it in the browser. The front-end reporting interface connects to the reporting database, retrieves the information you requested, and displays the information in your browser. You rarely have to wait more than a second to view the information you requested. You can access your reports via the administration screen shown in Figure 4.8.

Click on the name of an account, then click View Reports for the profile you want to use, as Figure 4.9 shows.

There is another way to access your data: Google provides an application programming interface, commonly called an *API*, that programmers can use to extract data directly from Google Analytics without using the reporting interface. Data in the API is the same data that you get in the reporting interface.

Now that you know all this, you can better communicate with your developer to ensure that data collection is happening properly. You also now have a better idea of where all the data comes from.

Here are the key takeaways to remember about data processing and organization:

FIGURE 4.8

To view reports, first choose an account to work with

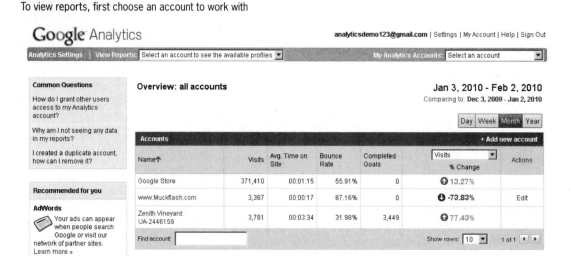

- Google Analytics data is processed in three steps: First, site search data is processed; next, filters are applied; and, finally, profile settings are applied.
- Google Analytics data is organized in a hierarchy. One Google Account can be associated with multiple Google Analytics Accounts, which can contain multiple Google Analytics Profiles.
- Once Google Analytics data is processed, it can never be changed. This makes it essential to ensure that your configuration is correct from the very beginning.

—

Installing and Administering Google Analytics

Explaining how to implement Google Analytics is no easy task. The reason is that every Web site is different. While sites can share similar characteristics, there is "no one size fits all" implementation plan. Our goal in this chapter is to explain how to plan your Google Analytics implementation. We walk through some of the basic configuration steps, then explain the more advanced implementation processes. Finally, we explain how to maintain your implementation to avoid potential issues with your data. Our goal throughout this chapter is to stress concepts that you can apply to your own configuration.

Planning an Implementation

Most people believe that installing Google Analytics is simply adding JavaScript page tags to your site. While it is true that you need to add some code to your site (we call this process *tagging*) an implementation is much, much more. Because Google Analytics collects data about your online business, the configuration must be aligned with your business goals. Furthermore, it must be configured to work with the technical architecture of your site. This combination of technical configuration and business configuration is what complicates an implementation.

But installing Google Analytics is not a daunting process. It just takes a little time and planning to identify potential issues and find the solutions to deal with them.

Before we dive into page tagging or configuration settings, let's talk about your Web site and the needs of your company. Remember, the implementation is all about aligning your business and your Web site architecture.

Gathering business requirements

We recommend starting your Google Analytics implementation by documenting the business needs of the people who will be using Google Analytics. You can't configure Google Analytics if you don't know what data you need.

Understanding the needs of those using Google Analytics to effectively plan how to install and configure the tool. Get out there and learn what metrics are important to them!

The best way to collect requirements is to interview the various groups and teams that will use Google Analytics or will be interested in the data. If you are a small company, you might interview yourself! But if your organization is larger, you may need numerous meetings with groups in different locations.

During these meetings, try to get an idea of what key performance indicators (or KPIs) and metrics are important to their job functions. Most people don't have outrageous requests. Most people in a marketing role need basic information about campaign performance, and so on.

- What metrics and KPIs are you currently using in your daily work?
- What metrics and KPIs would you like to have but cannot get?
- Do you have any reports that you can share with us?

It is important to collect the various metrics that people might use. You also need to decide how frequently the data consumers get the metric: daily, weekly, monthly? Do they provide the metrics to others on a regular interval? All this information can help when configuring the reporting features in Google Analytics.

Obviously the amount of effort it takes to uncover and document business requirements depends on the size of your organization. If you're a small business with 10 employees, you may uncover all the measurement needs in a one-hour meeting. But if you're a global organization with offices in multiple locations, it could take some time.

Sometimes, when the organization is new to analytics, it can be difficult to define metrics. However, all is not lost! Rather than defining metrics, try to answer a business question. For example, the organization may have no idea how well various marketing initiatives perform but could track this information in Google Analytics.

It may also be necessary for you to educate others about what data Google Analytics can provide and how it can assist them in their daily activities. It's your job to play the role of evangelist and promote analytics.

While you're interviewing users, it's also a good idea to organize users by their functional group, like marketing and IT, in the organization. You'll find that people in the same department or group often want to measure the same things. This information can be useful later when you're defining goals and setting up profiles because you can group Google Analytics settings by functional needs.

You may also uncover other needs unrelated to KPIs. For example, some people may be interested in viewing data for a specific section of the Web site. Or someone may specify that they need a specific report format delivered at a certain time. These needs are just as important as KPIs and should be captured during your interview process.

Your business requirements gathering should result in a fairly detailed document containing the KPIs and metrics of everyone using Google Analytics. You can find a sample business requirements spreadsheet at www.analyticsformarketers.com/s/business-requirements.

Gathering technical requirements

During the requirements gathering process, you must identify any features of your Web site that might cause issues with the Google Analytics configuration. This is a good stage to start involving your developer, who will be able to provide the technical support you need to handle these issues. As we explain in Chapter 4, Google Analytics uses JavaScript and cookies to track visitors. As a result, any Web site technology that can cause an issue with the Google Analytics JavaScript or cookies could affect your data.

Gathering technical requirements can normally be done in a meeting with the people who manage your Web site. Again, the participants will depend on the size and complexity of your organization. During this meeting you should ask those responsible for the site if:

- The Web site has multiple domains.
- The Web site has one or more subdomains.
- The Web site is dynamic (that is, uses query string parameters).
- The Web site uses a lot of Flash, Flex, AJAX, or Silverlight.
- The Web site makes extensive use of videos.
- The Web site is an ecommerce Web site that processes transactions.
- The Web site has a lot of non-HTML files, like PDF files and MP3 files.

TABLE 5.1

Common Web Site Configurations and Google Analytics Solutions

Configuration	Solution
The Web site has multiple domains.	Cross-Domain Tracking
The Web site has multiple subdomains.	Subdomain Tracking
The Web site is dynamic.	Basic Configuration, Exclude Query String Parameter settings
The Web site uses a lot of Flash, Flex, AJAX, or Silverllght.	Virtual Pageviews or Event Tracking
The Web site makes extensive use of videos.	Virtual Pageviews or Event Tracking
The Web site is an ecommerce Web site that processes transactions.	Ecommerce Tracking
The Web site has a lot of non-HTML content.	Virtual Pageviews or Event Tracking

These are the most common Web site configurations that cause problems with Google Analytics. While we do not describe why these items cause problems, we list where you can find solutions to each situation in Table 5.1.

It is important to remember that these issues must be documented during the requirements-gathering phase. Gather as much information as you can. For example, if you determine that the Web site has subdomains, find out what the subdomains are and why they exist.

A majority of these issues are advanced configuration issues and are covered in this chapter's "Advanced Configuration" section. Remember, it's important to identify these site attributes so you can deal with them during the implementation process.

Creating a Google Analytics Account

Once you've gathered and documented your requirements, it's time to start the implementation process. Sounds exciting, doesn't it! Let's start at the beginning by creating a Google Analytics Account. If you already have a Google Analytics Account, there is no need to read this section. You can skip ahead to the "Configuration Settings" section.

The first step is to determine if you have a Google Account. Remember, all Google services, such as Google Analytics, require a Google Account.

NOTE

If you have a Google AdWords Account for your company, you can activate Google Analytics from within your AdWords Account. Log into AdWords and choose Google Analytics from the Reporting menu. You will then begin the Google Analytics setup process.

If you don't have a Google Account, you need to start from scratch. Luckily, Google has combined the process of creating a Google Account and a Google Analytics Account. To begin, navigate to www. google.com/analytics. You'll notice a blue Access Analytics button at the top right. Just below the button is a link to Sign Up Now (as shown in Figure 5.1).

Google first walks you through creating a Google Account. All you need is an e-mail address and a password, as shown in Figure 5.2. After agreeing to the terms of service, click Continue.

Be aware that if you're creating an account for your entire company, don't use a personal e-mail address. We'll say it again: Google Analytics is a Google service and is connected to a Google Account, and a Google Account can have many services. It's best to use a generic company account when creating your new Google Account. Remember, a Google Account is *not* the same thing as a Gmail Account. A Google Account can be created for *any* e-mail address, not just a Gmail e-mail address. As long as you can receive and read the activation e-mail, you can use any e-mail address when creating your Google Account.

Once your Google Account has been created, you need to verify the e-mail address you registered as a Google Account. Google will send you a verification e-mail. Simply click the link in the e-mail to verify your account and you're ready to create your Google Analytics Account.

FIGURE 5.1

Click Sign Up Now to create your new Google Analytics Account.

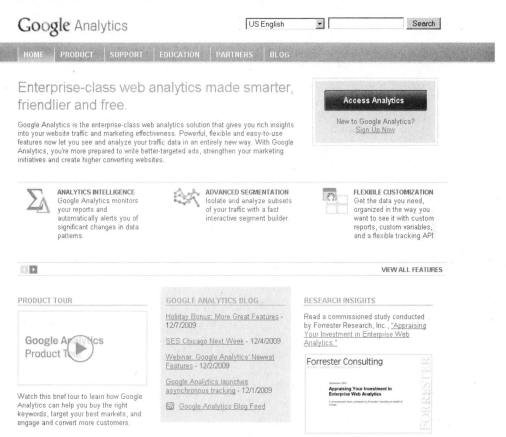

If you're having trouble remembering the difference between a Google Account and a Google Analytics Account, please refer to Chapter 4. You need to enter information about your Web site, specifically the Web site's URL. Google uses this information in the reports and performs quick scans to ensure that the tracking code was installed.

You'll also need to enter a name for your Google Analytics Account. Google uses the domain of your Web site as the default value. Using the real name of your company makes it easier to pick your account from a list of accounts.

After you enter the basic account information, you enter simple contact information — nothing too intrusive, just your name and country. On occasion, Google contacts Google Analytics users to gather feedback about the product.

Finally, you must agree to the Google Analytics terms of service (TOS). While most people rush through this step, it is a good idea to review the terms of service. You'll be surprised what it says. For example, it stipulates that any Web site that uses Google Analytics *must* post a privacy policy on the site that clearly states visitors are anonymously tracked using Google Analytics.

FIGURE 5.2

The first step in creating a Google Analytics Account is creating a Google Account.

Google accounts

Create an Account

Your Google Account gives you access to Google Analytics and other Google services. If you already have a Google Account, you can sign in here.

Required information for Google account

Your current email address: [   ]
e.g. myname@example.com. This will be used to sign-in to your account.

Choose a password: [   ] Password strength:
Minimum of 8 characters in length.

Re-enter password: [   ]

☐ Stay signed in

Creating a Google Account will enable Web History. Web History is a feature that will provide you with a more personalized experience on Google that includes more relevant search results and recommendations. Learn More
☑ Enable Web History.

Get started with Google Analytics

Word Verification: Type the characters you see in the picture below.

[   ] ♿
Letters are not case-sensitive

Terms of Service: Please check the Google Account information you've entered above (feel free to change anything you like), and review the Terms of Service below.

Printable Version

```
Google Terms of Service

Welcome to Google!

1. Your relationship with Google
```

By clicking on 'I accept' below you are agreeing to the Terms of Service above and the Privacy Policy.

[I accept. Create my account.]

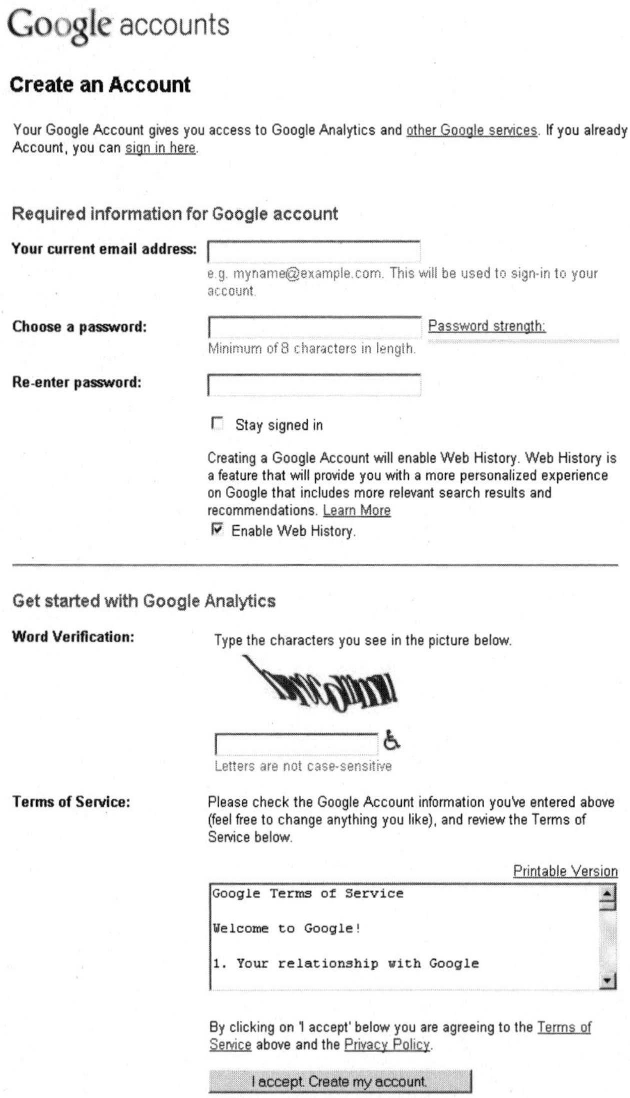

The terms-of-service step also contains information about data sharing. By default, Google shares your anonymous data in two ways. First, your data is shared with other Google products, such as AdWords and AdSense. This enables enhanced reporting across all Google products. If you're using any Google services, we recommend enabling this feature.

The second type of data sharing is anonymously sharing data with others. This setting is used for the benchmarking reports in Google Analytics. Google anonymously mixes your data with other Google Analytics data to create industry benchmarks.

We also recommend enabling this feature because the reports can be helpful during analysis. We explain more about benchmarking later.

NOTE

No matter which setting you choose, your data is only shared anonymously. No one outside Google will be able to access your data without your permission, and Google employees can only do so in accordance with a strict need-only policy. For more information, visit `google.com/privacy`.

Once you agree to the terms of service and specify your data sharing settings, it's time to configure the tracking code using the Tracking Code Configurator. This tool walks you through the JavaScript tracking code. You will need to change the Google Analytics Tracking Code (GATC) to accommodate technical issues that we identified during requirements gathering! Things like subdomains and multiple domains necessitate changing the standard tracking code. If your site does have multiple domains or subdomains, you should skip to the "Advanced Configuration" section and review the content that applies to your situation.

If your Web site does not have subdomains or multiple domains, consider yourself lucky! You can move to the next step.

Adding the Tracking Code

Once you have created your account, it's time to add the GATC to all your Web site pages. If you are not responsible for adding code to your Web site, it is a good idea to read this section so you understand what is involved in tagging your site.

First, retrieve the tracking code for your site. You can copy the tracking code from the Code Configuration Tool, shown in Figure 5.3. (If you ever need to find the tracking code again, click the Check Status link in the Profile Settings.)

Once you have the code, place it immediately above the closing BODY tag on all the pages of your site. Luckily, most Web sites today use template systems and you can simply add the tracking code to your footer template, or the element that provides access to the closing BODY tag, similar to the code below. This code has been modified to hide the Google Analytics Account number. Your code will have a number rather than the XXXXX-XX.

```
<!—Your Website Code -->
<script type="text/javascript">
```

```
var gaJsHost = (("https:" == document.location.protocol) ? "https://
    ssl." : "http://www.");
document.write(unescape("%3Cscript src='" + gaJsHost + "google-
    analytics.com/ga.js' type='text/javascript'%3E%3C/script%3E"));
</script>
<script type="text/javascript">
try {
var pageTracker = _gat._getTracker("UA-XXXXX-XX");
pageTracker._trackPageview();
} catch(err) {}</script>

</body>
</html>
```

Remember that if you're uncomfortable with this process, you should absolutely consult with your developer.

If you're using a content management system (CMS), you may not even need to modify any HTML. Many CMSs have plug-ins or extensions for Google Analytics. Depending on your CMS, you may only need to enter your account number and choose a few settings. It all depends on the plug-in. To see a list of CMSs and the plug-ins available, visit www.analyticsformarketers.com/s/cms-plugins.

Once the tracking code is on your site, you should start to see data in as little as three hours. How exciting! Five chapters into the book and you finally have data!

If you don't see any data in your account you may need to check your Web site pages to ensure that they are tagged correctly. There are many tools, both free and paid, that you can use to check your tags, which we talk about later in this chapter.

NOTE

If your Web site has extremely long pages, or if it takes a long time for your pages to load, you might consider using a different version of the tracking code. Google provides a fast-loading version of the tracking code called the Asynchronous Tracking Code. This version of the GATC can be placed at the top of the page and will not hinder the Web site's performance. You can learn more about the asynchronous version of the GATC at www.analyticsformarketers. com/s/async-code.

Configuration Steps

Once the tracking code has been installed, it's time to start working with the settings within Google Analytics. If you're still on the screen with your tracking code, click the Save and Finish button at the bottom of the screen. Or you can access all your Profile Settings by clicking the Edit link next to a profile, as shown in Figure 5.4.

FIGURE 5.3

Copy the Google Analytics page tag for your site from the Code Configurator. Remember: If your site uses subdomain or multiple domains, you should read the appropriate content in the "Advanced Configuration" section later in this chapter.

After you click Edit, you'll see all the settings for a profile. We've divided configuration settings into two groups: basic and advanced. Basic settings are things everyone can, and should, do. Advanced settings deal with many of the situations that come up in the requirements gathering process.

Basic configuration steps

Now that you've created your account, go through the following checklist of basic configuration steps with your developer's help. We'll walk you through each step.

1. Create three basic profiles.
2. Exclude query string parameters.

FIGURE 5.4

You can access Profile Settings by clicking on the Edit link from the main administration screen.

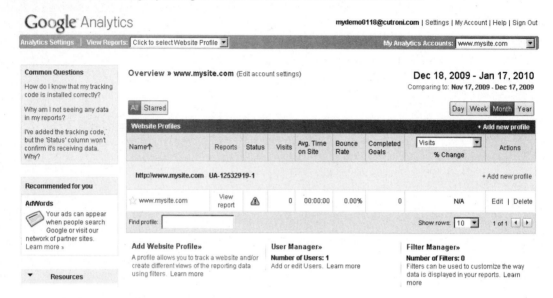

3. Specify the default page.
4. Configure site search reporting.
5. Define Conversion Goals.
6. Configure conversion funnels.
7. Normalize data with some simple filters.
8. Configure campaign tracking.

Create additional profiles

In Chapter 4, we explain how Google Analytics is divided into accounts and profiles. A profile is a collection of data and settings. This means that you can create multiple profiles for the same Web site and vary the settings from one profile to the next. This results in different sets of data for the same Web site. We recommend that you have at least three profiles for your Web site, as shown in Figure 5.5.

The first profile, the Raw Data Profile, is created when you create your Google Analytics Account. As the name implies, this profile should have no settings and will only contain raw data from your site. This Raw Data Profile is considered a fail-safe, or backup, of your data. If, for any reason, something goes wrong with the profile that you use daily, this profile will contain the missing data.

The second profile is the Test Profile. This profile should be used to test any new settings. As we explain in Chapter 4, once Google Analytics processes your data, it can never be changed. An incorrect setting can forever mar your data. To avoid mistakes, test all configuration settings or changes on your

FIGURE 5.5

Every Google Analytics Account should have at least three profiles.

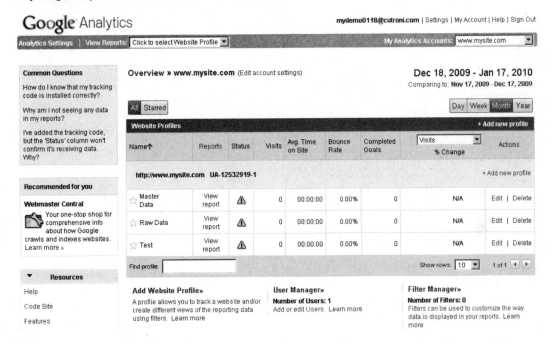

Test Profile and evaluate their impact on data before adding the setting to your production or Master Profile.

To create the Test Profile, simply click the Add Profile link found on the main Google Analytics administration page, as shown in Figure 5.6. When you create a duplicate profile for an existing Web site, Google does not copy any of the settings or data associated with the profile. It only starts collecting data for the site.

The final must-have profile, the Master Data Profile, should be used for reporting and analysis. This profile has all the appropriate settings to purify and clean the data. Whenever you need to add a new setting to Google Analytics, first test the setting on your Test Profile. Then, after you have verified that the setting will not negatively impact the data, apply it to your Master Data Profile.

Now let's look at some of the settings that should be applied to the Master Data Profile.

Exclude Query String Parameters setting

One of the most important settings in Google Analytics is the Exclude Query String Parameters setting. This setting is meant to deal with dynamic Web sites. (Remember: A dynamic Web site's configuration can cause issues with Google Analytics data. If your Web site is dynamic, pay attention to this section.)

A query string parameter is part of a URL. It is the part that appears after the question mark:

FIGURE 5.6

You can create a duplicate profile by clicking the Add Profile link for an existing profile.

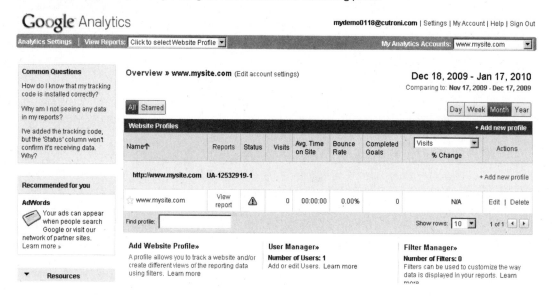

```
http://www.mysite.com/folder/page/index.html?id=23&jsesid=23jskdj568
```

The query string contains a series of name-value pairs separated by ampersands. These parameters usually serve a technical purpose, like identifying the content the visitor requests. But they can serve a business purpose. For example, in the URL above the query string parameter named id identifies which product is displayed on the page. As you can image, this parameter is particularly useful.

Query string parameters pose a problem because they can create duplicate data in Google Analytics. The three URLs below look different, but they are actually very similar.

```
http://www.mysite.com/page.htm?sessid=101
http://www.mysite.com/page.htm?sessid=102
http://www.mysite.com/page.htm?sessid=103
```

The query string parameter, which has no business value, causes Google Analytics to record the page multiple times. You can use the Exclude Query String Parameter setting to eliminate unnecessary parameters from Google Analytics, thus reducing duplicate versions of a URL.

To eliminate a query string parameter, simply add it to the field. To eliminate more than one parameter, separate each parameter using a comma, as shown in Figure 5.7.

Here's an easy way to identify all the query string parameters your site may use. After you've installed the GATC, wait a day or two and check the Top Content report. Sort the Pageviews column in

To eliminate more than one query string parameter, enter them as a comma-delimited list.

ascending order by clicking on the Pageviews Column Header. You should see something similar to Figure 5.8.

Notice there are a number of URLs with the parameter ? . This parameter does not look as if it serves a business purpose. So you can add it to the Exclude Query String Parameters setting and Google Analytics will remove it from all future data.

You should audit your content data and evaluate which query string parameters are needed and which are not. If none of the query string parameters on your site provides insight into visitor behavior, you can easily eliminate them all using a filter. Complete instructions can be found at www. analyticsformarketers.com/s/remove-qstring-filter.

We recommend removing all query string parameters that do not provide additional business insight. However, removing parameters may break certain reporting features in Google Analytics. Specifically, the Site Overlay report may not work if you exclude certain parameters from Google Analytics.

Don't worry, though: You don't need to choose between clean data and a functioning Site Overlay report. If you need both, you can always create an additional profile for site overlay usage. This profile should have the same configuration settings as the old profile except for the exclude query string parameters.

Specify the default page

The Default Page setting normally gets overlooked. It won't have a major impact on your data or analysis, but to be thorough and complete in your implementation, you should get this setting right.

The default page on your site is the page your Web server displays when no specific page is requested by the visitor. Normally the page the visitor would like to see appears in the URL. In the URL http://www.mysite.com/product.asp, the visitor is requesting the product.asp page. If

FIGURE 5.8

In the Top Content report, notice all the pages with query string parameters? We bet you can eliminate some of those.

there is no page specified in the URL, the Web server will return the default page. Even though no page is specified in the URL, there is an actual page on the server.

If the visitor requests http://www.mysite.com/, the server will still return a page. The problem is that Google Analytics will generate a pageview for /, not the actual page stored on the server. You will literally see / in the Top Content report, as shown in Figure 5.9.

FIGURE 5.9

It is possible to have multiple versions of the default page in your Top Content report if you do not configure the Default Page setting correctly.

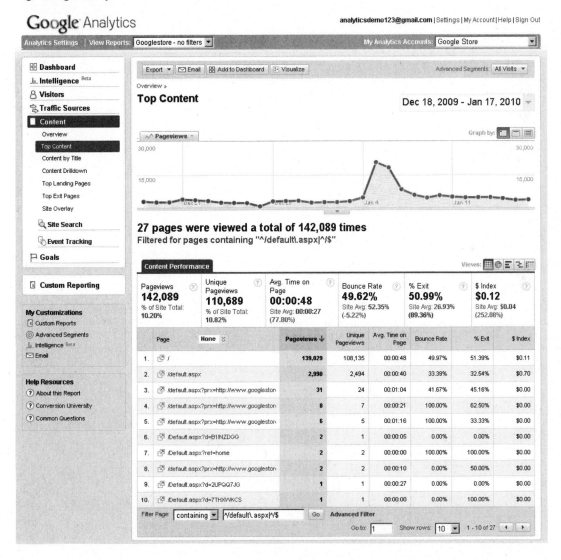

While Google Analytics may record / for your default page, it is also possible that it may record the actual name of the default page. For example, you may have `default.asp`, `index.php`, or another version of your default page in the data. Now there are two default pages in your content data, as shown in Figure 5.9. The result is separated data in the Content reports.

This is a simple problem to solve. First, determine whether you have multiple versions of the default page in your content reports by looking for / and your default page in the Top Content report. If you find both pages, add the name of your default page to the Default Page setting. This setting is part of the Profile Settings and is shown in Figure 5.10.

That's it; there is nothing more to do. Is this an earth-shattering change that will lead to impeccable data and unmatched insights? No. But to be thorough in your configuration, make sure you get the Default Page setting correct.

Not all Web sites have this issue. It is possible that your Web site is configured to always return the name of the page, rather than just a slash. This is a server setting that some system administrators configure.

FIGURE 5.10

Enter the name of your default page in the Default Page setting.

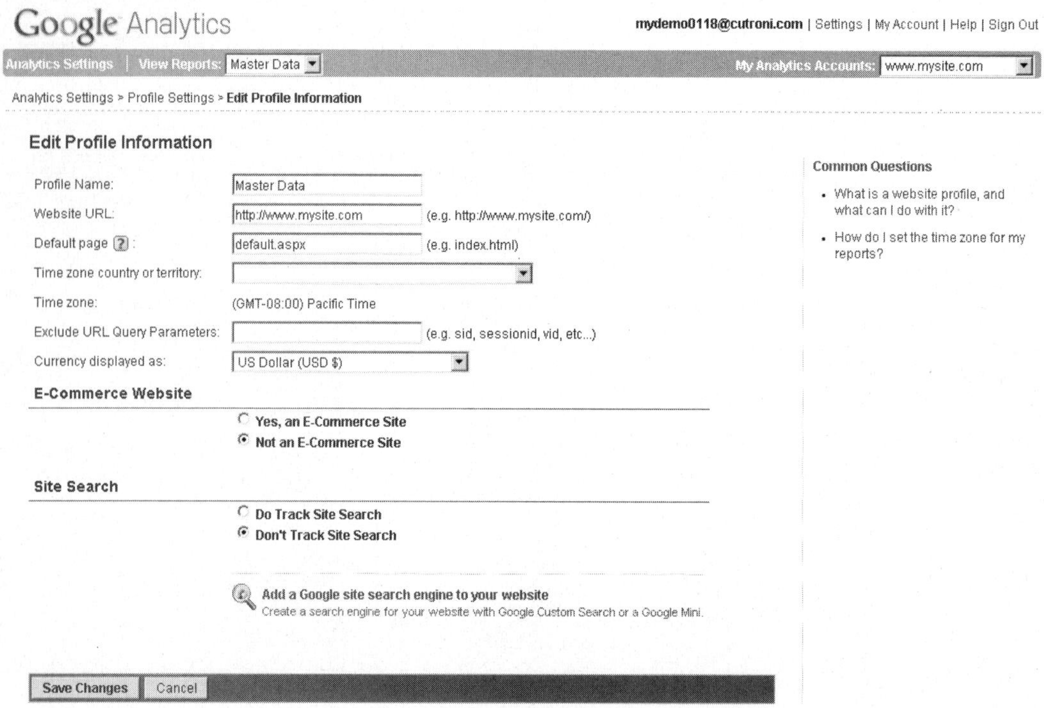

Configure site search reporting

Site Search reports provide valuable information about what people search for on your site. If you have a search tool installed on your site, you can track not only what people search for, but also other attributes of their search. For example, you can track where they start their search, what they do after they search, and ultimately if the people who search convert. In Chapter 8, we explore ways you can use this data to optimize your site. While it's not required to configure site search, the reports provide invaluable data and should be configured if possible. Plus, it's ridiculously easy!

To configure Site Search reports, begin by doing a search on your site. For example, we searched for "hats" on www.googlestore.com, as shown in Figure 5.11. Once the search is complete, look at the URL for the search results page. Can you see the search term in the URL? If so the configuration of site search will be simple.

Once you verify that the URL contains the search term, you must identify the query string parameter that contains that search term. The Site Search query string parameter is directly to the left of the search term. It will be separated by an equal sign (=), as in this URL:

FIGURE 5.11

Search results for the query "hats" on www.googlestore.com.

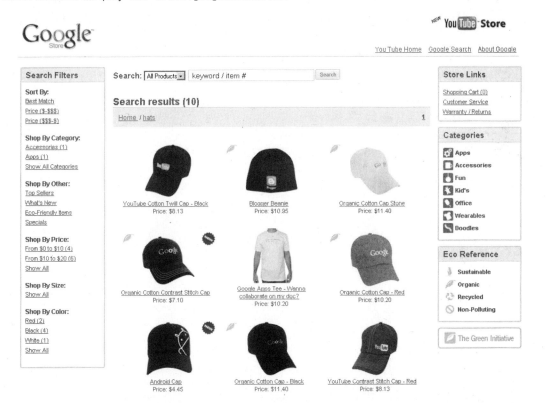

```
http://www.googlestore.com/googlesearch.aspx?q=hats&imageField.
    x=0&imageField.y=0&imageField=search
```

If your site doesn't have a query parameter in the URL, we give you a workaround later in this chapter. The next step is to enter the query string parameter into Google Analytics. The Site Search settings are found in the Profile Settings, as shown in Figure 5.12. Begin by selecting Do Track Site Search to display the Site Search settings.

Enter the query string parameter into the Query Parameter field. For our example, we use the letter q.

As Google process the data, it looks for the Site Search parameter. Every time it finds the Site Search parameter, it extracts the search term and populates the Site Search reports. It's that simple.

There are a two additional Site Search settings that can help normalize your data and provide more insights.

First, you have the option to strip the search term query string parameter from the URL. This setting strips the parameter that holds the search term after Google has processed the Site Search data. This setting is similar to the Exclude Query String Parameters settings we explained earlier in the chapter. It helps consolidate multiple rows of data in the content reports into a single line. For example, if you do not strip the search term parameter from the URL, you could end up with thousands of additional rows of data in your content reports because each search term could create a unique URL.

By stripping the query string parameter, Google Analytics consolidates all the search result pages in the Content report into a single row. You still get all the data from site searches in the Site Search report, but your Content reports do not contain thousands of search URLs.

We recommend you choose Yes for the Query Parameter setting because stripping the search parameter will clean up your data without reducing its ability to provide insights. All those juicy keywords will still exist in the Site Search reports.

The second optional setting you can configure for site search is a search category. Many Web sites allow users to search within different categories. If your site uses categories, you can track the categories in similar fashion to the search terms.

Examine the URL of the search results page. If it contains a query string parameter that holds the search category, you can use this setting. Just paste the query string parameter into a form, as you did for the search term. Figure 5.13 shows all the settings for search categories, which are exactly the same as the search term.

But what should you do if you can't see the search term in the URL? You can still configure site search, but you will require an advanced implementation. You need to create a virtual pageview and manually generate the needed data in Google Analytics. You can find instructions later in this chapter.

Set up some goals

Goals are arguably the single most important feature in Google Analytics and are used to track conversions and other business outcomes. There is no other setting in Google Analytics that closely aligns your business measurement with the Google Analytics configuration. For details on how to set good Conversion Goals for your Web site, refer to Chapter 2.

The Site Search settings can be found in the Profile Settings.

During the requirements-gathering phase, you should have documented the conversion activities you would like to track on your site. These activities could be buying a product, downloading a white paper, viewing a certain number of pages, and so on. It's time to take those requirements and implement them in Google Analytics.

There are two types of goals in Google Analytics: Threshold Goals (commonly called *Engagement Goals*) and URL Destination Goals. Threshold Goals are triggered when a visit reaches a certain threshold for visit length or pages viewed. A URL Destination Goal is triggered when a visitor sees a specific page on the Web site.

Goals are specific to a profile and are located in a profile's Profile Settings section, as shown in Figure 5.14. Each profile has four goal sets. Within each goal set there are five different goals. Google created goal sets as an easy way to organize goals in the reporting interface.

Before we explain the different goal types, there are settings that apply to all goals. First is the goal name, as shown in Figure 5.15. You can name each goal anything you want to help you identify the goals in the reports. Our suggestion is to use something short but descriptive. There is a limited amount of space in the reports, and long goal names can look horrendous.

Another common Goal Setting is an Activation Setting. This setting is basically an on/off switch that you can use to enable or disable a goal. Why would you want to turn a goal off? That's a good question. We've used this setting in the past to flat-line a goal when we want to replace it with a different goal. This setting is not used often, but it can come in handy when you want to create a goal and activate

FIGURE 5.13

Google Analytics tracks a search category as well as the search term. The settings for a search category are directly below the main Site Search settings.

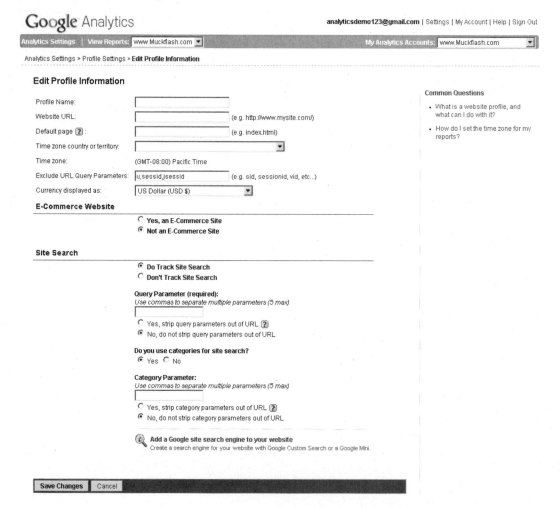

it in the future. For example, if there is a specific goal for a campaign, you can create the goal and then activate it when the campaign launches.

The final setting that is consistent from one goal to another is Goal Position. Remember, there are four sets of goals and each set of goals contains five goals. The purpose of the Goal Position setting is to specify the set where the goal will be created. For example, you may want to designate all goals in set 5 to be the CMO Goals, or all goals in set 2 as the Marketing Goals.

As of this writing, the Goal Set setting should not be used to change a goal's set. You cannot move goals from one set to another *and* maintain historical data! Moving a goal will result in losing previous

FIGURE 5.14

Goal settings can be found in the Profile Settings section of a profile.

conversion data. It is best to place all goals in their permanent location. When creating goals, try to place them into logical groups, either by reporting need or by business function, to help you avoid potential issues with moving goals.

Now it's time to choose a goal type. This setting is also shown in Figure 5.15. When you choose a specific goal type, the Goal Entry Form will change, based on the type of goal you choose. The configuration for each goal type is, as you might expect, different.

URL Destination Goals

URL Destination Goals have been part of Google Analytics since Day 1. A URL Destination Goal is triggered when a visitor reaches a certain page during a visit. The classic URL destination example is the thank-you page displayed after a visitor completes a purchase. By designating the URL of the thank-you page as a goal, Google Analytics will record a goal when a visit includes that page.

Configure a URL Destination Goal by choosing URL Destination as the goal type (see Figure 5.15). You'll notice that an additional field appears in the form. Next, navigate to your Web site and find the page that represents that goal and copy the URL. For example, if you want to configure your thank-you page as a goal, you would navigate to that page and copy the goal.

Next, paste this URL in the Goal URL field (see Figure 5.16) and delete everything up to the first slash after the .com, .net, or whatever the domain extension is. For example, if your goal's URL is www.mysite.com/pages/thankyou.htm, delete www.mysite.com so that only /pages/thankyou.htm appears in the Goal URL field. Google Analytics does not use the domain when calculating goals.

Once you have entered the goal URL, you can configure the optional settings for a goal. One setting specific to URL Destination Goals is the Match Type. This setting controls how Google Analytics applies

FIGURE 5.15

All goals have a name, a goal position, and an activation setting.

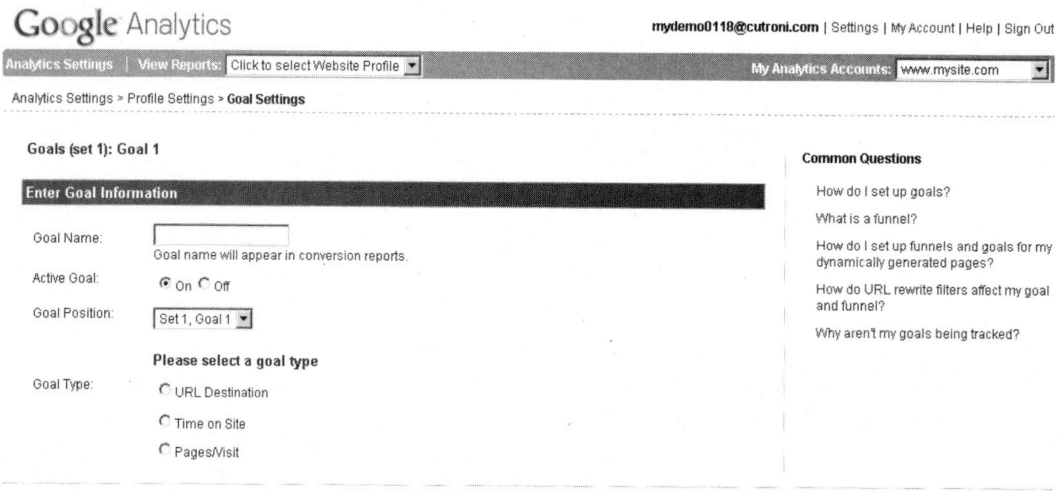

the information you entered in the Goal URL field to the data. There are three ways Google Analytics compares the Goal URL value to the data:

- Exact Match is the easiest match type to explain. If the Goal URL you enter does not exactly match the Request URI, a goal is not tracked.
- Head Match is the default setting and is the most forgiving of all the goal type settings. When using a head match, Google applies the value you enter into the Goal URL field to the Request URI. As long as the request URI starts with the value you entered, a goal is counted. It doesn't matter if the request URI contains extra information at the end.
- When you choose Regular Expression, Google applies the regular expression you added to the URL Goal field to the Request URI. If the regular expression matches any part of the Request

FIGURE 5.16

Settings for a URL Destination Goal.

URI, a goal is counted. Using a regular expression can come in handy when multiple URLs can count as the same goal. For example, if you want to create a generic goal to track PDF downloads, you could use a regular expression to match all values that end in .pdf, such as \.pdf$.

That's it for the common Goal Settings. Next we explain the different types of goals, starting with Threshold Goals. There are two types of Threshold Goals: Pageview Threshold Goals and Time on Site Threshold Goals. These goals are great for measuring general engagement with a site.

Time on Site goals

As the name implies, a Time on Site Threshold Goal is triggered when the length of a visit meets certain criteria. For example, you can configure a goal in Google Analytics to trigger when a visit is at least five minutes. You can also configure a goal to trigger if a visit does not meet a minimum length.

Time on Site goals are useful when trying to measure visitor engagement. If your business goal is to attract visitors and have them spend time on your site, Time on Site goals are a critical part of your configuration.

Configuring a Time on Site goal is straightforward. The interface is shown in Figure 5.17. All you need to determine is the time component of the goal. Once you enter the hours, minutes, and seconds, choose a condition (greater than or less than), and your Time on Site goal is complete.

Pages/Visit goals

Pageview Threshold Goals are triggered when a visit reaches a certain number of pageviews. For example, let's say you are a publisher and you make money based on how many pages a visitor views. You can probably calculate that visits of more than five pages are profitable. You could create a goal to measure what percentage of your traffic reaches that important threshold.

To add a Pageview goal, begin by clicking on Add Goal for a specific goal set. You'll see a new form with the basic settings for your new goal (see Figure 5.18).

You may have noticed that each Goal type can have a Goal Value. The Goal Value is a static value that Google Analytics uses as revenue every time a conversion occurs. This option is especially usefully for Web sites that do not have a traditional transaction, like lead-generation Web sites. Calculating a Goal Value does not need to be overly complex. But it's up to you to use your business data to calculate the value. Think about how much a conversion means to the bottom line of your company.

In addition to using Goal Values to attach monetary values to conversions, they can also be used as a means to index the importance of different visitor actions. For example, a Web site may have two goals, one for a newsletter signup and one for an RSS subscription. The newsletter signup may be more valuable to your company than the RSS feed, but neither is considered direct revenue. The differing value should be reflected in the Goal Values. You can simply input the value 5 for the newsletter signup and input the value 10 for the RSS subscription. The values 5 and 10 are arbitrary, but they indicate that an RSS subscription is worth twice a newsletter signup. Again, you need to decide the conversion values.

Regardless of how you use the Goal Value Setting, type the value you want to assign for your goal in the Goal Value field; it's that simple.

FIGURE 5.17

To configure a Time on Site goal, enter a time element and condition.

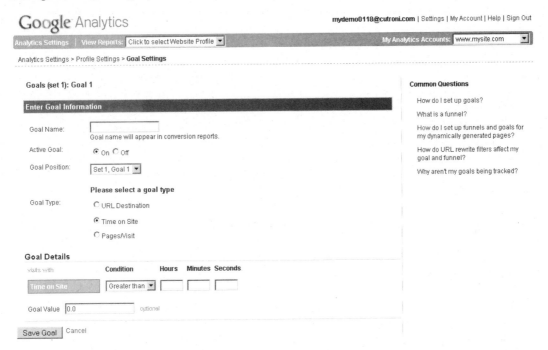

A final note about goals: It is only possible for a visitor to convert one time per visit. For example, if you create a goal to track newsletter signups, and a visitor signs up twice, Google Analytics will only track one conversion. Why? From a business perspective, most goals happen only once per visit, so it makes sense that Google only counts them once.

Configure funnels

As explained in the previous section, it is critical to measure Web site outcomes, and one way you can measure outcomes is using URL Destination Goals. These goals measure how often people complete your critical tasks. Just as important is measuring the processes that lead to these goals.

If a visitor is only a few clicks away from converting, you want to understand where the visitor had trouble with the process of conversion. We call these processes *funnels* and can measure how visitors move through them using the Funnel Visualization report shown in Figure 5.19. We talk more about funnel analysis in Chapter 8. But you want to optimize the processes that lead to conversion.

A funnel in Google Analytics is made up of a series of pages. You can create one funnel for each URL Destination Goal in Google Analytics. If you have 15 URL Destination Goals, you can create 15 funnels. Each funnel can have up to 10 steps. Why 10? Do you have any processes longer than 10 steps on your Web site? We didn't think so. Ten steps are adequate for most sites.

FIGURE 5.18

Settings for a Pages/Visit goal

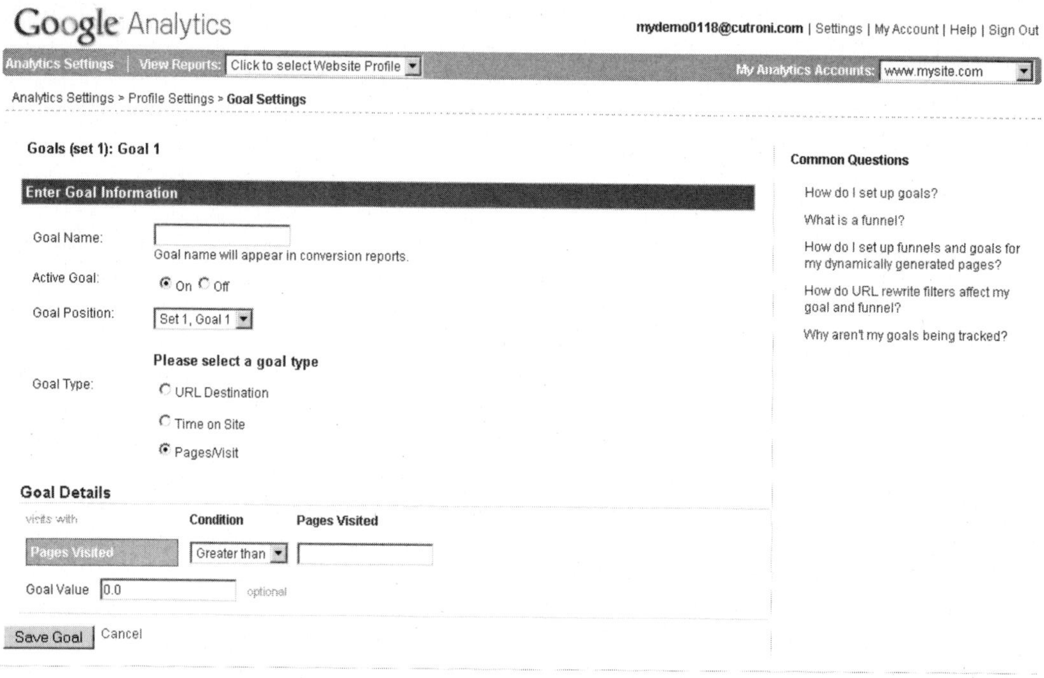

To begin setting up a funnel, you'll need the URL for each page in the process. You can simply navigate to your site and copy and paste the URLs from your browser to a text document. When you're finished, you should have a list of URLs that identify all the pages in your process.

Next, navigate to your Profile Settings and find the goal associated with the funnel you want to create. The Funnel Settings are located on the same page as the Goal Settings, as shown in Figure 5.20.

Begin by clicking Yes, Create a Funnel for This Goal to add a step to the funnel. You'll notice two text fields and a checkbox where you enter information about step 1 in your process. Continue to add steps to the funnel by clicking on the + Add Goal Funnel Step link until you have fields for each step in your process. You do not need to add your goal URL to the funnel.

Now it's time to start adding the details to your funnel. Start adding the URLs for each step in your funnel to the URL field for each step. You don't need to enter the entire URL, just the part of the URL that appears after your domain extension (such .net, .com, or .org). For example, if the URL for a step in your funnel is www.mysite.com/step1.html, you should enter /step1.html into the URL field. This is the same technique you used when you defined the goal.

In addition to the URL for each step, you must also enter a name for each step. The step name should be entered into the Name field. You should name each step something intuitive, but try not to make it too long. There is only so much room for the name in the Funnel Visualization report.

FIGURE 5.19

The Funnel Visualization report contains data if you configure a funnel.

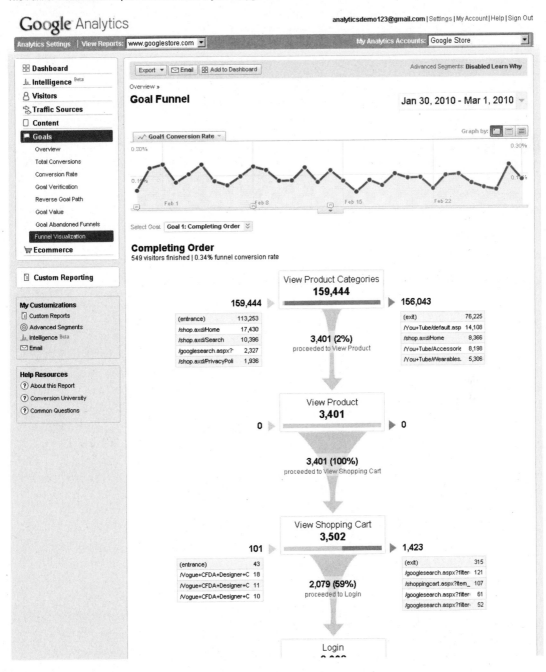

The Funnel Settings also share some Goal Settings. Specifically, a funnel uses the same match type as the goal. If you're using a match type of Head Match for your goal, Google Analytics also uses a Head Match when building your funnel. We most commonly see problems when people try to use a Regular Expression match type for their goal, and then try to use a Head Match for their funnel. Remember, the match type you define for your goal is also applied to the funnel.

The only other setting applied to a funnel is the Required Step setting. Defining this setting is simple. When you choose to make step 1 in your funnel a required step, the visitor must see that page at some point of their visit prior to converting. That's it. If they do not see step 1 at some point during the

---

FIGURE 5.20

The Goal Funnel configuration is below the Goal Information form.

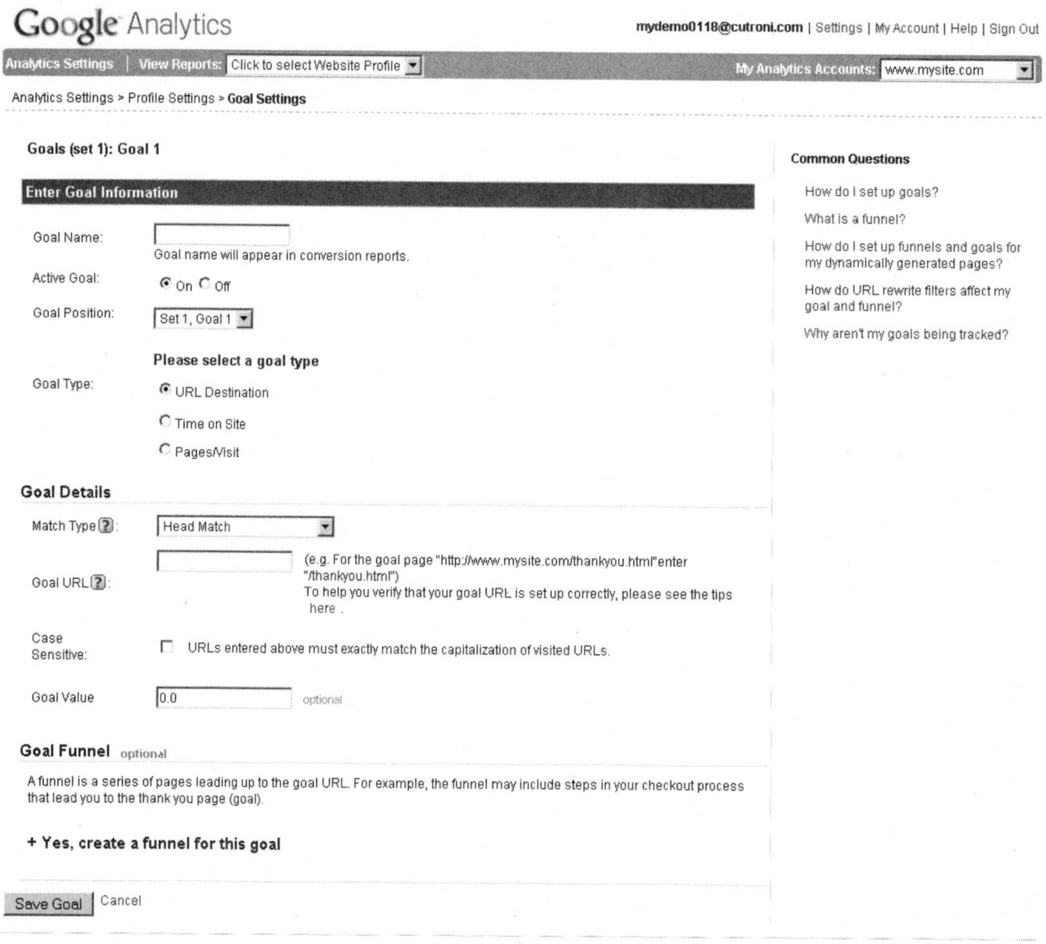

visit, a goal is be counted in the Funnel Visualization report. Google Analytics will still count a conversion in other reports, but not in the Funnel Visualization report.

There are situations where it is difficult to create a funnel. The most common problem is multistep processes that all have the same URL. While this complicates creating a funnel, it does not stop you. We explain a solution to this problem in the next section when we cover virtual pageviews.

Normalize data with simple filters

Once all the Profile Settings and Goals have been configured, it's time to move to filters. Filters are a way to apply logic or business rules to the data in a profile. Some filters are used to exclude data from a profile while other filters literally change how the data looks. Filters, like many of the other Profile Settings, are essential to data quality.

There are two types of filters; *Predefined filters* and *Custom filters*. Predefined filters are templates used to guide you through creating a filter. When you create a Predefined filter, you tell Google Analytics to include or exclude traffic that matches a specific condition. For example, you can create a Predefined filter to exclude all traffic from a specific IP address.

Custom filters are a more complex, but flexible, way to create a filter. We cover Custom filters in depth in the "Advanced configuration steps" section. Right now, we use a mix of Predefined filters and Custom filters to help normalize data.

Exclude internal traffic

The first filter you should apply is a filter to exclude internal traffic. Internal traffic is traffic generated by you, your employees, contractors, and so on. Why do you need this filter? When it comes to data, you don't count. You want to ensure that data from you and your employees is not included with real customer data. Thus you need to exclude any data from noncustomers.

The easiest way to exclude internal traffic is using a Predefined filter based on the IP address.

Begin by clicking the Add Filter link in the Filters section of the Profile Settings. Once you see the Filter form as shown in Figure 5.21, enter a name for your filter. Use a descriptive name so you and other users can identify the filter in a list and understand what it does. Next, choose Exclude from the first pop-up menu. This tells Google Analytics that this is an Exclude filter.

Next it's time to identify how you exclude traffic. We recommend using your IP address in the Exclude filter. If you don't know your IP address, you can find it using a service such as whatismyip.com. Simply enter your IP address in the IP address filed. See Figure 5.22 for the details of the filter. If you don't know your IP address you can try a service like `http://www.whatismyip.com` to find it.

Remember: Test this filter on your Test profile first. Once you see how it impacts your data, you can add it to the Master profile. Adding an existing filter to a new profile can be done quickly. Google stores all filters in a Filter Manager. When you want to add an existing filter to a new profile, simply navigate to the Profile Settings for the desired profile, click Add Filter and then choose Apply Existing Filter to Profile, as shown in Figure 5.23.

FIGURE 5.21

A Predefined filter is an easy way to exclude traffic from a profile.

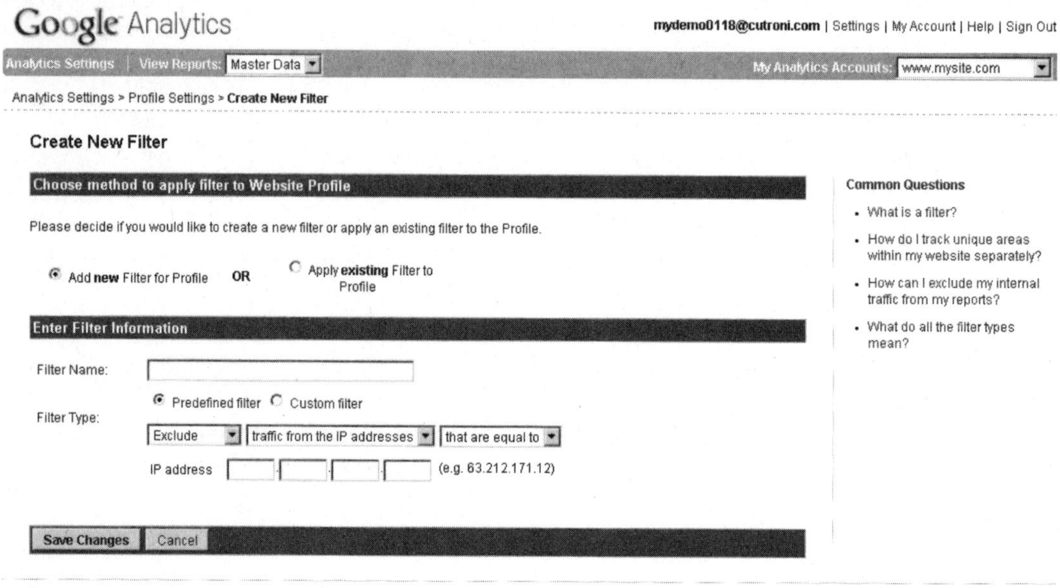

FIGURE 5.22

The specific settings to exclude traffic based on IP address.

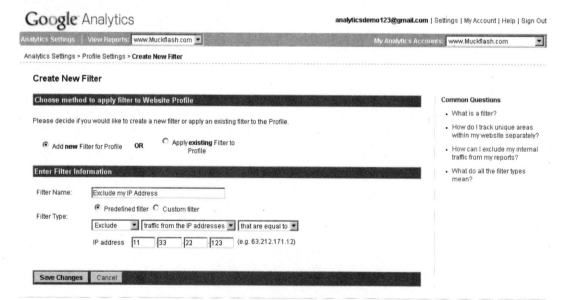

This technique only works if your company has a static, or unchanging, IP address. If your company does not have a static IP address, you need to exclude yourself from traffic using a different technique, which we describe at www.analyticsformarketers.com/s/internal-traffic-filter.

Force request URI to lowercase

Another filter that can help ensure data quality is the Lowercase filter. Unlike your filter to exclude traffic from an IP address, this filter is a Custom filter. The Lowercase filter forces the case or capitalization of your data to lowercase. Why is this important? Some Web servers serve the same URL in uppercase and lowercase.

Google Analytics is case-sensitive, meaning that two pieces of data that are exactly the same except for case are viewed as two different pieces of data in Google Analytics. Remember how we used the Exclude Query String Parameter setting to normalize data?

When creating a Lowercase filter, you need to identify the piece of information you want Google Analytics to force to lowercase. In this application, you want to make all the data in your content reports lowercase. In Chapter 4, we explain how Google creates data fields when processing data. Those data fields become the basis for all the reports in Google Analytics. The Content reports are built using a field called the Request URI. This field contains everything that appears after your domain extension (.com, .net, .org, and so on).

FIGURE 5.23

You can apply existing filters to new profiles by choosing the Apply Existing Filter to Profile radio button.

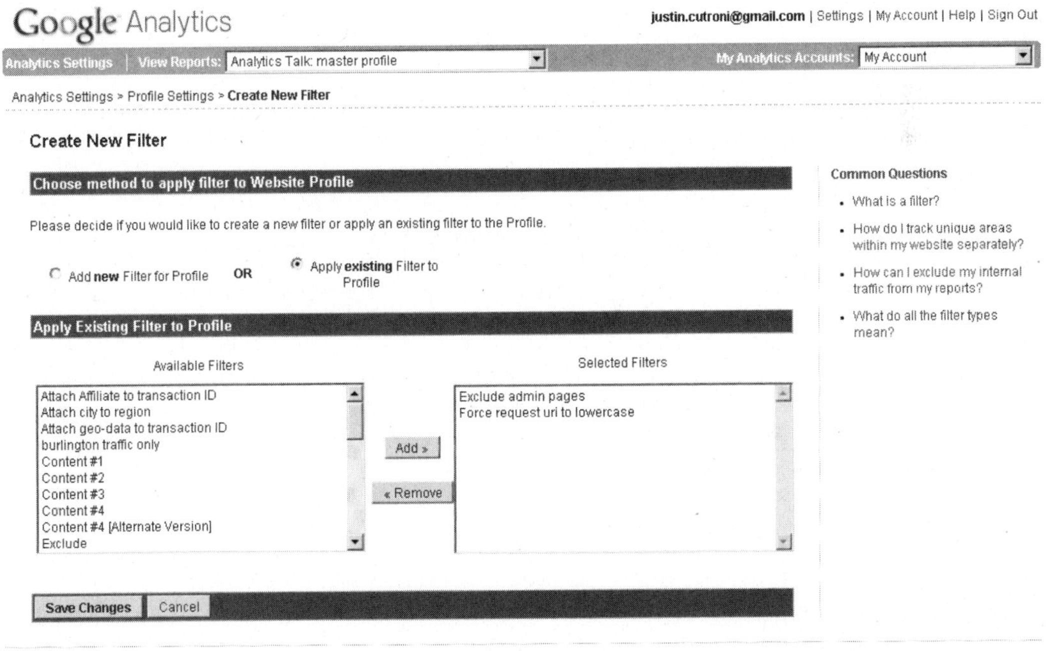

Figure 5.24 shows the setting for a Lowercase filter.

Once you configure a Lowercase filter for the Request URI, the data in your Content reports will always be lowercase and consistent.

Force campaign parameters to lowercase

In addition to applying a Lowercase filter to the Request URI field, it's also a good idea to apply a Lowercase filter to the fields that store information about your marketing campaigns. There are five parameters that store campaign information. Creating a Lowercase filter for each campaign, similar to those shown in Figures 5.25 and 5.26, ensures that you always have uniform information about your marketing campaigns. We explain more about marketing campaign tracking later in this chapter.

Configuring campaign tracking

Marketing campaign tracking is how you track different kinds of marketing campaigns in Google Analytics. It is a common misbelief that Google Analytics automatically identifies different traffic sources, like e-mail, paid search, banner ads, and so on. *You* must configure Google Analytics to identify these traffic sources. And if you do not configure them correctly, you will get dramatic inconsistencies in

FIGURE 5.24

The setting for a Request URI Lowercase filter. This filter helps normalize data by changing the case to lowercase.

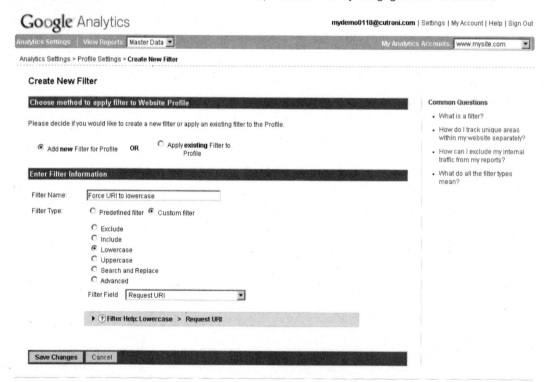

the data. The goal with campaign tracking is to identify not only which marketing activities are successful and which are not. You can use this information to promote marketing activities that work and fix marketing activities that do not work.

Campaign tracking is covered in later sections of this book, where we explain specific details for different types of marketing activities, like e-mail, paid search, and display advertising. This section provides an overview of how campaign tracking works.

Campaign tracking uses a technique called *link tagging* to identify types of marketing activities. Link tagging is the addition of query string parameters to the destination URLs used in your marketing materials. The values you place in each query string parameter are automatically pulled into Google Analytics, thus identifying marketing activities.

These parameters are added to the URLs in your marketing materials, not the URLs of your Web site pages. There is no special coding that has to happen on your site. You don't need to add extra JavaScript to pages. You must manipulate the links used in your display ads, CPC ads, e-mails, and so on.

When people click on a tagged link, they are directed to your Web site as usual. When they land on the Web site, the URL contains the link-tagging parameters. Your Web site ignores these parameters, but

FIGURE 5.25

Lowercase filter used to force a Marketing Medium Value to lowercase.

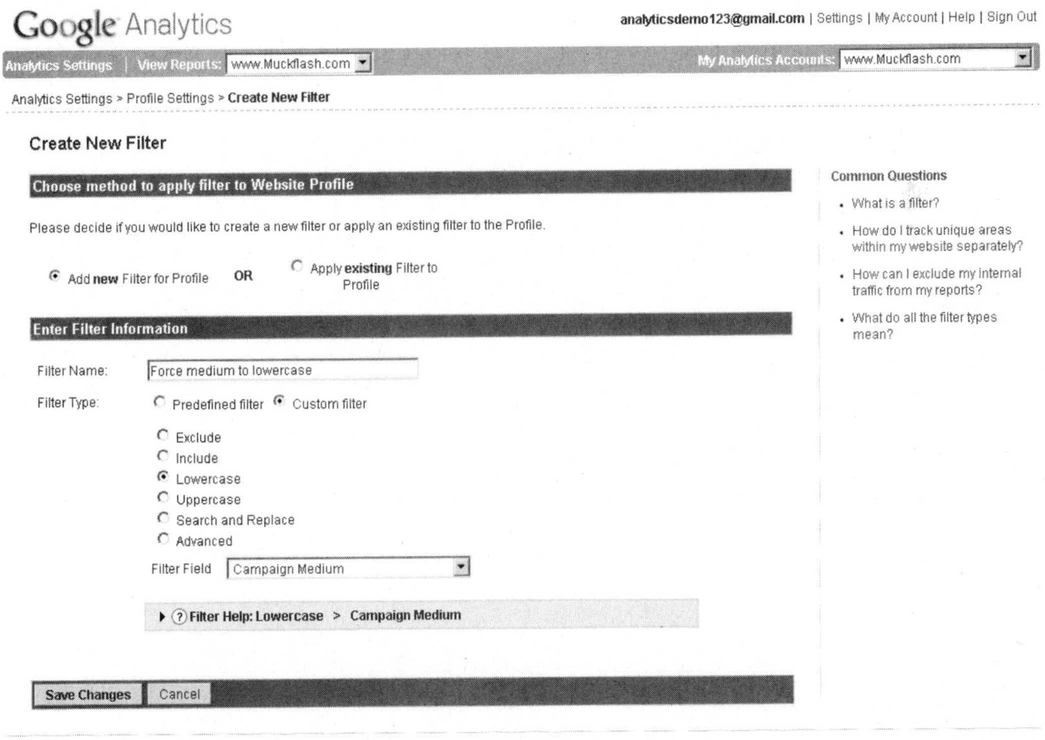

FIGURE 5.26

Lowercase filter used to force a Marketing Source Value to lowercase.

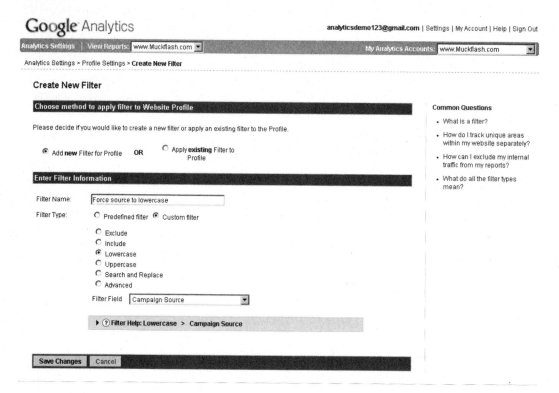

the GATC identifies them and recognizes that the visitor came from a marketing activity. The tracking code reads the values from the query string parameters and stores them in cookies on the visitors' computers.

Once the campaign information has been transferred to a cookie, all a visitor's actions are stored in the cookie on his or her computer. This cookie is critical, since it provides a way for Google Analytics to connect visitor behavior, like conversions, to marketing activities.

For example, to track visitors coming from an e-mail campaign, you need to manipulate all the links in the e-mail by adding additional query string parameters to the links. A link such as www. mysite.com/landing.html would be manipulated to look like www.mysite.com/landing. html?utm_campaign=camp&utm_source=source&utm_medium=medium&utm_ content=content. Remember: Every URL in the e-mail needs to be modified.

Notice all the parameters that start with utm. These parameters are the Google Analytics link-tagging parameters that hold information about your marketing activities. Don't worry about the parameters and what they mean. Just remember that the data in the parameters is pulled directly into Google Analytics. So where in Google Analytics do you find the data?

Figure 5.27 shows the Campaigns report. You can see not only the traffic each campaign generates using the Site Usage tab, but also the conversions or goals, using the Goal tabs. Almost all the data in this report comes from information you add to the destination URLs of your marketing activities.

As described in Chapter 4, all reports are created from fields or dimensions. The information from each campaign tracking parameter becomes a different field or dimension in Google Analytics.

There are many other reports and features that provide insights into how your marketing activities perform. We cover more reports and techniques later in the book.

There are five parameters that Google Analytics uses in link tagging. These parameters form a hierarchy of data that helps provide information about marketing:

- **utm_campaign:** The Campaign parameter is used to hold the name of the marketing campaign. Usually a marketing activity is part of a bigger marketing activity. You can use the utm_campaign parameter to identify marketing activities at a high level. This parameter becomes the Campaign Name field and Campaign dimension in Google Analytics.

- **utm_source:** The Source parameter provides more context to the information in the utm_ campaign parameter. For example, when you track paid search campaigns, you use the Source parameter to track which search engine is sending the traffic (Google, Yahoo, Bing, and so on). When tracking e-mail, you might use the Source parameter to track the type of e-mail you are sending (newsletter, special offer, and so on) or the segment of your e-mail list you are sending to (age segment, demographic segment, purchase history segment, and so on). We describe specific values for the source parameter in the "Online Marketing Activities" section of this chapter. The utm_source parameter becomes the Campaign Source field and the Source dimension in Google Analytics.

- **utm_medium:** Like the Source parameter, the Medium parameter provides more context to the marketing activity you are tracking. Medium describes how you are broadcasting your message. It literally describes the mechanism you use to send your marketing message. If you want to identify traffic coming from e-mail, use a value of email for the Medium parameter. If you want to identify traffic from display advertising, you might set the Medium parameter to display or banner. We explain specific values for marketing activities in later chapters. The utm_medium parameter becomes the Campaign Medium field and Medium dimension in Google Analytics.

- **utm_content:** The Content parameter is an exceedingly useful parameter and can be used to identify variations of marketing materials. For example, you may want to use different creative variations in your e-mail marketing. You can alter the value of the Content parameter from one e-mail variation to another to differentiate them in Google Analytics. The utm_content parameter becomes the Campaign Content field and Ad Content dimension in Google Analytics.

FIGURE 5.27

The Campaigns report contains data for all marketing campaigns.

- **utm_term:** The final marketing campaign parameter is the Term parameter. This parameter is traditionally used to hold information about keywords from paid search campaigns. Tracking paid search campaigns to the keyword level helps you understand which keywords are, and which are not, working. The utm_term parameter becomes the Campaign Keyword field and Keyword dimension in Google Analytics.

When used together, all the parameters provide information about the different aspects of marketing activities. You can identify which campaigns are working using data from the utm_campaign parameters, and which parts of campaigns are working using the Medium, Source, Content, and Term parameters. All the campaign data provides different segmentation options to help you analyze marketing activities.

Now that you know all the different parameters used to track marketing activities, you need to know how to add them to the links in your marketing. Google offers a form-based tool, called the URL Builder, shown in Figure 5.28 and found at `www.analyticsformarketers.com/s/url-builder`, that can be used to tag your links.

The URL Builder is fairly easy to use. Simply enter values for Campaign, Medium, Source, and any additional parameters, along with the destination URL used in your ad. Click Generate URL and the form returns a URL that can be used in the ad.

While this tool is adequate, there are better options. We suggest using a spreadsheet with an embedded formula to create the URLs for your marketing campaigns. A spreadsheet-based solution offers several advantages over the Google URL Builder.

First, it scales better. A single marketing campaign might have many versions of ads in different mediums. This variation can create a huge number of URLs that must be tagged. Manually submitting the Google URL Builder over and over again is too time-consuming. It is much faster to use a spreadsheet.

The second advantage is data consistency. Remember, Google Analytics extracts the data from the parameters exactly as they appear in the URLs. If the spellings and capitalization are different, each variation is captured, creating duplicate data in some reports.

It is much easier to record your link-tagging parameters in a spreadsheet and reference previously used values. Plus, if you have a number of people in your organization running different kinds of marketing activities, you can share the spreadsheet so everyone uses the same naming values and naming conventions. We've included a sample spreadsheet on our site at `www.analyticsformarketers.com/s/url-spreadsheet`.

Once you have all your marketing campaigns tagged, you have completed the basic configuration of Google Analytics. Congratulations! But you may not be finished with the setup. Depending on the structure of your site, you may have to tackle some advanced configuration steps. Remember the list of Web site pitfalls we compiled at the beginning of the chapter? Check the list for any additional work you may need to complete.

Advanced configuration steps

In this section, we address configurations that require advanced programming or Web site manipulation. Many of the Web site issues explained at the beginning of this chapter require an advanced solution. While you may not be responsible for this work, it's important to understand the concepts. This understanding will make it easier to explain potential data issues and understand why certain things are, or are not, possible. The most common advanced implementation items are:

- Tracking multiple subdomains
- Tracking multiple domains
- Tracking clicks and events with virtual pageviews
- Advanced site search tracking
- Ecommerce tracking
- Advanced filters

FIGURE 5.28

The Google Analytics URL Builder can be used to tag campaign links.

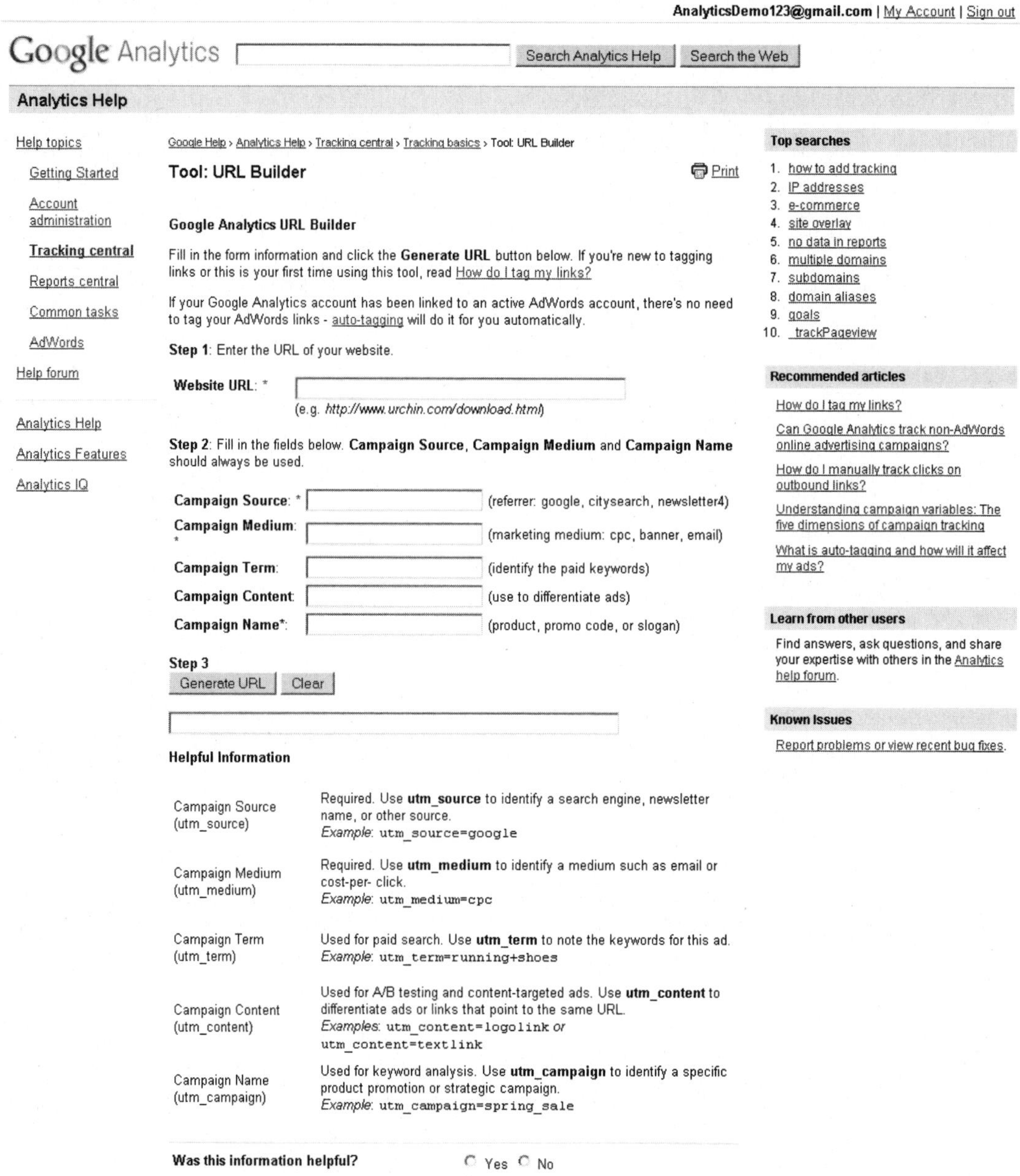

AnalyticsDemo123@gmail.com | My Account | Sign out

Google Analytics [   ] [Search Analytics Help] [Search the Web]

Analytics Help

Help topics

Getting Started

Account administration

Tracking central

Reports central

Common tasks

AdWords

Help forum

Analytics Help

Analytics Features

Analytics IQ

Google Help › Analytics Help › Tracking central › Tracking basics › Tool: URL Builder

Tool: URL Builder   🖶 Print

Google Analytics URL Builder

Fill in the form information and click the **Generate URL** button below. If you're new to tagging links or this is your first time using this tool, read How do I tag my links?

If your Google Analytics account has been linked to an active AdWords account, there's no need to tag your AdWords links - auto-tagging will do it for you automatically.

Step 1: Enter the URL of your website.

Website URL: * [   ]
(e.g. *http://www.urchin.com/download.html*)

Step 2: Fill in the fields below. **Campaign Source**, **Campaign Medium** and **Campaign Name** should always be used.

Campaign Source: * [   ] (referrer: google, citysearch, newsletter4)

Campaign Medium: * [   ] (marketing medium: cpc, banner, email)

Campaign Term: [   ] (identify the paid keywords)

Campaign Content: [   ] (use to differentiate ads)

Campaign Name*: [   ] (product, promo code, or slogan)

Step 3
[Generate URL] [Clear]

[   ]

Helpful Information

Campaign Source (utm_source)	Required. Use **utm_source** to identify a search engine, newsletter name, or other source. *Example*: utm_source=google
Campaign Medium (utm_medium)	Required. Use **utm_medium** to identify a medium such as email or cost-per- click. *Example*: utm_medium=cpc
Campaign Term (utm_term)	Used for paid search. Use **utm_term** to note the keywords for this ad. *Example*: utm_term=running+shoes
Campaign Content (utm_content)	Used for A/B testing and content-targeted ads. Use **utm_content** to differentiate ads or links that point to the same URL. *Examples*: utm_content=logolink or utm_content=textlink
Campaign Name (utm_campaign)	Used for keyword analysis. Use **utm_campaign** to identify a specific product promotion or strategic campaign. *Example*: utm_campaign=spring_sale

Was this information helpful?   ○ Yes ○ No

Top searches

1. how to add tracking
2. IP addresses
3. e-commerce
4. site overlay
5. no data in reports
6. multiple domains
7. subdomains
8. domain aliases
9. goals
10. trackPageview

Recommended articles

How do I tag my links?

Can Google Analytics track non-AdWords online advertising campaigns?

How do I manually track clicks on outbound links?

Understanding campaign variables: The five dimensions of campaign tracking

What is auto-tagging and how will it affect my ads?

Learn from other users

Find answers, ask questions, and share your expertise with others in the Analytics help forum.

Known Issues

Report problems or view recent bug fixes.

You will find more information on many advanced topics at the companion site for this book, www. analyticsformarketers.com.

Tracking subdomains

Web sites with subdomains need to be configured differently from sites without subdomains. A subdomain is the part of the URL that appears before the primary domain. In the URL sub.mysite. com, sub is the subdomain. The subdomain appears directly before the primary domain.

Subdomains can cause issues with the Google Analytics tracking cookies. Google Analytics uses first-party cookies to track visitors. When it sets the tracking cookies, it associates them with the domain of the Web site. The tracking cookies can only interact with the tracking code on that domain.

By default, Google Analytics includes the Web site's subdomain in the domain of the cookie. A tracking cookie set for a particular subdomain can interact only with the tracking code on that subdomain. If the visitor moves to a different subdomain on the site, or to the main domain of the site, Google Analytics thinks the visitor has left, which leads to problems with many of the metrics in Google Analytics.

For example, if Google Analytics sets the cookie on products.mysite.com, it will set a series of cookies for products.mysite.com and use those cookies to track the visitor when they are on products.mysite.com. If the visitor moves to checkout.mysite.com, Google Analytics sets another cookie to track the visitor. Now there is a single visitor with two Google Analytics cookies: The visitor is tracked as two different people. In addition, duplicate cookies cause inaccurate referral data in the Traffic Sources reports.

You can resolve issues with subdomains as long as you plan. When customizing the tracking code, notice a number of radio buttons on the Standard tab, as shown in Figure 5.29. When you select the radio button One Domain with Multiple Subdomains, Google Analytics changes the tracking code. The changes are subtle, but significant.

The new tracking code excludes any subdomains when setting the tracking cookies. The GATC sets one set of cookies that can be accessed as the visitor traverses all subdomains of the site, which is exactly what you want.

Tracking multiple domains

If your Web site visitors traverse multiple domains during a single visit, you could be missing critical information. When visitors leave a Web site, they leave their tracking cookies behind. And as explained in Chapter 4, Google Analytics cannot track a visitor without cookies. A multiple-domain situation is common for Web sites that use a third-party service such as a shopping cart. You can remedy this problem, but it takes work.

The solution for tracking Web sites with multiple domains is to attach the cookies to the Web site visitors, so as they move from one domain to the next, the cookies go with them. If the visitors always have their cookies, you can accurately track them with Google Analytics.

The issue with multiple domains is cookie portability. You need a way to transfer the cookies from one domain to another, using a process called *cross-domain tracking*.

Configuring cross-domain tracking is a two-step process. The first step is to modify the tracking code that appears on every page of both domains. This can be done directly from the Code Configurator using the radio buttons (see Figure 5.30).

FIGURE 5.29

The radio buttons in the Code Configurator provide options for tracking Web sites with multiple subdomains.

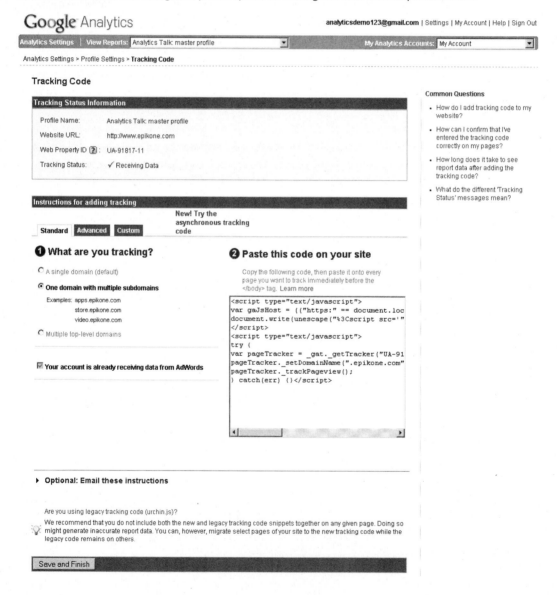

These code changes tell Google Analytics that your Web site has multiple domains and that you need to pass the cookies from one Web site to another.

The next step is to add code to all the links and all the forms that direct visitors from domain A to domain B as well as links that come back from B to A. The additional code passes the cookies from one domain to the next by adding the cookie values to the URL. Every link and every form that directs the visitor from domain A to domain B must be modified. This implementation sounds like a complete pain, and it is — but failing to add this code means that it impossible to accurately track visitors.

All standard links must be modified as shown below. Notice that the link has been changed to include additional JavaScript. Your job is to place the URL where you want the visitor to land, in the _ link() method. When a visitor clicks on the link, Google Analytics copies the cookie values, adds them to the URL that you place in the _link() method, and then forwards the visitor to the URL.

```
<a href=http://www.mysite.com onClick="pageTracker._link
    ('http://www.mysite.com');return false;">Checkout</a>
```

When the visitor lands on the URL, Google Analytics copies the cookie values from the URL and sets new tracking cookies from the original site. Now the visitor has two sets of cookies, one for each Web site domain. More important, the cookies have the same value. You have effectively transferred the Google Analytics information from one domain to the next, thus creating a seamless view of the visitor's interaction with your content.

In addition to changing all the links on your site that point from one domain to the other, you must also change all the forms. Why would a Web site use a form rather than a link to direct visitors from one domain to the next? The most common example is a Checkout Now button for a shopping cart —it's almost always a Submit button and not a link. But ultimately it all depends on the Web site architecture and platform. While the results of the implementation are the same, the code is different, as shown here:

```
<form name="checkout" method="post" onSubmit="pageTracker._
    linkByPost('www.mysite.com/step1.html');">
```

Notice that the modified form contains a method named _linkByPost(). This method, like _ link(,), copies the Google Analytics cookie values and passes them to the second Web site by adding them to the URL.

After you've made all the code changes to your site, the final step is to clean up the data with a filter. The filter adds the Web site domain to the content reports. Because you are tracking two Web sites within one profile, you're getting data from two domains. You may have some pages that share the same page name. For example, there may be an index.html on both domain A and domain B. But Google Analytic ignores the domain in the reports, so all you see is index.html, without knowing how many times index.html appears in the data for domain A or domain B.

To resolve this problem, you can add an Advanced filter that inserts the domain name into the content reports. The settings are shown in Figure 5.31.

FIGURE 5.30

The Code Configurator has an option for tracking visitors across multiple domains.

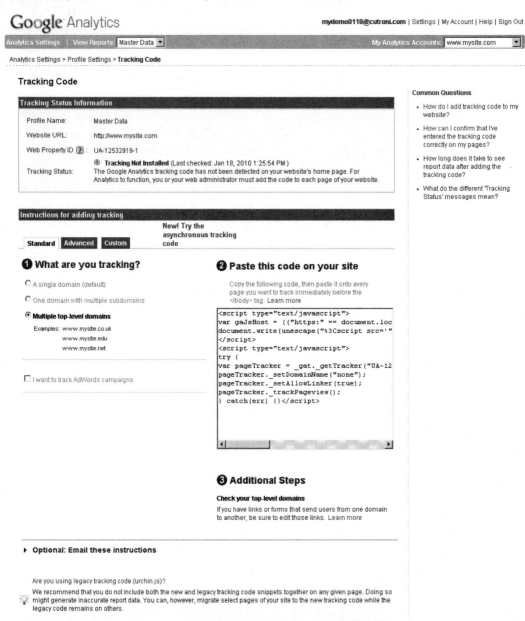

The virtual pageview

As you've seen in the previous sections, many Google Analytics settings depend on pageviews. URL Destination Goals, funnels, and site search are all features configured using pageviews. More specifically, most of these features require a specific piece of information in the URL. For example, to configure site search, there must be a parameter in the URL that identifies the search term. For URL Destination Goals and funnels to work, there must be URLs that differentiate a conversion page or funnel step from other pages on the site.

But what happens if these distinct URLs don't exist? What happens if there is no query parameter in the URL to identify a site search query? Or what if you want to configure a goal for a PDF download? How to you create a pageview for a PDF? Or what happens if the entire site is in Flash, or uses a lot of AJAX? In these cases, you can create a virtual, or fake, pageview that contains the information you need to configure a goal, a funnel, or site search.

Pageviews are created by the `_trackPageview()` method of the GATC. Every time this method is called, another pageview is created. Normally, this code only appears in the standard page tag, as shown in the code below. But you can add the `_trackPageview()` method to almost any part of a page. You can create a pageview any time you want.

```
<script type="text/javascript">
var gaJsHost = (("https:" == document.location.protocol) ? "https://
    ssl." : "http://www.");
document.write(unescape("%3Cscript src='" + gaJsHost + "google-
    analytics.com/ga.js' type='text/javascript'%3E%3C/script%3E"));
</script>
<script type="text/javascript">
try {
var pageTracker = _gat._getTracker("UA-XXXXX-XX");
pageTracker._trackPageview();
} catch(err) {}</script>
```

Once you create a virtual pageview, you can use it to create a goal, funnel, or site search configuration.

There are three steps to creating a virtual pageview. The first is to determine where to put the `_trackPageview()` method. This placement depends on why you're creating the virtual URL.

Second, you need to create the data Google Analytics will use for the virtual pageview. You can add the data that will be used to name the virtual pageview to the `_trackPageview()` method. You need to add the name of the virtual pageview to the JavaScript in the page.

There are not many restrictions on what you can name a page. We suggest you create a logical structure of data using a folder hierarchy. It's a good idea to place all virtual pageviews in a folder named `/virtual` to make them easy to identify in reports.

FIGURE 5.31

An Advanced filter can be used to add the Web site domain to the URI field. This helps differentiate duplicate pages that appear on both domains.

For example, let's say you need to create a virtual pageview to identify the end of the ecommerce checkout process. You might name the virtual pageview something like /virtual/checkout/ complete.

You might then name all the pages in the checkout process /virtual/checkout/step-1, / virtual/checkout/step-2, and /virtual/checkout/step-3.

Finally, you need to move the Google Analytics Tracking Code to the top of the page. You can place it in the <head> tag, as shown in the code below. While you don't need to move the tracking code to the top of every page on the site, it is often easier to move the tag to the top of the page for the entire site. It can be difficult to manage the tracking code if you move it to the <head> tag for some pages and keep it before the closing </body> tag for others.

```
<head>
 <script type="text/javascript">
 var gaJsHost = (("https:" == document.location.protocol) ? "https://
    ssl." : "http://www.");
 document.write(unescape("%3Cscript src='" + gaJsHost + "google-
    analytics.com/ga.js' type='text/javascript'%3E%3C/script%3E"));
 </script>
 <script type="text/javascript">
 try {
 var pageTracker = _gat._getTracker("UA-XXXXX-XX");
 pageTracker._trackPageview();
 } catch(err) {}</script>
</head>
```

The tracking code must be moved to ensure that the ga.js file has loaded in the browser before any Google Analytics JavaScript is called by the browser. If the ga.js file has not fully loaded in the browser, and the browser tries to create a virtual pageview by executing _trackPaegview(), the result will be an error.

Once you've added _trackPageview() to the necessary locations, you should start to see data in Google Analytics after a few hours. If you're creating a virtual pageview for a goal, you can now configure your goal as described earlier in this chapter using your virtual URL as the Goal URL. You can also use a virtual pageview to configure each step in a funnel. If you're using virtual URLs to capture simple things such as PDF downloads, you should start to see data in your various content reports.

While the virtual pageview is an effective workaround for challenging tracking scenarios, it does have a drawback: You're creating a lot of extra pageviews that will skew your pageview-related metrics. To mitigate this problem, you can create multiple profiles and apply Include or Exclude filters to include or exclude the virtual pageviews. For example, you may need the virtual pageviews to configure a goal for your Master profile. In this case, you need to include the virtual pageview for your goal. Other virtual pageviews, like file downloads, may not be as important and so can be removed from the profile using an Exclude filter. It's up to you to determine what's important.

Event Tracking tool

An alternative to using virtual pageviews is a feature called Event Tracking. Event Tracking is a flexible data-collection tool that can track almost anything on a Web site.

Event data is fundamentally different from other data in Google Analytics. Events are not pageviews and cannot be used for things like goals or funnels. So, if you need to track a PDF download as a goal, you need to use a virtual pageview, not an event.

Events are organized in a logical hierarchy of *categories*, *actions*, *labels*, and *values*:

- Categories are used to group different types of event data, such as video player events, click events, or widget events.
- Actions are a description of how the visitor interacts with a piece of Web site content, like clicking Play, Pause, or Complete.
- Labels provide more information about the action value. For example, it may not be enough to know that a visitor clicked Play on a video player. It would be more helpful to know the name of the video that was playing when the visitor clicked Play. A label can be used to track the name of the video that is playing.
- An Event Value is simply an integer that is associated with an action and label combination. Values do not have an associated unit, they are just numbers. Values can be used for almost anything, from assigning a value to events to counting how long an event lasts.

Like the virtual pageview, Event Tracking requires additional coding. To create an event, you must execute a line of JavaScript when the visitor executes an event. If you want to create an event when the visitor clicks the Play button on a video player, you must add the Event Tracking code to the Play button of the video player. If you want to track a file download as an event, you must add the Event Tracking code to the link the visitor clicks to download the file. You get the idea.

The Event Tracking code looks like this:

```
_trackEvent(category, action, opt_label, opt_value)
```

Each value in the parenthesis (called an *argument*) must be replaced by the value you want to use in Google Analytics: The value you use for `category` will be displayed in the Categories report; the value you use for `action` will be displayed in the Actions report; and so on.

While Event Tracking is a useful feature, it is definitely an advanced topic. We dig more into Event Tracking and how it can be used at `www.analyticsformarketers.com/s/event-tracking`.

Custom variables

One feature that we do not explain in this book is the User-Defined feature. That's because a new feature named *custom variables* was introduced to take its place. Custom variables are a way to bucket data based on your specific business needs. In this section, we provide a basic functional overview of custom variables.

You can have virtually unlimited numbers of custom variables, which means that the same visitor can exist as part of many custom variables. The old User-Defined feature allowed a visitor to be in only one segment at a time. This ability to have visitors be part of many custom variables is due to the structure of a custom variable.

Each custom variable has four parts:

- **Index.** Index slots go from 1 to 5; think of an index as a drawer in a filing cabinet.
- **Name.** A name could be something like `interest` or `pricing level`; think of name as the name of each drawer in the file cabinet.

- **Value.** A value could be something like `green initiative` or `on-sale`; think of value as the information in each drawer.
- **Scope.** This is an optional way to define if the variable should be page-level (defining information about a page), session-level (defining information about a visit), or visitor-level (describing information about a visitor). Think of scope as how often you clean out each drawer in the filing cabinet.

Both the name and the value of each variable are fairly easy to understand. The name and value will appear in the Custom Variables report. Every custom variable must have a name and value. See Chapter 7 for more information about analyzing data with custom variables.

The most complicated part of custom variables is understanding index, scope, and the interaction between the two. As defined earlier, scope is how long the variable should last. A visitor-level variable is set as a cookie and is associated with the visitor as long as the cookie exists. A visit-level variable lasts only for the duration of a visitor's visit. And a page-level variable lasts only during the pageview when the page-level variable is set. Again, scope is how long a variable will last.

Index is how the variables are organized. There are five slots in the index, which means that you can set up to five variables. Think of the index as the drawers in a filing cabinet. There are five slots in the index, so there are five drawers in this hypothetical filing cabinet. When using custom variables, you can place one variable in a slot. Or, using our example, you can place one variable in each drawer of the filing cabinet. Each slot can contain only one custom variable at a time.

Scope has a profound impact on the index. Scope controls how often each slot in the index is cleaned out. Again, using our example of the filing cabinet, scope controls how often each drawer in the filing cabinet is emptied. When you place a page-level variable in a specific slot in the index, like slot 1, that slot is filled and cannot be used again during that pageview. This means that you cannot set another variable in slot 1 during that pageview. However, when the visitor moves to a new page, Google Analytics empties slot 1 because the custom variable was a page-level custom variable.

Visitor-level custom variables behave in a similar manner to visit-level custom variables. When a visitor-level custom variable is set in a specific slot in the index, that slot can never be used again. That's because the visitor-level variable persists from one visit to the next. Using the filing cabinet example, when you place something in a specific drawer in the filing cabinet, that drawer is never emptied again, unless you want to delete what you have and replace it with something else.

Now you can see the challenge with custom variables. You must define the custom variables you want to use and identify the scope of each variable.

Custom variables are implemented, like all things in Google Analytics, using JavaScript. To create a variable, you must assign each variable at least three pieces of information: an index, name, and a value. Remember, scope is optional. Here's the basic code:

```
pageTracker._setCustomVar(index, name, value, scope_optional);
```

This code should be your site whenever you want to set a custom variable. It could be when someone logs into your site or it could be when a visitor submits a form. It all depends on the variable and the action the visitor must take to cause that variable to be set.

You can see that custom variables are very flexible and can be used to track almost anything. Planning what you want to track and how to implement your custom variables is critical to ensure good data. For more information about custom variables, visit `www.analyticsformarketers.com/s/` `custom-variables`.

Advanced site search tracking

There are not many things that can complicate the site search configuration. The most common implementation problem occurs when the site search term does not appear in the URL. Remember, Google Analytics requires the search query to appear in the URL in order to configure site search.

You can resolve this issue by creating a virtual pageview that includes the site search query as a query string parameter. Then the virtual pageview or, more specifically, the virtual query string parameter holding the search term can be referenced in the site search configuration. Basically you need to create a virtual pageview in this format:

```
pageracker._trackPageview('/virtual/search?searchQuery=boston');
```

The word "boston" was the search term entered by the visitor. How you populate the value of `searchQuery` depends on where you place this code and where you place this code depends on what you can change.

This code could be attached to a Submit Search button. When a visitor clicks the Submit Search button, a virtual pageview is created containing the keyword. If you use this approach, make sure you move the GATC to the top of the page before you create the virtual pageview.

Another option is to change the tracking code on the search results page to include the search term. You could use server-level code that manipulates the page tag or JavaScript that extracts the search term from the page HTML and creates a virtual pageview.

If your site search does not identify the search query as a query string parameter, you must create a virtual pageview that contains the search terms as a query string parameter.

Once the virtual pageview has been created, you can reference the query string parameter in the site search settings as you would normally.

Ecommerce tracking

Like many Web analytics tools, Google Analytics provides a way to track ecommerce transactions. This is critical because many commerce-based Web sites have commerce-based KPIs (like revenue and transactions).

Ecommerce data is collected with a special ecommerce page tag. This code must be placed on the thank-you page or on the page that signifies that a transaction has occurred. This page is often called the *receipt page*. When your receipt page is rendered, the ecommerce tag sends the transaction information to the Google Analytics servers by requesting the same invisible image file used for pageview tracking.

While this seems straightforward, the ecommerce tag is unique. This tag must be manipulated by your Web application, in real time when a transaction occurs, to include transaction details. Depending on your ecommerce platform, the implementation could require some server-side coding. Many ecommerce platforms have Google Analytics modules that automatically track ecommerce transactions. However, if you're using a homegrown commerce platform, you need to add server-side code to add transaction information to the Google Analytics commerce page tag.

There are two steps to implementing ecommerce tracking on a site. The first step is to enable the ecommerce reports in Google Analytics using the Profile Settings, as shown in Figure 5.32.

Simply check the Yes radio button and Google Analytics will add a series of ecommerce reports and an ecommerce tab to many of the reports in Google Analytics. Congratulations, you have completed the easy part of ecommerce configuration!

Step 2 is the addition of the ecommerce JavaScript tag to the thank-you page of your Web site. The actual ecommerce JavaScript is:

```
<script type="text/javascript">
  try{
   var pageTracker = _gat._getTracker("UA-xxxxx-x");
   pageTracker._trackPageview();
   pageTracker._addTrans(
   "A-7728", // order ID - required
   "Hats", // affiliation or store name
   "21.64", // total - required
   "0.65", // tax
   "10.00", // shipping
   "Boston", // city
   "Massachusetts", // state or province
   "USA" // country
   );


   pageTracker._addItem(
   "A-7728", // order ID - necessary to connect item with
  transaction
   "DD44", // SKU/code - required
   "Red Sox Hat", // product name
   "Hats", // category or variation
   "10.99", // unit price - required
   "1" // quantity - required
   );
```

```
pageTracker._trackTrans();
} catch(err) {}
```

Notice that the code is divided it into three sections. The first section contains the summary information for the transaction. Each piece of information in the _addTrans() section becomes a different field dimension or metric in Google Analytics. Google then uses each field to create a report. The Transactions report is based on the Transaction ID. The data from the Revenue field becomes the Revenue metric used in many reports, in Advanced Segments, and in the custom reporting interface. Your job is to ensure that there is server-side code to populate each field appropriately.

Note that the geographic information (city, state, and country) is no longer used by Google Analytics reports.

In addition to tracking basic summary information about a transaction, Google Analytics can also track details of a transaction, such as which products the visitor purchased and information about those products. This information is added to section 2 of the ecommerce code. Notice that you can enter a product name and category. Like the summary information, Google Analytics takes the product information and creates dimensions and metrics. This information is then used to create reports (such as the Products report or the Categories reports) and to create advanced segments and custom reports.

The final section of the ecommerce tracking code sends all the data to Google's servers.

As mentioned earlier, you don't just add this code to your receipt page; you must add server-level code to add all the appropriate values whenever a transaction occurs. Normally you must add server-level code that places the transaction information in the appropriate positions.

Creating server-level code that inserts the transaction data is the complicated part. If you are not a programmer, you should check with your IT department. Your job is to understand that adding ecommerce data to Google Analytics can be done, but it can require more time and effort.

Filters

The last advanced topic is filters. Earlier in this chapter, we explain basic filters used to normalize data. The filters were fairly simple, and we focused on how to add filters and not on how filters work. There are many kind of filters, called *custom filters*, you can use to manipulate data and data access.

Filters work on a simple premise: You enter a type of pattern into Google Analytics and tell Google Analytics to apply that pattern to a piece of data. If the pattern you entered matches the data, an action happens. While there are exceptions, most filters trigger an action.

The patterns used in Google Analytics are called *regular expressions*, or RegEx for short. A regular expression is a powerful pattern-matching language. It was developed by programmers and can be challenging to learn. We don't cover regular expressions in this book, but there is an excellent series of blog posts by LunaMetrics, a Google Analytics authorized consultant. You can find the complete tutorial at www.analyticsformarketers.com/s/luna-filter-tutorial.

The data part of a filter is called a *field*. The fields we explain in Chapter 4 are used in a filter. As data is processed, Google Analytics applies the regular expression you enter to the field you choose.

And what about the actions? There are a number of filter actions that appear as radio buttons in the Filter configuration page (see Figure 5.33).

FIGURE 5.32

Activate the ecommerce reports using the Ecommerce Web site setting in the Profile Settings.

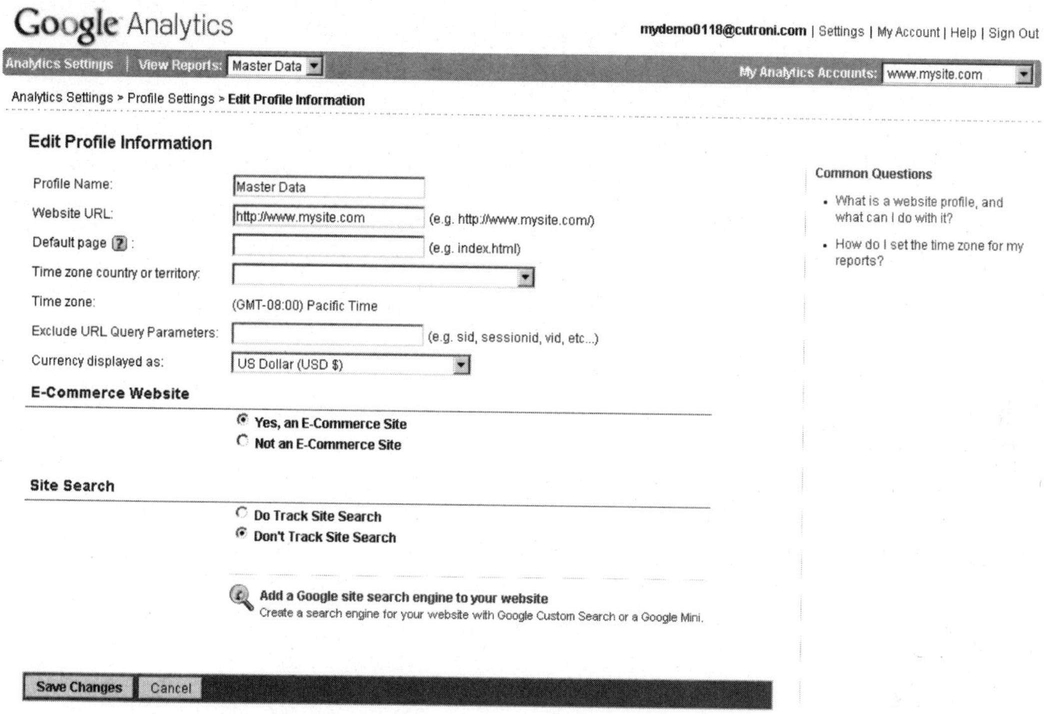

Include and Exclude filters

Include and Exclude filters are the most commonly used filters. When applied to a profile, they include data or exclude data. We touched on this concept earlier when creating IP-based filters to remove internal data from a profile.

Why would you want to include or exclude data from a profile? For example, you may want to include only data from a specific region of the country, such as a specific sales territory. You can create an include filter that contains a list of all the desired states (the pattern) and applies it to the Visitor's Region field. The settings are shown in Figure 5.34.

Notice that we used a regular expression to create the list of states we want to include. We did not create one filter for each state we wanted to include.

Once this filter has been applied, all future data in the profile will be from one of the specified states. If you use include or exclude to create modified data views, it is best to create additional profiles and then apply the filter to the new profile. As we explained earlier, it's a good idea to have multiple profiles for redundancy. If you want to create a profile with a modified data view, create a new profile, add all the settings of your standard reporting profile, and then add the Include or Exclude filter to customize the data.

Uppercase and Lowercase filters

Uppercase and Lowercase filters change the case of the field the filter is applied to. A Lowercase filter applied to the Page Title field will force every value of the page title to lowercase. An Uppercase filter applied to the Request URI will force every value of the Request URI to uppercase.

Why use an Uppercase or Lowercase filter? These filters normalize data as described in the "Basic configuration" section of this chapter. Remember, Google Analytics is case-sensitive and cannot differentiate between two pieces of data that differ only in case — for example, the keywords "Football" and "football."

Creating an Uppercase or Lowercase filter is easier than creating other filters. Uppercase and Lowercase filters require only choosing a field, as previously shown in Figure 5.24.

FIGURE 5.33

Filter actions are chosen using radio buttons in the Filter Type settings.

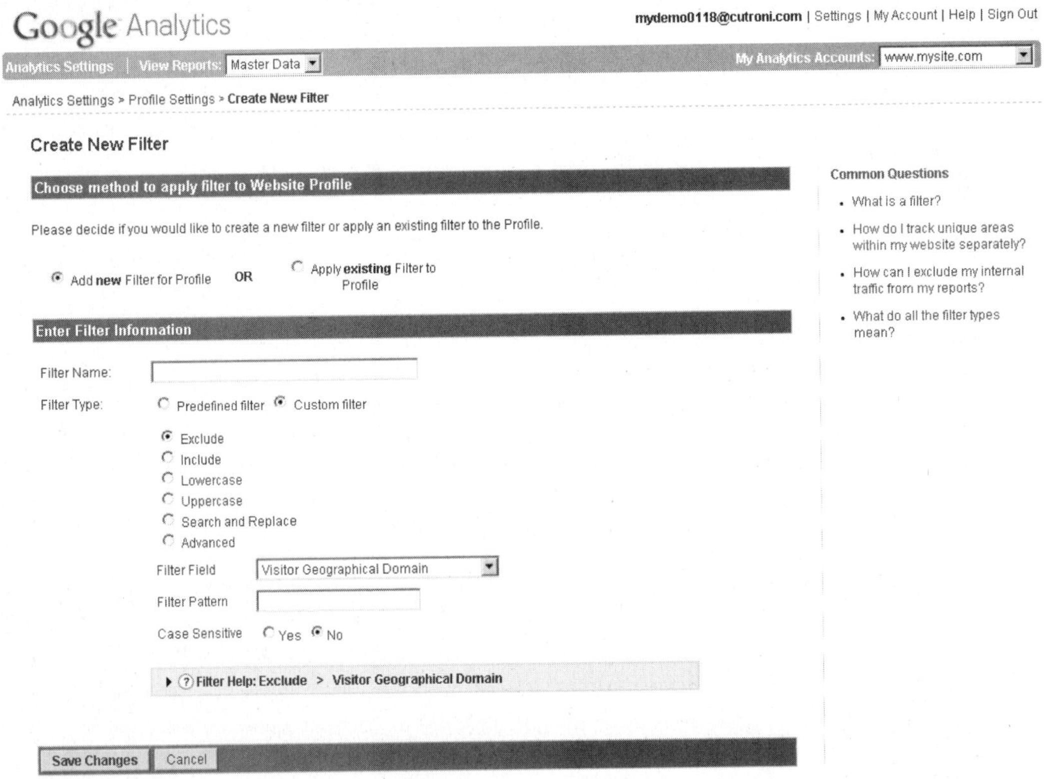

Advanced filters

As the name implies, Advanced filters are complicated! One look at the form used to create an Advanced filter and you can instantly see there is more to these filters than Include, Exclude, Uppercase, and Lowercase.

Advanced filters are primarily used to manipulate data. Specifically, they are used to concatenate different fields or rearrange parts of fields. Why would you ever want to do this? Think about the example we used describing the subdomain tracking and cross-domain tracking. Sometimes you need to add more information to the URI to provide more insights.

Advanced filters are used to normalize the Request URI field, which often contains excessive data that can make reports difficult to understand. Advanced filters can also be used in various hacks to add more data to Google Analytics.

The first thing you'll notice in the configuration form in Figure 5.35 are two fields: A and B. These are the standard fields used by all filters. Next to the field is a text box where you enter a pattern. As with

---

FIGURE 5.34

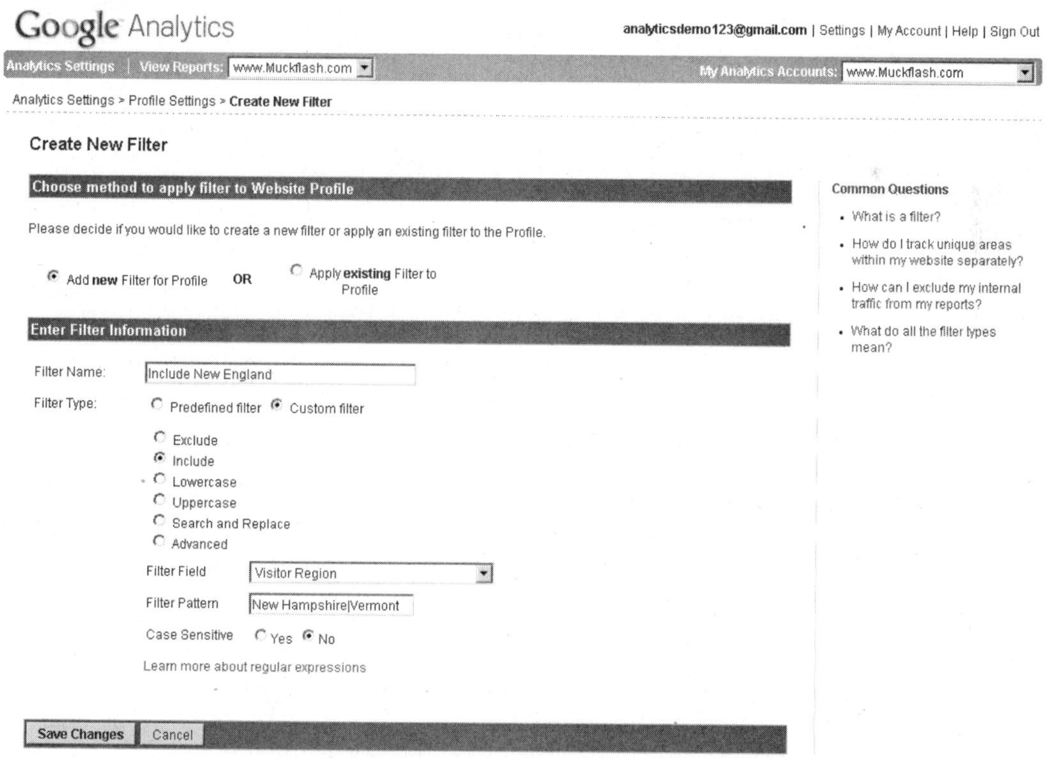

An Include filter to include only traffic from certain U.S. states

all filter patterns, the pattern must be a regular expression. What's special about the Advanced filter is that you can enter a pattern for each field. The pattern is then applied to the appropriate field.

Another unique feature of Advanced filters is that you can actually capture parts of each field using the pattern. Remember, Advanced filters can be used to concatenate fields or rearrange parts of fields. If you want to concatenate fields, you need to specify which parts you want to concatenate. You need to choose the parts of each field you want to put together using the pattern. Specifically, you use parentheses to capture parts of the field. Google Analytics stores the part of the field in the parentheses. You can then recall that piece of data when you want to add it to a different piece of data.

FIGURE 5.35

Setting for an Advanced filter

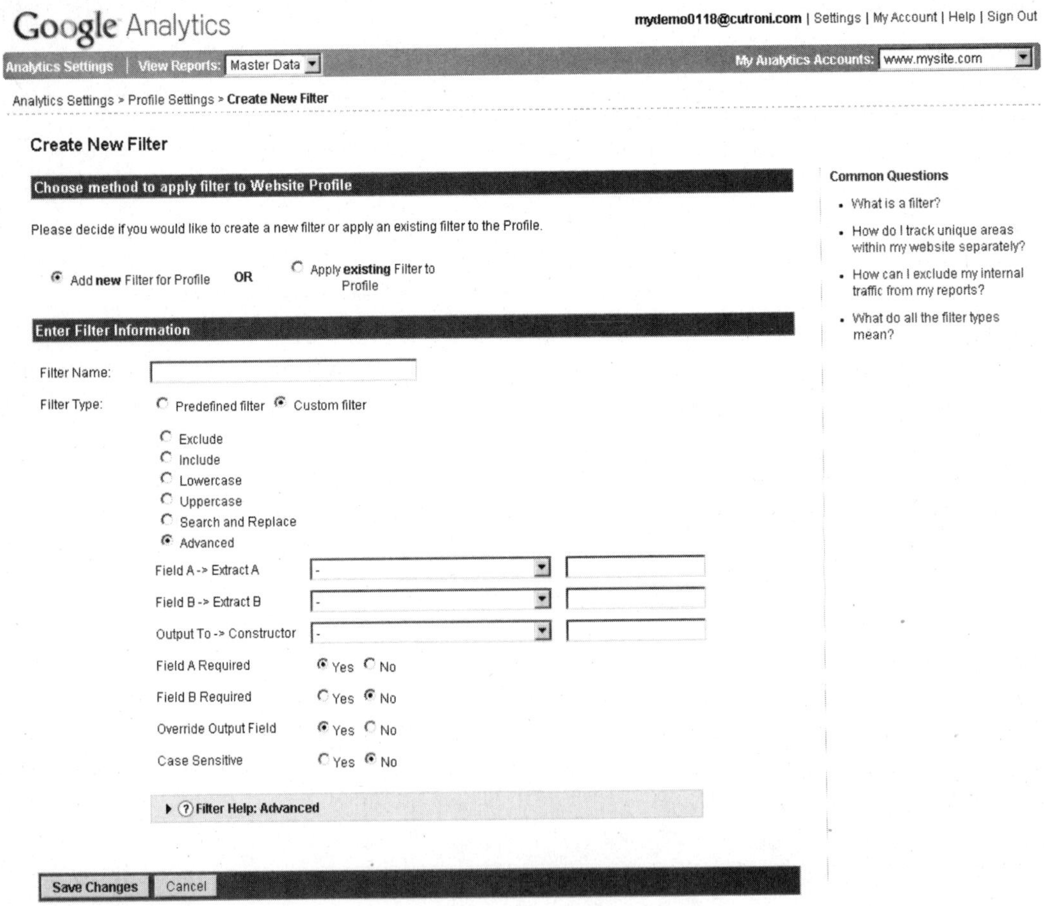

To put the data back together, you use the Constructor, also shown in Figure 5.35. The Constructor is also a field. You can output the parts of field A and B you captured using a special notation in the Constructor field.

For the most part, the standard implementation of Google Analytics does not include many Advanced filters. But now you should be able to modify or manipulate your data.

Maintaining Your Implementations

Once you have Google Analytics up and running, there is not much you need to do to maintain the implementation. It should run smoothly on a day-to-day basis. But there are things, like updates to a Web site, that can trip up Google Analytics and cause problems with your data quality.

Changes to GATC

For the most part, the Google Analytics page tags should not change or disappear from your site. Problems with the tags usually occur when you update, relaunch, or modify your site. Maintaining the tags is all about process and education. It is imperative that everyone who works on the site understands page tagging and the importance of maintaining the tags.

Most sites use templates, and you can add the tracking code to a common footer file. This makes maintenance easy because the tracking code is located in one place and not scattered in the HTML on different pages.

In addition to process and education, you can monitor your page tags using a tag-monitoring tool. There are many tools available, some more robust than others. As you can imagine, the price for these tools ranges from free for simple tools to extremely high for complicated tools. You will find a complete list of tag-monitoring tools at www.analyticsformarketers.com/s/tag-monitoring-tools.

These tools crawl your site and scan the resulting code for the Google Analytics tags. Depending on the tool, you will receive an alert if the tags are missing.

You can easily monitor your data quality using alerts. Alerts are part of Google Analytics' Intelligence features. As the name implies, alerts are e-mail from Google Analytics when a specific data condition has been hit. For example, you can create an alert when your Web site traffic has 0 visits per day.

While using alerts is a simple way to monitor data quality, especially when you do not log in every day, there is latency in this method: Alerts are sent once per day, so it is possible to have a data issue for many hours before it is notified.

Changes to Configuration Settings

Changes to any setting in Google Analytics, such as a filter or goal, can forever manipulate the data, which is bad. But there is a simple way to avoid issues with your Configuration Settings: Limit administrative access to a bare minimum.

There are two types of users: administrators and users. Administrators have access to every profile within an account. They also have access to every Google Account Setting and every Profile Setting. Basically an administrator can do anything to an account and to any of the profiles in an account.

By contrast, a user cannot change any Google Account Settings or any Profile Settings. Users can only access profile reports in Google Analytics. Furthermore, a user can only access profile reports he or she is authorized to access. An administrator must grant users access to specific profiles.

There are two simple rules to keep in mind when managing users:

- First, ensure that only authorized people have access to your data. Scan your account users to ensure that each user is appropriate. Delete any user who should not have access.
- Second, reduce the number of administrators to the bare minimum. Remember: An administrator can change any account or profile setting and even delete the account. The only way to reduce the chances of a configuration mistake is to reduce the number of people who can make configuration changes.

There is no other way to reduce the chance of a configuration issue than restricting the number of people with the capability to make changes to your settings.

Even if you limit the number of people who can make changes, mistakes can happen. To help mitigate issues when making changes, it's a good idea to apply your changes to a Test profile first rather than a profile used for analysis and reporting purposes, as we urged earlier in this chapter.

Once you add or change a setting in a profile, it is a good idea to have the administrator keep a detailed log of the changes made to the configuration. Google Analytics does not have a change log or an auditing system. One solution is to use a spreadsheet, preferably a Google spreadsheet, to record changes to the tracking code or settings in Google Analytics. A Google spreadsheet is helpful because it can easily be shared with users. But based on our experience, it can be difficult to get people to navigate from Google Analytics to Google spreadsheets to record their changes.

Another option to record changes to your Google Analytics setting is to use the annotations feature. Annotations are small notes of less than 160 characters that can be added to a profile. An annotation can be private (only visible to you) or public (visible to anyone with access to the profile). Annotations are located just below the data graph and can be accessed by clicking on the little arrow in the middle of the bottom axis (shown in Figure 5.36).

Incorrect campaign tracking

There is no shortcut to tracking marketing campaigns. While some marketing tools are integrated with Google Analytics, you may need to manually tag marketing campaigns. If you do not tag your marketing campaigns correctly, you will get bad data. It's that simple.

You must be diligent and ensure that all marketing activities are tagged before they are sent. Check and double-check that all campaigns are tagged properly to ensure data quality. The complexity of checking your campaigns increases with the number of internal or external teams you work with, but you must scale and continue to check all campaigns. If a campaign does slip through, be sure to add an annotation to Google Analytics explaining the change in traffic.

FIGURE 5.36

Annotations can be used to track changes to your Google Analytics Settings.

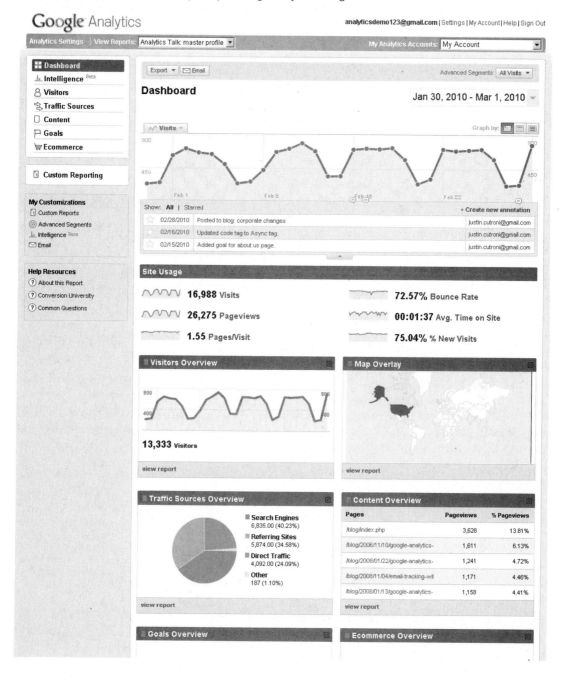

We explain other settings and configurations later in this book as they apply to different kinds of marketing activities. For a checklist you can use to keep you Google Analytics account running smoothly over time, visit www.analyticsformarketers.com/s/maintenance-checklist.

—

Basic Analysis Features and Concepts

Chapters 4 and 5 explain the essentials of how to deploy and configure Google Analytics. This chapter focuses on how to start analyzing data by walking you through the basics of using the Google Analytics interface. You'll see how to use features such as the Calendar and Data Table, as well as where to find the information you need among the many standard reports in Google Analytics. If you already have experience using the Google Analytics interface, you may want to skim through this chapter and focus your attention on the advanced features covered in Chapter 7.

Nine Tips for Becoming an All-Star Analyst

Before we jump into the Google Analytics interface, here's a quick word of advice on how to approach your analysis: Google Analytics contains lots of information, only some of which is relevant to your activities. Staying focused and avoiding the trap of report-surfing, where you browse your data aimlessly, can be tricky. The following tips will help you stay focused and build credibility as an analyst:

1. **Get your Google Analytics implementation right.** Don't start drawing conclusions from your Google Analytics data until you've followed all the instructions in Chapter 5, preferably with help from a developer. The worst thing you can do is report inaccurate numbers from Google Analytics and then reverse yourself later. Presenting new numbers will damage your reputation as an analyst and undermine the credibility of Google Analytics as a measurement tool.

2. **Define business goals for your Web site.** Without business goals your data is worthless! Worse than that, it's a distraction. What is the purpose of your Web site? Influence potential donors? Sell shoes? If you don't know the answer, refer to Chapter 2 for tips on defining conversion goals. Your *business goals* should always be the starting point to analytics.

3. **Identify the activities and business decisions you're trying to influence.** What is top of mind for your team members? Is it time to set the quarterly budget? As an analyst, pay attention to the business context and make sure you structure your analysis around the decisions your team is grappling with right now. If you're not sure what the team cares about, ask it! Timing is hugely important if you want to give voice to your data.

4. **Define research questions that can be tied to decisions.** This is term paper 101 in high school, and it still applies. Good questions make good analysts. For example, you might start with the question "Is my SEM campaign generating positive ROI?" If the answer is yes, you have a strong case to raise your budget. If not, you have a strong case to lower your budget or spend more time optimizing your campaign.

5. **Set a schedule.** Set aside 15 minutes a day or a couple of hours a week to tackle the business goals and research questions you've created in Google Analytics. A fixed schedule will help you use your time efficiently — get in, get out, and move on. Piano teachers have been drilling kids on this concept for hundreds of years, and the advice holds true today. Also, make sure you are aware of major decision points you can influence such as budgeting meetings, quarterly performance evaluations, major sales, and marketing events. These milestones are your time to shine as an analyst, so be sure to prepare for them in advance.

6. **Recognize your own bias.** If you have a vested interest in the outcome of a particular campaign or dispute, be aware that your analysis will almost certainly be biased. Take extra care in these cases to go into Google Analytics with a research question and an open mind rather than a goal of proving yourself right. Stay agnostic until you have looked at the evidence.

7. **Check your work.** One of the most difficult things for an analyst to do is gain the trust of team members. When you think you've found a killer insight, take the extra time to find supporting evidence. Cross-check your findings against other data sources such as your financials, CRM system, or advertising tools. Find a buddy to help you understand if your conclusions make sense. Be skeptical of your findings until you've seen them validated with as many data sources as possible.

8. **Socialize your findings.** Once you've developed an insight you feel is rock-solid, focus on getting it implemented and monitor the results of the change. This basic cycle of experimentation is *the most powerful concept in analytics*. If you can show positive impact from your recommendation, you'll win more resources for analytics and more trust from team members. Without socializing your findings, you can fill a book with great analysis and still get nowhere.

9. **Speak in plain English.** Express your findings in language that your team members can understand. Focus on business value and desired outcomes. Simple insights are often the most powerful. Don't use fancy terminology to show your intelligence. Take the time to convert

metrics such as conversions into financial terms and use visuals and examples to help communicate your message.

Taking into account this advice, remember the be-all and end-all question of Web analytics: What should my business do more of, and what should we do less of?

Google Analytics is full of data about how your visitors are using your Web site, where they come from, who they are, and so on. All this information is fun to look at, but none of it matters unless you can use it to make smarter decisions about where to place your energy. Analytics is a means to an end. It's a tool for gauging the effectiveness of your activities, prioritizing, and ultimately running a more efficient, more responsive, business. You need to maintain a healthy relationship between the analysis you do and the actions you take.

All action and no analysis leads to foolish decisions. Even worse, all analysis and no action leads to no decisions at all. As you approach your analysis, remember to stay focused on your business goals — always.

Navigating the Google Analytics Interface

To log into Google Analytics, you need a Google Account (a username and password) and an active Google Analytics Account, as Chapter 5 explains. You use a Google Account to access all Google's services such as Gmail and Google Calendar. Your Google Analytics Account is tied to the specific Web sites you're tracking.

Accessing your reports

Once you have a Google Account and linked it to a Google Analytics Account, navigate to www.google.com/analytics to access your reports. Just click the blue Access Analytics button.

If you're not already signed in, you're greeted by a page asking you to enter your username and password. If you forget your password, click the Can't Access Your Account? link.

After you are signed in, the Google Analytics Account Management Interface page appears. This page lists all the Google Analytics Accounts linked to your Google Account, as well as all the profiles contained in those accounts. For a primer on how to use the Account Management Interface to control access to your accounts, configure goals, set filters, and take care of important administrative details, refer to Chapter 5.

CAUTION

Before you start analyzing your reports, make sure you have applied the concepts in Chapter 5 with the help of a technical team member or outside expert. It is crucial that you have good, clean data to analyze.

Select the account you want to view and click the View Report link next to the Profile name. If you only have one Google Analytics Account, just click the View Report link. This link will open the Google Analytics Dashboard for the profile you selected. The Dashboard contains attractive graphs and tables showing summary information for your site, and it is always the first page you see when you open the reports.

We'll dive into the Dashboard shortly, but first look at Figure 6.1. This figure divides the Google Analytics interface into three main sections: the header, the navigation menu, and the Report view. The data shown is for Zenith Vineyard.

Using the header to navigate between accounts and profiles

If you have multiple accounts or profiles, use the navigation in the header to move between them. Use the My Analytics Accounts menu to switch among Google Analytics Accounts, and use the View Reports menu to navigate among the profiles you selected. Remember, in the Google Analytics hierarchy, accounts are first, so when you navigate to a new account using the Account pop-up menu, all

FIGURE 6.1

The three main sections of the Google Analytics interface: the header, navigation menu, and Report view.

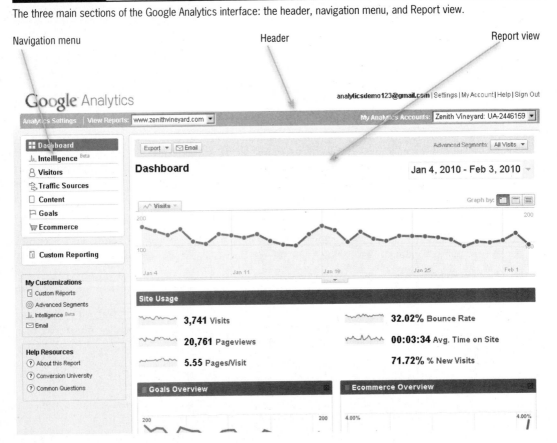

the information shown in your reports will also change. The profiles listed in the pop-up menu also change, because profiles are always contained within a specific Google Analytics Account.

If you get lost, you can always get back to the Account Management Interface page showing all the accounts you can access by clicking the Google Analytics logo in the upper-left corner. You can also use the links in the upper-right to access the Google Analytics Help Center.

Exploring basic Dashboard features

Now that you know the basic sections of the Google Analytics interface, let's take a look at the Dashboard. If you have just clicked the View Reports link, the Dashboard should be open. If not, click Dashboard in the navigation menu. The Dashboard in Google Analytics works like an executive summary for visitor activity on your Web site. It is a quick and easy way to see aggregate metrics about your Web site. Figure 6.2 shows the basic features of the Dashboard, many of which are common to all Google Analytics reports.

Looking over Figure 6.2, can you identify the most important elements visible in the screenshot? Hint: It's not the big Dashboard Summary table or the graph of overall visitors. It's the set of report summaries showing goal performance and ecommerce data!

Remember, it's important that you always approach your analysis from the perspective of a business problem or decision. The count of overall visitors to your site, bounce rate, and so on are interesting, but don't fall into the trap of settling for these aggregate metrics. Instead, treat the Dashboard as a jumping-off point to more detailed reports that help you answer your research questions. Let's take a closer look at some of the other tasks you can perform on the Dashboard.

Changing the date range with the Date Selector

In Chapter 4, we explain how the Google Analytics Tracking Code sends information to Google's servers each time someone views a page or triggers a tracking event on your Web site. You can use the Date Selector to filter your reports to include only the visitor activity that occurred during a specific date range. For example, when you first sign in, the Date Selector is set to a default 30-day date range. Figure 6.2's reports show the data for the date range (Jan 4, 2010 – Feb 3, 2010) set in the Date Selector.

Note that the default date range ends with *yesterday* not *today*. Remember from Chapter 4 that Google Analytics takes a few hours to process data, so today's data will always be incomplete. For this reason, the default setting does not include today's data. If you want to analyze today's data, be aware that it will change throughout the day, sometimes in unpredictable ways.

Also note that the beginning and end of each day in the date range is determined in accordance with the time zone you select in your profile. You can change this setting inside the Profile Settings of the Account Management Interface described earlier.

NOTE

If your Google Analytics account is tied to an AdWords account, Google Analytics always uses the time zone specified in your AdWords account to determine the beginning and end of each day.

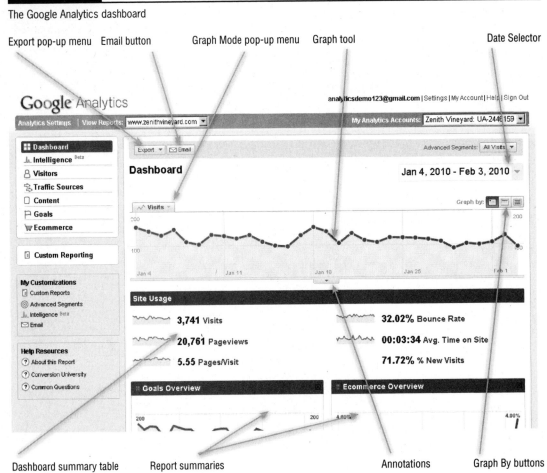

FIGURE 6.2

The Google Analytics dashboard

Export pop-up menu   Email button   Graph Mode pop-up menu   Graph tool   Date Selector

Dashboard summary table   Report summaries   Annotations   Graph By buttons

To change the date range, click the pop-up menu button (the gray triangle) to the right of the date range. The Calendar appears in the Date Selector window. You can change the starting and ending dates for the period you want to view by selecting days on the Calendar or by entering starting and ending dates into the text fields. Clicking the month title at the top of the calendar selects an entire month, while clicking the half-circle next to each week selects an entire week. Click the Apply button to make your final selection.

In the Calendar view, you can also select a date range by clicking Timeline. The Timeline includes a small graph you can use to reference trends in traffic you might want to analyze. It also includes a small scrollbar to navigate forward and backward on this miniature graph. When you find a period you want to analyze, click on it and drag the blue selector box over the specific date range. Click the Apply button to make your selection.

The date range you select persists as you navigate between reports. However, if you navigate to a new profile or account or log out of Google Analytics, the date range resets to the default 30-day date range.

Inside the Date Selector window, notice the Compare to Past checkbox. You can use this checkbox to compare traffic from one time period to another time period. To make your comparison, first use the Calendar to select the more recent of the two date ranges. For example, if you want to compare last month to this month, start by selecting This Month. Next, click the Compare to Past checkbox. Finally, use the Calendar to select Last Month, and click the Apply button. The Compare to Past feature is incredibly useful for putting a traffic spike or dip into context. It's also great for analyzing year-over-year or quarter-over-quarter performance.

CAUTION

To get the most accurate comparisons, make sure that both ranges have an equal number of days and that they start and end on the same days of the week. Traffic varies by day of the week, so if one range includes more weekend days, it will throw off your comparison. For this reason, it's better to use the Calendar rather than the Timeline for comparisons.

Try comparing data from this month to last month, or if you have just configured your Google Analytics account, try configuring yesterday's data with the same day in the previous week. When the Compare to Past feature is active, you'll see changes in the various metrics on the Dashboard quantified as a percentage change, reducing the need to jump to Excel to make that comparison.

Reading the Site Usage section of the Dashboard

The Site Usage section of the Dashboard displays aggregate metrics about your site. As we mentioned earlier, aggregate metrics are rarely actionable on their own, but it is important to understand what they mean. The following are basic definitions of the labels in Google Analytics:

- **Visits:** A visit consists of a single-user session. A session is defined as a period of interaction between a visitor's browser and your Web site, ending when the browser is closed or shut down, or when the user has been inactive on your site for 30 minutes.
- **Pageviews:** A pageview is an instance of a single Web page (such as your home page) being loaded by a visitor's browser. A visit can have multiple pageviews, but a pageview can be associated with only a single visit.
- **Pages/Visit:** The average number of pageviews per visit
- **Bounce Rate:** The ratio of single-page visits to total visits
- **Avg. Time on Site:** The average length of time a visit to your site lasts in hh:mm:ss format.
- **% New Visits:** The number of first-time visits to your site (as measured by the presence or absence of a Google Analytics cookie stored on the visitor's computer) divided by the total number of visits.

Clicking the graph to the left of each metric in the Site Usage section of the Dashboard brings that metric's info into the Graph tool without navigating away from the Dashboard. Clicking on the metric title navigates you away from the Dashboard and takes you to a more detailed report for that metric.

Manipulating data with the Graph tool

Take a look at the graph in Figure 6.3. Notice the *x*-axis shows the date range indicated in the Date Selector. The *y*-axis shows visits, as indicated by the Graph Mode pop-up menu in the upper-left of the graph. When you hover your mouse pointer over data points in the graph, you see the specific value displayed for the current data point. Most, but not all, reports in Google Analytics include a graph. You can display different metrics in the graph by clicking the Graph Mode pop-up menu at the top left of the graph, as shown in Figure 6.3.

The Graph Mode pop-up menu allows you to display different metrics on the graph's *y*-axis. You can also use the Graph Mode pop-up menu to compare two metrics in the same graph. For example, if you notice a traffic spike, you can quickly evaluate whether the spike consisted mainly of new or repeat visitors by first clicking Compare Two Metrics and then selecting both Visits and % New Visits.

Last, you can use the Graph Mode pop-up menu to compare a given metric to the site total or average. However, this comparison works only if you are viewing a report for a *subset* of total site traffic. Otherwise you are comparing data for the entire site to itself!

When you have finished making your selection, click the Graph Mode pop-up menu to close it.

FIGURE 6.3

The Graph Mode pop-up menu allows you to change the metrics are shown on the graph.

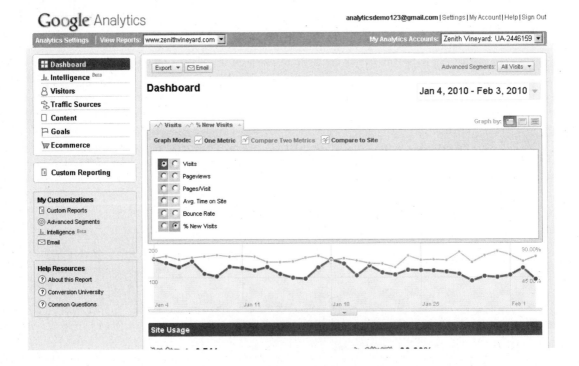

You can use the Graph By iconic buttons in the upper-right corner of the graph to change the scale on the *x*-axis to days, weeks, months, or, for some reports, hours. For example, when you look at information by the day, you see a regular drop in traffic on the weekends (this is normal for many sites). Toggling to weeks or months flattens traffic data and allows you to see broader trends, such as whether you get more traffic at the beginning or end of the month or if your traffic varies by season.

Customizing the Dashboard using report summaries

The gray boxes located below the Site Usage section of the Dashboard are known as *report summaries*. Each module summarizes a specific report in Google Analytics. You can move the modules by selecting the gray title bar and dragging them to a new location on the Dashboard. Clicking the Close box (the *x* icon) in the upper-right corner removes the report summary from the Dashboard. Any changes you make to the report summaries are tied to your Google Account (not your Google Analytics Account). If you share your Google Account with others — for example, if you use a generic company Google Account to log in — others who use that same account can see your changes. If you use your personal Google Account to log in, others who access the same Google Analytics Account *will not* see your changes.

TIP

If you want easy access to a particular report, you can bookmark the report in your browser. You can then skip the Account Management Interface page and go straight to your favorite reports.

If you're viewing a particular report other than the Dashboard in Google Analytics and want to add it to the Dashboard, click the Add to Dashboard button in the gray control bar at the top of the Report view.

Working with the Google Analytics Standard Reports

As Chapter 4 describes, each time a visitor loads a page or triggers a tracking event on your Web site, the Google Analytics Tracking Code sends information to Google's servers. From these events, Google Analytics calculates hundreds of metrics and dimensions about visitor activity on your site and organizes the information into a series of standard reports. This section provides an overview of the information contained in some of the most important reports and explains how to help when you are stuck.

Understanding terminology and definitions

The previous section introduced a handful of metrics and dimensions available in Google Analytics. However, as you navigate through your reports, you'll start seeing metrics and dimensions called Recency, Hostname, and % Exit. Some of these metrics and dimensions may appear obvious. Others may be more difficult to understand. If you want more information about what a number means in Google Analytics or how it's calculated, you can go to the following places for help:

- Click the ? iconic button located next to certain metrics throughout the reports to get more information about that metric.
- Click the About This Report link in the Help Resources section, located at the bottom of the navigation menu.
- Refer to this book's glossary.
- Do a search in the Google Analytics Help Center. You can access the Help Center by clicking the Google link in the upper-right of the Header.

Exploring the Google Analytics standard reports

Now that you have a basic understanding of the Google Analytics Dashboard and how to make sense of the metrics and dimensions, let's take a deeper look at the standard reports in Google Analytics. Use the navigation menu to drill down into the reports available from the six standard report categories (or in the beta and optional categories available in your account). The standard report you select displays in the Report view area, where you can sort, filter, and export data using features described later.

Google Analytics contains more than 60 standard reports covering a wide array of visitor behavior. The amount of information in these reports can be overwhelming. Going back to the analysis fundamentals explained earlier in this chapter, it is key to approach these reports with a research question that relates to your specific business objectives. An example research question might be "How effective was my direct mailing last week in driving newsletter signups on my Web site?"

TIP

If you get lost while navigating, you can use the breadcrumb navigation located in the upper-left corner of the Report view to help you find your way.

Your research questions should be specific, relevant to your business, and actionable rather than vague or generalized. For example, it's better to ask "What can my referring sites tell me about where to look for more traffic?" and "What impact did the redesign of my shopping cart have?" rather than "How many visitors did I have yesterday versus the day before?" Once you start looking at Google Analytics from this mindset, it will be much easier to zero in on the reports that are relevant to your business.

Table 6.1 outlines five standard report categories, the reports they contain, and examples of questions each report can help you answer about your Web site. We've marked some of the most useful reports with an asterisk. (Chapter 7 explains how to design your own custom reports.)

Take some time to exploring the reports listed in Table 6.1, especially those marked with an asterisk (*). Don't worry if you don't look at all the reports; not all the reports apply to your business. Also, many of the reports contain the same or similar information presented differently.

Working with data tables

Most standard reports in Google Analytics include a Data Table showing information organized into rows and columns. Figure 6.4 shows the All Traffic Sources report for Zenith Vineyard with some of the most important features of the Data Table called out. You can find the All Traffic Sources report under the Traffic Sources section in the navigation menu.

FIGURE 6.4

The All Traffic Sources Report shows where your Web site traffic originates.

Secondary dimensions   Scorecard   Column header   Table View iconic buttons

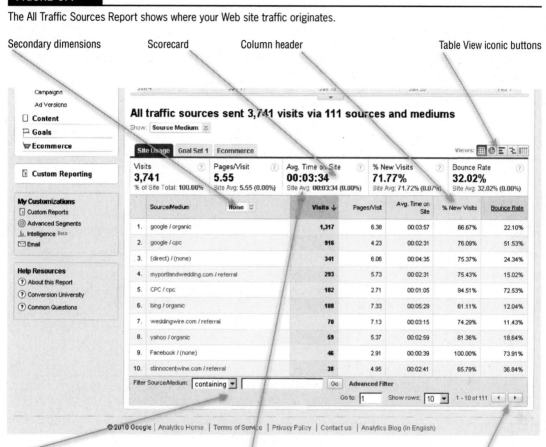

Filter Box   Comparison information   Paging options

Reading the scorecard

The row of numbers at the top of the Data Table is known as the *scorecard*. The scorecard figures are overall totals and averages of the data contained in the table. If you add the total number of visits displayed in each row of the table, the total equals the number of visits shown in the scorecard. Averages are calculated by dividing each column total by the overall number of rows in the table. (Remember that averages are calculated based on the total number of rows in the table, not just those rows visible on your screen.)

TABLE 6.1

Standard Report Categories and Example Questions

Category	URL	Report content and purpose	Example questions it answers
Dashboard	`analytics/a/ google.com/ reporting/`	Your Google Analytics "executive summary," where you can see an overview of major reports and customize them to meet your needs.	Anything new today?
Visitors			
*Visitor Overview	`/visitors`	Summary stats from key reports in the Visitors section.	
Benchmarking	`/benchmark`	Compare visitor statistics for your site to industry averages across the Web. Marginally useful for gauging performance.	Is my shopping cart converting well compared to others? Is my bounce rate high or low for a tech blog?
*Map Overlay	`/maps`	Visualize where your visitors are located geographically. See raw stats by continent, region, country, state and more.	Which city has the highest conversion rate? Which landing pages are people in the U.K. seeing?
*New vs Returning	`/visitor_types`	Compare visitor behavior for new versus returning visitors across a variety of dimensions.	Where are my new visitors arriving from? Are new or returning visitors more engaged with my site?
*Languages	`/languages`	Explore visitor behavior according to language defined in the visitor's browser settings.	Which languages are converting well? How are my translations doing?
Visitor Trending			
Visits	`/visits`	See how many visits your site gets over a given period.	When is the ideal downtime for site maintenance?
Absolute Unique Visitors	`/unique_ visitors`	Shows how many unique visitors arrived at your site over a given period.	Am I receiving more or less unique visitors since I started my advertising campaign?
Pageviews	`/pageview`	Shows how many pages were loaded by visitors over a given period.	Are pageviews for the site up or down?
Average Pageviews	`/average_ pageviews`	See the average number of pages loaded per visit over a given period.	What time of day is engagement highest on my site?
Time on Site	`/time_on_site`	See the amount of time spent on your site by visitors over a given period.	What time of day is engagement highest on my site?
Bounce Rate	`/bounce_rate`	Shows what percentage of visitors leave your site after viewing just one page.	Is my landing page optimization effort engaging more potential customers?

TABLE 6.1 (CONTINUED)

Standard Report Categories and Example Questions

Category	URL	Report content and purpose	Example questions it answers
Visitor Loyalty			
Loyalty	/loyalty	Get a sense for how well your site attracts repeat visits. Useful for content optimization.	Is my new newsletter helping to drive repeat visits? Do I need introductory content on my core content pages?
Recency	/recency	See how regularly users visit your site. Understand whether visitors are checking back often. Useful for publishers and online apps.	What percentage of my user base visits my site every day, or at least once per week?
Length of Visit	/length_of_ visit	Shows the average length of time for a single session on your site.	What's the engagement on my site over time?
Depth of Visit	/depth_of_ visit	Use as a secondary metric to supplement bounce rate. See a distribution of visit depth as opposed to an average as shown in the Average Pageviews report.	How many visitors are visiting three or more pages on my microsite?
Browser Capabilities			
Browers	/browsers	See what browsers your visitors are using across a variety of dimensions. Useful for design specifications.	Should I spend the extra time to do cross-browser optimization?
Operating Systems	/platform	See what operating systems your visitors use.	Do we need to create pages that are mobile-friendly?
OS Browsers	/os_browsers	Combines browser and OS report.	How tech-savvy is my audience?
Colors	/colors	See what color palette is supported by your audience.	What's the ideal color palette to optimize my site for?
Screen Resolutions	/resolutions	See a distribution of screen resolutions for your Web site visitors.	What's the ideal screen resolution to optimize for? Can I go one size up?
Flash Versions	/flash	See what versions of flash are supported by visitors.	What version of Flash should I optimize for?
Java	/java	See whether your visitors are able to load Java applets.	Is it safe to use Java on my site?
Network Properties			
Network Location	/networks	Find out the registered name of the ISP for any Web site visitors. This often include corporation names and other potentially useful info.	Has my competitor visited my Web site? Are visitors accessing my site at work or at home?

table continues

TABLE 6.1 (CONTINUED)

Standard Report Categories and Example Questions

Category	URL	Report content and purpose	Example questions it answers
Host Names	/hostnames	Use this report to identify which of your domains are being loaded by visitors. Most useful when tracking multiple domains/subdomains.	Am I tracking data for all my subdomains? Has my tracking code accidentally been copied outside my domain?
Connection Speeds	/speeds	Combine with page sizes to determine how quickly visitors are able to load your content.	Do I need to reduce the file size of any of my pages?
*User Defined	/user_defined	This report provides a breakdown of any custom metrics you've defined in Google Analytics. Custom variables are an extremely powerful function.	How much revenue did my campaign generate? What is the behavior of users who have completed a certain action on my site?
Traffic Sources			
Overview	/sources	Summary stats for key reports in the Traffic Sources section.	
Direct Traffic	/direct_ sources	See visitor stats for visitors that arrived at your site by typing in your URL, bookmarking or via an untagged email link. Good for tracking the success of offline activities and awareness campaigns.	Did my TV ad campaign increase overall visits to my site? Did my Bookmark This Site link have any impact on traffic?
*Referring Sites	/referring_ sources	This report shows you which sites on the Web are sending you traffic and how those visitors behave on your site.	Which Web sites should I reach out to so I can increase my exposure? Which sites might make good places to advertise?
*Search Engines	/search_ engines	See how many visitors are finding you via search engines, which keywords they arrive from, and how they behave.	How many people arrive on my site by searching for my brand name? How does the ROI on paid traffic compare with organic traffic?
*All Traffic Sources	/all_sources	Compare traffic source data across all your various mediums.	Which channels drive the most traffic? Which traffic sources have the highest ROI?
*Keywords	/keywords	Evaluate your search traffic at the keyword level across all search engines at once.	Which keywords should I optimize my site for? Am I delivering the right content for the keywords I'm found on?

TABLE 6.1 (CONTINUED)

Standard Report Categories and Example Questions

Category	URL	Report content and purpose	Example questions it answers
*Campaigns	/campaigns	Assess the ROI from marketing links you have tagged with campaign variables.	What's the ROI on my email campaign? What's the ROI on my co-marketing effort?
Ad Versions	/ad_versions	Track the performance of your AdWords ads, or other ads you tag with Google Analytics campaign variables.	Which ad creative in my display campaign has the highest conversion rate?
AdWords			
*AdWords Campaigns	/adwords	Evaluate all aspects of your AdWords campaign performance at the campaign, adgroup, ad or keyword level.	Which campaigns should I spend more on and which should I cut? Which keywords should I exclude and which should I raise budget on?
Keyword Positions	/keyword_ position	Provides a breakdown of how your position in the AdWords auction affects key site variables, broken down by keyword.	Are my ads more profitable when in the top or bottom slot on AdWords?
TV Ads	/tv	Shows performance metrics related to TV Ad Campaigns you ran through Google AdWords.	How many viewers are my TV ads reaching? What percentage of my audience is viewing the entire ad?
Content			
Overview	/content	Summary stats from key reports in the content section.	
*Top Content	/top_content	Provides a range of metrics on the performance of individual pages on your site, listed by URL.	Which pages have the highest bounce rate? Where do visitors spend time on my site?
Content Detail	/content_ detail	Access via the other content reports. Get summary stats on a given pages performance.	What does this page actually look like (click to view)?
Navigation Summary	/content_ detail_ navigation	Shows you how visitors arrived at a particular page and where they went next.	How many people left my site after viewing this page? Which pages do people view before reaching my registration form?
Entrance Paths	/content_ detail_path	Shows where vistors who entered your site through a given page went next on your site	How well is this page performing as a landing page for my site?

table continues

TABLE 6.1 (CONTINUED)

Standard Report Categories and Example Questions

Category	URL	Report content and purpose	Example questions it answers
Entrance Sources	`/content_detail_sources`	Shows what the sources of traffic were for visitors that arrived at your site via a specific page.	What caused a traffic spike to a particular page? Are the right landing pages showing up for each traffic source?
Entrance Keywords	`/content_detail_keywords`	Which keywords did people type in before they arrived on a specific page?	How well is an SEO effort on a particular page working?
Content by Title	`/content_titles`	Same as the top content report, but organized by page title instead of URL.	What is the performance of my site group according to title keywords? What is the performance for a particular page I don't know the URL for?
Content Drilldown	`/content_drilldown`	Analyze page performance based around the directory structure (real or virtual) you use on your site.	How do pages listed under `/product` on my Web site perform?
Top Landing Pages	`/entrances`	See which pages visitors see first when they arrive at your site?	Which landing pages should I optimize first to have the most impact on revenue?
Top Exit Pages	`/exits`	Shows which pages visitors view last before they leave your site.	Where am I losing the most traffic? Are there problems with those pages I can fix?
*Site Overlay Report	Not applicable	Visualize your site's performance by looking directly at the site itself. See where visitors go when they reach your site.	Is my primary navigation working as expected? Are visitors are taking surprising paths through my site I can capitalize on?
Goals			
Overview	`/goals`	Summary stats for key metrics in the goals category	
Total Goal Conversions	`/total_goal_conversions`	See a distribution of your goal conversions over a given period, including hour of the day.	What time of day yields the most conversions for a particular goal?
Goal Conversion Rate	`/goal_conversion_rate`	Track the conversion rate of your site over a given period.	Is my content optimization effort having a positive impact on my bottom line?
Goal Verification	`/goal_verification`	See which pages are being used to trigger your goals. Useful to ensure your Goals are functioning as expected.	Is my purchase goal being triggered only from my thank-you page?

TABLE 6.1 (CONTINUED)

Standard Report Categories and Example Questions

Category	URL	Report content and purpose	Example questions it answers
Reverse Goal Path	`/reverse_goal_path`	See which visitor pages viewed before they completed a desired action on your site.	What are the most important visitor paths leading up to a goal completion, and how can I optimize them?
Total Goal Value	`/total_goal_value`	Shows the dollar value of your goal completions across a given period.	Are my marketing efforts paying off in real dollars generated?
Abandoned Funnels	`/abandoned_funnels`	The inverse of conversion rate, distributed over time.	What percentage of visitors am I losing during my conversion process, and what does this mean in terms of lost revenue?
*Funnel Visualization	`/goal_funnel`	See where you're losing visitors in your conversion process and plan a strategy for raising your conversion rate.	Is my registration form too complicated for users? Are there any obvious problems with my shopping cart that can be corrected?
*key reports			

NOTE

If you select the Compare To Past checkbox in the Date Selector, you see comparison information for the two date ranges you selected instead of information for the site total or average.

Below each metric in the scorecard you also see information about how that metric compares to the site average or total. This comparison information is important when you use the Filter Box to filter the results shown in the table or look at a report that contains a subset of overall site traffic. In the All Traffic Sources report, for example, the percentage change shown below each metric in the scorecard is 0.00% because the All Traffic Sources report describes traffic sources for all site traffic.

Sorting and paging through table rows

You can sort data by clicking the gray column headers in the table. Unless you use a filter, you'll often need to scroll after sorting, to sift through extreme values at either end of the spectrum (bounce rates of zero or 100 percent, for example). To sort, open the All Traffic Sources report in your Google Analytics account and sort the rows to find which referral sources sent you the highest percentage of repeat visitors.

You can adjust the number of rows visible in your Data Table from the default 10 rows to a maximum of 500 rows by using the Show Rows pop-up menu at the bottom-right of the table. Expanding the table to 500 rows, however, makes the report load noticeably slower. You can also move a particular row to the top of the table by entering the row number in the Go To text field, or you can page through all the rows using the arrow buttons in the corner. Using the Go To text field, paging, or making a new selection in the Show Rows pop-up menu does not affect the overall totals and averages shown in the scorecard.

Changing table views

The icons visible in the upper-right corner of the Data Table are known as the Table View iconic buttons. Starting from the left, the first four buttons (Table View, Percentage View, Performance View, and Comparison View) allow you to easily compare one row of data in the Data Table to the rest of table. The fifth button (Pivot View) lets you compare multiple dimensions, both vertically and horizontally, in the same view. A sixth button (Detail View) is visible only in some reports; it loads more specific information about a given row in the table.

We describe applications for table views later in this chapter, but for now here is a general description of each view:

- **Table View:** Also known as the "Give me everything" view. Table View gives you data in its rawest form and is great for math junkies and code-breakers.
- **Percentage View:** This view allows you to examine each row as it relates to the total, displaying a pie chart to the right of the data. Once you've clicked on the Percentage View iconic button, look for the two arrows displayed in left-most areas of the gray column header. Use the ◄ pop-up menu to organize the rows along a given metric. Next, use the ► pop-up menu to assess the impact of a given row on the total for the entire table. This view is great for putting a particular row in context to identify its importance. For example, you can instantly use this view to visualize what proportion of the total minutes spent on your site can be attributed to people who arrived from Yahoo.
- **Performance View:** Similar to Percentage View, except that it uses a bar graph to present the data instead of a pie chart.
- **Comparison View:** Use this view to compare an individual row element to the site average (as opposed to relating it to the site total). This view is a great way to put a specific data point in the table into context. For example, use the Comparison View to see how the Pages/Visit data for Google traffic (a proxy for engagement) compares to the site average.
- **Pivot View:** An advanced view that lets you view multiple dimensions horizontally and vertically in the same view. Use this view to answer detailed questions such as how visits and pages per visit compare between Google and Yahoo in California versus New York. (Chapter 8 provides more information on multidimensional analysis.)

Navigate through the standard reports described earlier in this chapter and experiment with the different views to see how many ways you can get to the same insight.

Filtering data with the Filter Box

At the bottom-left of the Data Table is the Containing pop-up menu and text field. This set of options is called the Filter Box, as Figure 6.4 shows.

You can use the Containing text field to constrain the rows that appear in the Data Table. For example, looking at the All Traffic Sources report, enter `referral` into the text field and click the Go button. The data table adjusts to show only referral traffic (traffic that originated from another site linking directly to your site). Next, change the Filter Source/Medium pop-up menu from Containing to Excluding and click Go. You now see only the visits that *did not* originate from another site linking directly to yours.

Filtering with regular expressions

You can use a system of special characters, called *wildcards*, designed for advanced pattern matching known as *regular expressions*. Table 6.2 shows the key characters you can use in the text field to help you get started.

Filtering with the Advanced Filter tool

Click the Advanced Filter link next to the Filter Box to open the Advanced Filter tool. Use this tool to combine multiple criteria into a single filter, such as to include filtering by the primary dimension used in the report or by any of the metrics in the report. Filtering allows you to restrict the data in the data table to match any subset, removing the necessity to export the data to Excel or another spreadsheet application, as Figure 6.5 shows.

NOTE

You will find a more in-depth tutorial covering regular expressions online at `www.analyticsformarketers.com/s/regex`.

TABLE 6.2

Wildcard Characters for Regular Expressions

Wildcard	Regular Expression Meaning
.	Match any single character
*	Match zero or more of the previous item
+	Match one or more of the previous item
?	Match zero or one of the previous item
( )	Remember contents of parenthesis as item
[ ]	Match one item in this list
–	Create a range in a list
|	Logical OR
^	Match to the beginning of the field
$	match to the end of the field
\	Escape any of the above

FIGURE 6.5

When advanced filters are applied, the data in the report table is modified to show only the data rows that match the criteria defined in the filter. The report shows the criteria results for the keywords that have received 100 visits or more, and thus the Bounce Rate column shows conclusive data, revealing higher-volume keywords that have the highest bounce rates.

Search sent 7,677 total visits via 18 keywords
Filtered for Visits >= 100

Show: total | paid | non-paid

	Keyword	None	Visits	Pages/Visit	Avg. Time on Site	% New Visits	Bounce Rate
1.	mothers day brunch		115	1.63	00:01:05	99.13%	79.13%
2.	mothers day brunch portland		122	1.97	00:01:33	94.26%	74.59%
3.	(content targeting)		1,955	3.99	00:02:20	85.88%	51.82%
4.	wedding facilities		475	5.45	00:03:17	88.21%	38.53%
5.	winery wedding		127	5.72	00:03:45	85.83%	33.07%
6.	vineyard wedding		102	4.81	00:02:43	90.20%	30.39%
7.	wedding vineyards		112	5.93	00:02:54	76.79%	29.46%
8.	winery weddings		118	5.80	00:04:32	78.81%	28.81%
9.	zenith winery		559	5.46	00:03:48	54.92%	27.55%
10.	oregon vineyard wedding		227	6.17	00:04:09	66.52%	26.43%

Scorecard:

Visits	Pages/Visit	Avg. Time on Site	% New Visits	Bounce Rate
7,677	**5.35**	**00:03:31**	**69.47%**	**31.57%**
% of Site Total: 37.29%	Site Avg: 4.69 (14.23%)	Site Avg: 00:03:09 (11.67%)	Site Avg: 71.00% (-2.16%)	Site Avg: 38.76% (-18.54%)

Go to: 1   Show rows: 10   1 - 10 of 18

Filter
Visits | Greater than or equal to ▾ | 100 | Delete

For example, a common issue when working with data in the report table is dealing with data outliers. Consider the Keywords report: If you want to know what keywords have the highest bounce rates. you could sort the Bounce Rate column in descending order (largest to smallest). However, you'll soon find a long list of single-visit keywords with 100 percent bounce rates. Collectively, these keywords are a large chunk of traffic, but analyzing each one individually would be a challenge. By using the Advanced Filter to limit data in the table to keywords with 100 or more visits, you will avoid the "noise" of all those single-visit keywords.

Click the + Add New Condition link to add additional filters. Finally click the Apply Filter button to apply your filters to the table. Not only do the rows included in the table change, the totals and averages displayed in the scorecard also change.

Exporting and e-mailing reports

Now that you know how to read a Data Table in Google Analytics, chances are you have at least one colleague who won't be able to follow in your footsteps. Giving direct access to Google Analytics can often raise more questions than answers, so often the best way to share your findings is to export the data after you've applied the necessary sorts, filters, and table views to get to the information you want.

There are two main options for sharing your data. First, you can export the data to your local hard drive in a variety of formats (including CSV, XML, and PDF) and then print or otherwise share as you like. You can also e-mail a report directly from Google Analytics, or schedule it to be delivered to you or your colleagues automatically each day, month, week, or even quarter.

Exporting your data

You can export data using the Export menu located in the gray control bar at the top of the Report view (shown in Figure 6.2). You can export as a PDF, XML CSV, CSV for Microsoft Excel, or TSV file. A PDF file does its best to preserve the formatting in the report and look polished, while the other formats give you raw data you can import into Excel, a database, or other data-manipulation tool.

Once you choose the correct format from the Export menu, you are prompted to download or view the file. When you export reports, you are limited to 500 rows of data, so some larger reports may be cut short. To get around this limitation, team up with a programmer and use the Google Analytics API.

E-mailing reports

The most direct way to continually share your Google Analytics reports is to set up automatic e-mail delivery. You can have Google Analytics send reports to you or your colleagues on a daily, weekly, monthly, or quarterly basis in any of the formats described earlier. To schedule delivery of a report, click the Email button in the control bar to access the Send Now setup page. You can send an e-mail immediately or set up a recurring e-mail by clicking the Schedule tab (shown in Figure 6.6).

TIP

If you have developer support, you can use the Google Analytics Data Export API to automatically extract data from Google Analytics and insert it directly into your sales database, CRM system, or custom database. See Chapter 15 for more information on the Data Export API.

Enter the e-mail addresses of the people you want to receive the report; deselect the Send to Me checkbox if you don't want to be included. Add a subject to let everybody know what the e-mail contains. Whatever you enter in the Description field becomes the body text in the e-mail.

After you select the format of the report to be attached to the e-mail, specify how often you'd like the e-mails sent. Daily reports are sent in the morning, weekly reports on Mondays, monthly reports on the first day of the month, and quarterly reports on the first day of the quarter. To complete the scheduling, click Schedule. To delete a report after you've scheduled it, or to make changes to the contents of the scheduled e-mail, click the Email link in the My Customizations section at the bottom of the navigation menu.

E-mailing regular reports is a good idea for a number of reasons, and we encourage you to use this feature. The amount of data available in Google Analytics can be overwhelming, and well-managed e-mail reports are a great way to filter and share information for people who aren't as familiar with Google Analytics. The first step in this process involves figuring out what specific metrics are relevant to

FIGURE 6.6

Schedule reports to be e-mailed directly to you and your team members.

your colleagues. Next, determine the optimal delivery schedule. It's important not to overdo it. A monthly report may get more attention than a daily report that quickly becomes an annoyance. Last, check directly with the folks receiving the reports to make sure they can read them correctly and are getting what they need from them.

Advanced Analysis Concepts and Features

This chapter dives into concepts critical to successfully conducting advanced analysis and provides a practical review of the built-in tools in Google Analytics designed for this purpose. If you're not excited about reading this chapter already, then you should get excited now! Why? Because advanced analysis is where everything comes together and where the greatest value lies.

Think about it: Most valuable things take digging to find, like gold or diamonds — so why should Web analytics be any different? And in fact it isn't — the proverbial goldmine of insight from Web analytics is buried deep beneath the surface of the data just waiting to be found using advanced analysis techniques and tools.

Using Segmentation to Find Meaning in Your Data

Think of advanced analysis as an X-ray for your online marketing and Web site data, allowing you to peer inside and see what's really going on. Indeed, the picture you see from looking at the "outside" of the data (consider Figure 7.1) may be starkly different from what you'll find when looking beneath the surface (see Figure 7.2's segmented data). The tools covered in this chapter — Advanced Segments, Custom Reports, Advanced Report Filtering, Motion Charts, Secondary Dimension analysis, and Pivot Table reports — are like the X-ray machinery: To use them successfully, you must know both how to operate them and how to interpret what they produce.

FIGURE 7.1

The main graph shows unsegmented top-line visits while the data summary below the graph shows top-level metrics. How do you determine what caused changes in the reported data? Figure 7.2 shows segmentation at work, revealing what caused the changes observed in the top-line summary.

Understanding dimensions and segmentation: Thinking in 2D versus 3D

The ability to "look beneath the surface" is based on data dimensions — an aspect of how data is recorded, stored, and accessed in Google Analytics. Just like the metrics we cover in Chapter 6, dimensions are fundamental to the structure of the data collected by Google Analytics. Think of a dimension as a "category" for information, while a metric is a "fact" about information, and the thing in question is the "information" itself. Review Chapter 4 for details on how data is collected and processed into dimensions.

At a fundamental level, understanding how to use dimensions in Google Analytics effectively requires understanding the nature of multidimensional analysis. Looking at data in 2D versus 3D reveals a different view of the same thing.

Consider a page on your Web site — let's say the home page. The page is the object and it has a given name, homepage. There are facts about this page, such as how many times it was viewed (metric: Pageviews) and how many times it was the last pageviewed during a visit (metric: Exits). There are also

FIGURE 7.2

Segmentation at work: The main graph shows segmented top-line visits, illuminating what drove the overall changes in visits.

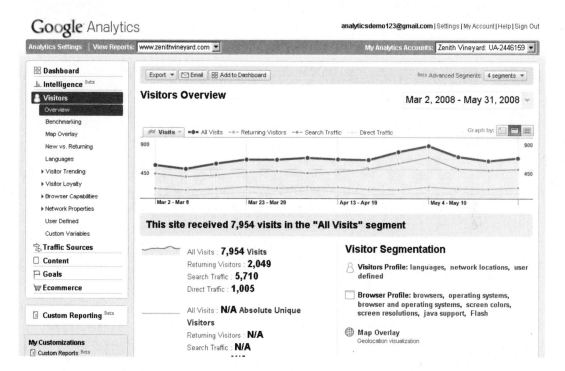

categorizations about this page: was it ever the first page viewed (dimension: Landing Page)? Was the pageviewed by new or returning visitors (dimension: Visitor Type)? In what cities were people who viewed this page (dimension: City)? Table 7.1 shows data collected about four visits and several dimensions for which data from those visits are reported.

The information in Table 7.1 results in the following metrics as "facts" about the multidimensional data collected:

TABLE 7.1

Multidimensional Data Collected from a Web Page

Visit Number	Landing Page	Source	Medium	Visitor Type	City
Visit-1	/index.html	Google	Organic	New Visitor	Seattle
Visit-2	/product1.html	Direct	None	Returning Visitor	San Francisco
Visit-3	/index.html	Facebook	Referral	New Visitor	New York
Visit-4	/fanpage.html	Facebook	Banner-Ad	New Visitor	San Francisco

- 4 total visits
- 2 entrances to /index.html
- 1 entrance to /product1.html
- 1 entrance to /fanpage.html
- 1 visit from organic search on Google
- 2 visits from the source Facebook
- 1 direct visit from San Francisco
- 2 total visits from San Francisco

The power of dimensions is that they enable analysis of data from a multidimensional perspective. If you're assessing the performance of a marketing campaign, the ability to determine visits that were from your campaign relies on dimensions. If you have a top-line metric, such as visits generated by the campaign, that's great to see, but you need to go below the surface: How many of those visits were from new visitors and how many from visitors who had already been to your Web site? There's a dimension for that. Of those who were returning, how many times had they visited the site before? There's a dimension for that, too. Were the visits received through your campaign from the geographic areas you expected? Look into the Country, Region, or City dimensions to find out.

Dimensions available in Google Analytics

Google Analytics has more than 50 dimensions. Some dimensions are available by default in all reports via the Dimension pop-up menu. Other dimensions are available only within certain reports, such as Event Category and Event Action, which are listed under Dimensions only in the Event Tracking reports. Still other dimensions are only available in Advanced Segments, Custom Reports, and the Data Export API. We list below all dimensions available in Standard Reports, Advanced Segments, Custom Reports, and the Data Export API as of this book's publication.

NOTE

The Dimensions and Metrics tables are constantly evolving as the Google Analytics product continues to be developed. The latest Dimensions and Metrics tables can be viewed online at www.analyticsformarketers.com/s/dimension-list.

- **Visitor:** City, Continent, Visit Count, Country/Territory, Date, Day, Days Since Last Visit, Hour, Language, Latitude, Longitude, Month, Page Depth, Region, Sub Continent Region, User Defined Value, Visitor Type, Week, and Year.
- **System:** Browser, Browser Version, Connection Speed, Flash Version, Hostname, Java Support, Domain, Network Location, Operating System, Operating System Version, Screen Colors, and Screen Resolution.
- **Traffic Sources:** Ad Content, Ad Group, Ad Slot, Ad Slot Position, Campaign, Keyword, Medium, Referral Path, Source, and Source/Medium.

- **Content:** Exit Page, Landing Page, Page, Page Title, Event Category, Event Action, and Event Label.
- **Ecommerce:** Affiliation, Days to Transaction, Product Category, Product, Product SKU, Transaction, and Count of Visits to a Transaction.
- **Internal Site Search:** Site Search Category, Search Destination Page, Search Term, Refined Search Keyword, Search Start Page, and Site Search Status.
- **Custom Variables:** Custom Variable Key 1, Custom Variable Key 2, Custom Variable Key 3, Custom Variable Key 4, Custom Variable Key 5, Custom Variable Value 1, Custom Variable Value 2, Custom Variable Value 3, Custom Variable Value 4, and Custom Variable Value 5.

Applying basic segmentation techniques for standard reports

You can access dimensions in Google Analytics in many ways. In fact, just about every report uses dimensions in displaying data. However, that data is only displayed in one-dimensional form unless you activate cross-dimension reporting.

The cross-dimension reporting tool

The most important basic analysis method for using dimensions is cross-dimension reporting. Cross-dimension reporting means analyzing data in one dimension and comparing it against another dimension. It makes it easy to dig into data to gain deeper insight and answer business questions.

For example, consider a marketing campaign for Zenith Vineyard aimed at connecting with new brides-to-be who are looking for a wedding venue. As a regional venue outside of Portland, Oregon, Zenith Vineyard wants to understand how Web site traffic through their campaigns differs between people within the region around their venue as well as regions outside the local area.

Dimension analysis can help to address these concerns and provide insights needed to optimize the advertising for Zenith by revealing the geographic locations of visitors coming through their campaigns. By using the cross-dimension reporting tool to analyze the City dimension when viewing the details for a campaign, Zenith Vineyard can determine how much traffic, engagement, and conversions are coming from people within their market area and how much from outside the region.

Figure 7.3 shows a report using cross-dimension analysis of Zenith's "special events" campaign analyzing the City dimension and displaying the percentage of new visitors from each city. This reveals the cities where more visitors are being introduced to Zenith Vineyard for the first time (New Visits) versus cities where more visitors have been to the Web site before (Return Visitors).

Accessing the cross-dimension feature

The cross-dimension feature is available for most reports in Google Analytics. You'll see it in three places depending on the type of report: below the main graph on the left side (see Figure 7.4), below the main graph to the right next to other drill-down and Data Selection options (see Figures 7.5 and 7.6), or in the column headings in the report Data Table (see Figure 7.7). Additionally, custom reports use

FIGURE 7.3

The result of drilling down and selecting cross-dimension analysis based on the City dimension is this report, showing the cities in which responders to the special events campaign were located. Furthermore, the report indicates performance based on the percentage of New Visits from each city.

Dimension

dimension analysis as a means of drilling down to additional dimensions contained in a custom report (custom reports will be covered in greater detail later in this chapter).

Using Secondary Dimensions

Secondary Dimensions provide the ability to simultaneously analyze two dimensions per row in a report table. This is a useful feature when you're asking business questions that bridge two topic areas, such as Traffic Source and Geography, Keyword and Landing Page, or products purchased via a Source/Medium.

The ability to access granular-level data looking at two dimensions has long been available by drilling down and conducting cross-dimensional analysis. However, combining the data in the Report Table and merging two dimensions in the Dimensions column is a more practical feature for everyday analysis because it saves considerable time by showing data next to each other on the same page.

FIGURE 7.4

Cross-dimension reporting option on Traffic Sources Detail report

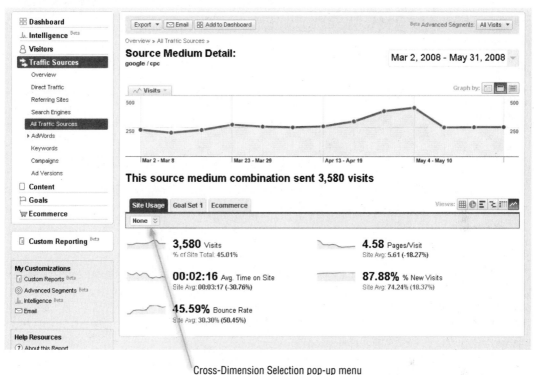

Cross-Dimension Selection pop-up menu

Going back to the Zenith Vineyard scenario of measuring the impact of advertising on local and nonlocal customers, Secondary Dimensions provide a means of easily understanding which keywords bring traffic from local verses non-local locations and what the volume and value of that traffic is.

Let's say you want to answer the question "What regions does traffic come from for each sponsored keyword?" Using Secondary Dimensions expedites accessing the data needed to answer this question. Without Secondary Dimensions, you would need to go to the Keywords report and drill into the details for each keyword, cross-segment the Region dimension, and export the results, repeating this for each of the dozens of keywords listed. But with Secondary Dimensions, you simply access the Keywords report and set the Secondary Dimension to Region, as shown in Figure 7.8.

Creating your own dimensions using custom variables

Custom variables are a powerful and advanced part of collecting data about your Web site in Google Analytics. Before the introduction of custom variables, Google Analytics supported only a single Custom dimension called User-Defined. This feature allowed you to define any value you wanted for this User-Defined dimension. However, each visitor could have only one value assigned to him or her. Unlike

FIGURE 7.5

Cross-dimension reporting option on Geographic Detail report

Cross-Dimension Selection pop-up menu

User-Defined segments, custom variables allow you to have multiple values for the same visitor at the same time using multiple scopes.

For example, if you wanted to segment site visitor interest and pricing level, the same visitor could have both an interest area and a pricing level value assigned to them with custom variables, while they could only be assigned to interest *or* pricing-level with a User-Defined segment.

How custom variables work

First, you can have virtually unlimited numbers of custom variables, meaning that the same visitor can exist as part of many segments created by custom variables. This capability to have visitors be part of many segments is due to the structure of a custom variable, which contains:

- An *index* (index slots go from 1 to 5; think of an index as a drawer in a filing cabinet)
- A *name* (such as "interest" or "pricing level"; think of *name* as a folder in the drawer)
- A *value* (such as "green initiative" or "on-sale"; think of *value* as a paper in the folder) paired to the name

FIGURE 7.6

Cross-dimension reporting option on Content Detail report

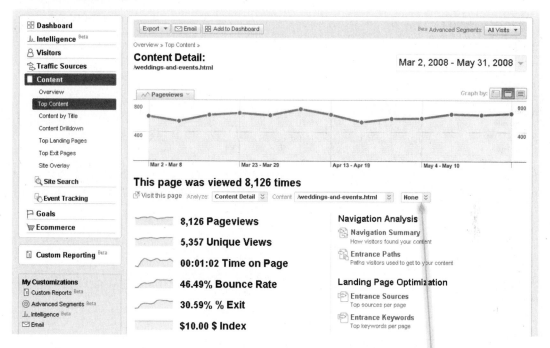

Cross-Dimension Selection pop-up menu

- A *scope*, an optional means of defining whether the variable should be page-level (defining information about a page), session-level (defining information about a visit session), or visitor-level (describing information about a visitor).

While the technical limitation of custom variable `name-value` pairs is the same as other dimensions — 50,000 unique records per day — there are functional limitations that affect the number of custom variables that can be set at any one time.

Custom variables are defined using the `_setCustomVar()` method and sent to Google Analytics when the next tracking call is made. As a consequence, a maximum of five custom variables that can be sent at any one time. Each custom variable is further limited to 64 bytes in the `name=value` string.

Scope is the second major factor for custom variables, creating a multilevel data model. Custom variables exist at visitor, session, and page levels (also known as scope). While the technical aspects of scope get complicated quickly (see Chapter 5 for details on how custom variables work and how to implement them on your Web site), it simply means that the visitor-level scope remains constant and persistent for the *person* (visitor), the visit level refers to the *session* (a defined period of ongoing

FIGURE 7.7

Cross-dimension reporting options in the Report Data Table

Cross-Dimension Selection pop-up menu

interaction), and the page level scope relates to a single point of interaction and is impartial to visit or visitor. Figure 7.9 illustrates the three levels used in custom variable scopes: visitor, visit, and page.

An example of the multilevel scope data model in action might involve describing information about a visitor, a visit session of that visitor, and a pageviewed by that visitor. For example, you might want to know the breakdown by gender for your registered Web site users (presuming gender is something they've provided, perhaps via profile information), interest in a particular offer, and exposure to a piece of content. Gender should be set using the visitor-level scope, since it is fixed and won't change per visitor. Interest in a particular offer is something that, once defined, becomes fixed for that visit (session), and thus interest should use the visit-level scope. Last, content viewed is really just informational and not specific to the visitor or visit — you simply want to know what content was accessed, so content should be set using the page-level scope.

To put this in action, you would see a `male` gender visitor view the `on-sale` offer and then access information about various products by viewing pages of content. The gender is recorded to the visitor-level scope, the `on-sale` offer to the visit-level scope, and as pages are viewed, each page is reported as a page-level scope noting the page accessed.

The Keywords report with the secondary dimension set to Region reveals the regions that traffic came from through each keyword in one report Data Table.

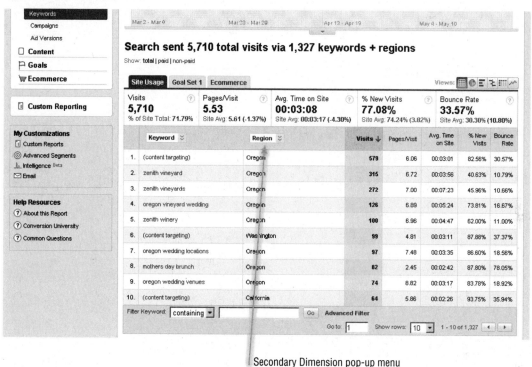

Secondary Dimension pop-up menu

Custom variables are powerful, and more complicated than User-Defined segments or standard trackers for pageviews or events. To take advantage of this capability, you'll need to thoroughly understand the many facets of planning your data model and implementing code to collect data using custom variables.

Understanding and analyzing Custom Variable reports

Custom variables drastically shift the paradigm for Google Analytics from collection of information based on a page loading, an interaction with an element of the site, or a purchase, to collection of rich data about what is being viewed, who the viewer is, and everything in between. The key to understanding and analyzing custom variables lies in the multidimensional concepts explained early in this chapter. Custom variables increase the effective dimensions beyond the predefined values listed earlier to values that you define. The predefined dimension names are the equivalent of custom variable "names" and the value corresponding to a predefined dimension name is equivalent to the "value" of a custom variable "name=value" pair.

FIGURE 7.9

Custom variables have a multilevel data model scoped to Visitors, Visits, and Pages.

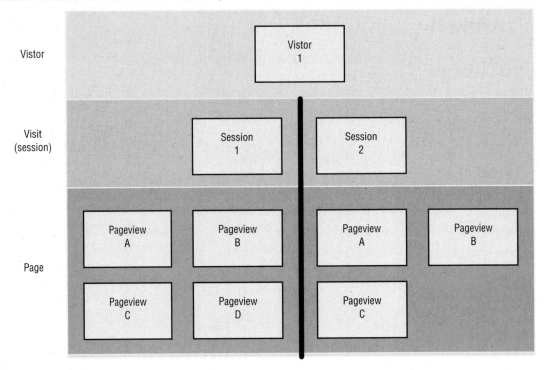

Custom Variables reports reside in the Visitors report section and are also accessible via Custom Reports (see Figure 7.10) and Advanced Segments (see Figure 7.11). (Advanced Segments and custom reports are covered later in this chapter.) When you access the standard Custom Variables report, the initial list you see is the list of custom variable names (see Figure 7.12). Clicking on a name drills down to the values for that custom variable name and reveals all the values and corresponding metrics for each value. From this point, you can begin to cross-segment against other standard dimensions.

Common uses for custom variables

While you can use custom variables for just about any imaginable analysis, the best approach begins with planning. As with your entire Web analytics implementation (see Chapters 1 through 3), you must determine what *business questions* need to be answered.

Some potential uses of custom variables to categorize data include:

- Products viewed
- Product categories viewed
- Cross-sell and upsell exposure (related or suggested products)
- Shopping cart contents

FIGURE 7.10

Custom variables are accessible under the Visitors report. The initial screen of the Custom Variables report shows the list of variable names that have been defined. Clicking on a name accesses the values associated with that name.

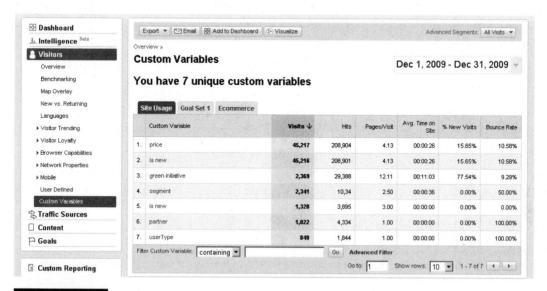

FIGURE 7.11

Custom variables are also accessible under Advanced Segments and custom reports. Simply build a custom segment or custom report using your selection of criteria based on custom variable names, values, and other dimensions and metrics you want to include.

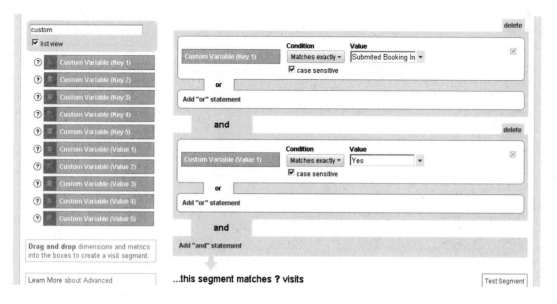

- Shopping cart abandonment
- Newsletter subscribers
- RSS subscribers
- Customer class (first-time buyer, returning buyer, discount buyer, etc.)
- Membership status
- Constituent group
- Market area or postal code
- Download materials and what was downloaded
- Content group analysis
- Language selections
- Rich content interaction
- Campaign history (first campaign, second campaign, etc.)
- Ad exposure history (ad versions viewed)
- Promotion code users and promotion codes used

FIGURE 7.12

This custom report is designed to analyze Custom Variable Index Slot #1 by selecting the dimensions for Custom Variable (Key 1) and Custom Variable (Value 1).

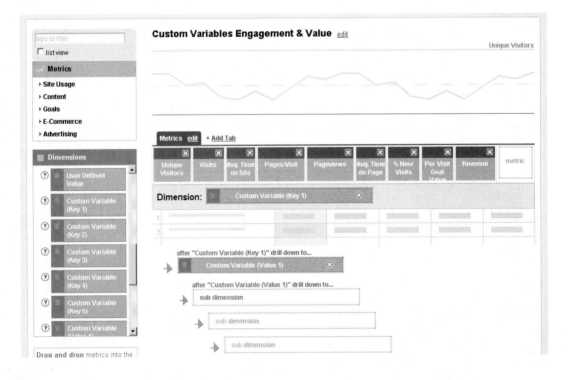

TABLE 7.2			

Example Data Model for Content Group Custom Variables

Index	Name	Value	Scope
1	section	market	3
2	group	boats	3
3	sub-group	yachts	3
4	pagename	40' yacht	3
5	productViewer	yes	1

Analysis scenario: Content optimization through content grouping

The business case in this example is to understand more clearly what content visitors accessed and interacted with. Many Web sites lack page URLs that provide useful, descriptive information about what content is on the page and where that page sits within the hierarchy of the site. For example, consider this URL: /modules.php?name=Marketplace&file=item&ItemID=602492. Standard Google Analytics tracking would report exactly that URL — not terribly insightful as to what content the visitor was viewing. To make this information more useful, you could instead use custom variables to create content group names. Table 7.2 shows an example content group model.

The data model in Table 7.2 articulates a means of recording section, group, subgroup, page name, and tag data on a page-level scope when the page is viewed, and setting a visitor level-scope to identify that this visitor has viewed a product. Consider creating a similar data model before implementing any code for custom variables to plan requirements, opportunities, and analysis methods.

Custom variables are a feature that is truly enterprise-level and thus implementation requirements should not be taken lightly — poor planning of custom variables will result in poor data, while thorough evaluation of needs and precise implementation of this feature will yield powerful insights. You can learn more about the technical side of custom variables in Chapter 5 and visit www.analyticsformarketers.com/s/custom-variables for links to additional online resources.

Analyzing Data with Advanced Segments

The Advanced Segments capability is arguably the most useful advanced feature built into Google Analytics to date. The Advanced Segments tool is essentially an easy-to-use but extremely powerful data mining and segmentation tool. Before this feature was introduced, the capability to perform advanced, real-time segmentation of Web analytics data was reserved for the highest-end Web analytics tools and came with a hefty price tag.

Advanced Segments in Google Analytics lets you perform virtually infinite levels of analysis on your Web analytics data, slicing and dicing any combination of dimensions, metrics, and values. As

Figure 7.13 shows, you can create any number of custom Advanced Segments and apply up to four at the same time, allowing you to quickly compare data from selected segments.

FIGURE 7.13

Advanced Segment Builder: Creating a segment for new visits from Portland.

Using Advanced Segments to answer business questions

Advanced Segments are best used when answering business questions — for example, "Should we expand our physical locations to a certain area, say, Portland, Oregon?" Based on this business question, you can create Advanced Segments that provide further insight into the Portland area and fuel the analysis of whether expansion into that area is a good business decision.

Note how this approach is different from asking a direct numbers question such as "How many visits did we get from Portland?" If that is the question you use to approach Advanced Segments, you of course can create a segment that provides that number. However, you could have already accessed that particular number via the Geographic reports in Google Analytics. The business question "Should we expand our physical locations to a certain area, say, Portland, Oregon?" requires the analyst to create a more complex segment, or multiple segments, and analyze the resulting data at a much deeper level than had a nonbusiness question such as "How many visits did we get from Portland?" been asked.

Understanding how Advanced Segments work

Advanced Segments are based on restricting the data reported to a limited set of visits or sessions in the selected time period based on the criteria defined for the Advanced Segment. Similar to the concept of filtering, Advanced Segments can include or exclude visits from the segment based on your chosen criteria. However, Advanced Segments differ from profile filters in that they apply to historical data and can be modified at any time.

When you create an Advanced Segment, the criteria, or rules, defined by the segment govern what visits get included. For example, you could create an Advanced Segment to answer the question "How many visits came from Portland, Oregon" by using the criteria "City dimension matches exactly 'Portland' and Region dimension matches exactly 'Oregon.'" This segment would thus include only those visits recorded as having the Region name of "Oregon" and the City name of "Portland." Defining Region in this case is important because there are multiple cities with the name "Portland."

The key segmentation concept: Selection of data

Every Advanced Segment is based on a selection of dimensions and metrics. Selected dimensions or metrics have required conditions and condition values. Condition values include:

- Does/doesn't match exactly
- Does/doesn't match regular expression pattern
- Does/doesn't contain
- Does/does not start/end with
- Less than/equal to/greater than a value

Conditions can be combined into logical statements using AND and OR operators; for example, "Where City matches 'Portland' and Region matches 'Oregon.'" To put this concept of Advanced Segments into a tangible perspective, think about it as a pack of Skittles candies. Without segmentation, you just have a pack of candy. But apply segmentation based on the criterion of "color matches purple" and you have a much smaller subset of candies from the pack. Now if some purple candies are sweet and some are sour, you could apply the additional criterion of "flavor matches sweet" to select only the sweet, purple candies. If you didn't care what the color was and rather wanted any color of candy, provided it was sweet, you could remove the criterion of "color" and be left with all the candies that are sweet.

A great way to visualize Advanced Segments is with a Venn diagram, as Figure 7.14 shows. Venn diagrams are a perfect way to visually think about advanced segmentation. Each circle in the diagram represents a part of the "pool." The overlap of circles, when many circles are used, becomes the values returned by the Advanced Segment.

FIGURE 7.14

Visualizing Advanced Segments as a Venn diagram segment for new visits from Portland, Oregon. The darkest area in the middle illustrates where the three sets of criteria overlap to create the pool of visits that will be included in the advanced segment.

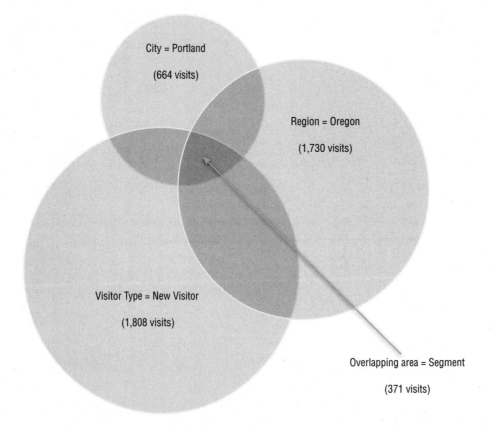

City = Portland

(664 visits)

Region = Oregon

(1,730 visits)

Visitor Type = New Visitor

(1,808 visits)

Overlapping area = Segment

(371 visits)

Limitations of Advanced Segments

There are limitations for Advanced Segments. At the time of this writing, Advanced Segments can apply only to 500,000 visits or fewer. If the data you segment exceeds 500,000 visits, data sampling is used to estimate the metrics shown in reports generated when that segment is applied. Thus, if the segment "visits from Portland, Oregon" had 800,000 actual visits, advance segments would use only the first 500,000 and would estimate metrics across all 800,000 visits based on the sample of metrics from the first 500,000 visits.

Additionally, it is important to note that Advanced Segments apply only to *visits* and not *visitors*. The database structure for Google Analytics contains Unique Visitor IDs. Each unique visitor may have many visits, and each visit is sourced by its own Visit ID. When Advanced Segments are applied, they do not evaluate data based on the Unique Visitor IDs, but rather on Visit or Session IDs. As a consequence, certain metrics can't be determined using Advanced Segments, such as the number of unique people from Portland, Oregon, in a given time period. The only way to derive metrics of unique visitors on a dimension-specific level is to create a profile that uses filters to limit the data processed in that profile to the desired dimensions and values. (See Chapter 6 for a more in-depth explanation of visits and visitors.)

Furthermore, there is another distinction with Advanced Segments that needs to be understood. The distinction between visits and pageviews often causes confusion. If you create a segment with the setting "page matches exactly `index.html`," then why would you see lots of pages that are *not* `index.html` in your content reports? Because the *sessions* (or visits) that included pageviews on `index.html` also included pageviews to lots of other pages.

Using Advanced Segments

Keep in mind the following techniques when using Advanced Segments.

Combining dimensions and metrics for selection criteria

In addition to adding dimensions, you can also add metrics as selection criteria to an Advanced Segment. For example, you may want to see visitors who were really engaged on the site, whether first-time or returning visitors. You could add a selection statement with the values of "time on site greater than 30 seconds or pages viewed greater than 5." This statement would result in visits that lasted more than 30 seconds on the site or viewed more than 5 pages being included in the segment.

Inverse inclusion

An advanced technique for Advanced Segments that can provide answers to extremely difficult questions is to cleverly exclude data in an inverse fashion. For example, let's say you want to know the conversion rate on purchases of a particular product. The direct approach would be to create a segment that *includes* purchases of the given product. However, if you have a goal configured for completion of an order and apply a segment that includes only those visits that bought a certain product, the resulting data will, by design, only include visits that completed an order — and thus the reported Goal Conversion Rate would be 100 percent.

TIP

Try nesting metrics-based and dimensions-based criteria in the same Advanced Segment and use inverted metrics statements for "less than" analysis.

Now, let's take a back-door approach and apply the principle of inclusion by exclusion. If you create a segment that *excludes* the visits that purchase products *other than* the given product, the resulting visits left in the segment would include all visits — those that purchased and those that did not. The outcome for the Goal Conversion Rate reports is to calculate the Conversion Rate based on the visits contained in the segment. By design, the only visits in the segment that would have completed a purchase would be those that purchased the product in question.

Behavioral segmentation

Behavioral segmentation means analyzing data based on the displayed behavior. This behavior could include viewing certain pages or groups of pages, spending a certain amount of time on a page or set of pages, or coming from or going to a particular location on another Web site. If the behavior is tracked in Google Analytics, you can segment based on it.

Let's say you are a school wanting to increase new student applications. You could begin your analysis by creating a segment that targets visits that display a high interest in admissions. Using segmentation based on behavioral criteria, you can learn about what content these visitors view and value the most. Through careful analysis, you'll discover what content you should produce more of — videos, virtual tours, PDF brochures, student testimonials, faculty bios, and so on. Analyzing the behaviors of a segment of visits that you know converts can yield insights into what content compelled the visitors to take the desired action. Learning what content compels conversion actions should help you create more such content and position it more effectively on the site.

Consider Zenith Vineyard's wedding business. A desired behavior is for visitors to inquire about a particular date for their wedding. A behavioral segment that would provide insight into these visitors would be based on visits where "Page matches `booking-complete.html`." This would produce a segment showing the activities — the pages viewed, traffic sources, landing points, and so on — of those who submitted a booking inquiry.

A second segment could look at "those visits that viewed the Page that matches `weddings-and-events.html` and viewed the `booking-form.html` page and did *not* view the `booking-complete.html` page." This segment reveals those visits that showed interest in wedding event information and in inquiring about a date, but that did *not* complete the inquiry.

Managing and sharing Advanced Segments

When Advanced Segments are created, they are tied to the Google account of the person who created the segment (see Chapter 4 for a review of Google accounts). Each user's segments are available in all Google Analytics Profiles and Google Analytics Accounts to which they have access. Furthermore, Advanced Segments can be hidden from or tied to a specific profile, a capability that makes handling large numbers of Advanced Segments across dozens or even hundreds of profiles possible. Figure 7.15 shows an example of the Advanced Segments management interface.

FIGURE 7.15

The Advanced Segments control panel shows segments applied to the current profile and a link to share a segment. Advanced segments are specific to each Google Analytics user's individual user account, not the Google Analytics Account or Profile. However, you can share segments across profiles that you have access to, and send segments to other users using the Share link.

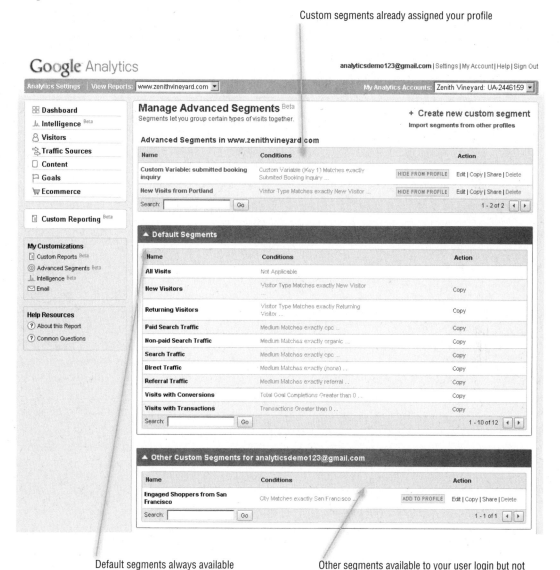

Custom segments already assigned your profile

Default segments always available

Other segments available to your user login but not applied to this profile

However, even with the ability to manage Advanced Segments access, keeping track of all the segments you create over time can get tiresome. We strongly recommend using a consistent naming pattern when creating Advanced Segments. Consider something such as *Web site name: description of segment*. This naming convention makes locating Advanced Segments designed for a specific Web site much easier.

In addition to accessing any segments you have created from any profile, you can also share an advanced segment with another user using the Share link. To share an Advanced Segment, simply click the Share link and copy the URL from the pop-up menu and send it along (see Figure 7.15).

Bringing Together Key Metrics and Dimensions with Custom Reports

The Custom Reports tool in Google Analytics allows you to create a report with up to 10 columns of metrics and five nested drill-down dimensions. In addition, each report can have multiple tabs for metrics, expanding the potential number of metrics. The purpose of custom reports is to provide a means

FIGURE 7.16

The custom report building interface allows you to create reports that have combinations of dimensions and metrics that aren't available in other standard reports.

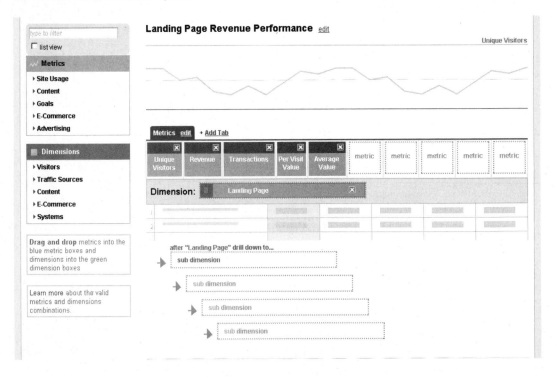

FIGURE 7.17

The result of the custom report, showing revenues and other commerce-related metrics as they relate to landing pages. This report shows data that you can't get in any of the standard Google Analytics reports.

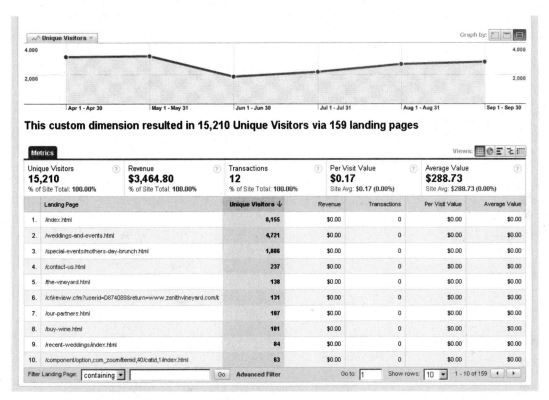

This custom dimension resulted in 15,210 Unique Visitors via 159 landing pages

	Landing Page	Unique Visitors ↓	Revenue	Transactions	Per Visit Value	Average Value
1.	/index.html	8,155	$0.00	0	$0.00	$0.00
2.	/weddings-and-events.html	4,721	$0.00	0	$0.00	$0.00
3.	/special-events/mothers-day-brunch.html	1,886	$0.00	0	$0.00	$0.00
4.	/contact-us.html	237	$0.00	0	$0.00	$0.00
5.	/the-vineyard.html	138	$0.00	0	$0.00	$0.00
6.	/cf/review.cfm?userid=D8740893&return=www.zenithvineyard.com/c	131	$0.00	0	$0.00	$0.00
7.	/our-partners.html	107	$0.00	0	$0.00	$0.00
8.	/buy-wine.html	101	$0.00	0	$0.00	$0.00
9.	/recent-weddings/index.html	84	$0.00	0	$0.00	$0.00
10.	/component/option,com_zoom/Itemid,40/catid,1/index.html	63	$0.00	0	$0.00	$0.00

of reporting combinations of dimensions and metrics not available in the predefined reports. A powerful technique is to use custom reports and Advanced Segments together by building a custom report designed specifically to complement an advanced segment.

Figure 7.16 shows the custom reporting building interface, while Figure 7.17 shows the result of a custom report.

Example uses for custom reports

The reports you could create with the custom reporting engine are virtually endless based on the ability to combine 10 metrics in one report with up to five dimension drill-down levels. You can get creative when making custom reports, but remember to always keep the business question in mind. It is all too easy to get caught up in "Wow, I can do *this!?*" when "this" really isn't important or valuable.

Here's an example of a custom report designed to meet a business need: The business engages in trade shows to promote its products to target customers. At the trade shows, it distributes flyers that contain a promotion code that can be redeemed on the Web. Ideally, the promotion would be tracked as part of a campaign, but given the nature of handing out flyers, providing a vanity URL isn't likely to attract a high percentage of responders. However, the promotion code is a sure-fire way to measure those who were contacted at the trade show.

The business question is ultimately "Did the investment in the trade show pay off?" The means of assessing this investment relies on measuring sales that used the promotion code furnished at the show. The ecommerce integration on the site in this example has been customized to pass the promotion code to the Ecommerce Affiliation data field, which in turn populates the Affiliation dimension. A custom report can then be created that shows Visits, Sales, and other insightful metrics beginning with Affiliation and drilling into other aspects of the visit's response, such as Traffic Source/Medium and Visitor type, as Figure 7.18 shows.

The outcome is a report that easily shows how many visits and how much revenue was derived from the promotion code, as well as determining other engagement metrics around this trade show that can be compared to future trade shows.

FIGURE 7.18

Building a more advanced custom report using the ecommerce Affiliation field, a dimension not accessible in any standard report.

Managing and sharing custom reports

As with Advanced Segments, custom reports are tied to each user account and available in any profile that user can access. To share a custom report with another user, you must use the Share link, similar to that for Advanced Segments, to send a URL that will create the report in the other user's account.

Limitations of custom reports

There are a couple of key limitations for custom reports.

First, you cannot combine certain dimensions with certain metrics. For example, if you select Visitors as a metric, the only dimensions you can add to the report are Day, Week, and Month, as Figure 7.19 shows.

FIGURE 7.19

Not all dimensions and metrics can be used together. Here the Visitor dimension has locked down use of almost all the other metrics and dimensions because the Visitor dimension is compatible only with dimensions related to time. Note that grayed-out dimensions in the list can't be dragged into the Custom Report building canvas because they aren't compatible with the selected metric of Visitors.

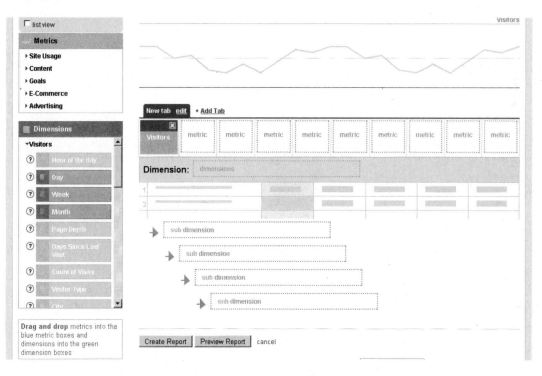

NOTE

Google may change the dimension and metric compatibility over time. You can find the latest combination compatibility on the Google Analytics API documentation site for valid combinations at `www.analyticsformarketers.com/s/valid-combos`.

The second limitation, as of this book's publication, is that you cannot create custom metrics. Custom metrics (the ability to, in the interface, create a new metric based on a combination of other metrics and a defined calculation) would be an extremely powerful feature, and one that is often presumed to be part of a custom reporting engine. However, the vast majority of analysis doesn't require the creation of custom metrics and can be completed with the existing tools. If creating custom metrics is truly essential, the Data Export API, explained in Chapter 15, provides a means of exporting data into external systems and doing what you want with it — such as creating custom metrics.

FIGURE 7.20

This motion chart shows keyword performance over time. Each dot represents a keyword. The line shows a "trail" for a selected keyword showing trends and associated values. The size of the dots is based on visits; the half-circle indicates that the largest size equals 648 visits.

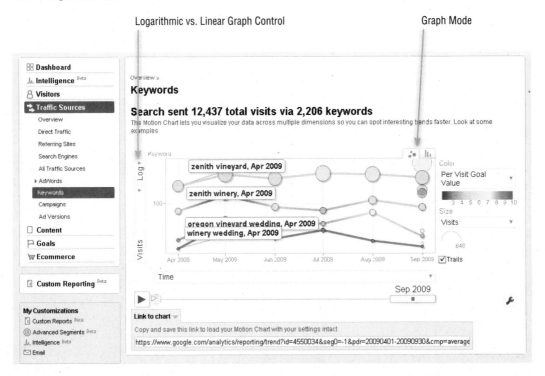

Visualizing Data Across Multiple Dimensions with Motion Charts

Motion charts are an advanced analysis tool designed for analysis of relationships among dimensions, metrics, and time in an interactive and visual interface. Motion charts are built on the Trendalyzer Flash widget integrated into Google Analytics. Trendalyzer was built by the Gapminder Foundation and acquired by Google in March 2006. With motion charts, you can analyze up to five dimensions of data simultaneously and view the relationship between these dimensions as time progresses.

As Figure 7.20 shows, this is a fantastic tool for detecting anomalies, opportunities, problems (one-time events or things that jump out — and they will literally "jump" out on the motion chart!), and tracking trends over time. Motion charts aid in analyzing an enormous amount of data quickly to find these outliers and develop useful insights.

Understanding the key features of motion charts

Motion charts have several controls that help more effectively present their results.

X and Y axes: Linear or logarithmic, time-based or metric-based

The motion chart's X and Y axes can be configured to use either a metric or time as the basis of measurement for the axis. If a metric is selected, you have the option of using a logarithmic scale or a linear scale. Linear is the default and represents the literal numbers in the metric you selected. Logarithmic uses a mathematical formula to normalize, or "level," the metric's data so trends are more visible and huge swings or spikes in figures are avoided.

Time slider

The Time slider allows you to graph the figures over a given timeline. You can adjust the playback speed for animating how data changes over time, controlling whether the Time slider plays the motion quickly or slowly through the data timeline.

The timeframe used in the Time slider is set to the active date range used in the reports before activating motion charts. Thus, if you want to analyze an entire year, you need to set your data range to a year before activating the motion chart feature.

Another consideration is that the timeframe uses the daily, weekly, or monthly data display option used on the previous report. For analysis of several weeks, months, or years, it is best to set the data display to weekly or monthly before activating the motion chart feature to prevent the overwhelming granularity of dozens or hundreds of daily data points.

Chart modes: Dots or bars

You can display data in the graph as circles, dots, or vertical bars. Vertical bars provide better visualization when you need to compare a handful of values side by side and see how they change against one another rather than evaluating the time-based trends of each point on the chart individually.

Coloration and size

Color and size are used to help differentiate data displayed in the chart. The size can represent bigger or smaller numbers or values, and color can be set to represent stronger or weaker performance.

Dimension selection

With motion charts, you can select up to five dimensions. One dimension is time and the other four can be dimensions available from the report you were viewing. You can use size, color, X axis, and Y axis to each have a different factor based on dimension or metric.

Trails

Trails are a graphing mode using dots (circles) to help differentiate the trend of one dot from another. Trails are very useful, but they can add noise to the report if not used selectively.

Other resources for motion charts

Motion charts are a powerful analysis feature but can be a challenge to learn. Thinking in 2D versus 3D is hard enough — so learning to think in 5D with the visual elements of time, color, and size might take some time to master. Check out the following resources from the official Google Analytics blogs to learn more about motion charts and to access additional examples of how to use motion charts.

- Basics of using motion charts: `www.analyticsformarketers.com/s/motion-chart-basics`
- Mastering trend analysis with motion charts: `www.analyticsformarketers.com/s/motion-chart-trends`
- Advanced analysis techniques with motion charts: `www.analyticsformarketers.com/s/advanced-motion-charts`

Grouping and Analyzing Data with Pivot Tables

Pivot tables are a method of analyzing large sets of data; many people are familiar with the pivot tables in Microsoft Excel or IBM Lotus Notes. Pivot tables are known for their ability to organize and report large sets of data in a combined and grouped fashion. With a pivot table, you can effectively analyze three, four, or even five dimensions of data at one time.

Let's say you've been asked to provide a report showing products sold, revenues earned for each product, and the geography and marketing channels that contributed to sales for the previous month. This request is a perfect candidate for a pivot table report.

The first step to building this report is to determine the dimensions and metrics you'll need. In this case, you need to analyze the Product Name, City, and Medium dimensions, and the Product Revenue and Unique Transactions metrics (for a point of comparison).

To generate the report, start by going to the Ecommerce reports section. Under Product Performance select Product Overview. Click the Pivot View button to activate the Pivot Table report.

FIGURE 7.21

The Pivot Table report feature allows you to analyze data within Google Analytics using the popular pivot table style commonly used in Excel and other spreadsheets. This pivot table shows products purchased and revenue by visitor type (new or returning) and region by using a primary dimension of Products, a secondary dimension of Region, and pivot table columns of Visitor type.

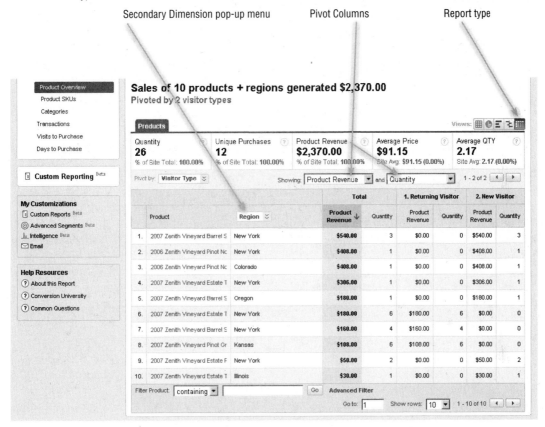

Secondary Dimension pop-up menu   Pivot Columns   Report type

Next, set the Pivot By dimension to Medium, the secondary dimension to Region, and set the column views to show Product Revenue and Quantity.

The report will show each combination of product and region in a row and columns for each value in the Medium dimension. Each column will have two subcolumns, one for each metric selected — in this case, Product Revenue and Unique Purchases. The Pivot Table report can be exported in various formats just like other reports in Google Analytics. The CSV for Excel export renders the columns ready for an Excel pivot table, letting you conduct further analysis.

Figure 7.21 shows a pivot table in action.

Note that Google Analytics' pivot tables aren't as flexible or as robust as a pivot table in a spreadsheet application. However, the ability to build a basic pivot table with three dimensions and two sets of metrics in Google Analytics is likely sufficient for the majority of pivot-style reporting. Dimensions and metrics available in a pivot table vary depending on the report you're viewing. Additionally, as of this writing, Advanced Segments are not available in a Pivot Table report.

Measuring Spikes and Trends with Intelligence Reports and Custom Alerts

The word "intelligence" comes from the Latin verb *intellegere,* meaning "to understand." Intelligence reports and custom alerts are two intertwined features that help you find the proverbial "needles in the haystack" or the "known unknowns" and "unknown unknowns" so you can more easily and more rapidly understand the data contained in your Google Analytics.

As former Defense Secretary Donald Rumsfeld put it, "There are known knowns; there are things we know we know. There are known unknowns; there are some things we do not know. But there are also unknown unknowns — the ones we don't know we don't know." Within Google Analytics, there are literally millions of data points. Advanced Segments help you peer beneath the surface of your reports and cross-dimension analysis empowers you to drill into data points, but digging through all that data day-in and day-out is laborious.

Furthermore, even with hours of slicing and dicing data, what about all the things that you didn't find? Are there nuggets of insight sitting right next to your favorite report under a few layers of data? Avinash Kaushik wrote on his blog in October 2009, "I wish the tools would use an algorithmic approach to highlight the things an analyst needs to know, give 'em some starting points. Why make people dig for hours?" That is where Google Analytics' Intelligence reports come in.

A simple four-value grid illustrates the challenge of data with Web analytics tools. Collecting data is no longer the issue; it is finding the data that matters and understanding it to gather insights. In most cases, you operate in the realm of the "known knowns" — you know what you want to learn and you found the data that provides that learning. The "known unknowns" are things you know you need to know but are not yet known. The unknown unknowns are things you didn't even know you needed to find out. Figure 7.22 shows an example.

How Intelligence reports work

Intelligence reports are based on a complex algorithm that sifts through millions of data points in Google Analytics and finds things that fall outside the expected range. This algorithm operates against dozens of dimensions, the values under each dimension, and the corresponding metrics related to each dimension/value combination being analyzed.

Using advanced statistical modeling, the Intelligence reports capability identifies a range that would be expected for a given dimension, value, and metric combination. When a given dimension, value, and metric combination changes significantly from the expected range, the Intelligence capability creates an automatic alert.

FIGURE 7.22

Intelligence reports find the "unknown unknowns" in your data — the things you weren't looking for and didn't know were there. The main graph line shows changes on some days and no significant changes on other days, but alerts are triggered on both days since there are significant changes occurring in the data.

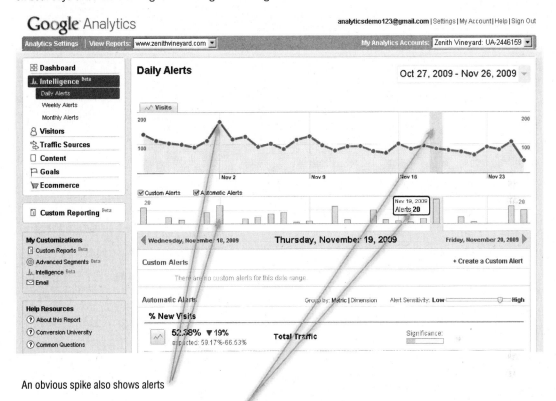

An obvious spike also shows alerts

The main graph line doesn't seem to indicate any major changes, but there were 20 alerts on this day

The significance can be adjusted to find only extremely large changes or more subtle variations. The slider is called Sensitivity, but the concept is better described as tolerance for variation. For example, if new visits from San Francisco are normally 180 to 220 per day and then spike to 400 on one day, the Intelligence reports algorithm will find the change because it is significant. But if the change was to 220 visits, the algorithm would be unlikely to detect it because it is within the expected range.

Using Intelligence reports intelligently

Intelligence reports *won't do your job for you*. They won't magically find important data, analyze it, define what action should be taken, and communicate that information to the right people. Intelligence reports *will* make your job easier and faster, and they will increase your efficiency and effectiveness

FIGURE 7.23

Intelligence reports have five key parts: alert basis (Daily, Weekly, or Monthly), Sensitivity, Alert Grouping, Alert Trend Analysis, and a quick Custom Segment link for an alert.

Show Trend button

when conducting analysis. Instead of staring at the big blue line on your Google Analytics Dashboard and beginning the process of understanding "What made this change?" using data-range comparison, Advanced Segments, and endless dimension drilling, simply open the Intelligence report set and click the day of interest.

You can choose several options when working with Intelligence reports, as shown in Figure 7.23:

- First, Intelligence reports make calculations at three levels of granularity on daily, weekly, or monthly data. You can select Daily, Weekly, or Monthly from the navigation menu — just make sure your date range is appropriately set (don't try to use Monthly for one month of data).
- Second, you can set the Alert Sensitivity from high to low — high sensitivity will find small changes while low sensitivity will alert you only to very large changes.
- Third, you can adjust the grouping of alerts from Metric to Dimension. Grouping by metric will report any alerts about the Bounce Rate under the Bounce Rate grouping, detailing the dimensions where Bounce Rate has changed (for example, that Bounce Rate from San

Francisco decreased by 80 percent). Grouping by Dimension results in alerts being organized by the dimension they relate to, regardless of the metric (that is, Visitors from San Francisco: Bounce Rate decreased 80 percent, New Visits increased 18 percent).

- Fourth, see the trend for a given alert by clicking the Graph icon on the left of each alert row (be sure to scroll to the top of the page to see the main graph change).
- Fifth, on the far right of each alert's row, you can click the Create Segment link to create an Advanced Segment for the alert's criteria and conduct further analysis.

The ideal "intelligent" analysis process should follow this pattern:

1. Identify the time period to analyze.
2. Set the alert basis (Daily, Weekly, or Monthly).
3. Intelligence reports tell you all the things that changed during that time period.
4. Look through the alerts and find ones that stand out.
5. Click the Advanced Segments button to create an advanced segment and conduct further analysis.

The old process, *sans* Analytics Intelligence, follows a path similar to this:

1. Identify the time period to analyze.
2. Look for signs of a big change — check Traffic Sources, Goal Conversions, Sales, Pageviews, Bounce Rates, and so on and hope to find a metric that stands out.

FIGURE 7.24

Custom alerts work like automatic alerts, except that you define the conditions and criteria that result in the alert, and you can choose to be sent an e-mail when the alert is triggered.

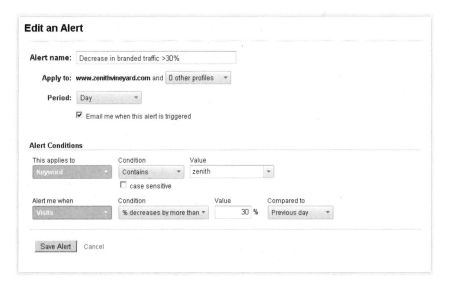

3. If you find a change, set the date-range comparison to try to spot what changed.

4. Presuming you find a cause for the change, create an advanced segment or drill down further to find out more about the data.

Managing Intelligence alerts

Intelligence alerts are automatically generated and there are few options to manage their settings. However, under the Custom Alerts link there is an option to set the Default Sensitivity for automatic Intelligence alerts. To reduce the number of alerts shown by default, simply change this setting to "lower" sensitivity. For more alerts, raise the sensitivity to a higher setting. You can adjust alert sensitivity on the Intelligence reports screen at any time, but only changes to this setting will persist for future visits to the Intelligence Reports section.

Using custom alerts

If automatic Intelligence alerts are insightful, the custom alerts built into the Intelligence report section are powerful. They operate in a similar fashion to automatic alerts generated by the algorithm in that they look across all the data in your profile. Where custom alerts differ is that the criteria for evaluating data are based on what *you define* rather than what the algorithm is programmed to find. Further, you can set an alert to send an e-mail when the alert is triggered. Figure 7.24 shows an example.

The key concept for custom alerts is to capitalize on the "known unknown" — when you know what you don't know. For example, you might setup a daily alert on referral traffic from Twitter, alerting you to spikes of 50 percent or more.

Creating custom alerts is straightforward: After naming the alert and selecting additional profiles you want applied to the alert, the first option is setting the alert period (to Day, Week, or Month). After setting the period, select the Conditions to trigger the alert. You must define both a dimension and corresponding value and a metric that, when changed by the defined pattern, triggers the alert.

Custom Alert Settings are similar to Advanced Segments: You must define a dimension and value, but you can do so using the same set of criteria: matches exactly, does not match exactly, contains, does not contain, matches regular expression, does not match regular expression, starts with, does not start with, ends with, and does not end with. Criteria for metrics (numbers) are less than, greater than, decreases by more than, increases by more than, percentage decrease, and percentage increase.

Custom alerts are listed above the automatic alerts and are also indicated in the main alerts chart with a blue bar instead of a green bar.

—

PART

III

Controlling Costs and Planning Profits

Maximizing Web Site Performance

Imagine that your Web site draws 10,000 visitors every month, and 100 visitors buy your product. If you want to increase sales, you can either raise the number of visitors coming to the site through inbound marketing, or you can make better use of the traffic you already have and focus on converting more visitors into buyers. The latter approach is often cheaper and easier than attracting more visitors, and it has the added benefit of raising satisfaction with your Web site and raising ROI on your advertising spend long into the future.

Increasing the efficiency of your Web site as a sales and marketing tool is often called *Web site optimization* or *conversion optimization*. This chapter explains how you can use Google Analytics data and voice-of-the-customer research to identify problem areas on your site and mount a successful optimization effort. It will also introduce Web site testing, a scientific way to use data to educate design decisions.

Understanding Core Optimization Concepts

In September 2009, a retired statistics professor and winemaker named Robert Hodgson dropped a bombshell on the fast-growing community of expert wine critics and reviewers. After a careful study of data from *The California Grapevine* tracking the results from hundreds of wine competitions, Hodgson found that the probability a wine would win a gold medal in a competition was roughly equal to what would be expected if medals were awarded by chance alone. Joshua Greene, editor and publisher of *Wine and Spirits Magazine*, provided a surprising response, declaring, "It is absurd for people to expect consistency in a taster's ratings. We're not robots." Hodgson's findings echoed those published by dozens of others, including a study by the University of California at Davis in 1963 showing that experts could be fooled into believing wines were much sweeter than they actually were simply by adding color.

So in the face of all this evidence, why do consumers continue putting so much stock in the experts' opinions? First and foremost, it's because the subjective experience of taste is nebulous enough to allow room for error. Second, if consumers threw out the expert rating system, they'd have to find another way to make quick decisions as they wander the aisles.

It's our view that Web site design today suffers from many of the same problems as the world of fine wines, namely confusion over how to evaluate quality, a lack of accountability, and a lot of poor decisions. Fortunately, Web analytics offers an escape from this mindset.

NOTE

The term *Web site optimization* is sometimes used to describe the process of trying to increase your site's visibility in search engines, also known as *search engine optimization (SEO)*. We'll deal with this process in a later chapter.

Web site optimization is a data-driven methodology you can use to make your Web site more efficient at enticing, cajoling, and otherwise encouraging visitors in order to reach your desired outcomes. In a nutshell, it involves identifying areas for improvement on your site using Web analytics data, voice-of-the customer research, and best practices, and then systematically evaluating alternatives using a performance-testing platform. Amazon.com, Google, Walmart.com, and countless other Web giants all use Web site optimization to strengthen their offerings, raise customer satisfaction, and drive revenue.

Over the long haul, this data-driven approach to design will keep your site moving toward consistently higher returns on your marketing efforts and help you avoid debating questions that can be better answered by your site's visitors. With that in mind, let's look at some of the concepts you'll need to become an optimization superstar.

Getting into the optimization mindset

Your Web site's conversion rate serves as a multiplier on all your inbound marketing efforts. If you can double the effectiveness of your Web site as a sales tool, you can double the ROI on inbound marketing. Looking at the basic concepts we cover in Chapter 2, a visitor has *converted* when he or she completes an action that drives business value, such as completing a purchase. Web site optimization is about raising the business value generated from each visit to your site by raising the percentage of customers who convert, or by raising the value of a single conversion. If your site is driven by engagement rather than transactional goals, this might mean enticing visitors to spend more time engaging with content.

Before we dive into the specific ways you can use Google Analytics to boost conversion rates on your site, we want to offer some ideas on how to mentally prepare for the effort.

As a starting point, you'll have more success with Web site optimization if you stay open-minded about your site's visitors and acknowledge early on that *you are not your customer*. Remember the Curse of Knowledge concept from Chapter 1: As long as you've been in business and as hard as you try to anticipate what visitors need and want, your understanding will always be incomplete. It's no surprise that when you're new in town, you tend to notice things that locals don't. After you've worked with your Web site for a while, it can be hard to shake your assumptions, so do your best to throw them out right now.

Remember also that your Web site visitors are not just numbers on a page; they're people. Each carries his or her own unique perceptions, motivations, and assumptions. Some visitors have been comparison shopping for weeks and are ready to buy. Others have no idea who your company is or what it does. Some enter from the home page, but many more enter from all kinds of pages you don't anticipate.

By staying curious about what it is your visitors need and want and challenging your colleagues to do the same, you'll have an easier time shedding your assumptions and finding more creative ways to strengthen the performance of your site.

Second, to make real strides in optimization, you need to be creative about the copy, imagery, workflow, functionality, pricing, freebies, and tactics you use to move visitors through the *conversion funnel*. Throughout this book we've described the need to be goal-driven and analytical when it comes marketing, but when you develop the actual messaging and assets, it is as important as ever to be creative in identifying what works for your audience. Learning how to be creative and still keep your site simple and usable is a hallmark of good Web site design. This is where strong tacticians such as Web designers, copywriters, user experience designers, and information architects come into play. Customer insight serves to enhance your efforts, but without effective specialists who can translate that insight into actual pages and site elements, you won't get far.

Last, as you approach the task of Web site optimization, it's important to adopt a mindset of *continuous improvement*. Going back to our analogy of the online marketing system, it is important to view the site as something that's constantly evolving. Competitors' sites change, tastes change, and traffic patterns change. Your Web presence needs constant nurturing. Don't neglect it! By advocating this view, you can prepare yourself and your organization for the long haul of true optimization.

In our experience, the biggest gains come from the incremental improvements of this type of long-term effort, similar to the way that evolution happens in the real world. In the words of Jan Carlzon, "You can't improve one thing by 1,000 percent, but you can improve 1,000 little things by 1 percent." To succeed over the long haul, you'll need to enlist the support and cooperation of the people in your organization that control the Web site code, brand guidelines, and so on. For some tips and advice on how to gather support, refer to Chapter 3.

Key optimization tools and methods

In Chapter 2 we present a diagram of a typical online marketing system, shown again here in Figure 8.1.

NOTE

Once you've configured your goals, you need to validate the goals against other data sources such as the shopping cart, list management tool, or order-fulfillment system to ensure they are working properly. If you run into difficulties, get help from someone with technical expertise such as your IT contact or Web developer. You can also look at the Goal Verification report in the Google Analytics Goals section to see which pages are being counted as completed goals in Google Analytics. Note that 100 percent accuracy is unlikely due to the issues covered in Chapter 4, but you should try for 95 percent accuracy or better.

FIGURE 8.1

Components of a typical online marketing system

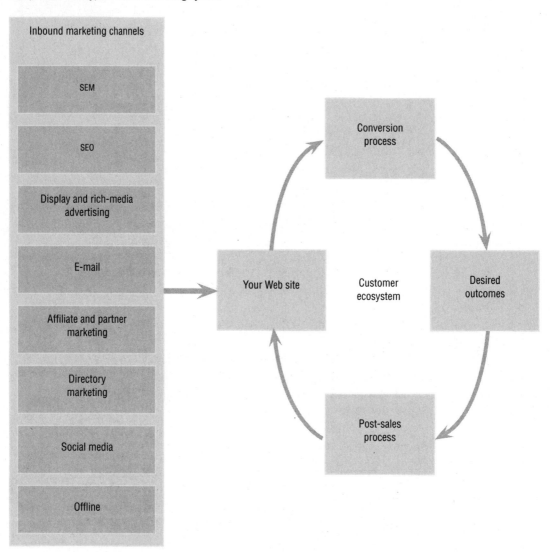

You can apply optimization techniques to each element in this system, but in this chapter we are focusing on the Web site. We explain how to measure and optimize the inbound marketing channels such as e-mail marketing and search engine marketing in later chapters.

The most efficient and effective way to continuously refine and improve Web site performance is by deploying a *Web site testing tool* to run with Google Analytics. Web site testing tools allow you to display one or more variations of a Web page (called *A/B testing* or *split testing*) — or multiple combinations of specific page elements (called *multivariate testing*) — to find the optimal variation to maximize Conversion Goals. There are several tools available to choose from, including a free tool from Google called Google Website Optimizer. Our advice is to select a tool that can integrate with Google Analytics.

We can't hope to cover all the details of deploying a Web site testing tool, so instead here's a list of resources to get you started:

- *Always Be Testing: The Complete Guide to Google Website Optimizer* by Brian Eisenberg and John Quarto-von Tivadar with Lisa T. Davis.
- *Landing Page Optimization: The Definitive Guide to Testing and Tuning for Conversions* by Tim Ash.
- Google Website Optimizer Official Blog (`http://websiteoptimizer.blogspot.com`).
- Google Website Optimizer YouTube channel (`www.youtube.com/user/websiteoptimizer`).
- *Creating Your First Google Website Optimizer Experiment Video* by David Booth (`www.youtube.com/watch?v=uPtsrCqUKL8`).

Now it's time to take a look at how you can use Google Analytics and voice-of-the-customer research to identify what to test.

Evaluating Web Site Performance

Thinking back to Robert Hodgson and his quest to help wine drinkers find the perfect vintage, you are faced with a similar challenge in evaluating the performance of your Web site. Now that you've made the decision to move beyond subjective analysis, what's next? Figure 8.2 shows some of the major areas you'll need to consider as you look for ways to improve your site and boost your conversion rates.

Analyzing goal performance in Google Analytics

To assess how well your site is performing, you first need to clarify your business goals. Second, you need to recast your business objectives as measurable Conversion Goals in Google Analytics. In Chapter 2, we presented two types of Conversion Goals: Engagement Goals and Transactional Goals. In Chapter 5, we explain how to configure Google Analytics to track Conversion Goals using the Goals feature. If you haven't completed this configuration, you should do so now. Without measurable Conversion Goals, it is more difficult to quantify the business impact of your Web site.

As you define the Conversion Goals in Google Analytics using the information in Chapter 5, ask the following questions.

- What effect does this Conversion Goal have on the site's revenue, costs, or customer satisfaction?

FIGURE 8.2

Focus areas for evaluating Web site performance

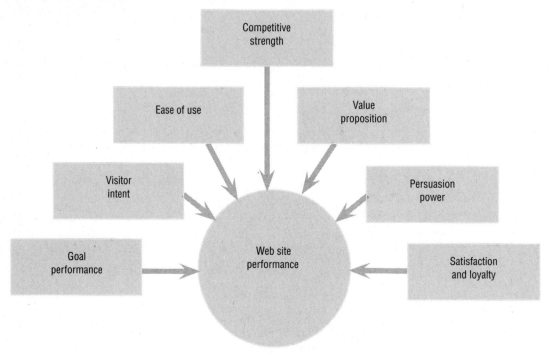

- How much is one converted visit worth in financial terms?
- Are there any offline processes (such as a sales process) required to turn a converted visit into revenue? How does this affect the value of the Conversion Goal?
- Are there any offline processes I can move online to create a new Conversion Goal on the site? For example, implementing phone tracking (covered in Chapter 15) or moving a registration form online.
- Which Conversion Goals drive the most business value?
- Which Conversion Goals do my colleagues and manager value most?
- Is there a clear winner in terms of which Conversion Goals to focus on first?

The more closely you can identify the dollar value of a conversion, the more effective you will be at optimizing. If you can point to evidence that you generated a specific dollar amount for your organization, it will be easier for them to understand the value behind optimizing the site. This will help you win the resources to expand your optimization effort down the road.

Key goal performance measures

The metrics used to understand goal performance in Google Analytics depend on the business model being used. Ecommerce sites can use a specific set of ecommerce metrics to analyze purchase behavior. Ad-serving sites can define Threshold Goals that serve as a proxy for engagement and tie closely to revenue. Here are some of the most important metrics in Google Analytics for analyzing goal performance. Note that these metrics can be tied both to Transactional Goals and Engagement Goals by using the Threshold Goals feature:

- **Goal Completions:** The number of *visits* that include at least one completed goal.
- **Total Goal Value:** The total value of all goal conversions. You can use this metric as a proxy either for profit or for revenue, but we recommend using revenue because this number is generally more steady than profit.
- **Goal Conversion Rate:** The percentage of visits to a site that result in a Conversion Goal being reached.
- **Per-Visit Goal Value:** The Total Goal Value divided by Total Visits. This metric (combined with Total Goal Value) is the best indicator of success from goals because it provides a composite index of value. With goal conversions, you may have two goals that are not of equal value, but the Goal Conversion Rate or Total Conversions treats them the same. The Per-Visit Goal Value weights the value by the related importance of the goal.

If you've configured the Ecommerce feature in Google Analytics, you have access to some additional metrics useful for analyzing overall site performance:

- **Transactions:** The total number of ecommerce transactions processed through your site.
- **Ecommerce Conversion Rate:** This is the rate at which visitors become purchasing customers. This metric is a key indicator of success for Web site optimization.
- **Average Order Value:** The average value of an ecommerce transaction. While the Ecommerce Conversion Rate tells you when you're getting more people buying, it doesn't tell you if those orders are more valuable. If you can increase the Average Order Value *and* your Conversion Rate, you're really in business.
- **Purchased Products**: The total number of products sold. It is useful for zeroing in on revenue-driving products.
- **Total Revenue**: Total of quantity of products sold multiplied by the price of all items. Be aware that revenue doesn't equal profit!
- **Per Visit Value**: Total Revenue divided by Total Visits. Again, this doesn't equate to profit per visit, since it doesn't account for the cost of delivering goods.

Using the Google Analytics interface to analyze goal performance

With your Google Analytics Goals defined, it's time to get comfortable analyzing your site's goal performance. This means being able to answer simple questions such as "How many conversions did my site generate this month?" and more complex ones such as "What was the overall contribution of the Web site versus offline marketing toward this month's revenue?"

The easiest place to start analyzing goal performance is to examine the reports in the Goals section in Google Analytics. If you have the Ecommerce feature configured, you can also begin by looking at the Ecommerce reports. Figure 8.3 shows the Goal Detail report for the booking form at Zenith Vineyard, an online form visitors can use to book reservations for special events. You can open the Goal Detail report by clicking on any of the items listed in the Goals Overview report, which is the first report shown when you navigate to the Goals section.

Figure 8.3 shows that 110 visits included a completion of the booking form by a Web site visitor over the time period shown (Total Conversions). This means that 5.09 percent of visits resulted in a booking (Conversion Rate). Bookings are a good success metric for the Zenith Web site, but it's important to remember than bookings do not equal profit or even revenue. Each booking must be processed by the reservations manager, and due to cancellations, only some bookings result in a sale.

The reservations manager could manage this discrepancy by using an historical average to define the goal value of an online booking to match the revenue generated by each booking. This would allow the vineyard to optimize the Web site against Goal Value per Visit on a daily basis. The manager could also schedule a report to be delivered weekly that could be combined with sales records to calculate

FIGURE 8.3

The Goal Detail report for the Zenith Vineyard booking form

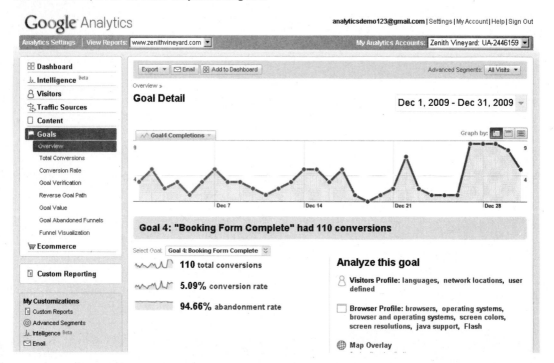

Goal Value per Visit and profit with even more accuracy. For details on how to assign goal value to a goal, see Chapter 5.

As you're examining your site's Conversion Rate, try to focus more on the impact of your efforts over time, rather than looking at the absolute percentage. A 5 percent Conversion Rate for a site of this nature is actually very respectable. Last, remember that the two most important metrics in analyzing goal performance are Goal Value per Visit and Total Goal Value — *not* Conversion Rate.

Open your Google Analytics account, load your Goal reports (located in the Goals section of the navigation menu), and see if you can answer the following:

- How many conversions did my site see in the last week (or since Goals was first configured)?
- How is this number trending over time?
- What is the Conversion Rate and Total Goal Value for each goal?
- How does the goal value defined relate to revenue and profit?
- Are there any spikes in conversions that correspond to a particular marketing activity or Web site change?
- What is the most important Conversion Goal on the Web site in terms of business value?

Segmenting goal performance

Like most metrics in Google Analytics, conversion data becomes more useful as you break it down. For example, it is more useful to be able to compare the goal value generated by one class of marketing activity (such as SEM) versus another (such as e-mail marketing) than it is to look only at an aggregate measure. From the perspective of Web site optimization, you need to be able to segment goal performance so you can cut through the noise and evaluate the impact of specific changes made on the site.

In Chapter 7, we describe several ways to break down metrics such as Conversion Rate and Goal Value along different dimensions in Google Analytics. One way is to navigate to a particular report such as the All Traffic Sources report and look for a Goal Set 1 or Goal Set 2 tab located above the scorecard. Figure 8.4 shows the All Traffic Sources report for Goal Set 1 at Zenith Vineyard. The Table View has been adjusted to Comparison View (using the icon in the upper-right corner) to show which traffic sources yield the highest Goal Value per Visit. Note that some of the metrics have been adjusted so they can be shared publicly.

Figure 8.4 shows that MyPortlandWedding.com generates a considerably higher Goal Value per Visit than most traffic sources shown. Clicking Myportlandwedding in the table reveals the actual Goal Value per Visit to be $3.03. Multiplying $3.03 by the Total Visits from MyPortlandWedding.com yields a Total Goal Value of $721.14 for that traffic source.

After adjusting Total Goal Value for costs to determine profit, the advertising manager from the vineyard can use this figure to evaluate whether the listing on MyPortlandWedding.com was profitable or not. He or she can also compare this figure to other mediums to determine whether MyPortlandWedding.com outperforms or underperforms them.

Goal Set 1 for the Zenith Vineyard's All Traffic Sources report

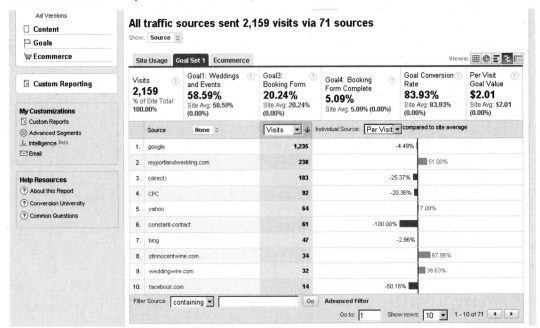

A second method for segmenting goal performance is to configure an Advanced Segment that filters traffic by a particular dimension (such as local versus out of state traffic) and then examine the reports in the Goals section. Once you have the Advanced Segment applied, all the reports in the Goals section will apply specifically to the portion of traffic defined in the Advanced Segment. Figure 8.5 breaks out visits made from within Oregon to those made out of state. The report shows that Oregon visits generate more than 70 percent of the goal value created through the booking form.

A third method for breaking down goal performance is to create a custom report that includes the goal values you want to segment and the metrics and dimensions you want to use to segment them. Creating your own report is a great way to tailor performance data that can be published to individual team members each month. For more information on how to create a custom report, refer to Chapter 7.

Regardless of how you segment the goal performance, you'll need to apply a variety of metrics and dimensions to identify which of your Web site optimization efforts are generating the most value. Here are some suggestions for good dimensions for segmentation you can use to get started:

- **Traffic Source:** Traffic sources often correspond to the marketing channels covered in Chapter 2. By separating goal performance from these channels, you can start weighing their importance against one another to figure out where to focus your efforts.

FIGURE 8.5

Zenith Vineyard's Goal Value report with Advanced Segments applied

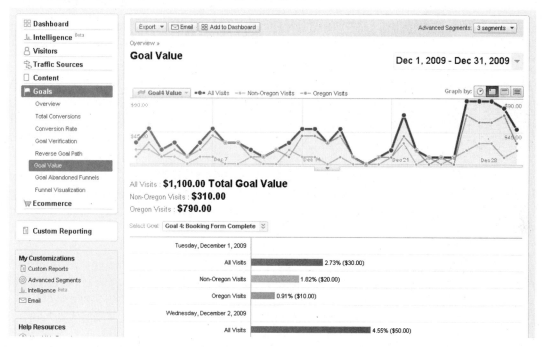

- **Paid Versus Unpaid:** You can group multiple traffic sources to reflect a mix of paid advertising versus organic traffic. The specific categories you use, which might include grouping individual referral sources or different source and medium combinations, depend on how you're allocating your advertising spend.
- **Time:** Your business may be affected by seasonal changes. Looking at change over time can give you a sense of the way your site's performance is trending and the time of the year the site has the most success.
- **Geography:** When your marketing activities are focused on particular geographic areas, you can analyze the impact on each regional activity.
- **New Versus Returning Visitors:** To understand how your customers make decisions, you could compare the Conversion Rate of New Visitors versus Returning Visitors.

Take time to experiment with these methods to see if you can break down the aggregate goal performance metrics you looked at previously and see how they correspond to your current marketing activities.

FIGURE 8.6

The psychological breakdown of the conversion funnel

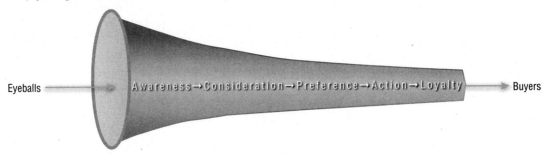

Eyeballs — Awareness→Consideration→Preference→Action→Loyalty — Buyers

Understanding your conversion funnel

Now that you understand how to monitor a site's overall performance as well as the performance of individual segments of traffic on the site, it's time to break down goal performance along one more dimension that's crucial in Web site optimization. This process involves looking at the required steps a visitor must go through to convert on your site, as well as the steps your organization needs to go through to turn a conversion into revenue. We call this structured set of steps surrounding a Conversion Goal a *conversion funnel.*

You can look at the conversion funnel in two ways. First, you can define the funnel in terms of the mental progression a visitor must go through before they make the final decision to convert. Figure 8.6 shows a traditional marketing funnel defined in this way.

Your inbound marketing and word of mouth generates awareness of what your site offers and drives users into the funnel. Your Web site encourages interest, preference, and action. The post-sales process and overall satisfaction drive loyalty. From the perspective of Web site optimization, you need to ensure that the Web site is meeting the needs of visitors at every stage in this conversion funnel.

You can use the concept of a funnel to give added depth and sophistication to an optimization effort. Instead of defining an objective such as "the marketing team must drive 10 percent more conversions this quarter," you can use the concept of a funnel to define more focused goals such as raising the percentage of visitors from search advertising who go from casual interest on the site to serious consideration, as measured by the time spent or content viewed.

See if you can use your existing knowledge of your customers to give added depth to this notion of a funnel. Are there clear steps all buyers must go through before purchase? Do any of the stages in this process align with specific actions visitors can take on your Web site? For example, if you're running a blog, you may view the conversion funnel in terms of engagement. A useful goal in this case might be to convert regular readers into commenters, or to raise the percentage of visitors who subscribe to your RSS feed.

A second useful approach to understanding your conversion funnel involves focusing on specific *actions* users need to take before they can convert. This framework is most useful in evaluating your checkout process or any other structured process on the site that leads to a conversion. This action-based

TABLE 8.1

Sample Conversion Funnels

Action	Measure
Shopping cart purchase	
Add item to cart	Visit to `add_cart` redirect page
Enter checkout	Visit to `checkout.html`
Enter shipping info	Visit to `shipping.html`
Enter billing info	Visit to `billing.html`
Confirm purchase	Visit to `confirmation.html`
Redeem coupon	
Visit microsite	Entrance on any page on site
Select coupon offer	Visit to `coupon.html`
Enter e-mail to receive coupon	Visit to `email_received.html`

framework drives the Funnel Visualization report in Google Analytics. In preparing your funnel, we strongly recommend that you go through the conversion process and take screen shots at each specific step (including the browser's address bar to refer to the URLs). You can use these screen shots later to explain the process to colleagues and discuss potential improvements in a group setting. Table 8.1 provides more examples of action-based conversion funnels best suited for Google Analytics.

Chapter 5 provides instructions on how to configure Google Analytics to display each step in the conversion funnel. Figure 8.7 shows an example of this report for the booking form at Zenith Vineyard. You can see from the report that 25 percent of the visitors who arrive at the booking form actually complete it. Raising this percentage would be a good goal for optimization, because it would have a direct positive impact on both Conversion Rate and Total Goal Value. The report also shows where visitors go after viewing the form, which can provide clues for understanding where they might be having trouble.

To construct a conversion funnel that will make sense for your business, you can often deepen your understanding by looking at all the steps necessary after a Conversion Goal to generate revenue, as mentioned earlier. For example, before a wedding happens at the vineyard, an event planner offers visitors options for enhancing their experience. Looking at the Conversion Rate and value generated from this portion in the funnel may suggest that it makes more sense to begin optimizing here.

The takeaway is that it's important that you never lose site of the end goal (in this case, profit) when you're trying to decide which part of the funnel deserves the most attention.

Now that you have a conceptual understanding of Conversion Goals and conversion funnels in Google Analytics, see if you can answer these questions about your site:

- What are the principal steps in the conversion funnel that correspond to specific pageviews on the site?

FIGURE 8.7

The Funnel Visualization report for Zenith Vineyard

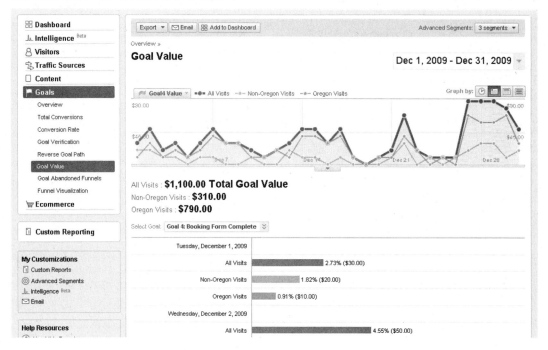

- What's the overall Conversion Rate of visitors who enter the conversion funnel?
- Are there any steps in the conversion funnel where you lose a surprising amount of visitors?
- How do different conversion funnels on the site compare in terms of the percentage of visitors converted?

With these questions answered, you should begin to regularly check on the overall business value generated by the site, as well as the value for individual segments of traffic. This will provide the foundation needed to evaluate whether new inbound marketing efforts are having a positive impact, or whether your overall optimization effort is leading toward a positive trend in your bottom-line objectives.

Understanding visitor intent

Moving away from Conversion Goals toward the next focus area, it's time to put your own business goals aside and try to understand what it is your *visitors* want to accomplish. On the Web, users rule. Here are three methods you can use to learn more about why visitors come to your site and what they expect to find. You'll use this information later to identify any disconnects between what the visitor expects and what the site has to offer.

Method 1: Inbound traffic analysis

One of the quickest ways to understand why visitors come to your site is to look at the inbound traffic using the Traffic Sources reports. You will find clues about what people are doing before they arrive at the site, what context they are in when they first encounter what you offer, and why they click through to visit the site.

You can also learn about visitor intent by analyzing keywords from the search engines visitors use to find the site. Look at the Keywords report in the Traffic Sources section. (We cover the Keywords report in more detail later.)

We describe the basic terminology used to describe inbound traffic in Chapter 5. In this chapter, we focus on analyzing traffic from the *referral* medium and save the other mediums for subsequent chapters. At the most basic level, referral traffic includes visitors who arrive at the site from another Web page by clicking a link. This link could be a mention of your business in a blog, in a directory, or anywhere accessible through the browser (excluding search engines). You can identify which sites are sending traffic by visiting the Referring Sites report found in the Traffic Sources section of Google Analytics.

FIGURE 8.8

The Referring Sites report for Zenith Vineyard

Figure 8.8 shows the Referring Sites report for Zenith Vineyard. The Data Table lists all the domains sending referral traffic to the site, as well as the Bounce Rate, % New Visitors, and other metrics. Clicking the Goal Set 1 tab shows how many bookings were generated by each of the referral sources.

By selecting one of the domains in the Data Table, you can see the *referral paths* on that domain that were responsible for sending visitors to the Zenith Vineyard site. For example, if a user clicks a link at www.mysite.com/mylinks.html, the domain is listed in the referring sites report as mysite. com and the referral path shown when you click that domain is /mylinks.com. Notice the small arrow icon to the left of each referral path. Clicking this icon shows you the actual page responsible for sending traffic (where available).

You can drill down still further by clicking on one of the referral paths in the Data Table to take you to the detail report for that referral path, as shown in Figure 8.9; specifically weddingwire.com/ biz/zenith-vineyard. Clicking the link icon shows that Zenith's site has been indexed and placed into the listings at WeddingWired.com, a site that helps brides find locations and resources for their weddings. Visitors from this referral source are evaluating Zenith Vineyard as a potential wedding

FIGURE 8.9

The Referring Site Detail report for a referral path in WeddingWire.com

location. Getting back to the goal of understanding visitor intent, this has provided some useful context around this portion of Zenith's traffic.

Take a look at the Referring Sites report for your site, and visit as many of the major referral sources as you can, paying special attention to the following:

- How is your site being positioned to incoming visitors?
- What do visitors appear to be looking for before they arrive at the site?
- Are there any clues you can use to identify how far along they are in the buying process?
- What information about your business have they been exposed to during their search?
- What aspects of your brand are being stressed and which are being downplayed?
- Which other sites tend to be classified alongside your site? How does your Web site compare to theirs?

As you start to uncover more about the referral sources, be on the lookout for any disconnects that exist between how your site is being positioned to incoming visitors and how your site greets visitors as they arrive on the site. We call the process of optimizing the first page users see on a site *landing page optimization*.

Method 2: Internal site search analysis

If you have a search engine on your site, whether from Google (such as Google Site Search) or one of the other tools out there, you can use Google Analytics to track and analyze what the visitors type into the search box. (The steps for configuring internal site search are covered in Chapter 5.)

You'll need to wait until Google Analytics has populated your Site Search reports with data before you can open them under the Content section in the navigation menu. Note that these reports appear only in the profiles for which you have configured Site Search.

Figure 8.10 shows the Site Search Terms report for the Google Store. It shows the search terms that visitors typed into the site's search engine, how often they were entered, how often they led to additional searches (search refinements), how often they led to a conversion, and so on.

In Figure 8.10, it's immediately clear that a large number of visitors are searching for the term "blogger" in the store, but a huge percentage leave immediately after just one search. After applying the Secondary Dimension of Source, it's clear that most of these visitors are arriving via a link that says "gear" in the footer of Blogger.com. This explains why the volume of queries is so high, but the store is still doing a poor job converting these gear seekers into revenue. This is a good example of one place the Google Store could optimize some of its offerings.

Take a look at your reports and try to answer the following questions. Be sure to use the skills we teach in Chapters 6 and 7 to apply Secondary Dimensions such as Source and Medium, apply different Table Views, sorts, and filters. If you're curious about the results for a particular query, type it into your site and see what turns up.

- What do people seem to be searching for most on your site?
- How often are people searching for things your site doesn't offer?

FIGURE 8.10

The Site Search Terms report for the Google Store.

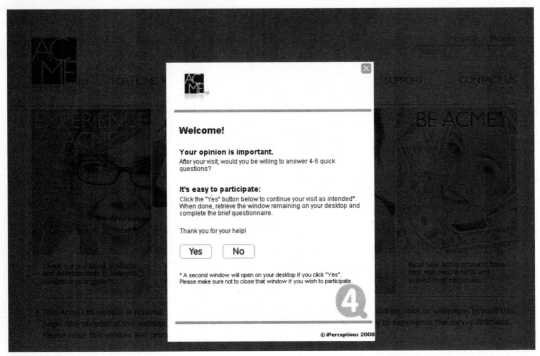

- How often are people searching for things offered that are underrepresented or hard to find on your site?
- Is there any nonobvious content on the site that visitors are not searching for at all? Are you sure your site needs that content?
- Are visitors using synonyms for terms described differently on the site? Could this be causing confusion? Think also about adding these keywords to your AdWords campaign.
- Where do people appear to be experiencing unsatisfactory results (a high percentage of search exit, or a high percentage of search refinement and low goal completion)?

If you click a search term, you can also open the Search Term Detail report for that term. You can then use the Analyze pop-up menu above the scorecard to see how users refined their search after typing in that term, which can give an even better sense of what users are searching for. All this should give you a better sense of why users are coming to your site and how well the site is satisfying them. The availability of this data is a great reason to add a search engine if your site doesn't have one. Both Google and Yahoo offer great options free of charge.

Also consider adding a Category pop-up menu to your site's search engine, which allows you to group keywords together into meaningful categories for analysis. For example, Amazon.com allows visitors to designate a category such as "Books" when searching. This can help give your visitors better search results — and give you more powerful data to analyze.

Method 3: Interrupts and exit surveys

Employees at the drugstore chain Walgreens are trained to ask customers at checkout whether they were able to find everything they were looking for in the store. This gives managers a useful means to identify any disconnects between what visitors want and what they're able to find in the store.

You can accomplish the same kind of analysis on your Web site by implementing a third-party tool that surveys a portion of your users to answer a few specific questions about their visit as they leave the site (or by building one with the help of a developer). For example, iPerceptions offers a simple tool called 4Q (www.4qsurvey.com). 4Q gives users a four-question survey designed to help you understand the following:

- What are visitors trying to accomplish on my site?
- Are they completing what they set out to do?
- If not, why not?
- How satisfied are my visitors?

Figure 8.11 shows what the survey questionnaire looks like.

FIGURE 8.11

The 4Q Exit Survey questionnaire

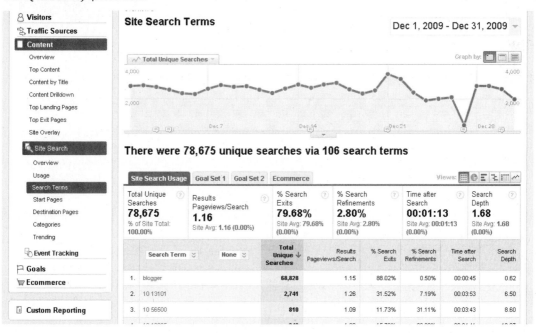

After you've deployed 4Q, it collects responses and makes them available via an online interface. This data can be a great source of insight about visitor intent. You may decide that these surveys are too annoying to visitors, but remember: If you have enough traffic, you can get away with showing the survey to only a portion of your visitors. You can also deploy the survey for a limited time and retire it for a while after you have enough responses to digest. If you don't like 4Q's implementation, ForeSee Results (www.foreseeresults.com) offers another popular option. Or work with your developers to create your own.

Identifying basic usability problems

Once you've gathered enough data on why visitors are arriving on the site, the next step is to begin identifying how you can help them achieve their goals with the minimum amount of mental energy. This branch of research is generally called *usability testing* or *user experience research*.

Because of the incredible amount of choice and information on the Web, visitors are unbelievably stingy with their attention. From the moment a visitor arrives at a site, the frustration meter starts ticking. If it gets high enough, the potential customer is out the door in seconds.

Now that you know what it is the visitors are trying to do, you can start looking at how easy or hard it is for them to do it. This is a crucial dimension in evaluating your Web site's performance.

Note that Google Analytics can sometimes offer clues. For example, search queries that include a large amount of refinement and a low goal-completion rate can often indicate problems. So can visits to error pages, a high Refresh Rate (Pageviews divided by Unique Pageviews), and unexpectedly high Bounce Rates or Exit Rates. Nonetheless, as outlined in Chapter 2, to really understand why visitors behave as they do, you need to move beyond the analytics data and into the realm of voice-of-the-customer research. For a deeper understanding, go to Appendix A for some suggested additional reading.

Giving users a way to complain

For usability assessment, there's no substitute for actual feedback from visitors. Exit surveys are one method for gathering customer data that you can use to improve a site. Another, less intrusive method is to provide users with a persistent link they can use to report problems.

Two companies, Kampyle (www.kampyle.com) and OpinionLab (www.opinionlab.com), offer excellent tools for collecting and analyzing voice-of-the-customer data on your site. Kampyle's tool, shown on the left side of Figure 8.12, combines a colorful prompt on the corner or edge of the page with predefined categories that make it easy to process feedback.

Kampyle also allows you to combine the feedback reported through the tool directly to your Google Analytics data using a prebuilt integration, which allows you to connect qualitative feedback with key segments in the Web traffic with minimal development. For example, Twiddy & Co., one of our success stories from Chapter 3, used an integration between Google Analytics and Kampyle to identify a frustrating disconnect between a print ad promoting a discount and an out-of-date product page.

OpinionLab uses a somewhat subtler prompt in your Web site's footer, shown in bottom-right corner of Figure 8.12.

FIGURE 8.12

Left: Kampyle's feedback prompt. Right: OpinionLab's feedback prompt the + symbol at the lower right).

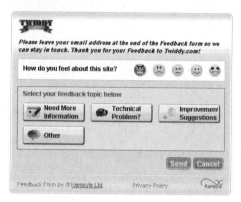

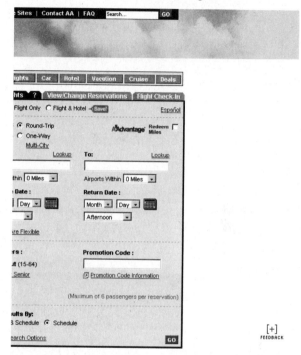

Both Kampyle and OpinionLab automatically generate reports that can help you understand key points of feedback and segment feedback along several dimensions. You can use these reports to gather site-wide feedback and to gather data on specific pages on the site.

You can also gather feedback on your site in more traditional ways such as e-mail surveys and telephone surveys of existing customers, in-person conversations, and regularly talking to your sales people. Even easier, you can add a Give Us Feedback e-mail link to a point of focus on the site and begin collecting data right away. The advantage of this method is that you can respond to users and make them feel heard.

No matter how you go about it, the important thing is that you give customers an easy outlet to voice their concerns and then respond to their critiques. From an optimization standpoint, if users identify a functional error or point of confusion on the site, they're doing you an immense favor, so make it effortless for them.

Running task completion tests

A second, extremely powerful option is to run some simple usability tests on the site either on your own or with the help of an expert. This test involves recruiting a small number of target audience members to perform the tasks you've identified as being important for visitors. By monitoring their session and asking them to think out loud as they perform each task, you can often identify major points of confusion with the site. You can also include quantitative measures such as time to completion to benchmark your improvement efforts. From an optimization standpoint, correcting problems identified during these tests is often the single most effective way to boost Conversion Rates.

If you're interested in conducting some simple tests, we provide recommended reading in the Appendix A to help you get started. An easy way to conduct simple tests is by using a third-party service. UserTesting.com is one of the best-known services and has put together a distributed panel of testers who can quickly provide feedback. As always, as you uncover issues, be sure to focus on elements that are likely to impact your goal performance *and* help visitors.

Applying heuristic analysis and best practices

Last, if you have budget available for a usability assessment, you can benefit from a growing body of best practices and research by hiring an expert. Professionals in this area are generally called *user experience researchers, usability researchers, usability experts,* or something along those lines. They have been trained to look for common issues based on foundational principles in human-computer interaction and information architecture, as well as their own experience. Some examples include diagnosing many of the following pitfalls:

- **Too much clutter:** On the Web, less is often more. Conversion Rates can often be improved by simplifying long text blocks with bullets, eliminating distracting links and images, adding white space, and boiling down arguments to the bare essentials.
- **Browser compatibility problems:** Try loading your page in multiple browsers. You may uncover glaring errors that could be costing conversions. You'd be surprised how often designers overlook this simple step.
- **Unclear call to action:** Visitors should always have a clear sense of what they should do next, whether it is to sign up for a newsletter or download a white paper. If the pages lack a strong call to action repeated multiple times, the site may be losing potential conversions. Experimenting with the text around a call to action, button design and color, references to timeliness, reassurances, and so on can be a powerful way to impact Conversion Rates.
- **Industry jargon:** Sometimes marketers assume visitors understand certain terminology that they may not.
- **Confusing navigation:** If the site uses an unconventional layout, lacks a search engine, uses fanciful instead of descriptive text for menu items, or lacks a clear structure, consider these potential problem areas where you should begin optimizing.
- **Slow load time:** If your site includes lots of heavy imagery or you are using a slow hosting service, you're likely losing potential conversions on every pageview. This slowness is often one of the easiest and most straightforward problems to correct.
- **Functional errors:** Your Web developer or hosting platform can sometimes provide server logs indicating when errors were triggered on the site. If you're not logging errors, start doing so.

- **Overly long forms:** On the Web, you should collect only the information that's needed. Visitors are turned off by requests for unnecessary information and by forms that don't provide clear progress indicators. Simplifying the checkout process can be a great area to start testing.

Our advice in selecting the right professional is to find someone with strong references and who can point to specific insights they have given customers and specific sites they've helped optimize. Once you've found that person, it's extremely important to hold him or her accountable from Day 1!

You now know how to analyze how many visitors are converting and the value you're generating from those conversions. Make these goals clear and evaluate the impact of recommended changes on those goals.

Examining your value proposition

If you can make serious improvements in the usability of the site, you can often move leaps and bounds ahead of your competition. However, even after you've made the site more usable, you still need to make a separate effort to ensure that you're communicating the benefits of your product or service well, and that those benefits hold real value for visitors.

In the offline world, if you are a restaurant owner, improving usability might mean making it easier to book reservations, to park, to understand the menu, and to find the restroom. Creating a strong *value proposition,* on the other hand, involves bringing together those benefits patrons look for in a restaurant, such as convenience, delicious food, prompt service, appropriate pricing, and a good ambiance. It also involves communicating those benefits in language that visitors understand.

In evaluating the strength of your site's value proposition, you need to be sure to compare what you're offering to what competitors offer. Visitors rarely visit just one site and then make a purchase there. To gain insight into how your site can be improved, you need to examine it from the perspective of someone browsing multiple sites in your category. Here are a few ways to get started.

Evaluate your site against competitors

You can begin your evaluation in Google Analytics, which provides a useful feature called Benchmarking that is designed to help place your site's performance in competitive context. Google Analytics aggregates and organizes data across thousands of accounts that have opted into data sharing, offering you the ability to see how specific metrics for your site compare to category averages.

You can find the Benchmarking report in the Visitors section of the navigation menu. Figure 8.13 shows the Benchmarking report for Zenith Vineyard.

Looking at the Visits module, it's clear that the surge in visits Zenith saw on December 27 was part of an industry-wide traffic pattern. It looks like visitors stayed away during the holiday but came back in full force shortly thereafter. This provides useful context around a jump in conversions that otherwise might have been difficult to explain. The other modules in the report also offer a good starting place for comparing your Bounce Rate and Time on Site with those of competitors. You can use these measures to help set your targets for improvement. To view the appropriate metrics for your site, be sure to click the Open Category List link at the top of the report to select the category that best matches your site.

FIGURE 8.13

The Benchmarking report for Zenith Vineyard

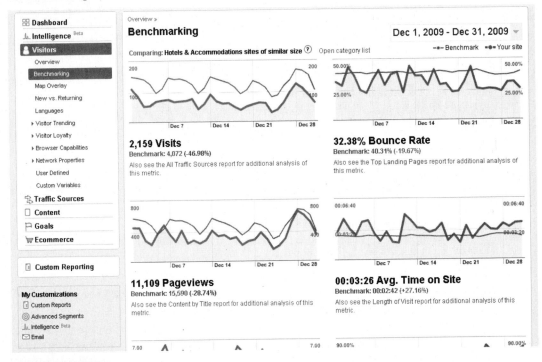

Next, set aside a couple of hours and visit your online competitors and do some basic comparisons. You can identify online competitors by surveying your existing customers, by browsing the top results in your product category on Google, by looking through industry sources, or by relying on your own knowledge of the market. Here are some useful questions to think about as you look through competing sites:

- Do they have a tagline or positioning statement?
- What are the three most important benefits or features they present about their offering?
- How strong is the evidence supporting their claims?
- Do they say anything explicitly about your brand on their site?
- How does their pricing structure compare to your site?
- How does their site organization compare to your site?
- Where do they choose to offer the most in-depth information?
- What are their main conversion actions? Do these match your site?
- What do their conversion processes look like?

Once you have some basic ideas about each area, a good next step is to locate potential buyers and see what they think. Ask target audience members to spend three to five minutes on each site as if they were considering a purchase, record their browsing activity, and see what they can recall about their experiences. You should get a sense for which aspects of the site's value proposition (benefits offered) are coming across strongly and which are being ignored, and where the site's strengths and weaknesses lie with respect to competitors.

The social Web is another great resource for competitive analysis. Online buyers often ask for help and advice before making a purchase and will discuss their experiences after they've converted. If you have ever visited TripAdvisor or Yelp, you have read this kind of commentary. Take a look at some of the following social media search engines and see if you can uncover any conversations about your brand or competing brands. These tools regularly index user-generated content to make it available to searchers in near real time.

- BlogPulse (`www.blogpulse.com`)
- HowSociable (`www.howsociable.com`)
- Google Alerts (`www.google.com/alerts`)
- Technorati (`www.technorati.com`)
- Twitter Search (`search.twitter.com`)

If you're not able to turn up anything, you can also browse your referring sources to uncover niche community sites or directories that include reviews or comments from customers about your brand. In the case of Zenith Vineyard, MyPortlandWedding.com includes several reviews from past brides as well as chatter about the wedding venues in the Portland area. As long as you disclose who you are, you can even join the conversation and ask for feedback directly.

For a more quantitative picture of your site's popularity, stickiness, and even demographics, the Web also boasts several third-party rating services. These services mine ISP or customer panel data to track visitor activity across the Web. Some of the most popular options are Nielsen NetRatings, Hitwise, ComScore, Compete.com, and Quantcast.

Using Compete.com's free service, for example, you can see what search terms and referral sites visitors used to reach your competitors Web sites as well as your site. You can see how the site's popularity is trending versus competitors and which competitive site is attracting the most attention. Take a look at some of these services and see what you can uncover. On the other hand, note that the data provided is never perfect, and so it should be used more as a general guide rather than as a central measure of performance.

Combine experimentation with best practices to find what works

One of the most direct ways to enhance your site's persuasive power is to use the flexibility of a Web site testing tool such as Google Website Optimizer to try out ideas on actual visitors. By testing multiple variations of key site elements, you can gradually learn which element has the most persuasive effect on the visitors. The beauty of this method is that you don't need to invest too much time understanding why a particular variation works to know that it's the best.

FIGURE 8.14

The LIFT model for evaluating power of persuasion

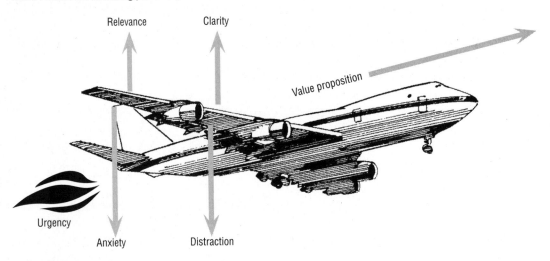

FIGURE 8.15

An example LIFT analysis report of a BabyAge.com product page

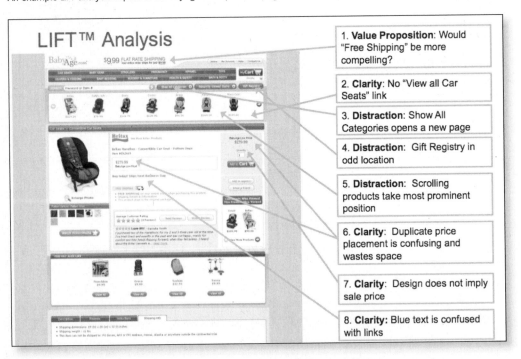

As with usability analysis, professionals employing this method have developed lots of different heuristics to evaluate what to test. For example, Wider Funnel, a Vancouver marketing agency specializing in Web site optimization and testing, has developed the LIFT model (shown in Figure 8.14) to evaluate the persuasive power of a site and identify elements to test.

Wider Funnel has applied LIFT to develop hypotheses for a variety of clients including BabyAge. com. Figure 8.15 shows a LIFT analysis of one of its product pages.

After applying the analysis to the BabyAge.com site and running a series of A/B tests, Wider Funnel was able to raise the percentage of visitors converted to sales by 22 percent.

No matter who you talk to in the testing industry, you'll find dozens of examples of companies that have made incredible gains on their sites from heuristic analysis and controlled testing, ranging from Netflix to the Obama presidential campaign. Methodologies vary widely, so if you're considering expert help, we suggest looking at firms among those listed in the Google Website Optimizer authorized consultant program. We provide additional resources in Appendix A for an in-depth picture of heuristic analysis.

Go deeper into the hearts and minds of customers

Our final recommendation for evaluating the strength of your value proposition and offering is to look at the traditional methods developed by market researchers over the past several decades. These include ethnographic research, lab studies, in-depth surveys, and even brain scans. You'll need a budget or a great deal of time if you head down one of these roads, but the research can yield a depth of understanding that's difficult to gain on the Web alone. Whatever you discover, be sure to use a testing tool to put your insights into practice.

Optimizing through Continuous Improvement

You've done it! You now have over a dozen methods at your disposal to identify ways to improve your site and measure progress. On the other hand, in many ways your work is just getting started. Customer insight will help you execute better on your vision and strengthen your marketing system, but you still need to execute. What follows are a few last words on how to keep moving in the right direction as you set out down the road of continuously improving your site along the dimensions we've outlined.

Zeroing in on high-impact pages and elements

By now you have identified what it is visitors are trying to accomplish on your site, where they're having functional difficulties, and some of the reasons they may not be enticed by what you're offering. To get the most bang for your buck, it's important for you go through the process of prioritizing what to improve so you can attack the biggest problems first. Here are tips for how to use Google Analytics to help you:

- **Target your templates.** If your site loads content dynamically into one or more templates, you may be able to get a substantial gain from improving the design of common elements in your template rather than improving an individual Web page. For example, the template that drives your product pages might be a good option to test.

- **Identify your top landing pages, and the pages with the high Bounce Rates.** Google Analytics includes a report called Top Entrances (it's in the Content section). Note the pages that serve as the most common entry points to your site. Were the pages designed to receive new visitors? If not, you could include these pages in the consideration set. Also take a look at the pages that have a high number of Visitors and a high Bounce Rate, since these may also indicate room for improvement.

- **Identify popular conversion paths using the Reverse Goal Path report.** Available under Goals in the navigation menu, the Reverse Goal Path report shows the sequence of pages navigated by visitors before completing the conversion action. These pages are common waypoints used by visitors who eventually convert. Many of these pages should overlap with what you defined in your conversion funnel, but you may find some surprises as well.

- **Identify high-traffic pages.** This one may seem obvious, but it's nonetheless a good idea to open the Top Content report in the Content section to find the pages that are viewed the most. You should also pay attention to these pages.

- **Focus on optimizing traffic for select traffic sources.** As you look through the reports listed in the Traffic Sources section, you can identify the traffic sources sending you the most visitors and work on optimizing the user flow specifically for these visitors by creating tailored landing pages and other personalized elements.

- **Target high-drop-off points in your conversion funnel.** Use the Funnel Visualization report to find the pages with the highest rate of abandonment and work to improve them.

- **Find pages with a high Refresh Rate:** We call the ratio of Pageviews to Unique Pageviews for a given page the *Refresh Rate*. A page in the top content report with a high Refresh Rate can indicate that people are looking for something on this page they can't find, or that the page is an important gateway between two other pages. These can sometimes be good pages to improve.

10 tips for continuous improvement

Here are 10 tips to help you make optimal use of your analytics data as you execute on Web site changes with a Web site testing tool:

1. **Involve users early in the design process.** Put together a panel of users from your target audience and ask them to provide feedback on new designs before you get to the process of coding and deploying the design. You may be able to eliminate subpar changes early, save time, and get fresh new perspectives.

2. **Educate designers on your goals.** When you're discussing improvements with your design team, use the sharing functionality in Google Analytics or walk through the analytics reports

with them to show how the site is performing. Ensure that everyone understands the main tasks that visitors are trying to accomplish and what the Conversion Goals are for the site.

3. **Hold your team accountable.** Set quantitative goals for improvement and then hold team members accountable. You can publish Google Analytics reports regularly and share results in team meetings to ensure everyone is on the same page. Don't let your team wriggle out from under these targets with polish and sizzle. Be confident in your data.

4. **Iterate before a complete redesign.** It's often tempting to upend your entire site and redesign from scratch, but this can be risky. You might improve in some areas but degrade performance in others. You will also learn less about how specific elements on the site are contributing to overall performance. If the redesign is a flop, you're often left with nothing. Before you undertake a complete redesign, consider trying some basic iterations instead.

5. **Don't sweat aesthetics too much.** Your Web site is a system for moving visitors toward a desired outcome — not a piece of art! Avoid investing too much time in minor aesthetic points and focus the energy in making your site clear, quick-loading, and straightforward. Use testing to settle the details.

6. **Keep a change log.** Use the annotations feature in Google Analytics to track changes to your site, or use a simple spreadsheet. It is of the utmost importance that you log the exact dates you make changes so that you can understand their impact later.

7. **Look hard at competitors.** Competitive and market analysis can be a great way to uncover new ideas to improve the site. If you see a workflow or site element your competitors do well, don't be afraid to replicate it or learn from it. Just don't get carried away and don't break any laws!

8. **Strive for simplicity.** Complexity is a liability on the Web. Simplify your site wherever you can.

9. **Move fast.** You want to create new variations and get them out as quickly as you can. Strive for a quick turnaround cycle (four weeks, for example) to deploy changes in a testing tool and evaluate results. At the same time, be cautious about assuming too much over a short period (such as a few days).

10. **Segment, segment, segment.** Work hard to break down your visitors and the site into manageable chunks rather then trying to tackle everything at once. Lots of incremental improvements often add up to more than one major change.

—

Search Engine Marketing (SEM)

There are two ways to increase your organization's visibility in search engines. You can use search engine optimization (SEO) to raise your ranking in organic (unpaid) results, or you can bid against other advertisers to secure paid (sponsored) listings on keywords relevant to your product or service. This chapter explores the latter method, showing you how you can use Google Analytics to track and optimize your search advertising campaigns on Google AdWords, Microsoft AdCenter (for Bing), Yahoo Search Marketing, and other sponsored search providers.

Search Engine Marketing Basics

The Web has given consumers access to an amazing breadth and depth of information online, provided they can find what they're looking for. Each time users enter a keyword into a search box, they offer a clue to their intent. Taken together, these billions of search queries have created a tremendous opportunity for advertisers, who can finally target their message based on people's stated intentions instead of the demographics or other poor predictors of purchasing behavior they've been forced to use for decades. Even better, each time a searcher clicks one of these ads and makes a purchase, advertisers can track the result, making search engine marketing (SEM) the most measurable and targeted form of advertising ever devised.

It's no surprise then that SEM has grown into a $12 billion industry in the U.S. in a little over a decade, making a fortune for Google and rocketing businesses like Zappos to international prominence. With little competition, companies that jumped on the SEM bandwagon early were able to attract traffic at rock-bottom prices, leaving others in the dust.

Today, online competition has heated up dramatically, driving the cost of acquiring clicks and customers ever higher. There are still great returns out there, particularly if you've found a strong niche. But to get the most from your SEM campaign, you need to be smart about which keywords you bid on, how much you pay, what text is used in ads, what hours of the day, days of the week, and times of year ads are allowed to run, and where ads are shown geographically. You need to do all this in addition to building a strong value proposition and a fiercely persuasive Web site using all the avenues we explored in Chapter 8.

SEM works on an auction-plus-quality model. Advertisers that deliver the most relevant ads at the highest price win. While the bid price is straightforward — the higher bid wins — the aspect of "most relevant" is what makes up quality. Quality is determined by an algorithm that evaluates several factors, including click-through rate, relevance of ad copy, and landing page contents to the keywords for which ads are being run.

In case you're not familiar with how the search auction works, here's a quick summary. (SEM veterans can skip this and move ahead to the next section.) For this summary, we use Google's AdWords platform. Other search engines offering sponsored listings operate in a similar fashion, although AdWords is undoubtedly the most advanced when it comes to factors such as quality score and relevancy matching.

NOTE

For the purposes of this chapter, we use the term *search engine marketing* to mean the same thing as *paid search engine advertising, pay-per-click (PPC)*, and *cost-per-click (CPC) search marketing*. The term SEM is sometimes used to describe the process of increasing visibility in organic listings, which we refer to as *search engine optimization (SEO)*.

Figure 9.1 shows Google results for the keyword "search engine marketing." Notice the Sponsored Links area at the top and to the right of unpaid (*organic*) listings. These sponsored listings include a title, ad text, and a destination URL, displayed only for search queries that advertisers bid on using Google's advertising platform, Google AdWords.

Each time a user clicks a sponsored listing, the advertiser receiving the click pays Google. The amount the advertiser pays for the click depends on how much other advertisers are willing to pay for the same keyword and the quality score of the ad, as determined by the AdWords platform. More competition for a keyword results in more competitive bidding, higher bid prices, and ultimately higher costs for that keyword.

The rank or order in which the ads are listed has a powerful effect on how many clicks each advertiser gets. Rank order in the auction depends on two key factors: bid price and quality score.

First, the bid price offered by advertisers for a given keyword allows an ad matched to that keyword to be considered for higher placement, all other things being equal.

Second, quality score is calculated based on two primary factors: 1) search ads that capture more clicks and engagement from users are considered more relevant by Google and given higher placement, all other things being equal, and 2) the landing page quality (the "landing page" is the destination URL for the ad; that is, the page you reach when you click the ad). Landing page quality is evaluated algorithmically and, in some cases, by people to determine whether the keyword and ad pointing to that

FIGURE 9.1

Google search results for the keyword "search engine marketing." Sponsored links are shown above and to the right of unpaid (organic) listings.

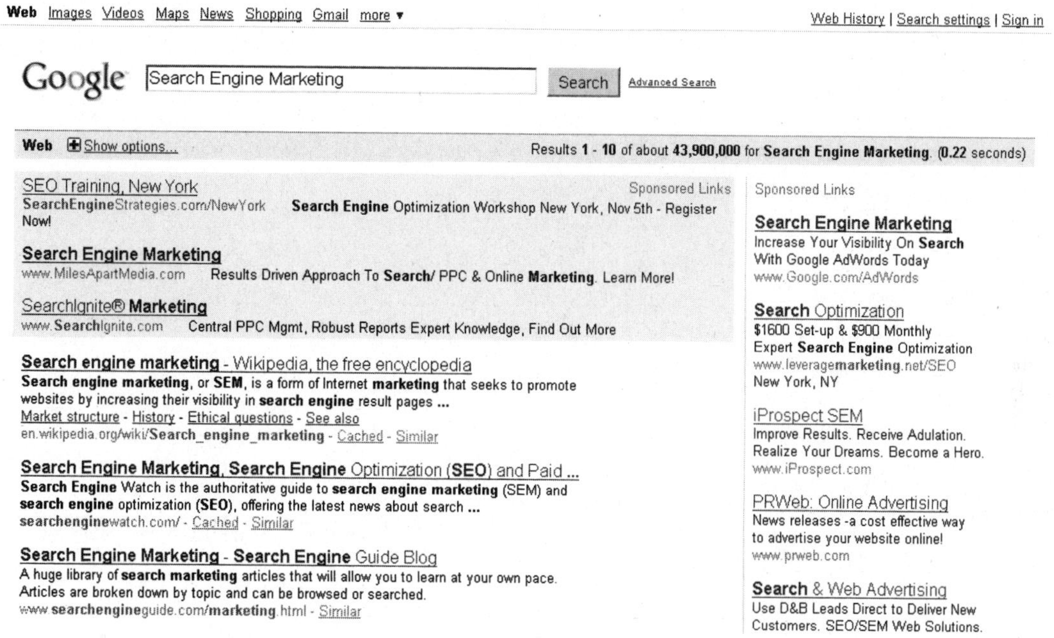

page are well matched to the contents of the page. Greater relevancy increases the ad score, while less relevance reduces the score.

If your ad is about vineyard weddings and your keyword is "vineyard weddings" but the page is about a hotel, not a vineyard, it won't be considered very relevant. Quality scores ensure that searchers are not exposed to ads that would more likely be perceived as irrelevant and thus unwanted. Keeping quality and relevance of the search experience high is what keeps searchers happy, and happy searchers keep the search engines in business.

The key to winning this auction is to streamline your bidding process, ad text, and Web site to allow you to generate more value from your advertising than competitors, which will lead to a more profitable and competitive business. Winning with sponsored search is what the rest of this chapter is about!

Strengths and weaknesses of SEM as a marketing channel

There has never been an advertising medium as measurable and targeted as SEM. It is most powerful as a direct response medium where you are given incredible control over your exposure, where you can change your ads and budget whenever you like, and where you can tie converting visitors directly back to your advertising spend.

SEM can be used for branding as well when ads are prominently and consistently shown for a wide set of keywords. For example, if a shoe manufacturer is always listed at the top of results when searches for or related to shoes are conducted, it can support the brand by relating that company as a leader for shoes.

Table 9.1 summarizes some of the most important pros and cons of SEM as a marketing channel.

To understand SEM in the context of other marketing channels, think back to the concept of the conversion funnel explained in Chapter 8: Potential buyers must first become aware of your product, at which point they may review it more carefully, form a preference for it, and eventually make a purchase.

SEM is an ideal tool for encouraging users who are at all levels of that funnel because it provides immediate, measurable, controllable, and accountable exposure on search engine result pages — the

TABLE 9.1

Pros and Cons of Sponsored Search Engine Marketing (SEM)

Pros	Cons
Easily measurable. Google AdWords include its own conversion system called Conversion Tracking and can be configured to work directly with Google Analytics with little effort.	**Competitive.** If your competitors have deeper pockets or higher conversion rates, they can snap up the best inventory of clicks and placements to keep you locked out.
Controlled. You can control which keywords your ads show for, as well as where and when they show, at an incredible level of detail and control.	**Low emotional appeal**. It can be hard to engage with users on an emotional level with just a few lines of text. It is easier to do on your site, but it can be difficult to capture the attention of flighty surfers long enough to deliver a powerful emotional message.
Flexible. Change your ad text, bids, or exposure at a moment's notice.	**Branding.** If you are focused on building brand awareness, it can be expensive and impractical to pour money into semirelevant, general keywords where you will see little direct impact on immediate sales.
Wide reach: Billions upon billions of queries are conducted annually, allowing you to reach hundreds of millions of Internet users all across the world (provided they are searching for relevant content).	**Demanding.** Because SEM allows constant changes, it also requires constant monitoring. When you are not optimizing, your competitors are. Bid management tools make this easier, but the battle never ends.
Self-service. Unlike traditional media, you can access and manage your campaigns directly.	**Ongoing costs**. Building a strong presence in organic listings through SEO can pay dividends over the long haul, but as soon as you stop bidding on SEM, you stop getting traffic.
Low startup cost. Start experimenting with as little as $5 with no outside creative agency and see your ads appear the same day.	**Click fraud.** Fraudulent clicks — clicks that are made by someone or something (a computer program) who clicks on an ad solely to drive up costs for the advertiser or generate more revenue for the seller of the ad — have been a problem for SEM from the start. However, big advertising providers have invested heavily in detection and prevention of these clicks so that advertiser dollars are not wasted.

TABLE 9.2

Major Search Engines' Reach and SEM Tools

Search Engine	U.S. Market Share	SEM Platform
Google	72 percent	Google AdWords (`adwords.google.com`)
Yahoo	16 percent	Yahoo Search Marketing (`advertising.yahoo.com`)
Microsoft Bing	9 percent	Microsoft AdCenter (`adcenter.microsoft.com`)
Ask.com	3 percent	Ask Sponsored Listings (`sponsoredlistings.ask.com`)

intersection of consumer interest and intent. You can focus SEM efforts on different levels of the funnel through the types of keywords you run ads for: More general terms (such as "shoes") are usually searched by people earlier in the conversion funnel, while more specific, longer search phrases (such as "men's size 12 running shoe") are commonly used by someone later in the conversion funnel, ready to purchase. However, because SEM relies on a constant stream of budget to keep it going, you should be sure to conduct SEO efforts, as Chapter 11 explains, to increase exposure through organic listings in parallel with your SEM investments.

Major SEM platforms and tools

Table 9.2 shows the share (according to a late 2009 report from Hitwise) and SEM platforms for the four major U.S. search engines:

For the purposes of this chapter, you'll need at least basic familiarity with one of these platforms. If you're not currently using any of the platforms, we recommend opening a Google AdWords account and setting up a starter campaign. Without an active SEM account with at least one of the search engines, you won't be able to take advantage of the techniques we show you for optimizing your SEM using Google Analytics. Also note that many of the topics explored in this chapter are specific to Google AdWords because it is more closely integrated with Google Analytics than other platforms.

Planning for Success with SEM

Planning a successful SEM campaign is critical to achieving the best performance and value for your advertising spend. In short, good planning leads to good performance. Analysis and optimization are critical, but without a good plan, analysis only tells you things are going badly. In this section, we cover principles for creating a campaign plan that yields better results from the start and leads to more actionable and fruitful analysis and optimization.

The best plans are made using great tools. While there are countless toolsets from companies like SEOmoz.org, Bruce Clay, and Wordtracker, there are excellent free tools that are often overlooked or underused. These tools, when fully used, provide innumerable insights for planning a successful campaign as well as optimizing an existing one.

Conducting keyword research

SEM is all about keywords. Thus, when planning, begin with keywords. This process should start with brainstorming the terms that you think are relevant for your business. Google provides a number of excellent tools. (We recognize we may be a bit biased toward Google, but this book focuses on Google Analytics after all! And, in fact, these tools are some of the best available, especially given that they are free.)

Google Insights for Search

The Google Insights for Search tool (`www.analyticsformarketers.com/s/insights`) is a keyword and topical analysis and comparison tool. It provides data going back to 2004 as well as forecasts for the next year based on statistical models. As illustrated in Figure 9.2, Google Insights provides comparisons of up to five keywords at a time plus industry benchmarks, news mentions, geographic interest, related terms, and rising related searches. Use Google Insights as a tool for validating whether a keyword or topic is a good fit for your business and for understanding a more complete picture of what's going on in the world in relation to the keywords you are considering.

Also, note that there is a difference between the Google Insights tool and Google Trends, another tool for evaluating the trending of interest in particular keywords over time: Google Trends does not provide the news, geographical, and industry-related data that Google Insights provides.

Google AdWords Keyword tool

The AdWords Keyword tool has been improved over the last several years and now provides an incredibly powerful means of generating keyword ideas. You can easily build campaigns based on the keywords you find with this tool. The tool is straightforward: Either enter keyword ideas to get data about those terms and, optionally, have the tool return related terms, or enter the URL of a page (such as your Web site's home page) or a block of text, and get recommendations of keywords people would use to try and find that content.

There is one specific and often overlooked use for this tool: the ability to get search traffic estimates for a specific list of keywords. This option is found under the Filter My Results link when using the Keywords Analysis option (not the URL/Text option). When you select Don't Show Ideas for New Keywords, the results contain only data for the list of keywords you entered. The best approach is to begin with the keywords from your brainstorming. Enter these words and you'll get lots of ideas back. Use the Add button to collect the keywords that stand out as relevant to your campaign. Once you've reviewed and added relevant terms, download the selected keywords in Excel format. Figure 9.3 shows a sample search for keywords and the results returned by the Keyword tool.

NOTE

In addition to basic keywords and search volume data, the AdWords Keyword tool provides insight into seasonal search volume trends, the market bid prices for top positions, and the relative competition for each keyword. Keywords with high search volume, low competition, and low bid prices provide the perfect scenario of value, so bidding on keywords with these characteristics is valuable.

FIGURE 9.2

Google Insights for Search results comparing the keywords "Web analytics" and "Google analytics" over the past several years.

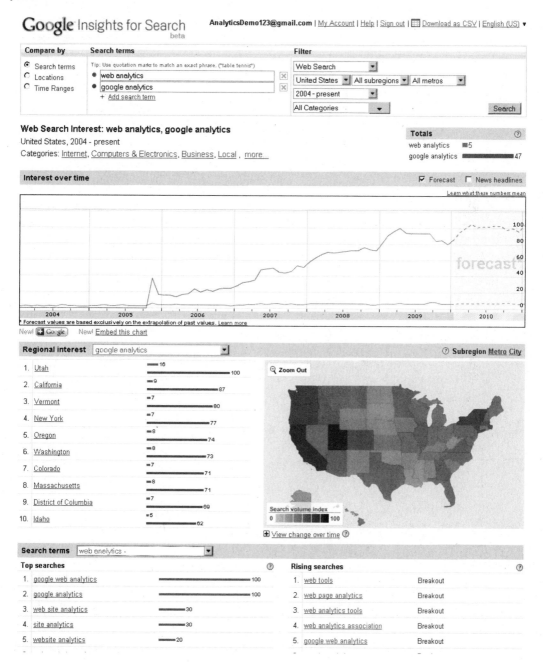

FIGURE 9.3

The Google AdWords Keyword tool allows you to research new keyword ideas and get search traffic estimates for specific keywords.

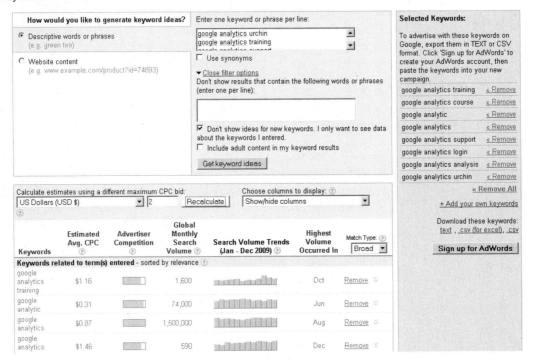

Once you've downloaded the Keyword tool's results, open the Excel spreadsheet, copy the list of selected keywords, and paste them back into the Keywords field in the Suggestion tool. Then, click the Filter My Options link and select the Don't Show Ideas for New Keywords checkbox. Click Get Keyword Ideas to get results that you can download, inclusive of search query volume, cost estimates, seasonality, and global versus local search volumes that are specific to just the keywords you entered.

You can find more information and tips for the Google Keyword tool at www.analyticsformarketers.com/s/keyword-suggestions.

Other tools

Google doesn't corner the market on good tools. There are several additional tools and providers. Some of our favorites for SEO and SEM are built by SEOmoz.org. Bruce Clay's SEO ToolSet is another fabulous resource. Additionally Microsoft AdCenter Labs provide great tools for keyword discovery and analysis. In addition, providers of competitive intelligence such as Compete.com and Quantcast offer tools for Web site traffic volume, related Web sites, and search keyword discovery and competitive intelligence. Visit www.analyticsformarketers.com/s/sem-tools for links and more resources for SEM tools.

Structuring campaigns for success

Before we get into more specific analysis techniques, there is an important overarching principle to master: structure. While it is easy to get started with SEM campaigns, optimizing performance and scaling campaigns to greater size while maintaining performance is actually a more complex task. The extreme competition inherent to the auction model of buying SEM media makes maintaining top exposure and performance a challenge, especially in competitive industries.

Structure is critically important for several reasons.

First, structure provides a means of budgetary control. AdWords and other SEM providers have the ability to set per-click and per-campaign daily or monthly cost limits and ensure that the budget is metered so that ads are seen throughout the day. However, throttling the spend for "head" keywords that may have huge search volume and thus potential click volume versus the "long tail" and typically lower-cost terms can't be done within a campaign. Thus, you can easily end up in a situation where a handful of keywords consume the majority of your budget, starving long-tail, low-cost, high-value keywords from seeing the light of day (see Chapter 11 for the details of long-tail keywords).

Second, well-structured campaigns afford a means of targeting. Targeting for geography, networks (the search engine's direct results, search partners, content network, and content partners), device targeting (within AdWords), demographic targeting, day-part targeting, and other options are all set at the campaign level. By creating campaigns that are focused on a specific geography, network, devices, demographics, and so on, you can vastly improve the performance of your overall investments in SEM.

FIGURE 9.4

An optimal campaign structure will control budget and targeting as well as afford more granular organization of ad groups and keywords.

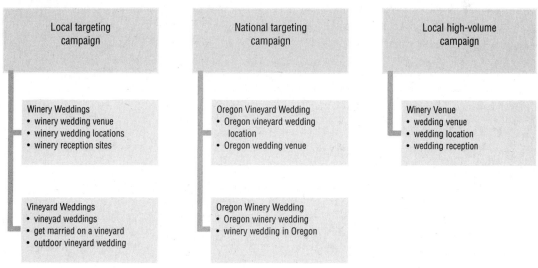

Local targeting campaign	National targeting campaign	Local high-volume campaign
Winery Weddings • winery wedding venue • winery wedding locations • winery reception sites	**Oregon Vineyard Wedding** • Oregon vineyard wedding location • Oregon wedding venue	**Winery Venue** • wedding venue • wedding location • wedding reception
Vineyard Weddings • vineyad weddings • get married on a vineyard • outdoor vineyard wedding	**Oregon Winery Wedding** • Oregon winery wedding • winery wedding in Oregon	

We'll get into more details about how to analyze performance by geography, device, seasonality, and so on later in this chapter.

Third, structured campaigns afford an opportunity to optimize the topics of your campaigns at a more granular level. Each campaign can include many ad groups; however, controlling, targeting, and budget for different topics is a prudent practice. By creating campaigns that focus on clusters of topics, you can more effectively control the investment into and results derived from a given topical area.

Under each campaign you should leverage ad groups to combine similar keywords and optimize the copy of ads. You will receive higher quality scores by structuring your ad groups and optimizing ad copy to keyword relationships at a more granular level because closer matching of ad copy to keywords in an ad group generally yields better click-through rates.

Figure 9.4 illustrates an optimized campaign structure using multiple campaigns, ad groups, and keywords. The local targeting campaign uses geographic targeting to limit reach to the local market area while the ad groups arrange keywords by topic. The national targeting campaign uses a nationwide geotargeting setting, limits display of ads to prime conversion points, and structures keywords underneath relevant ad groups. The local high-volume campaign focuses on the local market just like the local targeting campaign, except that it contains keywords that are more generic and thus higher in search volume, allowing budget control to ensure that the core, most specific "vineyard" and "wedding" keywords have the greatest amount of exposure.

Preparing to Measure SEM with Google Analytics

One of the great appeals of SEM is its inherent measurability. Because the advertising is purchased on a cost-per-click basis, the money spent is always tied to a measurement of results. However, all too many marketers stop after measuring impressions and clicks. As with display, e-mail, organic SEO, and other forms of marketing, the emphasis on "traffic" is great but the emphasis on *results* is typically much lower. This is due to a common yet incorrect assumption that more traffic equals more business, and also the fact that pay-per-click media creates a natural emphasis on the click and thus focuses on the number of clicks received. When the cost of traffic is so clearly visible and so easily controlled, a fixation on getting the most clicks for your money is understandable.

Although more traffic equaling more sales is likely to happen in a physical store, the Internet is different because it is so easy for all that traffic to leave with the click of the Back button or the keystrokes of a new search query. Thus, simply measuring the number of clicks isn't enough — you *must* measure *beyond the click*. This is where Web analytics tools come into the picture.

Understanding the role of Google Analytics

Google Analytics isn't a click measurement tool. You'll have to rely on your SEM platform to tell you how many *clicks* occur on your ads. Google Analytics records *visits* generated by SEM campaigns. Sometimes customers make multiple clicks on your SEM ads during the same visit. What Google

Analytics does record is everything *after the click*, as well as subsequent visits after that visitor came through SEM (as long as the visitor doesn't delete his or her cookies or enter the site through another marketing campaign). It is through this post-click measurement that engagement, value, and return on investment (ROI) are calculated.

There are two approaches to post-click measurement: point of conversion and complete interaction measurement.

Google AdWords and other SEM platform providers have their own systems for conversion-tracking measurements of when someone completes a specific action, usually completing an order or submitting a contact or lead capture form. The downfall with this kind of point-of-conversion SEM measurement, and indeed any online advertising, is that you see only part of the picture.

What happens between the click and the conversion? Knowing what keywords drive final conversions is better than simply measuring which keywords bring the cheapest traffic, but how many of those visits result in near conversions? Do they leave immediately after clicking, or do they view a few pages? Do they make it part of the way into the purchase or inquiry process? Where do people bail out of a purchase process? Did they fail to convert because they landed on a page that was not relevant for their search query? Did they perform a search on your Web site's internal search engine? From what page did they end up leaving the site?

These are all questions that can and should be answered, and questions that Google Analytics — when set up to track your SEM campaigns — helps you answer through complete interaction measurement.

NOTE

While Google Analytics (at the time of this writing) supports only cost-data importing for AdWords, the software counterpart to Google Analytics, Urchin Software from Google, *does* import both AdWords cost data and cost data from other SEM providers. Urchin can process cost information from other SEM providers against the same data collected by Google Analytics, and it can generate a similar set of ROI and SEM analysis reports that Google Analytics provides for AdWords. Find out more about Urchin via `www.analyticsformarketers.com/s/urchin`.

It is important to note that Google Analytics can track *any* SEM platform, not just Google's AdWords platform. Tracking SEM ads is done in the same fashion as tracking other types of marketing with Google Analytics: by setting up campaign tracking tags and supplying the values you want used for the Source, Medium, Campaign, Ad Content dimensions, and specific to SEM, Keyword. However, there are additional data points that include impressions, number of clicks, click-through rate, cost per click, and more available for Google AdWords traffic thanks to the advanced integration options between AdWords and Google Analytics.

Setting up tracking for AdWords

As you might expect, Google Analytics is designed to integrate closely with Google AdWords. There are two ways to track AdWords in Google Analytics: One, you can set up standard campaign tracking tags. Two, you can set up Auto-Tagging and Cost-Data Importing for AdWords. When the Auto-Tagging and Cost-Data Importing features are correctly activated, Google Analytics creates reports showing traffic from AdWords as "paid" search engine traffic and records the paid keyword bringing the traffic, plus the Campaign Name, Ad Group, Ad Position, and Ad Slot Position for each ad generating clicks. Additional data collected includes Impressions, Clicks, Cost per Click, and calculated metrics for ROI.

Setting up the full AdWords integration requires three steps.

1. Auto-tagging must be enabled by setting the Auto-Tagging option under the Tracking portion of the Account Preferences page in the My Account section of the AdWords interface.

2. The AdWords Account and Google Analytics Account must be linked. If you signed up for Google Analytics from within AdWords, the link is automatically created. If you're not sure whether your accounts are linked or you know that they are not linked, go to the Google Analytics link under the Reporting menu in the AdWords interface. If no Google Analytics Account is linked to your AdWords Account, you can create a new Google Analytics Account or link an existing one. Note that you *must* be logged into AdWords with a Google Account that is also an administrator-level user in your Google Analytics Account. If your AdWords login is not an administrator-level user under your Google Analytics Account, you won't see an option to link your AdWords and Google Analytics Accounts (you'll see only an option to create a new Google Analytics Account).

3. After enabling Auto-tagging and linking your AdWords and Google Analytics Accounts, you need to activate Cost-Data Importing for your profiles. Enabling Cost-Data Importing adds the Clicks tab under the special AdWords report suite in the Traffic Sources section of Google Analytics. The Clicks tab is populated with Impression, Click, Cost-per-Click, and ROI metrics based on actual AdWords data. In some cases where you have a profile for an external vendor or employee who is not authorized to have access to actual spending data, you may not want to make cost data available in the reports for that profile; in those cases, don't enable Cost-Data Importing.

In addition to importing Campaign, Click, and Cost data from AdWords into Google Analytics, AdWords provides a feature for importing Conversions data from Google Analytics into AdWords. This feature provides Conversion Rates, numbers of Conversions, and Cost-per-Conversion figures based on your selected Google Analytics Goals and displays them in the AdWords interface, making campaign management infinitely easier.

NOTE

The processes for automated AdWords tracking and advanced data-import integration have changed and may have changed again by the time you read this. Visit www.analyticsformarketers.com/s/adwords-setup for the latest about how to conduct AdWords integration with Google Analytics. Additionally, bear in mind that some users may need to link multiple AdWords accounts with the same Google Analytics Account, a process that requires the assistance of a Google Analytics authorized consultant or AdWords account specialist at Google to complete.

The only drawback is that you can't enable Google Analytics goals as conversion points in AdWords until there are conversions occurring on those goals by visitors from AdWords. You can activate this feature in AdWords by choosing Reporting ❯ Conversions. The resulting Conversions has an option to import from Google Analytics if you have goals configured within Google Analytics and AdWords visitors are converting on those goals. We recommend you *only* import *Primary Conversion Goals* — that is, lead capture, contact, purchase, and so on — and not Engagement or Step Goals, because the AdWords interface does not differentiate conversions from Engagement versus Primary Goals within its reports.

TABLE 9.3

Dimensions Used for Sponsored SEM Tracking

Dimension	Recommended Use	Tracking Tag Parameter
Medium	Always set Medium to cpc. Some articles and tools (such as the URL builder from Google) recommend using ppc, but because AdWords autotagging uses cpc and that can't be changed, use cpc for manually tagged SEM campaigns so Medium is recorded consistently.	utm_medium
Source	Set Source to the search engine that brings the traffic: google.com, yahoo, bing, and so on. Source should be used to define where traffic comes from; in the case of SEM traffic, that place is the search engine where you are running the ad.	utm_source
Campaign	With AdWords autotagging, Campaign is set to the name of the campaign in AdWords. With search engines other than AdWords, set this value to match AdWords' campaign names, or otherwise be consistent with campaign names used in other media and descriptive of the marketing effort the ads in the campaign support.	utm_campaign
Keyword	The Keyword field must always be defined for SEM traffic and should be set to the keyword or phrase you are buying on the SEM platform. For example, if you have the keyword "oregon vineyard wedding" in your keywords, you should set the Keyword dimension to that keyword phrase.	utm_term
Ad Content	The Ad Content field is optional but highly useful. It is best used to define the ad being served. All major SEM platforms allow the simultaneous testing of multiple ad versions. Ads with better click-through rates (CTRs) are scored higher and rank better. However, optimizing for CTR alone is risky because ads may be successful at garnering more clicks but may have far worse bounce, engagement, or conversion rates. Thus, setting the Ad Content value to the text of the ad or some other identifier (perhaps the title of the ad) such that you can compare CTR performance as well as value measurements is critical.	utm_content

Setting up tracking for other SEM providers

There is a common misconception that Google Analytics is only for measuring and analyzing Google traffic. That is simply not true. Measuring traffic at other search engines relies on the creation of tracking tags with values for campaign-related dimensions, as Table 9.3 lists.

Overcoming the issue of scale with SEM campaign tracking tags

A common challenge for tracking SEM campaigns is the sheer scale at which many are operated. If you've built a large account with well-structured campaigns, ad groups, and keywords, you may have thousands — even tens of thousands — keywords. Applying manual campaign tagging principles would require you to create a unique destination URL for *each and every keyword*, its Ad Group, Campaign, Source, and the cpc Medium. That is a rather daunting task to consider! However, there is hope: Both Yahoo Search Marketing and Microsoft AdCenter provide a means to add dynamic elements to their destination URLs that limit the need to create custom URLs to the ad group level rather than the keyword level.

With Yahoo Search Marketing, you can add dynamic parameters to your destination URLs that are automatically filled in when an ad is clicked. To automate tagging and avoid creating unique URLs per keyword, simply set the utm_term parameter in your ad destination URL to the value {YSMKEY}. For match type and network, you can use {YSMMTC:standard:advanced:content}, which for a standard match would result in standard being present in the destination URL. There are many additional dynamic parameters you can use with Yahoo Search Marketing. For details on these parameters, search the Yahoo Search Marketing help center for "tracking urls" or follow the link in the note later in this chapter.

Microsoft AdCenter and Yahoo Search Marketing have similar dynamic parameter capabilities. AdCenter's parameters to use for Google Analytics tracking are {keyword} for the search term in your ad group search term and {MatchType} for the network match type. You can also use {QueryString} for the actual search term. We recommend defining Campaign Name, Medium, Source, and Ad Content manually in each ad's destination URL and using utm_term={keyword} for the Keyword field.

Avoiding data accuracy pitfalls with SEM tracking

You may be tempted to forego tagging your Yahoo, AdCenter, and other SEM campaigns because of the extra effort involved in creating the tags for campaigns with hundreds or thousands of keywords. When SEM traffic isn't tagged for tracking, it is reported under the organic medium. Having SEM traffic attributed to the medium for SEO work is a particularly bad problem because it corrupts the integrity of organic search traffic data and your ability to accurately measure SEO efforts. Chapter 11 covers this problem and other causes of inaccuracy around SEO measurement.

NOTE

As with Google AdWords, the settings for Yahoo Search Marketing and Microsoft AdCenter change from time to time and may have changed after this writing. Visit www.analyticsformarketers.com/s/other-sem-tracking for the latest on automating SEM tracking tag creation for non-AdWords providers.

Also, if you use a third-party bid-management tool or other tracking system, these tools sometimes strip out the campaign tracking tags from your destination URLs or append additional query parameters to your destination URLs. When this occurs, it effectively destroys your ability to measure and thus manage SEM efforts using Google Analytics. If you've set up campaign tracking tags in your ads, and you *don't* see cpc Medium traffic or notice an inexplicable increase in reported organic Medium traffic, you are likely suffering from this problem. A simple test is to click one of your ads that is live on a search engine; if your Google Analytics tracking tags aren't visible in the browser address bar of the landing page after you click your ad, something has gone wrong. Talk with your tool provider to find out if it can support tracking tags.

Configuring settings in Google Analytics

There are a few settings that are important to configure that preserve the integrity of your SEM campaign data in Google Analytics.

First, make sure you set up the Exclude Query Parameters option under the main profile settings to exclude query parameters that may be added to destination URLs such as Yahoo's Tracking URLs. While these parameters may be used by other measurement tools relying on your Web site's code, they're not necessary in Google Analytics and only hamper landing-page analysis.

Second, ensure you've applied Lowercase filters for the following fields: Profiles: Campaign Source, Campaign Medium, Campaign Term, Campaign Content, Request URI, and User-Defined.

Third, ensure that you've set up goals and, if applicable for your site, ecommerce reporting in your profile. (See Chapters 5 through 7 for more information on goal configuration.) The remainder of this chapter assumes that you have created goals that are appropriate for your business.

A final tip for setting configurations within Google Analytics is to create a dedicated SEM analysis profile. While advanced segments have generally ruled out the need for medium-specific profiles, there are still advantages to having a profile that is filtered to include only traffic from your SEM medium. To create such a profile, start by creating a duplicate profile based on the Web Property ID of your main Web site profile. Once it's created, configure appropriate Profile Settings and goals and general filters. Then add a filter with the following settings: Filter type of Include, Filter field of Campaign Medium, and Filter field value of cpc|ppc. The result is a profile that matches your main profile but contains only data for visitors from your cpc- or ppc-tagged campaigns.

Quick checklist for SEM tracking setup

The following is a quick checklist of actions for setting up effective tracking for SEM campaigns:

- Activate AdWords auto-tagging.
- Link your AdWords and Google Analytics Accounts.
- Apply AdWords cost data to your profiles.
- Set your primary Google Analytics Conversion Goals to be imported into AdWords as Conversions.
- Set up manual tracking tags for non-AdWords SEM providers.
- Exclude unnecessary query parameters.

- Ensure that appropriate goals and goal values, ecommerce tracking, and site search tracking are set up.
- Create a profile for SEM traffic only.

Analyzing and Optimizing SEM Campaigns

Once you have established comprehensive, consistent, and reliable tracking for traffic generated by your SEM campaigns, you can begin the process of optimizing your sponsored search marketing efforts.

One of the most important things to bear in mind is that SEM optimization is a *process* — it's not going to happen overnight, in a week, or even a month. In fact, it will never really end. SEM, by nature, must be constantly evolving and changing as your business changes, as your customers change their search behaviors, and as your competitors position and reposition themselves within your industry.

Understanding key dimensions and metrics in the context of SEM analysis

When analyzing SEM traffic, you need to pay close attention to key dimensions. They are:

- **Medium:** For search, Medium should be either `organic` or `cpc` (for SEM traffic).
- **Source:** Sources are search engines referring traffic, such as `google.com`, `yahoo`, and `bing`.
- **Campaign:** Campaign relates to the unique campaign name you assigned in your tracking tags or inside AdWords.
- **Keyword:** Keyword is the search term that you bid for with the search engine (the "actual" search term used by the searcher rather than the bid term can be found by using a filter, as explained later in this chapter).
- **Ad Content:** This dimension should relate to the text ad you've created (note that you have to use the `utm_content` tracking tag).
- **User-Defined:** This dimension is useful if you have applied the Actual Search Term Discovery filter covered later in this chapter.
- **Geographic:** The Country, Region, and City dimensions are useful for analyzing the performance of SEM providers, campaigns, ad groups, and keywords based on geography (for example, if you sell a coffee thermoses, you will probably see higher conversion rates from North Dakota than Florida during winter months).
- **Other dimensions in custom reports:** Other useful dimensions not listed in the standard cross-dimension menu or used in standard reports include Ad Slot, Ad Group, Ad Position, Visit Number, Depth of Visit, and Length of Visit.

Likewise, there are a number of metrics that are critical to analyze when optimizing SEM efforts. They include:

- **Visits and Unique Visitors:** The Visits metric is a key point for measuring traffic while Unique Visitors (available only in custom reports you create) helps to assess the reach of your SEM efforts.

- **Percent of New Visits:** This metric is important because, in most cases, SEM campaigns should be focused on reaching new customers in new markets rather than customers who already know about you. This isn't to say SEM can't be used to market to existing customers or returning visitors, but when you're paying for each click, it is generally more desirable to see returning visitors click through from a branded organic term or simply type in your URL. If SEM is reaching a percentage of new visitors that is lower than average, you should look closely into what keywords are driving this and consider adjusting your campaigns.

- **Bounce Rate:** Bounce Rate is a pivotal metric to assess initial reactions of your visitors, with SEM. A higher than average (considering "average" in the context of landing pages on your site) Bounce Rate signals a mismatch between the ad copy and keyword and the appeal of your landing page.

- **Average Time on Site and Pages/Visit:** These metrics are engagement measures and are important to gauge effectiveness of attracting customers who engage with your Web site.

- **Per Visit Goal Value:** This metric, activated by setting values when configuring goals, provides the most important overall measure of value and effectiveness from SEM campaigns, ad groups, ads, keywords, landing pages, and so on. Per Visit Goal Value and Per Visit Ecommerce Value are considered by many search marketing professionals to be the most important metrics in measuring and managing SEM campaigns.

- **Goal Conversion Rates:** This metric measures the performance of keywords against specific goal conversion rates and illuminates terms that drive those conversion goals. However, be cautious to not overrely on single goal conversion rates and thereby overlook terms that drive preconversion interest.

- **Ecommerce Per-Visit Value:** Rely on this metric to indicate keywords that, on average, drive more revenue per visit. If that revenue is greater than your cost per click, it indicates a cash-positive return on ad spend. But be sure to pay attention to profit margin: If you spend $1 to make $1 in revenue but have a 70 percent cost of goods sold, you can really afford to spend only $0.30 to make $1.

- **Average Revenue per Order:** This metric is important because lots of orders for low-revenue items may be less valuable than fewer orders for much higher value items.

- **Ecommerce Conversion Rate:** This metric is an indicator of the propensity for a keyword to drive a transaction. While useful for finding terms that drive more purchases, it must be evaluated in the context of revenue generated per visit. This revenue-based evaluation is critical because a keyword that drives a high rate of low-revenue conversions may not be as valuable as a keyword with a lower conversion rate but higher average order value.

Differentiating sponsored (SEM) from nonsponsored (organic) search traffic

The first step in analyzing your SEM traffic is to make sure you're analyzing traffic from *sponsored* search and not from all search engine referrals. To do this, you first need to ensure that all your SEM campaigns are tagged appropriately; otherwise their traffic appears as part of the `organic` Medium. To begin isolating your SEM traffic, you need to understand a few key principles, features, and reports.

Using the Search Engines report

The Search Engines report consolidates data from known search engine sources. This report, by default, shows all search traffic, organic traffic, and SEM Mediums (SEM Mediums in this report require `cpc` or `ppc` as the Medium value). Note that throughout Google Analytics, you will see SEM referred to as "paid" traffic, and organic search (traffic from SEO efforts) as "non-paid" traffic. Thus, in the Search Engines report, there is the Show: Total | Paid | Non-paid option (see Figure 9.5). This is called a data slice. When Total is selected, the data in the Search Engines report includes both paid and non-paid traffic. When Paid or Non-paid are selected, the report shows only data for those mediums. The Paid slice includes the Medium values of `cpc` and `ppc`. The Non-paid slice includes the Medium value `organic`.

FIGURE 9.5

The Search Engines report consolidates data about visits from search, both paid and non-paid.

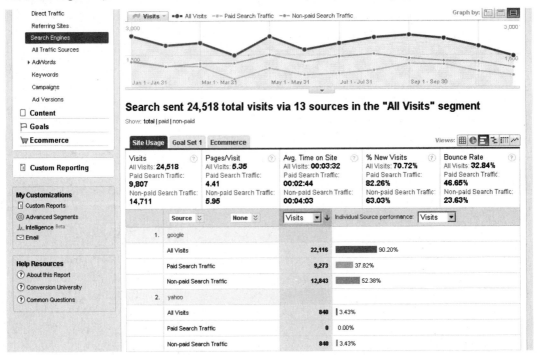

The Search Engines report shows traffic starting with search engine names (Source), from which you can drill down into a specific search engine and view the keywords that are generating traffic from that search engine. Figure 9.5 shows the search engine sources bringing both paid and non-paid traffic. This report provides a quick means of assessing which search engines bring the most Traffic, Goal Conversions, Goal Value, and Ecommerce activity. By changing the Show option among Total, Paid, and Non-paid, you can quickly get a picture of the contribution SEM efforts are providing to overall search engine exposure and Web site performance.

Using the Keywords report

The Keywords report, which displays all search keywords bringing traffic to the site, works like the Search Engines report insofar as its "slice" capability. By default, the Keywords report shows all keywords, whether from SEM or organic search. The Show option lets you slice the data by Paid and Non-paid just as the Search Engines report does.

This report is great to help you get a picture of keyword traffic and metrics regardless of the search engine involved. Use it to measure the Total Traffic, Engagement, and Value from top keywords using the Total slice option, and then quickly narrow to SEM traffic using the Paid slice. From here you can then drill into a particular keyword or filter the list using the Report Table filter. If you drill into a keyword, you can then choose to segment by dimensions such as Source (to see all the search engines that brought traffic through that keyword), Geography, and Landing Page.

Using Default Advanced Segments to your advantage

Google Analytics provides the Default Advanced Segment for Paid Traffic option for reports. When activated, all the data visible in your reports is limited to SEM traffic (that is, paid traffic, meaning the Medium value is cpc or ppc). When you start honing in on what to change *within the context* of your SEM campaigns, use the Paid Traffic Advanced Segment.

However, *don't* use Advanced Segments when conducting initial analysis, because you'll lose the comparative perspective afforded by seeing SEM data next to other data. For example, if you want to compare the Per Visit Goal Value from SEM traffic versus all traffic mediums, you'll need data in your reports that includes all mediums as opposed to SEM alone.

In addition to the Paid Search Traffic Advanced Segment, there is a Search Traffic Advanced Segment that, just like the Total slice of the Search Engines report, includes data for both paid and non-paid search engines. The Search Traffic Advanced Segment is a great segment to apply when analyzing SEM efforts against search traffic in general. Even if you receive traffic for the same keyword from both paid and non-paid search listings, you will likely see a difference in the behavior of visitors and thus a difference in Engagement, Conversion, and Value metrics. With the Search Traffic Advanced Segment applied, the comparison and contextual data points in reports provides an easy comparison of the difference in impact from SEM versus organic search activities when evaluating dimensions such as Keyword and Source.

For example, Figure 9.6 shows the Keywords report with the Comparison View When No Advanced Segment filter is applied versus when the Search Traffic Advanced Segment filter is applied. Notice the difference in the visualization of the report as well as the overall Bounce Rate metric. With the Search

FIGURE 9.6

This figure illustrates the impact of using the Search Traffic (top) versus Paid Search Traffic (bottom) advanced segments when analyzing keyword performance. Comparing bounce rates to the site average reveals two different perspectives of keyword bounce rates.

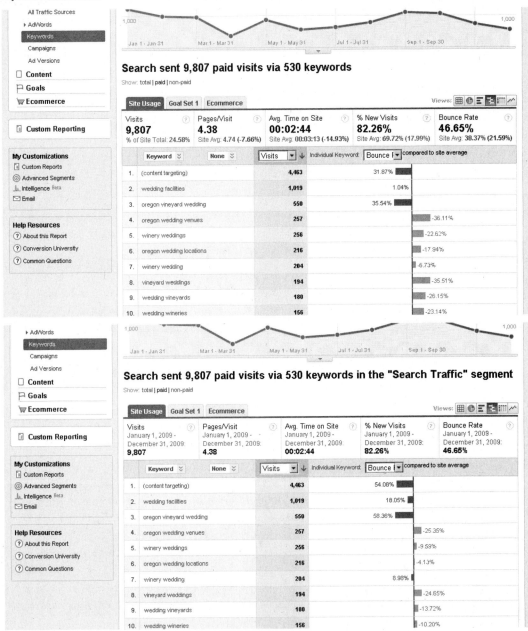

Traffic Advanced Segment filter applied, the Site Average Bounce Rate is 33.77 percent and the Bounce Rate for the slice of data shown (paid keywords) is 52.35 percent, a full 55.05 percent higher than the "average." Average in this case, though, is limited to paid plus non-paid search engine traffic. This figure shows that the Bounce Rate for paid traffic is significantly higher than that of non-paid traffic and points out the keywords where the higher Bounce Rate is taking place. Keywords where Bounce Rate is far worse should be flagged for review.

Compare these results with the same view but without the Search Traffic segment applied, and the metrics change noticeably — the Site Average Bounce Rate goes down to 30.95 percent and the comparison of keywords shows greater extremes of variance. This is because the "average" used for comparison purposes is based on the totals for data currently active for the reports. When the Search Traffic segment is active, the data set is limited to visits from search and carries with it the metrics associated with those visits. When the All Visits segment is active, the "average" includes many more visits and dilutes the point of comparison by introducing the additional non-search visits and their corresponding metrics into the calculations.

Standing in the intersection of interest and intent: Principles for SEM analysis

In Chapter 11, we explain the principles for defining your SEO measurement framework. Those principles are completely relevant to SEM optimization, but they vary slightly in application because of the differences between SEM and SEO efforts. SEM should serve as a means of positioning your business at the *intersection of interest and intent* for keywords that can't or don't have an organic position. SEM is also useful in cases where you do have an organic presence but want to provide a dual message or more refined landing page experience than your organic listing affords (such as with branded terms).

Focus on the keyword level

Analysis of campaigns and ad group performance is important as well. However when it comes time to optimize efforts, your actions will be oriented to keywords: either by moving keywords around as you optimize campaign structures, ad groups, and ad copy, or by changing bids and adding and removing keywords. Ultimately, SEM comes down to the keyword level and how keywords relate to ads, landing pages, and campaign structure.

Goal Value measures

First and foremost, if goals are set up appropriately, the Per Visit Goal Value metric should be your primary judge of a keyword's performance. We recommend reviewing the "Defining your SEO measurement framework" section in Chapter 11 for principles on this topic, as well as the "Key goal performance measures" section in Chapter 8. When measuring your SEM traffic, you need a solid framework of goals configured for both engagement and conversion points. Specifically, we believe that, at a minimum, you should establish goals that match the following areas and contain goal values based on an indexed scale. Note that this index-based goal value model differs from traditional evaluations of goal value based on an estimated dollar value for completing a certain action. Table 9.4 shows a suggested goals framework.

TABLE 9.4

Example Goals Framework for SEM Optimization

Goal Description	Goal Value
Reaching a general section of your site, such as a category in your store or section overview on a noncommerce site	0.5
Reaching a specific product or service detail page or, for media sites, an article or show-detail page	1.0
Reaching the shopping cart, the first step of a registration, or lead-capture process	3.5
Completing a purchase, registration process, or lead-capture form	10.0
Spending more than 30 seconds on the site	0.2
Spending more than 3 minutes on the site	0.8
Spending more than 10 minutes on the site (highly engaged)	1.5
Viewing 2 or more pages (nonbounce)	0.2
Viewing 5 or more pages (engaged)	0.6

Visit www.analyticsformarketers.com/s/goal-planning for additional resources to aid goal planning and value setting, including an interactive worksheet. Once your goals framework is defined, you can begin analysis of your SEM based on goals and goal values.

The Per Visit Goal Value metric should form the basis of measurement. Figure 9.7 shows the Keywords report analyzing the Per Visit Goal Value metric with the Comparison View activated. In this example, there are several goals — three of which are engagement steps and the fourth is the point of tangible conversion. Not all visitors convert on the fourth goal — in fact most don't, but many convert on the Engagement Goals. Because the goal values for the three Engagement Goals are far less than the fourth goal (Tangible Lead Completion), keywords that fail to drive conversions of the lead goal won't be given as high a goal value. However, they will be rewarded to the extent that they move people toward that end goal. Keywords with very low Goal Value hardly drive conversions on any of the goals and should be removed from the campaign.

Relying on Goal Value is superior to relying simply on Goal Conversion Rate for your primary goal. Consider Figure 9.7 where the Comparison View shows a primary Lead Completion Conversion Rate versus Goal Value–based effectiveness. Notice how the Goal Conversion evaluation shows some strong winners and some strong losers (Visitors). However, the Goal Value–based report reveals a different picture — one where all the keywords are contributing toward goals with some scoring higher than others.

Engagement analysis

Analysis of engagement is a secondary area on which to focus. Engagement is simply a leading indicator of the effectiveness of your SEM to reach and captivate your customer. Poor Engagement metrics for Average Time on Site and Pages per Visit are indicators that your keywords are not connecting with your audience, your ads present the wrong message and thus attract the wrong visitor or

FIGURE 9.7

Analysis of Keywords by Per Visit Goal Value using the Comparison View reveals keywords that are strong winners (highest goal value), successful in moving people toward conversion (average goal value), or losers (fail to drive any significant volume toward goals). The top image uses the Goal Conversion Rate metric for a single goal whereas the bottom image uses the Per Visit Goal Value metric, revealing a different picture.

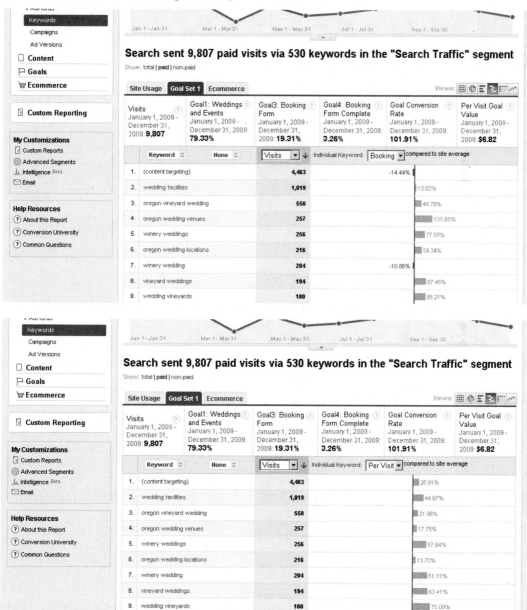

an undercommitted visitor, and your landing pages don't create a strong connection with your visitors or draw them deeper into the site.

Often, poor Engagement metrics are associated with badly targeted destination URLs, such as buying a specific keyword like "men's cross-trainer shoes" and landing the visitor on the store's home page, forcing them to search and browse the site once again to find what they had already searched for. That's a sure-fire way to drive people to bounce right off your site, and you'll see it with high Bounce Rate and low Engagement metrics.

Ecommerce analysis

Analyzing Ecommerce metrics for SEM takes basically the same shape as analyzing other mediums for ecommerce performance. When working to optimize your SEM campaigns for sales, the main focus and attention should rest in the Per-Visit Value metric. This metric combines the Revenue Generated, Average Revenue per Order, and Ecommerce Conversion Rate (or Sales Rate) into one number and shows the opportunity for incremental revenue generation. If your Per-Visit Value is $3 and your Cost per Click is $1, you have a practical printing press for cash. Simply relying on Total Revenue, Ecommerce Conversion Rate, or Average Value can lead to misconceptions and suboptimal performance.

For example, if a given keyword drives 60 percent of the revenues because it receives the majority of ad spend and generates the majority of traffic, but 10 other keywords that each receive one-tenth the traffic have twice the Per-Visit Value (creating a combined volume of traffic the same as the single keyword driving 60 percent of traffic), shifting the spend from the one "big revenue" term to the many "lower revenue" terms would *double* the total revenue from the same budget. The point here is to recognize and take advantage of opportunities to optimize the performance of money invested in advertising by analyzing keywords on an individual as well as aggregate basis against the ecommerce revenues generated by visits from those keywords.

Analyzing geographic performance and value

Geography can, and in most cases will, affect returns from your SEM investments. If you are running a national or multinational targeted campaign, the data in the Search Engines, Keywords, and even AdWords reports by default combine data across all geographies. However, when peering beneath the surface, you will likely see large, even extreme variations among geographies. This may change over time due to seasonality. For example, if you sell insulated travel coffee mugs and thermoses for drinks and soup, you will likely see higher performance from northern U.S. states and Canadian provinces than from southern U.S. states.

TIP

Consider the following custom report example for enhanced engagement analysis!
Custom Report for Engagement and Goal Performance Side by Side:
• **Dimensions:** Medium, Source, Campaign, Keyword
• **Metrics:** Visits, Pages/Visit, Time on Site, Bounce Rate, Per Visit Goal Value, Engagement Goals
• **Report Link:** www.analyticsformarketers.com/s/ch9-report1

FIGURE 9.8

The map at top is colored using the volume of visits. The map at bottom uses a per-visit goal value to indicate states with higher per-visit value.

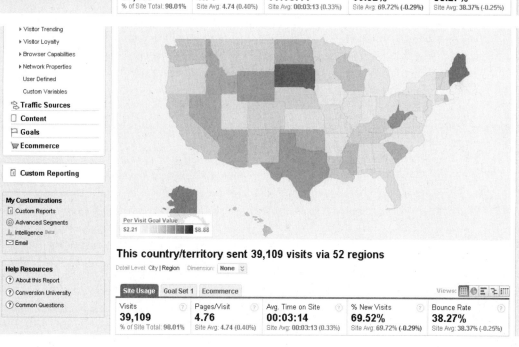

To optimize for geographic targeting, follow this general process: First activate the Advanced Segment for Paid Search Traffic to ensure that the data in your reports is limited to SEM traffic only. Second, browse to the Map Overlay report under the Visitors report section and change the map visualization to use Per Visit Goal Value rather than Total Visits for geographic reporting. The map colorization will instantly reveal states that have the highest Per Visit Goal Value. Figure 9.8 shows an example of Visits volume versus Per Visit Goal Value. The left side shows visits and the right shows goal values. Also, use the Data Table below the map details to conduct further analysis using the available reporting and analysis tools.

Understanding landing page performance

Landing page performance is critical for SEM campaigns. This importance is because search is inherently "unsticky." The browser's Back button is ever-present and readily used by visitors who hope to find what they're looking for, describe that intent with keywords, review and select a results listing, and expect to find what they're looking for once they click. If there is a mismatch between what they see on the landing page and what they expected to see based on their declared intent (declared by the search query used), they'll hit that Back button faster than you can say "bounce rate"!

There are two approaches to landing page analysis: One, find the landing pages that are performing badly and then find the keywords related to them. Two, find the landing pages a given keyword drives traffic to and analyze the performance of those pages. In either scenario two good metrics to start with are the Bounce Rate and Per Visit Goal Value. The reports to focus analysis on are the Top Landing Page report under the Content section and the Keywords report under Traffic Sources section.

When evaluating these reports, begin by applying the Paid Search Traffic Advanced Segment to limit data shown to SEM traffic sources. Next, analyze the Bounce Rate using the Comparison view to identify losing landing pages or keywords. Look for patterns: Do certain pages or keywords stand out? Once you identify pages or keywords, drill in one by one and cross-segment by keyword (if drilling in from the Landing Pages report) or landing page (if drilling in from the Keywords report). Look for continuation of the pattern of high bounce rates. Sometimes the aggregate Bounce Rate for a landing page or keyword is pulled down by a bad performer revealed through drill-down analysis. Look for these nuggets of insight to stand out using the Comparison View.

A power technique to quickly identify a set of poorly performing keywords and their related landing pages is to use the Secondary Dimension option and Advanced Report filters. Figure 9.9 shows the Keywords report with the Paid Search Traffic segment applied, the Secondary Dimension set to Landing Page, and an Advanced filter created to include only keyword/landing page combinations with more than 10 visits per combination and above-average Bounce Rates. This combination of settings provides an easy list of data for export to Excel or analysis right within Google Analytics.

AdWords-specific report analysis

Google Analytics provides a suite of enhanced reports for analyzing AdWords traffic. These reports, when enabled, provide data specific to AdWords about the exposure (Impressions), Clicks, and Costs of your campaigns and their Ad Groups, Ads, Keywords, Positions, and more. Much of the data in the

FIGURE 9.9

This report uses Secondary Dimensions, Advanced Segments, and Advanced Report Filters to return a list of keywords and corresponding landing pages that have high bounce rates.

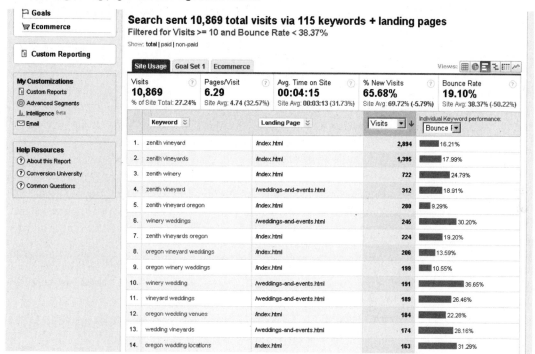

AdWords reports is already available in the standard All Traffic Sources, Search Engines, Keywords, Campaigns, and Ad Versions reports. However, the AdWords reports provide a unique and valuable resource because they contain data specific to the exposure and costs of your SEM campaigns running on Google and its network.

Leveraging the Clicks tab

The main difference between the AdWords Campaigns report and other search engine–related reports is the Clicks tab. This report gives the Impression, Click, and Cost Data imported from AdWords via the Account link (as explained earlier in this chapter). This report is useful for assessing keywords that are costing you a lot of money yet delivering suboptimal performance and those keywords that drive the greatest value for your business.

One limitation of this report, however, is that it does not include goal and engagement metrics on the same report. We find this inability to see goal data next to cost data a shortcoming in that a useful comparison is to be able to create lists of winners and losers that includes cost information. You could create such a winners-and-losers list by applying an Advanced Table filter with settings that include only the rows where metrics meet thresholds you define. We recommend you identify poorly performing keywords that consume large amounts of advertising budget. You can add a further layer of analysis by activating the Secondary Dimension and setting it to Campaign or Ad Group.

The result will be a list of keywords and (if selected, their ad groups or campaigns) that have significant enough volume to merit some level of certainty about the results that are poor performers and consume a disproportionate amount of the advertising budget.

Analyzing the Keyword Positions report

Keyword Positions is a report that is exclusive to Google Analytics' AdWords reports. It is powered when your AdWords and Google Analytics Accounts are properly linked. Once set up, the Keyword Positions report reveals metrics from a given keyword in various positions in which it was shown in AdWords. Positions are shown in a visually rich tool that mimics the Google search results page and shows the metrics you've selected in each of the positions, as illustrated in Figure 9.10.

In addition to the fixed Keyword Positions report, you can also create reports that include position dimensions using custom reports. These extra keyword dimensions are specific to AdWords and focus on placement. They are Ad Slot and Ad Slot Position. Ad Slot is either Top or Right Hand Side. Slot position means the position within the slot. Thus, Ad Slot Top, Position 3 means the ad appeared in the

---

FIGURE 9.10

The Keyword Positions report uses the Per Visit Goal Value metric to indicate which positions for a given keyword are most valuable. Notice how positions on the right are almost as valuable as the top-slot positions, which typically cost much more.

top ad display area's third position. Ad Slot Right Hand Side, Position 2 would actually be considered Position 5 by the AdWords average rank figure. This within Google Analytics would be considered the right-hand-side position No. 2.

Tracking the "actual" search query for a purchased keyword

A common and highly useful analysis is to determine the "actual" keywords that bring traffic to your site from a broad- or phrase-match bid or purchased keyword. For example, the purchased keyword might be "wedding facilities" and an actual search term used and matched to that bid term might be "top wedding sites in Portland, Oregon." The ability to assess the actual search queries used for a given sponsored keyword is helpful in a number of ways:

- Identifying new terms for phrase- and exact-match buys
- Discovering terms that should be negatively matched
- Determining the length of the long tail for a given purchased keyword

This filter originated as part of a two-part filter created by the team at Omega Digital Media and has since been refined by the Google Analytics community. Note that this filter could be broken easily if search engines change how they report referrals. Also, note that you can't use this filter in conjunction with the User-Defined field via the _setVar() tracking script method.

The filter is an Advanced filter that looks for the actual search term string in the referral portion of the utm.gif hit and copies it into the user-defined field. Filter field settings include:

- Filter type: Advanced
- Field A extract field: referral (this is the utmr value of a utm.gif hit — if there was a referral, the first utm.gif hit of the session will populate this field)
- Field A extract pattern: (\?|&)(q|p|query|encquery|s|qt|terms|kw|qs|wd|w|text)=([^&]*)
- Field B extract field: medium
- Field B extract pattern: cpc|ppc (this ensures you run this filter only if Medium is cpc or ppc — you don't want organic or other mediums)
- Output to field: User-Defined
- Output pattern: $A3
- Field A required: yes
- Field B required: yes
- Overwrite output: yes
- Case sensitive: no

—

Measuring and Optimizing Display Advertising

Online advertising includes banner, rich media, and other forms of visual online ads. Display ads are one of the oldest forms of online advertising and certainly the most famous — and perhaps infamous. The early Internet was flooded with banner ads, pop-up ads, pop-under ads, and the like. You may remember annoying ads with bright flashing banners or "punch the monkey" ads glaring across the Internet and your Web-based e-mail inbox in 1997.

Today, display advertising is still a prolific form of online marketing. However, in the age of a search-driven Internet and the application of performance marketing, traditional display ad paradigms must be rethought. Traditional display advertising metrics have focused on impressions as a primary means of gauging value and performance. This has been partly due to the means through which display ads were, and largely still are, purchased: a fashion similar to traditional offline media where media planners select sites intending to reach a certain demographic, then negotiate the purchase of a certain number of impressions, bought by the thousand impressions (or CPM).

This model of purchasing makes true performance marketing difficult, because taking action on what can be learned about performance is hard, if not impossible. However, new technologies from leading advertising networks and publishers have shifted display advertising to operate on a basis more like sponsored search, where campaigns can be planned, targeted, measured, and revised easily, in near real time. With the ability to purchase display advertising that can actually be held accountable and rapidly iterated, a new and powerful marketing opportunity is available to advertisers who embrace the process of applying performance marketing principles to display advertising.

Display and Rich Media Advertising Basics

Online display advertising has come a long way from the rudimentary banners that characterized the early Web. Once upon a time, if you wanted to run an online display ad, your only option was to call a site with traffic (called a *publisher*), negotiate an *insertion order* (a contract specifying how often ads would appear and under what circumstances), deliver your *creative* (your actual ad), and wait until you got a report back to gauge the results.

As an advertiser today, you can choose from hundreds of *ad networks* instead of going directly to each publisher. You can use simple tools to develop your own ads and receive instant metrics on how often they are viewed, clicked, played, moused over, or otherwise engaged by Web visitors. You can even use the same Google AdWords account you use for search advertising to run display ads.

Some publishers still require advertisers to go direct, but the bottom line is that there are lots of options to choose from for large and small advertisers alike.

Major display and rich media advertising formats

Here are some of the main options for online advertising:

- **Static display and simple Flash.** Static display ads can be run in a variety of sizes and are visible all across the Web. They generally follow a set of standard guidelines created by the Internet Advertising Bureau (IAB) and are supported in most major online advertising platforms including Google, Yahoo, Microsoft, and AOL. Note that numerous studies have shown that Web visitors have learned to ignore ads created in this format in a phenomenon called *ad blindness*.

- **Rich media.** Rich media is a more complex format of display ad that can support audio/video, expandable formats such as page take-overs, and sophisticated interactivity. The IAB defines rich media as "advertisements with which users can interact (as opposed to solely animation and excluding click-through functionality) in a Web page format." Developing and trafficking rich media ads often requires more manual work on the part of the advertisers and publisher as this format catches up to traditional display ads.

- **In-page/click-to-play video.** In-page video may be considered a subset of rich media. This format allows advertisers to embed video directly into a Web page, encouraging users to watch or simply playing when loaded.

- **In-stream video.** Ads embedded into online video content run either before a video is shown (pre-roll), midstream (during the video), or after a video has ended (post-roll). In-stream video is one of the fastest growing formats of online advertising, benefits from increased availability of premium online video content made possible by sites such as Hulu.com. Advertisers may also display text overlays directly in the video play partially obscuring video content.

- **In-stream audio.** Online radio stations, podcasts, music streaming sites such as Pandora, and even Voice-over-IP phone companies offer advertisers the ability to insert ads directly into audio streams. This is another rapidly growing segment of online advertising and boasts higher recall rates than traditional display ads.

- **Branded content.** Advertisers frustrated by ad blindness on the Web have increasingly turned to product placements, sponsored games, branded widgets, and other less direct forms of advertising to deliver a message. This may range from developing a Facebook game to distributing free instructional videos on YouTube.

It's possible to use these formats to drive activity at all stages of the marketing funnel, from basic awareness to direct response ads geared toward driving immediate conversions. On the other hand, display and rich media are typically associated with top-of-funnel awareness campaigns and often have a hard time competing with search advertising on a cost-per-acquisition basis. You can learn more about the strengths and weaknesses of display advertising, as well as how to get started with a campaign, by exploring offerings from the leaders in this space linked from www.analyticsformarketers.com/s/display-ads.

Pre-click metrics for evaluating display and rich media advertising performance

As display and rich media advertising have matured, so have the metrics used to evaluate success. This chapter focuses primarily on how you can use Google Analytics to analyze what happens *after* a user clicks on an ad that points to your site (post-click metrics). However, be aware that each ad format also includes several *pre-click* metrics used to understand performance. Here are plain-English definitions for a sample set of metrics:

- **Impressions:** The number of times an ad is served to the user's browser.
- **View-through rate (VTR):** The percentage of users who view an ad and then go on to convert on the advertiser's site later, as measured by the presence of a cookie on the user's computer indicating they viewed the ad. This metric is problematic to calculate due to the issues associated with third-party cookies.
- **CPM:** Cost per thousand impressions associated with running an ad.
- **Click-through rate (CTR):** The number of times an ad is clicked divided by the number of times the ad is served to the user's browser (clicks ÷ impressions).
- **Interaction rate (IR):** The proportion of ad views that result in users moving their mouse over an ad. This tracks user engagement with rich media ads.
- **Expansion rate:** The proportion of ad views that result in a user clicking to expand a rich media ad.
- **View-to-completion rate:** The percentage of video plays that reach the end of the video.

You can find more specific technical definitions and details on how each metric is calculate on the Internet Advertising Bureau's Web site (visit www.analyticsformarketers.com/s/iab).

As you navigate the advertising platforms recommended in the preceding section, you will see emphasis placed on pre-click measures. These measures are crucial in understanding your campaign performance, but as an analytical marketer, you need to consider the whole picture. Google Analytics can help you move past these metrics to evaluate the impact of your campaign on conversion goals, visitor behavior, branded queries, and other important indicators.

Pitfalls of measuring display and rich media

The king metric of display ads has historically been the *impression*. Impressions were the metrics by which ads were bought and sold, that is, on the basis of CPM. In a CPM model, the advertiser bears the risk that an impression will not result in a click, or worse, that an impression will go unnoticed. A false assumption has been made, and indeed continues to be made, that an online display ad impression has intrinsic value in the same way an impression of a radio or TV ad is thought to have value.

Making impressions that count

The difference is that an impression on radio or TV is a calculation of a listener or viewer *seeing* or *listening to* the ad, while an impression in the online context is merely measured by the ad *being present* on the page. An ad placed at the bottom of a page and never seen by the viewer who doesn't scroll all the way to the bottom is still counted as "impressed" in traditional display metrics. Buying display and rich media ads on a CPC (cost-per-click) basis or a CPA (cost-per-action) basis plays in favor of the advertiser, ensuring that they only pay when certain a interaction occurred (a click) or something of value was completed (an action).

The fallacies of view-through measurement

Another pitfall of display ad measurement is the more recent development of view-through conversion tracking. The view-through tracking concept is supposed to work by registering when a visitor views an ad, but may not click on it, and later visits the site for the ad and performs a conversion action. When such a visit or conversion occurs, a view-through visit or conversion is reported, rewarding the display ad with a new level of perceived value. The problem with this form of measurement is that a "view" may not mean much. It presumes a relationship between viewing the ad and the visitor later going to the Web site, when there may well be little or no such relationship.

Considering the case of the impression that doesn't count (that is, one that isn't actually seen by the visitor), it is entirely possible to reward display ads for view-through visits or conversions that the ad really had nothing to do with. Furthermore, view-through tracking relies on third-party browser-based or Flash-based cookies, which are prone to much higher deletion and blocking rates than first-party cookies. Thus, a significant portion of those who view ads and later visit a Web site isn't likely to be counted. Overall, while the concept of view-through measurement is fantastic, the technology can be misleading when too great an emphasis is placed on it. View-through measurement should be used, but not as a primary metric for evaluating display and rich media advertising performance.

Understanding Display Ad Tracking with Google Analytics

By now it shouldn't be new to hear that Google Analytics can be used to track *all* your marketing and advertising, including online display (or banner) and rich media advertising. In fact, tracking your display and rich media ads with Google Analytics is critical to the integrity of your data about traffic sources. When display and rich media aren't properly tagged for tracking, they are typically reported as part of the referring Medium with Source set to the domain of the ad-serving platform or as part of the `direct` Source and `none` Medium, not the site or Medium through which the ad actually ran. The result is pollution of your Referring Sites reports and the loss of valuable details about display and rich media performance.

Avoiding the death of your data

Google Analytics is designed around a concept of "name it like it is." Many other Web analytics tools and campaign tracking systems, as well as direct mail and other forms of marketing, often use campaign codes or something similar to denote what the campaign was for. That campaign code must then be looked up against a table or database of campaign codes before anyone knows what campaign it was for and what ads it represents. That means more work when analyzing performance — which doesn't lend itself to rapid analysis and response or democratization of data.

By naming ads and campaigns using a natural-language convention, analysis is easier and information about campaign and ad performance can be more easily shared because the interpretation of the data doesn't require a cipher to go along with the report. If the reported campaign name is `spring-newsletter-2010` versus `code:5242`, the recipient doesn't need to refer to a de-coder to understand which campaign the data is for.

Additionally, by using descriptive names, your data is easily understood, especially as the people using your Google Analytics account and analyzing its contents change over time. When data becomes relevant and understood by only one or two people within the organization, that information often becomes meaningless and valueless when those individuals leave. By using names that are naturally descriptive, you avoid this peril permanently.

Using the right dimensions for display ad tracking

Chapter 7 explains the multidimensional nature of Google Analytics. As Chapter 5 notes, Google Analytics campaign tracking provides for as many as five dimensions. When tracking display and rich media ads, four of the five dimensions should be fully leveraged, however the Term (or Keyword) dimension should not be used for display or rich media ads because the media is not search engine based.

- **Medium:** First, consider the Medium dimension. Medium is designed to work as the broadest or highest-level dimension for campaign tracking. For display and rich media, Medium should be set to `display` or `rich media`, or perhaps `banner` if you have used `banner` in the past.
- **Source:** After Medium, the Source dimension is most important. Source should simply denote the place the visitor responding to the ad comes from. Typically you should set this to the Web site on which the ad is running, or in rare cases, set it to the network or trafficking partner running the ad. However, setting Source to the actual Web site domain name (such as `yahoo`) ensures that you can properly compare the performance of different Web sites within a display ad network.

- **Campaign:** After Source, consider the Campaign dimension. Campaign is an ad hoc field that should be used to define the marketing initiative or campaign of which the ad is part. For example, you might be running an ad as part of the Spring 2010 campaign. Therefore, you should define the Campaign dimension value for the ad as `spring-2010`. By consistently using the same campaign name in other mediums and sources, you can easily measure the aggregate performance of all media that is part of a campaign as well as compare mediums, sources, and ads within the campaign. For example, do display ads perform better than other mediums for the Spring 2010 campaign?
- **Ad Content:** Last but not least is the Ad Content dimension. Ad Content should be used to differentiate one ad from another. This is best used as a compound-value dimension; that is, one where you have multiple values combined using a common syntax. Within Ad Content for a display ad, you should record information about the size of the ad, the offer or call to action proposed in the ad, and something to differentiate or describe the creative or visual concepts of the ad. For example, you could use the syntax `banner_468x60_free-shirt_white-bg` for a banner ad that is 468-by-60 pixels in size with a free T-shirt offer and using a white background in the ad itself.

Tying together the Medium, Source, Campaign, and Ad Content dimensions produces the multidimensional view of advertising performance that yields the deepest insights. With four dimensions, associated metrics will stand out and point to opportunities for optimization. So, for that T-shirt offer campaign, you might have the following dimensions set: Medium to `display`, Source to `nytimes.com`, Campaign to `spring-2010`, and Ad Content to `banner_468x60_free-shirt_white-bg`.

Setting Up Your Ads for Tracking

The process for tracking display and rich media ads with Google Analytics involves creating tags that are added to the destination URLs (links) of your ads. However, before we get into the details of creating and managing these tracking tags, there are a few important best practices to follow. The values that go into the campaign tracking tags are recorded in the Google Analytics campaign-tracking cookie and then passed to Google Analytics and displayed in the reporting interface. In short, what goes in the tag goes into the cookie, and what goes in the cookie goes in the reports.

Planning your naming conventions

What's in a name? A lot. The four primary dimensions that should be used for tracking display and rich media ads need to be assigned names. Planning the names you will use is important for a number of reasons.

Using data-rich values

First, within the naming convention you apply, be sure to use rich, descriptive data. Descriptive names are critical and can be extended further by using structured naming schemes. A structured naming scheme includes multiple pieces of information within one dimension value.

For example, in the Ad Content dimension, it is useful to include information about the type of display ad (banner, animated banner, Flash banner, interactive, and so on), the size of the ad (width and height), the creative contents, the offer or message, and the placement on a page. Remember to maintain the brevity of the Medium dimension, which should be used solely for high-level analysis. Source can be used to add multiple values if there is no specific Web site to which the ad can be attributed, while Campaign and Ad Content can, respectively, have more information included in them without fragmenting the data. We advise you to maintain consistency with the campaign so you can see the performance of an entire campaign. Avoid using the Campaign dimension as a location where you stuff lots of information unless there truly are different campaigns.

Before you start creating tags (covered next) and running ads, spend time outlining the kind of information you want to capture. Consider the types of ads you will be creating and define a naming convention for each of the four dimensions used for display and rich media measurement. Document this naming syntax and ensure others who may create and run ads use the same syntax. We recommend using a spreadsheet or similar tool. The Web-based Google Spreadsheets makes an excellent resource for sharing between a team or even disparate individuals across your company and external agencies and partners.

Consistency is critical

Second, using a consistent naming convention for the values of the campaign tracking dimensions is absolutely critical. The reason is that inconsistent naming conventions lead to data fragmentation. Consider Figure 10.1, which shows two rows in the Traffic Sources report where the Medium name for sponsored search has been named `cpc` in one case, `PPC` in another, and in yet another case `Ppc`. This difference in case causes the data to be fragmented, making it harder to know the total traffic from sponsored search investments and difficult to compare the performance of sponsored search versus other mediums.

Rules for consistency include:

- Always use lowercase in naming conventions (and consider using a lowercase filter on campaign tags in case anyone in the organization forgets to use lowercase names for their campaign names).
- Avoid spaces — use hyphens instead (for example, `spring-2010` instead of `spring 2010`).
- Use underscores to separate different sets of information within one dimension. For example, in the Ad Content dimension, use an underscore to separate the ad type from the ad size (for example, `banner_468x60`).

FIGURE 10.1

Notice how the inconsistent naming of `cpc`, `PPC`, and `Ppc` fragments the metrics for sponsored search; mediums should all be combined into one Medium name such as `cpc`.

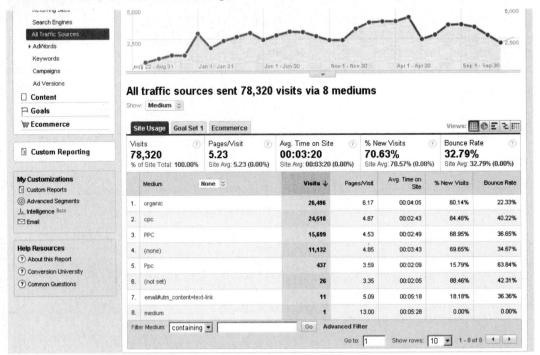

- Once you set the convention, don't *ever* change it! After you start using a naming convention, stick with it because changing tags in new ads won't change the data already recorded in Google Analytics, but it will hamper historical performance analysis.

Creating and managing campaign tracking tags

After defining your campaign-tracking tag-naming convention, you must create the dimension name and value pairings. This is best done using a spreadsheet with a column for each dimension and a row for each destination URL+dimensions+values variation you create.

Creating your tags begins with understanding the tag fields for each of the corresponding dimensions accessible in the Google Analytics reports. Table 10.1 outlines the tracking tag fields and corresponding dimension.

Integrating tracking tags into ads

Once you've defined the values that you will use for each of the four dimensions, you need to finalize the complete tag that will be appended to the ad's destination URL. You do this by combining the

TABLE 10.1

Dimension Values and Tracking Tag Fields

Dimension	Tracking Tag Field	Tracking Field Value	Example Tag String
Medium	utm_medium	display	utm_medium=display
Source	utm_source	nytimes.com	utm_source=nytimes.com
Campaign	utm_campaign	spring-2010	utm_campaign=spring-2010
Ad Content	utm_content	free-shirt	utm_content=free-shirt

tracking tag fields into a tracking tag string. The example in Table 10.1 would result in the following tracking tag string:

```
utm_medium=display&utm_source=nytimes.com&utm_campaign=spring-
    2010&utm_content=free-shirt
```

This tracking tag string must then be appended to the ad's original destination URL (the link that an ad will point to). However, there are two options for appending the tracking tag string that you should consider. It is important to know that these tracking tags can be created as query parameter strings as well as anchor strings. The difference is that a query parameter becomes part of the actual, indexable URL. A query parameter string is what comes after the ? in a URL and is made up of one of more parameters and corresponding value pairs.

For example, in www.analyticsformarketers.com/page.php?pageid=123, the query parameter string is ?pageid=123, the parameter is pageid, and the corresponding value is 123. The only major disadvantage of query parameters is indexing of your campaign destination URLs into search engine results (see the explanation in Chapter 11 of indexed custom campaign URLs).

An anchor string is what comes after the # in a URL. For example, in www.analyticsformarketers.com/page.php#some-anchor, the anchor string is #some-anchor. The advantage of using an anchor string is that it is not recorded in a search engine index and so does not fragment the link if the ad's destination URL becomes indexed by a search engine. However, some ad-serving platforms are not compatible with anchor strings; they remove the anchor string from the destination URL of the ad. You can easily check for this by setting up a test ad and destination URL and appending a dummy anchor string — if the anchor string is removed, your ad management or ad-serving platform is probably not compatible with anchor strings.

NOTE

A number of tools are available for creating campaign-tracking tags. Visit www.analyticsformarketers.com/s/campaign-tracking for more resources and links to tools.

By default, Google Analytics requires query parameter strings for campaign-tracking tags. However, with the addition of the _setAllowAnchor(true); customization to the Google Analytics page tag, you can use the anchor string approach without problem. Thus, a complete tracking tag string using the query parameter method would look like this:

```
http://www.analyticsformarketers.com/landingpage.html?utm_
    medium=display&utm_source=nytimes.com&utm_campaign=spring-
    2010&utm_content=free-shirt
```

A complete tracking tag string using the anchor string method would look like this:

```
http://www.analyticsformarketers.com/landingpage.html#utm_
    medium=display&utm_source=nytimes.com&utm_campaign=spring-
    2010&utm_content=free-shirt
```

Validating that ad tracking is working properly

Once you've defined complete campaign tracking tags for your ads, the next step is to validate that they are indeed working correctly. This can be done with relative simplicity by setting up a test ad using a destination URL with the tracking tags appended and then clicking on it. Once you reach the ad's destination URL in your browser, check to see that the tracking tags appear in the address bar of the page just as you've defined them. If they are missing or mangled, something is wrong!

If they are present, you can be 99 percent sure that tracking will happen properly. The only remaining check is to ensure that the values defined in the tags actually made it into the Google Analytics cookies. To check the cookies, simply use your favorite cookie-checking tool or utility (or go to www.analyticsformarketers.com/s/debugging-tools for recommendations), find the cookies for your domain, and look at the contents of the __utmz cookie. For the example noted in Table 10.1, the __utmz cookie contents would contain the values defined in the tracking tag, similar to this:

```
utmcsr=nytimes.com|utmccn=spring-2010|utmcmd=display| utmcct=free-
    shirt
```

If the destination URL click or cookie tests fail, there are a few common issues to consider. These issues are also commonly found for other kinds of ads and traffic sources (e-mail, sponsored search, organic, and so on):

- **Redirects**: Many ad management and ad-serving platforms use redirects to run ad clicks through their tracking systems. In some cases these redirects fail to pass along any query parameters or tracking tag strings.
- **Missing Google Analytics page tag**: If you have built a landing page for your ad, be sure to verify that the Google Analytics page tag was included in the page by viewing the page's HTML source and looking for the Google Analytics page tag.

- **Wrong Google Analytics page tag settings**: If the page tags are using the wrong settings, such as the wrong `_setDomainName()` method or the absence of `_setAllowAnchor(true)` method when it should be present, the cookies may not be set properly.

Tracking Flash ads

Google Analytics supports measurement of interaction within a Flash object through an integrated Flash tracking library. This facility is perfect for Flash sites or Flash objects that are embedded in other sites, such as a video player or widget. However, to track ads that are Flash-based, the integrated Flash tracking isn't typically a viable solution because ad-serving platforms and networks rarely allow any kind of reporting of user interaction within a Flash ad distributed through their systems. Thus, tracking Flash-based ads remains the same as the approach for non-Flash display ads covered in this chapter; that is, using tracking tags on ads' destination URLs.

Measuring display and rich media campaign history

Standard campaign tracking in Google Analytics operates on a "last-in" basis, which means that a visitor's current activity is attributed to the most recent campaign, source, and medium set for that visitor. This approach rewards the latest campaign and advertising source for any activity and conversions that might occur, preventing earlier campaigns from being rewarded for their contribution to engagement and conversion. But what if the awareness was created by a display or rich media ad? It would not be rewarded for a conversion or even repeat engagement, and the final campaign source would get all the glory.

However, you can break free from the tyranny of the "last-in" campaign source with custom variables. While prescribing the precise code for implementing custom variables to track first-in or contribution to conversion is beyond the reach of this chapter (see Chapter 7 for an overview of how custom variables work), what we can say here is that it is possible.

In short, we recommend implementing code that detects when a visitor enters the site from a display or rich media ad and, upon detection, sets a visitor-level custom variable denoting that the visitor has come through the display or rich media medium and recording the source and ad, if space allows. By setting the custom variable to the visitor level, it attaches information about the display-ad entrance to the permanent user-defined cookie for the visitor, persisting across future sessions and existing independent of the standard traffic source cookie. Once implemented, it lets you determine the impact of past display or rich media ad exposure on those visitors who convert on your Web site.

Analyzing Display Ad Performance

So far this chapter has covered how to set up tracking for your display ads. Without proper tracking in place analysis can't happen, but once you have added well-planned tracking tags to your ads and campaigns, what do you do? Begin analysis!

Assessing display ad performance at a high level

At a high level, measuring the performance of display ads follows the same principles as measuring the performance of any kind of advertising or traffic source: It's about value, not just impressions, clicks, visits, or pageviews. However, value with display advertising must be considered in light of the contribution that visually rich marketing exposure brings: an emphasis on branding rather than the more direct response of specific conversion actions such as buying a product or filling out a form.

Traffic generated from display ads differs from e-mail-based or search engine–based traffic in part due to the nature of display in the online experience. Typically, direct performance measures for display ads are much poorer than for, say, sponsored or organic search traffic. For example, the Bounce Rate will often be 50 percent higher for display ad traffic than for sponsored search, while pages per visit may be 80 percent lower.

Why is this the case? Users who view and respond to display ads are passively engaged, compared to a user who is actively searching for a topic, evaluating links on a search results page, and choosing to click through your link or ad. Display ads capture latent interest and complement active interest through search. The Atlas Digital Marketing Insights report on the combined impact of search and display ads studied the relationship between display ads and search-based ads and found a 22 percent lift in conversion rate for visitors who had been exposed to a display ad and later searched versus those who had searched but not previously seen a display ad.

Consider a newly engaged couple browsing a Web site with information about planning a wedding. A display ad for the Zenith Vineyard wedding venue may appeal to the couple and elicit a click, but it interrupts what they were doing — reading about wedding planning. That click may result in a few pageviews, but is unlikely to lead to an immediate booking request.

However, when the couple decides to choose a venue, the *branding value* of the display ad will surface. The couple may have bookmarked the site or may remember "that Zenith Vineyard wedding venue" and go back to the Web site directly. Or, if they don't respond directly but instead do a search, they will have greater affinity for Zenith Vineyard if they find it on a search results page full of other wedding venues.

If the display ad was rewarded only for driving a conversion, it would appear to have contributed nothing in this scenario and search would get all the credit. However, if you plan to gauge the value for display ads based not only on conversion but also on engagement, display ads will be properly rewarded and you will be able to assess the true value contribution from them.

Comparing display ads to other mediums

Once tagged appropriately, display ads can be easily analyzed by starting with the Medium name or names you used for display and rich media ads. Figure 10.2 shows the All Traffic Sources report with the Show option set to Medium, showing only the high-level mediums that receive traffic. In this report, you can quickly compare the overall performance and value of direct, organic, sponsored search (cpc), and other mediums.

From here you can drill into the display medium and begin to evaluate by sources, campaigns, ads, and so on for visits that came via display.

FIGURE 10.2

The All Traffic Sources report showing Medium makes comparing performance and value of the `banner` Medium to other mediums easy. This figure compares each medium's Per Visit Goal Value metric against the site average, revealing that the `banner` Medium underperforms significantly.

Analyzing campaign outcomes

The beauty of the multidimensional approach to campaign tracking in Google Analytics is that it allows you to look across data dimensions more easily. When it's used properly, analyzing the outcome of a campaign becomes easy at the aggregate level as well as the granular level. For a campaign that contains display ads, you can measure the results not only of that campaign in general, but compare elements of the campaign against each other, drill into the results for display ads, view sources, and compare ad versions, landing pages, and more.

Overall performance

Remember that with display ads, it is important to keep in mind the branding impact of a display campaign. Display ads usually underperform other mediums because of the passive appeal and less-engaged mindset of users who do respond to the ads with a click.

That aside, the principles for analysis of display campaigns remain the same as those you would apply for other ads: Look for areas of strength and weakness. If the overall Bounce Rate is 80 percent at the aggregate level for the `display` medium, don't conclude that all display ads are terrible: Drill into the details for the medium and evaluate the sources, landing pages, and ads involved — perhaps there is a site that performs really well and some that perform abysmally. Use drill-down analysis and comparison to determine the winners and losers, then prune out the losers while rewarding the winners.

Overall performance for display traffic should begin with total traffic generated (visits). Traffic volume should be considered in light of the volume of impressions (which isn't available in Google Analytics — you'll need to conduct visits-to-impressions analysis outside of Google Analytics) and the cost for that exposure. If you spent $10,000 to drive 1 million impressions and received only 1,000 visits, that equates to a cost per visit of $10, which is pretty high. Of course, compare that in the light of the cost of traffic from other mediums before making final conclusions on this top-line analysis.

First stop: Analyzing the Bounce Rate

The Bounce Rate is a first-stop metric for just about everything. With display ads, the Bounce Rate is no less important, but it should not carry quite the same significance as you would give it for a more direct-response-driven medium such as search or e-mail marketing.

NOTE

Remember, Bounce Rate indicates the immediate reaction of a visitor — the higher the rate the more visitors left without viewing another page or conducting any other measured interaction on your site.

When evaluating Bounce Rate, be sure to consider all levels of data — don't just look at the top-line Bounce Rate and make a conclusion — drill into the data and compare sources and geographies to find the big winners and losers. Additionally, with display ads, comparing Bounce Rate between ad versions is critically important. Unlike organic search, your landing pages for a campaign are more limited to display ads because the media is more brand-focused as opposed to hyperspecific. Thus, comparing Bounce Rate by landing page isn't likely to be revealing.

However with display ads, the creative content of the ad *is* likely to have an impact on bounce Rate. Why? Because of the nature of the media: People may click because the creative is compelling, yet once reaching the site leave immediately. As Figure 10.3 shows, evaluating the Ad Content dimension against Bounce Rate reveals the relationships between ad size, placement, creative, and content (provided you included identifiers for each of these areas in your Ad Content field).

Engagement performance

Engagement is certainly a buzzword, but it shouldn't be overlooked. Display advertising generates interest and, if effective, engagement. When considering engagement with display ads, pay particular attention to Time on Site and Pages per Visit.

Seeing high levels of engagement from display ads is a *really* strong indicator of marketing effectiveness. It is dangerous to expect immediate conversion with display ads, so engagement *should* be given more weight. If a display ad version, source, or the medium in general results in poor engagement, count it as a strong indicator something is wrong. Evaluating the sources of display medium traffic often reveals surprising outcomes: Some sites where you run ads bring visitors who remain engaged, while others don't. Judge poor engagement harshly when evaluating display ad sources and ad versions.

FIGURE 10.3

Comparing Bounce Rate for display ads reveals the relationship between the size, placement, creative, and contents of an ad and the propensity of that ad to attract visitors who stay on the site.

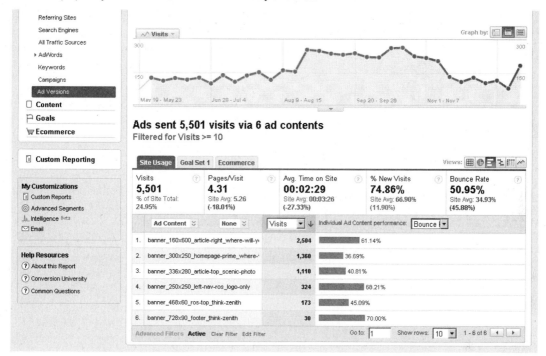

Goal performance

Goals can be tricky with display ads. There are two critical rules for goals when measuring display advertising. First, rather than judging display ads against specific point-of-conversion goals, set up a series of goals that relate to engagement levels, or reaching an area of the site or section, or type of content. The Goals feature in Google Analytics allows creation of goals that are matched against content (reaching a page or set of pages) and interaction (viewing a certain number of pages or spending a certain amount of time on the site).

Second, each goal can have a goal value associated with it. Setting a goal value results in the Per Visit Goal Value metric being populated. The Per Visit Goal Value is calculated when the sum of all goals reached during visits under a particular dimension value is divided by the number of total Visits for that dimension value. If you have 100 visits from the `display` medium and 10 visits each complete a goal worth 2.00 goal value, you would have 20.00 points of goal value points and a Per Visit Goal Value of 0.20 points.

When Goal Values are set, and goals are defined for engagement points and levels, the picture of display ad performance sharpens considerably. Figure 10.4 contains the same list of sources for display

FIGURE 10.4

Judging sources of display ad traffic by Goal Conversion Rate (top) versus Per Visit Goal Value (bottom) is starkly illustrated by the contrast between the two reports in this figure.

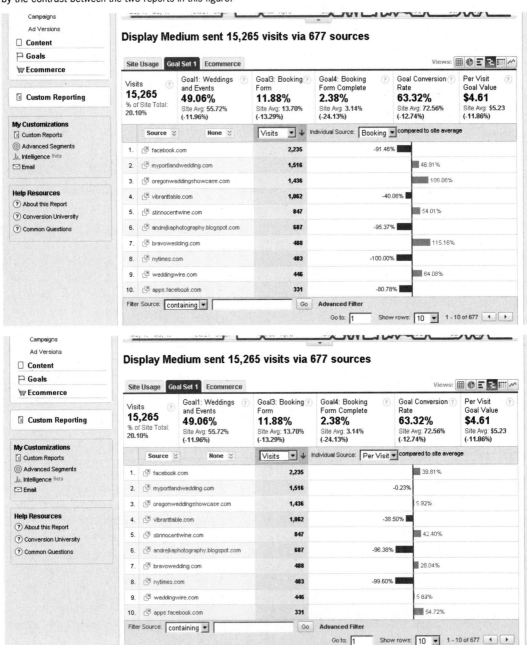

ads, with the top section showing performance based on the overall goal-conversion rate versus goal value on the bottom.

Ecommerce performance

Measuring ecommerce performance driven by display ads should be undertaken in the same fashion as goal performance measurement. The type of ad and the creative message and call to action in the ad drastically impacts the propensity for ecommerce conversion. For example, if a display ad promotes longboards for sale with an offer of "Buy one longboard and get a free skateboard — today only!" and lands the visitor on a longboard purchase page, the likelihood for an immediate purchase is much higher than an ad with impactful creative and a message that says "The world's best longboards!" One ad provides a purchase call to action and the other is focused on branding.

Using Advanced Segments to analyze display ads

Advanced Segments provide a means of digging into the granular details of your display advertising with great precision. First, begin by creating an Advanced Segment that incorporates all the Medium names for your display advertising (such as `banner`, `display`, and `rich-media`). Apply this Advanced Segment to your reports. Once it's applied, only visits that came from one of the included Medium values will be reported.

You can take your Advanced Segments a step further. After creating the Advanced Segment for the Medium values of your display ads, copy the segment and create a version that includes visitors from display ad mediums that stay more than 5 seconds, more than 10 seconds, and more than 30 seconds. You can do this easily by copying the initial display Advanced Segment and simply applying a criterion for Length of Visit greater than 5 seconds, 10 seconds, and 30 seconds, respectively.

Using custom reports with display ads

Custom reports are phenomenally useful for display ad measurement because of the ability to evaluate different dimensions and metrics all on one screen. One of the best purposes for custom reports, with regard to display ads, is creating a report that combines Visit, Bounce, Goal, Engagement, and Commerce metrics into one Data Table that you can easily export to Excel and combine with other display ad metrics such as Impressions and Clicks from advertising providers and networks. The value here lies in creating combined reports that factor in the value of the wide exposure afforded by display ad impressions.

Custom reports can be, well, custom. It is great to experiment with Google Analytics' Custom Report Builder and create reports that meet your specific interests. The following are recommended custom report dimension and metric combinations that build on the techniques described in this chapter.

- Display campaign medium, source, and ad content analysis:
  - **Dimensions:** Campaign, Medium, Source, Ad Content
  - **Metrics:** Unique Visitors, Visits, Pageviews, Pages/Visit, Time on Site, Avg. Time on Site, Avg. Time on Page, Bounce Rate, Per Visit Goal Value
  - **Report Link:** `www.analyticsformarketers.com/s/ch10-report1`

- Display medium loyalty analysis:
  - **Dimensions:** Medium, Count of Visits
  - **Metrics:** Visits, Pageviews, Pages/Visit, Time on Page, Avg. Time on Page, Time on Site, Avg. Time on Site, Bounce Rate, Total Goal Value, Per Visit Goal Value
  - **Report Link:** www.analyticsformarketers.com/s/ch10-report2

Troubleshooting Common Display Ad Tracking Problems

Early in this chapter, we covered the process for correctly setting up tracking for your display ads. However, how do you know if things have indeed been set up correctly? What if you don't have direct control or influence over defining and integrating the necessary tracking tags for display ads? This section covers a few best practices for addressing display ad tracking issues.

Tracking Engagement at PBSkids.org

In December 2009, PBSkids.org launched a new preschool video portal offering video clips and playlists from preschoolers' favorite PBS Kids programs. In January 2010, PBS Kids launched an online banner campaign on various kids' sites to drive traffic to the new preschool video portal. The goal of the campaign was to increase new visitors, expose visitors to the video portal, and circulate those visitors to other areas of the site.

The Web analytics team, working with the PBS Kids team, created a set of Engagement Goals using Google Analytics:

- User visits the Preschool Video page
- Time on Site exceeds the overall site average of 15 minutes
- User visits more than one page
- User visits more than the site average page depth of 15 pages

The team also evaluated campaigns against whether the % New Visits metric exceeded the previous month's site average for the New Visits metric. The results:

- Average daily visits to the site increased 25 percent during the campaign.
- New Visits increased 5 percent.
- Total Unique Visitors to the site increased 28 percent.
- Overall Pageviews on the site increased 20 percent.

The analysis showed that some ad placements that sent a lot of traffic to the site did not perform as well in getting new users to the site. However, the users from those sites tended to be more engaged than users from the other placements, perhaps due to their previous familiarity with the PBSkids.org site. While this particular campaign was fairly short, the find-

What happens when ads aren't tagged

When display ads aren't properly tagged for tracking using the dimensions recommended in this chapter, the visits they generate are still tracked by Google Analytics; however, they are generally attributed to the `referral` Medium, and the Source recorded for these visits is usually not the Web site where the ad was displayed and the click came from, but rather the ad server. In some cases untagged display ads are recorded to the `(none)` Medium and `direct` Source.

You may be tempted to forego the work of tagging display ads for measurement upon hearing that the visits will still be counted. But before you head out of the office for an early happy hour, consider that untagged display traffic will pollute the purity of data of Referring Sites and Direct Traffic data. It is critical to maintain the purity of these two mediums because they are so important to social and viral media measurement (Referring Sites) and offline marketing (Direct Traffic). Mixing in traffic from display ads will increase the volume of traffic attributed to these mediums, as well as skew the metrics for Engagement, Goal Conversion, and Value because display media tends to attract traffic that views fewer pages per visit, converts less on goals, and drives less goal value in trade for the wider branding impact of the display advertising.

ings from this experiment will be used to optimize future media buys, applying a "measure, learn, optimize" process to improving display advertising investments.

We recommend you put in the extra time to tag your display campaigns and *then* head out for that happy hour — and you will be much happier knowing that the integrity of your traffic source data is preserved.

Identifying problems at the ad-server level

Some of the most common barriers to tracking display ads with Google Analytics are problems that arise with ad serving and media management platforms. If you have added the necessary tracking tags to your display ad destination URLs, but are not seeing the data in Google Analytics reports under the Medium, Source, Campaign, or Ad Content values you defined in your tracking tags, chances are the ad-serving or media-management platform is interfering.

The simple test is to find one of your ads running in the real world, click it, and see what happens. If your tracking tags aren't visible in the URL (browser address bar) of the landing page, then they were removed in the process.

The next step, after conducting this simple test, is to use a tool such as Live HTTP Headers for Firefox or Fiddler2 for other browsers. These tools monitor the behind-the-scenes communications between your browser and the Internet (visit www.analyticsformarketers.com/s/http-tools for links to download these tools). Open one of the tools and go through the same process of clicking one of your ads on a live Web site. Once loaded, you can search through the header requests to see if your link at one point had the utm_ tracking tags. Watch for 301, 302, and meta-refresh redirects that may not pass along these query parameters.

Avoiding common, costly mistakes

Mistakes provide great opportunities for learning, but if you can avoid them it is all for the better. For display ads, running a display ad buy with a large budget and no flexibility to change it is inherently incompatible with the notion of performance marketing. If you can't make changes based on observed performance feedback and hold the advertising accountable, you can't optimize it.

As with any advertising you should be measuring results, and if you are measuring and the data clearly points to a problem, you should investigate. If the problem is indeed grievous, such as terribly targeted display ads, poor creative, or other issues, and you can see it but are unable to do anything about it, anxiety levels will rise!

A good practice is to either buy display media through a provider that allows easy changes to the campaign structure, budget commitments, creative, and targeting such as Google AdWords' display ad network or AdReady. If you are buying through a traditional direct buy on a Web site or small network, negotiate to hold at least 50 percent of your budget in reserve pending feedback from analytics data. Sponsored search marketing (known as SEM and covered in Chapter 9) has been heralded for years for its performance. Although it is fundamentally different from display media, a large part of the difference in performance is due to SEM's ability to easily modify search ads and eliminate ad budget being wasted on badly performing campaign elements.

—

Growing Organic Search and Conversions

Search Engine Optimization (SEO) and Google Analytics

Search engine optimization, commonly referred to as SEO, could be defined as the art and science of optimizing Web sites for improved exposure in search engines. It was probably less than a week after the first public Internet search engine was developed that SEO came into existence. Why? The search engine result page is the intersection of interest and intent, the Holy Grail of marketing.

While this is not a book about search engine optimization, this chapter is! We believe it is important to understand how search engines work at a high level, the history behind search engine optimization, and why the traditional means of measuring the success or failure of search engine optimization is no longer relevant and new methods of measuring SEO success are needed — and available — with Web analytics tools.

Knowing Truth from Fiction with SEO

There are two approaches to SEO. The first works to increase ranking and exposure of a site artificially, often without doing anything to improve the true importance, relevance, and competitiveness of the business behind the site. In short, this erroneous approach to SEO is rooted in trying to trick the search engines into ranking a site higher than it really should be ranked. It is like putting a thick layer of beautiful frosting on a cake that tastes bad. The frosting makes the cake look more attractive, but it doesn't do anything to solve the fundamental problem: a badly executed recipe.

The other approach to SEO begins with taking into account the often-overlooked fundamentals of the search engine: The purpose of search isn't searching; it's finding.

Google has gained and maintained a position as the best search engine because it consistently helps people *find* what they are looking for. Thus, Google's business is predicated on searchers becoming finders and coming back to Google the next time they need to find something online.

This "other" approach to SEO puts the needs of the searcher first, just like the search engines do. This shifts the emphasis away from trying to figure out what a search engine algorithm is looking for and trying to match it to the pursuit of a better business and building a better Web site.

In our view, the right approach to SEO begins with making your business better — understanding your customers and their needs — then building your Web site in a fashion that serves your customers better than any competitor *and* building it in a way that search engines can easily recognize what a great business you have.

Search engines, at least the ones people use regularly, are good at figuring out the best Web sites and ranking them at the top of a search results page. Billions of dollars are at stake. If Google were to fail at providing relevant results, at helping you to *find* and not just *search*, how long would you keep using it? SEO should not be in opposition to search engines; rather, it should work *with* search engines because there is mutual success and failure in the balance. Some companies rank at the top of popular searches without doing any SEO in a traditional sense, while corporate behemoths with gross sales larger than the GDP of some nations utterly fail at being found when people search for their brand and product names.

How search engines work

The Internet's first search engines were, in comparison to today's engines, simple — and easily manipulated. Early search engines analyzed only a few factors in their algorithms and could only "crawl," or find, certain types of pages. You commonly had to submit your pages to these early search engines to even have your pages crawled and eventually added to the index.

The basic algorithms looked at factors such as the number of times a certain keyword appeared on a page to determine the keyword density and thus the relevance of that page for that particular keyword. `Meta` tags were the basis of what the search engines looked at — some not even analyzing the full text of the page. As a result, one could easily manipulate the results and thereby optimize the ranking of a site. Some of these techniques included stuffing keywords into pages and `meta` tags by repeating words over and over in hidden elements — parts of the page that users normally wouldn't see but search engines would see and evaluate in their algorithms.

At a high level, search engines have four basic parts:

1. The bot, also referred to as a *spider*, *crawler*, and robot. Search bots are basically computer programs that scour the Internet and collect content for the search engine's massive cache and index.

2. The index and cache: The cache contains copies of the text and code on each page discovered by the bot. This cache is then indexed, much like a book's index, except that it contains *billions* of pages and *every* word on those pages is in the index, referenced to the pages at which each word can be found. For example, at the time of this writing, the word "analytics" returns

96,500,000 pages in the Google index. That's *96 and a half million pages* that contain or are related to the word analytics.

3. The algorithm is the "secret sauce" of a search engine: It determines the relevance of each page found in the index that is related to the search query used, then ranks the results from most relevant to least relevant. Without the algorithm, that list of 96.5 million results would be impossible to use because the relevant pages — the ones you want to *find* — would be buried like needles in the proverbial haystack of other results.

4. The results page: This is what you see after conducting a search. It presents the list of results from the search engine's index as ranked by the algorithm.

Keep in mind that this description of how a search engine works is a greatly simplified description of what is a complex technological exchange. But that complex technological exchange is also the beauty of search — it works and doesn't require a PhD in quantum physics to use. And, contrary to what many preach and believe, optimizing a site for search engines isn't a mysterious black art known to only a few people on the planet. Rather, SEO is about following a few best practices that the majority of Web sites ignore and having a great business model that competes in the real world.

An arms race with robots, spiders, and spam

Just as we all hate unwanted e-mail in our inbox, search engines hate irrelevant listings in their search results, a.k.a. search engine spam. Yes, spam is not only a food substance and the bane of your inbox — it has found its way into search engines. Search spam is a page that is irrelevant for a given search query and undesirable to a searcher. If you search using the keyword "coffee" and the top results were obscure companies you had never heard of or, worse, for something else entirely, you would think something was wrong with the search engine and probably click to another search provider.

As early search engine technology improved and SEO "experts" took advantage of what they could, it sparked an arms race of sorts between search engine providers and many SEO practitioners. Search engine providers sought to improve the relevance and accuracy of search results while at the same time including as much of the rapidly growing Internet in their index as possible. Meanwhile, SEO practitioners sought to keep their clients' sites on top of the growing pile of search results in an effort to garner more traffic, often to the detriment of true relevance. Search engines consider these fake results as spam, because the results are generally not useful to the searcher.

Keep in mind that we're not saying that all SEO techniques and companies, consultants, and practitioners who specialize in SEO are bad or have used tactics that create search engine spam. In fact, in recent years more and more SEO experts have emphasized best practices for optimizing and avoided questionable ones. However the history of the search engine business and SEO as a practice reflects a problematic past. When approaching SEO, whether it is something you will do yourself or hire an employee, consultant, or agency to assist with, we cannot emphasize enough the importance of applying only the best practices and avoiding the questionable ones.

Driving true success with SEO

We advocate SEO that builds lasting value and long-term equity. While not necessarily complicated, conducting effective *good* SEO is hard to do, so don't take lightly the need for knowledgeable experts to assist you. However, we urge extreme caution when evaluating so-called SEO providers because there are many who practice tactics that are outdated, ethically questionable, and not rooted in furthering the mutual success of your business, a search engine's business, and ultimately the customer who is trying to find you.

Here is a framework for SEO that we recommend following — as you'll see, it leads into the critical component for success with search optimization: measurement.

Follow the unique-authoritative-relevant principle

To attain and sustain top exposure in search engines, your site needs content that is unique, authoritative, and relevant.

This means that pages on the site should not be redundant — and by "page" we mean URL — a technical term for pages on a site. You might have the same page available under multiple URLs. For example, if you have `www.brandsite.com/shoes.html` and `www.companyname.net/shoes.html`, or `www.site.com/store.aspx?product=123` and `www.site.com/products.aspx?id=123`, and the pages contain the same content, you have what is considered *duplicate content*. Content should be unique to your business and differentiate you from competitors and your pages from other pages online. Visitors and search engine algorithms alike appreciate content that is unique and relevant to your company.

Authoritative means you need to know what you're talking about. Simply regurgitating information doesn't carry authority. Authority takes time to build through creating credibility and reliability. Being an authority requires hard work and usually doesn't happen overnight.

Relevant means that each page on the site needs to be clearly about what the visitor wants to find. It also needs alignment of technical factors as well as knowing your customers and industry. Relevance also requires recency or "freshness" — building a site and not adding new, fresh content ensures irrelevance because the rate of change on the Internet is accelerated far beyond what existed before the Web.

Putting the customer first

As we've said, for a search engine to remain successful it must ultimately help people find what they are looking for quickly and simply. Thus, successful SEO begins with knowing your customer and putting their interests first. Online customers are always a button-click away from leaving your Web site and going to the competition. Knowing and appealing to your audience with desirable products and services is paramount to success.

Using the right words

All too often companies use "internal-speak" online. For example, you have a clever brand name for a useful microwaveable travel coffee mug. Your expert product marketing team came up with a catchy name that's great for in-store product packaging and traditional offline advertising, but online it doesn't matter. When someone wants to buy a coffee mug for traveling that they can heat in a microwave before they walk out the door, they won't search for an unknown product name — they'll search for what they want, describing the product with commonsense words.

Therefore, you *must* use the words your customers will use to describe a product. Don't strip all branding from your Web site — branding is important once someone finds you — but put the words searchers use when trying to find your company, brand names, or products first, and use product names, catchy slogans, and internal-speak last.

Building it right

One of the top reasons companies need to hire an SEO specialist is to fix problems built into the site since its creation. Many sites were built in a way that actually creates a barrier to search engines finding and indexing content. Your Web site might have the best, most unique content, be insanely relevant, and be the most credible authority in the world, but if your site can't be crawled and indexed by a search engine's robots and if your pages don't provide a clear picture of what they are about, you'll just be one of the tens of millions of results found for most searches and not listed on the first results page where most people start — and stop — looking.

Building a site correctly begins with the underlying technology powering the site — usually a content management system (CMS). However, not all CMS platforms are created equally: Some are outright incompatible with publishing content in a manner that search engines can reasonably index. Others try to provide SEO features but in doing so cause more harm than good (such as providing a "search-friendly" URL feature that fails to redirect the "nonsearch-friendly" URLs to the "friendly" ones, causing duplicate content problems). Still other CMS platforms are built by developers who rightly understand what search engine technology needs to easily identify and accurately rank pages according to relevance and build that into the foundations of their platform. Our rule: Select a system built with SEO as key *forethought* in system design, not an afterthought. (See `www.analyticsformarketers.com/s/seo-cms` for a few of our favorites.)

Last, the critical component to building a site the right way for search engines begins with proper planning. It's always harder to change the foundation after the building has been built. The same is true for a Web site. A site's technology and information architecture must be built in a fashion that creates unique, relevant, and authoritative pages that are well-matched to keywords and phrases customers use when searching for what your site offers.

A practical example is this: If your company has several store locations, the store locator section of the site should not only list each store but have a dedicated page for each location. On each dedicated page should be information such as the address and telephone number, neighborhood and surrounding area names, main street names, nearby attractions and even competitors, hours of operation, and top products or services available at that location. If you are a restaurant in Bellevue, Washington, that serves a breakfast truly worth getting out of bed at 5 a.m. for and you create a dedicated location page for your Bellevue breakfast diner, you'll have a page that is relevant, unique, and authoritative for people looking for "breakfast restaurant in Bellevue" — they will find your page much more easily when searching and you'll convert them to a customer. Multiply this scenario by other meals, food types, and hundreds or thousands of locations, and you've created a gigantic new channel of Web site traffic.

Understanding the Case for Web Analytics and SEO

Just as we advocate a perspective on SEO that differs from commonly held assumptions about what SEO is and isn't, our approach to measuring SEO may seem a bit unconventional as well. In the same way that we have seen many approaches to SEO, some of which we consider hurtful to your business, we have also found there are many notions of how to measure SEO "success": Some are outright false, others misguided, and still others are accurate and helpful in making sound business decisions.

Dispelling the fallacy of "top ranking"

When measuring organic SEO, most people talk about "rank" or "position." Advertisements promote "top rankings" and everyone wants to be No. 1 on the results page. Companies often hire and fire SEO firms over the rankings they see when plugging their desired keywords in Google and looking at where their site ranks. Numerous software programs can be purchased to monitor and measure ranking on an automated basis and provide reports of rank by keywords and changes over time.

While all these are legitimate measures in some sense, when it comes to SEO we don't believe in ranking as the ultimate measure. Just as horsepower was once considered the status of a car's quality, today most people measure cars by their MPG ratings.

"Ranking" is dead

Why do we say rank is no longer the most important measure of success for SEO? Because rank as we knew it is dead. Yes, we said dead, and it's due to one word: personalization. Personalized search, as it's called, means search result rankings are tailored to each searcher. This is done through analysis of data a search engine has available about a searcher's interests.

In 2005, Google brought a new feature out of its labs: personalized search, which provided tailored results for those users who activated a "search history" feature. In 2007, the "personal search" algorithm was extended to run for users who didn't have "search history" enabled when signed in to their Google account. In December 2009, Google began applying personalized search to searchers who aren't even signed in to a Google account.

The purpose of personalized search is the same thing search engines are always after: making it easier to find the things you want. One example Google uses to explain how its personalized search system works considers the keyword "bass." Using the keyword "bass" as a search term could mean many things — information about specifies of freshwater fish, music, or something entirely different. If Google knows I am interested in fly-fishing, salmon, steelhead, and boats, the results can be tailored to favor bass fishing rather than subwoofers or bass guitars. Notice that in Figure 11.1 the results at the top of the page focus on bass fishing, followed by results related to other topics based on the word "bass."

FIGURE 11.1

Google's personalized search algorithm tailors the results to each user based on their search history. Here the top results are oriented to bass fishing, not bass guitars and other meanings of the word "bass."

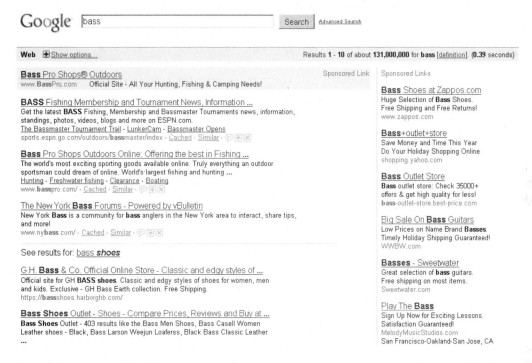

Personalized search is like an attentive concierge who notices subtle points of fashion to improve his restaurant recommendations.

The point is this: Ranking of results you see when conducting a search is likely unique to the searcher. Thus, relying on the observed rank of a search isn't a reliable means of measuring whether or not your SEO efforts have successfully increased exposure for keywords that matter. Relying on ranking will simply lead you in the wrong direction, because ranking at the top for nonpersonalized searches, or for the searcher's individual profile, doesn't mean you'll be found by your *customers*. Success happens when customers find your products, and that usually happens when the site is listed at the top of the results page. However, thanks to personalized search, the ranked "list" of results is no longer static — it is dynamic and changes for each searcher. What matters is what appears at the top of each individual customer's results page.

We need a new measure of success!

Looking beyond rank as a measure of SEO success

So other than ranking, how can a marketer measure the success of SEO? There are two options.

FIGURE 11.2

Google's Webmaster Tools system allows Web site owners and managers to see ranking and other diagnostic information about their site. The keywords report shows the *average* of all positions after the variations introduced by personalized search are factored in, revealing an accurate measure of a site's ranking for a given keyword.

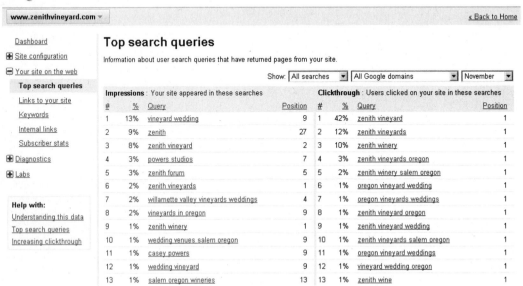

First, Google and Bing (the current incarnation of Microsoft's search engine) provide Webmaster Tools. Google's Webmaster Tools are arguably better than those Microsoft offers at this point, but that should (we hope) change with time.

Google Webmaster Tools provide a report showing the *average rank* of keywords for which your site is both listed and clicked through from (as shown in Figure 11.2). When it comes to rank, the only reliable measure is this "average ranking" report, which can conveniently be measured over time so that changes in average ranking can be measured as efforts are made to improve the relevance of the site for customers.

Aside from Webmaster Tools, and more important in our opinion, the key measure of SEO success is how people who come from search engines interact with your site. More than just traffic, you must measure metrics such as engagement, conversion rate, or revenue. Even if your site always ranks at the top for all your important keywords and has all the traffic in the world, it won't provide much value if that traffic bounces off the site like water off a duck's back. Ultimately your business grows through strengthening relationships with existing customers and acquiring new ones, so measuring factors that drive deeper engagement and customer acquisition is what matters.

Defining your SEO measurement framework

As explained in previous chapters, defining measurement needs should start with determining what drives your business, not just measuring abstract numbers. Thus, defining your measurement framework for SEO must ultimately be about what drives your business. If you have not worked on definitions and set goals, we recommend reviewing Chapter 2.

Determining your measures of SEO success

For SEO, we've focused on measuring the success of your SEO efforts in increasing traffic and business value. Optimization success measures provide insight into what techniques are working to increase site exposure through organic search (that is, search conducted by people on their own, not triggered by some campaign). Business value measures relate to the business impact of that exposure. Knowing the difference between these measures and understanding how they affect each other is key.

Measuring the success of optimization is something we cover in great depth later in this chapter. At a high level, measures of optimization should not be based on ranking but on the following areas:

- **Total traffic from organic search.** Ultimately, the top-line measure of SEO work today should be total traffic from organic searches. Thanks to personalization algorithms, companies can't rely on an observed rank, and thus traffic must be used as the basic measure.

- **Organic search traffic from branded versus nonbranded terms.** SEO efforts should work to increase the traffic you receive from keywords that don't contain your brand name or branded product names. It is a big problem if your site is not readily found in searches using your brand and product names. Once you've covered your bases and are consistently found and receiving traffic for branded searches, you should be looking to nonbranded keywords to generate the majority of your traffic. For most businesses, 20 to 40 percent of your traffic should come from branded keywords. If your business has little to no brand equity, or has a brand name that is generic or easily confused with another name (such as if your company name is San Francisco Plumbers), you may have significantly less branded traffic.

- **Organic traffic from head versus long-tail terms.** "Head" terms are keywords that receive lots of visits ("lots" being a relative term to the total traffic received from search engines), while the "long-tail" terms are the hundreds, thousands, or even millions of unique keywords that receive only a handful of visits. You don't want all your traffic coming from either head terms or long-tail terms. Having the right ratios for head versus long-tail traffic indicates healthy SEO, while unbalanced ratios indicate an SEO problem. For most Web sites, 40 to 60 percent of Web traffic should come from head terms.

- **Number of unique keywords referring traffic.** As the optimization of your site improves, the number and variations of keywords bringing traffic to your site should increase. Look at your current Keywords report in Google Analytics — you will likely see hundreds or thousands of queries that bring only one or a handful of visits. It may seem insignificant to have a keyword that only brought one visit, but having a million unique keywords each bringing one visitor equates to, well, a million visits. All those single-visit keywords add up! Successful SEO will result in a continuing expansion of the number of unique keywords that bring traffic to your site.

- **Organic traffic landing on the home page versus deep-content pages.** Because search engines work to match people with the pages they're looking for, the home page is rarely the ideal landing page. Good SEO efforts should result in more traffic landing on pages deeper in the site. How many times have you clicked on a search result looking for something specific and been taken to a page that forced you to search all over again? It's not a pleasant experience!

- **Bounce rate of organic search traffic.** The bounce rate for organic traffic is a sign of SEO health. When bounce rate increases, it indicates that the site is failing to provide the desired information the searcher is looking for, despite the success of getting the visit from a search engine. When bounce rate increases for search-related traffic, it is a major warning indicator of an impending drastic drop in organic exposure because your site is failing to appeal to customers. When your site fails to appeal to customers, it usually won't appeal to search algorithms either.

- **New visitors versus returning visitors from organic search**: Ideally your SEO efforts will open new markets and bring new visitors, and not simply be a means for users who already visit your site to navigate their way back.

So which metrics are the most important?

- If you are just starting SEO, you should focus on maximizing brand-related traffic. The worst place to be is one where people search for your company or products by name and don't find you! You'll want to watch the traffic from branded terms and traffic landing on your home page for upward trends.

- If you've mastered the branded searches, focus on expanding the long-tail search terms. You'll want to see the number of unique keywords increase month over month.

- Next, focus on increasing exposure for primary head terms. Watch for the volume of traffic to increase from the top 10 to 25 nonbranded keywords.

- Finally, once you're maximizing traffic generation, focus on optimizing what happens after people find you. Look at the bounce rate by keyword and landing page. You can often reduce bounce rate by identifying high-bounce pages and running tests using Website Optimizer (see Chapter 8 for more on optimizing your Web site using this tool) that will lead to improvements in the user experience.

Consider this scenario: If you optimized exposure and doubled your traffic but saw a 50 percent drop in the conversion rate, you have not actually improved your business. Despite doubling the number of visits from SEO traffic, the decline in the associated conversion rate reveals a drop in the quality of traffic. Fantastic traffic growth — as well as the costs associated with driving it — hasn't helped bring more business.

When planning your SEO success measurement framework, take into consideration the following metrics (also, review the coverage of key goal performance measures in Chapter 8):

- **Goal Conversion Rate for leads.** If you capture leads or have other measurable points of communication, watch the Conversion Rate for these leads. The fastest way to increase your business is usually to increase the Conversion Rate for leads rather than trying to get more traffic at a lower Conversion Rate.

- **Value of completed goals.** Define a value for each goal and watch the Total Goal Value generated from SEO traffic. See the coverage in Chapter 5 on setting up a Goal Value framework. By using Total Goal Value, you can readily assess the contribution from SEO to your overall Web site value based on this objective measure.

- **Per Visit Goal Value.** As explained in Chapter 8, this metric is one of the best indicators of success because it provides a measure of the value of all goals combined. When analyzing SEO, identify the keywords with the highest Per Visit Goal Value and work to increase traffic from these keywords.

- **Total Goal Completion.** Ultimately, you want the number of completed goals to increase.

- **Ecommerce Conversion Rate.** If you sell through your Web site, watch the Ecommerce Conversion Rate metric as a leading indicator for SEO success. If this metric decreases as traffic increases, it indicates that you're getting lower-quality visits from your search optimization efforts. Also, drill into your Keywords report and measure the Ecommerce Conversion Rate on a per-keyword basis. Focusing optimization efforts on terms or groups of terms with the highest Ecommerce Conversion Rates will lift overall sales from SEO.

- **Total Revenue.** At the end of the day, the metric that matters most is Total Revenue. Are you making more money than before? Google Analytics will show you Total Revenue from organic traffic under the Non-paid slices of the Keywords or Search Engine reports. Also be mindful of what it *doesn't* show you: your profit margin on products. If your SEO work brings in more sales from lower-margin items, you may end up with less profit.

- **Average Revenue per Order.** This metric takes into account the relationship between transaction value and revenue generated. While the Ecommerce Conversion Rate tells you when you're getting more people buying, it doesn't tell you if those orders are more valuable. Having 1,000 orders for a $10 item is usually worth less than 100 orders for a $200 item. You want Average Revenue per Order holding steady or improving as your SEO traffic increases — if not, it is cause for alarm. When analyzing keywords or groups of keywords, use this metric as a primary judge of where you should focus your optimization efforts.

Defining your business measures is only the first half of the picture. Later in this chapter we explain in detail specific metrics that gauge the effectiveness of optimization work.

Ensuring accurate SEO data is collected

Once you've identified your critical measures for success, you must have confidence that the data in your reports is reliable. While a multitude of scenarios can corrupt your data, there are common issues that will most likely impact your analytics data.

Differentiating sponsored from organic search. The first major issue with accurately measuring traffic from SEO is to avoid polluting your organic search traffic with traffic from sponsored search campaigns. Without fail, sponsored search traffic will *always* be attributed to `organic` rather than cost-per-click (CPC) unless you have identified the sponsored search traffic as sponsored.

With AdWords, it's as simple as enabling the Auto Tagging setting. For other providers like Yahoo Search Marketing and Microsoft AdCenter, you'll need to set up campaign tracking codes. (See Chapter 9 for more specifics on how to track sponsored search campaigns properly.)

When sponsored search is attributed to the `organic` Medium, it will skew the success metrics, and depending on how much sponsored traffic your company is buying, that skew could be significant. If you're trying to ascertain the success of the SEO investments and you see a 300 percent quarter-versus-quarter increase in nonbranded search traffic, you might want to throw a party for your SEO team. However, if the Sponsored Search team launched a new campaign this quarter and didn't tag its traffic as CPC, you would be throwing a party for the wrong team and investing in the wrong traffic-generation channel.

Home page and other redirects. Run a quick check by going to the company home page and typing `www.yoursite.com` (or whatever the home page URL is). Once the page loads, notice the URL in the address bar of your browser. Is it still `www.yoursite.com`, or has it been *redirected* to another URL? If the address is, say, `www.yoursite.com/site/home.aspx`, you likely have a redirect in place.

A redirect isn't *necessarily* a problem —it depends on the kind of redirect. There are redirects that are handled by the Web server and use a "301" (permanent redirect) or "302" (temporary redirect) status code (see `www.analyticsformarketers.com/s/redirects` for information about redirect types). Other redirects are performed with JavaScript or a `meta refresh` tag. Redirects handled by the server (called *server-side redirects* or *response redirects*) don't usually cause problems for Google Analytics, but a `meta refresh` or JavaScript redirect wreaks havoc on Google Analytics for measuring organic search by causing organic search traffic to appear as `direct`, or `self-referral` (referred from your own domain), traffic.

The reason JavaScript and `meta refresh` redirects cause problems is because the `document.referrer` JavaScript field isn't passed by the `meta refresh` or JavaScript redirect. Thus, once you reach the "real" home page URL or the destination of the redirect, the referrer information that Google Analytics looks at to determine an `organic` search engine source is void of the information needed to determine the organic search source and thus Google Analytics determines that the referring source is `www.yoursite.com` or `direct`.

Detecting a problematic redirect requires a technical explanation beyond the scope of this book. If you do observe a redirect, ask your Web master or Web development team for assistance to determine what kind of redirect is used. Alternatively, look for the key symptoms of problematic redirects: extremely low `organic` traffic and high `direct` traffic, and little to no traffic recorded for your brand-name keywords. In Google Analytics, it you choose the Search Engines report, change the primary dimension to Landing Page, and see little or no traffic reported for the home page, you probably have a "bad" redirect interfering with correct traffic attribution to the organic medium.

Indexed custom campaign URLs. A less common but nonetheless problematic issue is when custom campaign URLs get indexed and ranked in organic search engines. For example, let's say your e-mail vendor sent out a special offer announcement with a link to your Web site, properly tagged for e-mail:

```
http://www.yoursite.com/?utm_source=customers&utm_medium=email&utm_
    campaign=spcl
```

The vendor then posts a Web version of this mailing in the E-mail Newsletter Archive section of your Web site and includes the same link complete with campaign tracking codes. The next day a search engine happily discovers this link during its next crawl and adds it to the index. Once indexed, the link can appear in search results. If users click this link, they will come from a search engine but land at a URL with the custom campaign tracking codes, which override detection of the referral from organic search.

Detecting this issue within Google Analytics is difficult. For this reason, pay close attention to not publishing links with custom tracking codes into HTML pages that can get indexed. Alternately, you can completely avoid this issue by using the `#tag` method for campaign tracking URLs. See Chapter 5 for more details on this campaign tagging option.

Improperly implemented subdomain and cross-domain code. Another common cause for corrupted and unreliable organic search metrics is the use of subdomains and third-party domains when your Google Analytics page tags aren't configured properly for the domain architecture of your site. Symptoms of this issue are noticeable in the Referring Sites report: If you see your site listed as a referring source and it brings more than 2 to 3 percent of the total site visits, you likely have an incorrect configuration.

To resolve this issue, you need to correctly implement the Google Analytics page tags on your site. (See Chapter 4 for a background on the cookies and scripts involved in Google Analytics and Chapter 5 for specifics on how to configure your page tags properly.)

Site-search data pollution. Internal site search tools are a critical feature for most Web sites. However, in certain cases the internal site search engine can look like an external organic search engine. This most commonly happens with internal search tools that use "search" or "google" in their URLs — for example, `search.yoursite.com` or `googlemini.yoursite.com`. When this happens, the visitors who perform a site search will have their Google Analytics traffic source cookie set to the keyword used for the internal site search and be recorded as a new organic visit.

Detecting this problem is relatively easy: Look at your Keywords report for keywords that are unlikely to actually bring organic traffic. For example, a private school Web site finds one of its top keywords under Google Organic is "calendar." Hmm ... personalization or not, it is unlikely *anyone* is using the keyword "calendar" to locate this site!

Resolving this problem usually requires custom scripting beyond the scope of this book. Because this issue has the potential to (and most likely does) render your organic search reports completely unreliable, we strongly recommend resolving it quickly once detected. For professional assistance, contact a Google Analytics authorized consultant in your area (see www.analyticsformarketers. com/s/gaacs for Google's list of consulting partners for Google Analytics).

Measuring Effectiveness of SEO Efforts with Google Analytics

We now focus on how Google Analytics can be used to directly measure SEO efforts rather than solely looking at the business value from SEO. We focus less on business value measurement and more on practical, specific reports to set up and monitor. Since the death of ranking, the following reporting techniques provide the most reliable method for measuring effectiveness of SEO efforts.

Trends matter more than metrics

When conducting SEO work, it's foolish to expect fast changes. SEO done correctly typically takes time to build, but it grows like a snowball rolling down a hill. Therefore, conducting analysis on a day-by-day basis is not productive, while analyzing weeks or months can reveal if you're headed in the right direction. On a daily or weekly basis, it is important to watch for precipitous drops in traffic from organic search that would signal a massive problem, such as a directive inadvertently added to the robots.txt file (a file that defines what search bots can and cannot access) that tells search engines to stop crawling and delete all pages for the site from their index (yes, this has been done!).

TIP

Use the Custom Alerts portion of Google Analytics' Intelligence reports to set up daily monitoring of organic traffic to your site that alerts you of a decrease greater than 50 percent. See Chapter 7 for more information about Intelligence reports and creating custom alerts.

When analyzing SEO, the Search Engines and Keywords reports in the Traffic Sources report section are the primary reports you will work with. Under Traffic Sources, the Search Engines and Keywords reports should become your new best friends. In addition, don't overlook the All Traffic Sources report, choosing Medium View from the Show pop-up menu. Figure 11.3 shows the All Traffic Sources report.

CAUTION

When using weekly or monthly graphing views it is best to select time ranges with full-week (Sunday through Saturday) or full-month periods. If partial weeks or months are used in a weekly or monthly graphing mode, the data will appear falsely low in the trend pattern.

Viewing trends by week and month, not day

Trends inherently imply a period of time. Effective trend analysis in Google Analytics is difficult do over a long period of time when the graph lines indicate day-by-day data. Therefore, it is best to use weekly or monthly graphing modes when conducting trend analysis. For example, in Figure 11.4 the top graph shows organic traffic over a 12-month period graphed on a daily basis, while the middle shows

FIGURE 11.3

The All Traffic Sources report showing mediums with an Advanced Segment for organic search traffic reveals the growth trend of organic search engine traffic compared to all site traffic over several months.

weekly, and the bottom graph reports data on a month-by-month basis. The daily view (top) shows when wild daily variations occurred, which is common. By using weekly (middle) or monthly (bottom) views, identifying when true trends begin is easier.

Comparing time periods

Google Analytics has built-in time-range analysis tools to easily compare one time period to another. Chapter 6 has details on using the Date Selector tool and Compare to Past feature. Using the Compare to Past feature for SEO measurement is important because it eliminates the need to manually calculate the difference between two time periods.

When comparing time periods for analyzing SEO efforts, be mindful of the effects of seasonality, cyclicality, and external events. For example, if your site is highly sensitive to day-of-week cycles and traffic is low on weekends, comparing month versus month can be misleading. If one month contains an extra weekend it will have noticeably lower monthly traffic than a month with more weekdays. This time-period comparison would indicate a significant improvement in month versus month traffic and point to "success" with SEO efforts, when in reality one month simply had more traffic-producing days and actual effectiveness of SEO efforts may have decreased.

FIGURE 11.4

Organic search engine traffic over a year graphed by day. Single-day swings in traffic clutter the reports (top). Weekly views (middle) have more fluctuation but also show the trend more easily. In monthly Graph Mode (bottom), it is easy to see the macro trend over several years. However, identifying the precise time when the change started is harder. The weekly view (middle) is generally best for identifying the more precise timeframe when trend changes began.

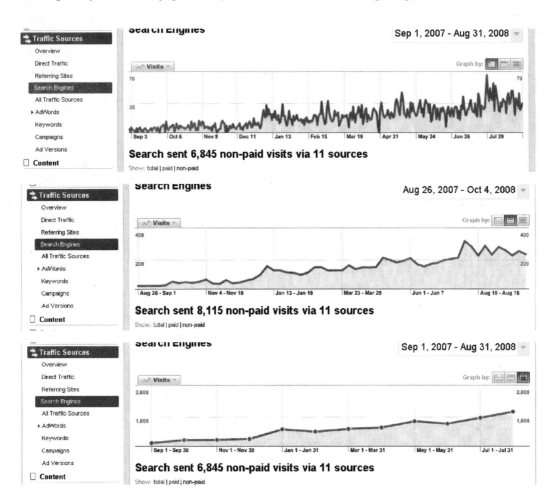

When measuring SEO effectiveness, focus on the % Change between the two time periods. The percentage change is automatically calculated for all metrics in a report when the Compare to Past feature is activated. If the percentage change is negative (for example, total traffic decreased by 8 percent) it is cause for concern, whereas if the change is good (traffic increased 12 percent) it is cause for elation. Note that when comparing absolute metrics such as Visits and Pageviews, you must compare equivalent periods of time and account for seasonality and cyclicality.

Two kinds of time-period analysis are typically the most useful: back-to-back and this-versus-last. Back-to-back analysis examines two adjoining time periods such as last month versus two months ago, while this-versus-last analysis examines the same time range in two different periods, such as October of this year versus October of last year.

There is a propensity to default to month-versus-month analysis because it is a round time period, but this time period (month versus month) analysis should be avoided unless you are comparing at least three months at one time. Week-by-week is favorable because it more accurately accounts for day-of-week cyclicality. For example, many ecommerce sites have found Tuesdays are typically the highest sales days. If your site is viewed more on Tuesday and significantly less on a Friday and Saturday, time-period comparison should maintain an equivalent set of weekdays (that is, always include a Tuesday and a Friday). Comparing one seven-day period with two Tuesdays versus one with only one Tuesday would likely show a larger difference in metrics — yet the cause would likely be due to the difference in day-of-week cycles than to the overall difference of the one seven-day period versus the other. Figure 11.5 shows how comparing a full-month versus a 28-day period can reveal significantly different comparison calculations.

Traffic metrics that matter

What should you use to measure whether SEO efforts are working: optimization or business? Business measures are ultimately the most important because they relate to business value — the end-of-the-day thing that matters most. Optimization measures are the focus of this section — specifically those relating to traffic generated from organic search.

Total traffic from organic search

The first traffic metric to watch is the Total Visits generated by organic search. There are a number of ways to view traffic from search engines, but all begin in the Traffic Sources section in Google Analytics. In the Search Engines report under Traffic Sources, you'll see a list of search engines and the traffic from each. Be sure to select the Non-paid option below the graph to ensure you're seeing traffic from organic search. Figure 11.6 shows this report selected, listing search engines in the standard Table View.

TIP

Click the Add to Dashboard link in this report to make it easily accessible from your Dashboard and provide a Summary view of organic search engine traffic in e-mailed Dashboard reports.

When analyzing total traffic from organic search, you should focus on the overall trend over several weeks and months, perform time-period comparisons, and look for single-day changes that would relate to a major event or external factor affecting the number of times people who find your site in search results.

As an alternative to using the Search Engines report, you can view the same set of data with different options by choosing All Traffic Sources ⬧ Show and choosing Medium rather than showing Source/Medium on the same row. Once Medium is listed, click on Organic to view the list of search engines. You can now drill down into a specific search engine or change the Primary or Secondary Dimension to other options.

FIGURE 11.5

Top: The graph line and scorecard shows organic search traffic comparing one month versus the preceding month. The percentage change in Total Visits is misleading because the months do not contain equal day-of-week periods. Bottom: The graph line and scorecard is based on comparison of two four-week periods and shows a more accurate representation of percentage change between the time periods. Scheduling a report to be e-mailed on a weekly basis showing last week versus two weeks prior will include two full Sunday-through-Saturday periods and is a fantastic means of gaining insight into rolling changes in search traffic. Daily reports showing time comparisons are not as useful because day-by-day fluctuations can result in a wild percentage of change from one day to the next that is perfectly normal given day-of-week cyclicality.

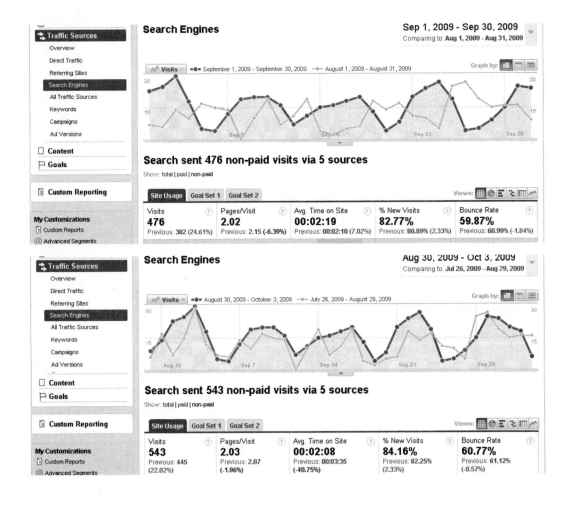

Traffic from each search engine

Another traffic-based measure to watch is the volume from each search engine. As with percentage of total traffic from organic search, this means of measurement is an indicator of SEO health — too much traffic from one search engine or too little from another indicates problems with your SEO strategy or execution. Ideally the traffic you receive from each search engine should follow roughly the same percentage share as search engines in the worldwide marketplace.

At the time of this writing, Google's market share is around 75 percent, Yahoo between 10 and 15 percent, and Bing at about 8 percent. Thus, the percentage of traffic from Google to your Web site should be about 70 to 80 percent of all search, Yahoo around 12 percent, and Bing under 10 percent. If the percentages are significantly different, it indicates a particular search engine is not indexing your site or not providing consistent exposure for your site equivalent to the exposure gained in other search engines. (See the pie chart in Figure 11.6 for an example of how the share of traffic from each search engine is reported.) An SEO expert will be particularly helpful in determining the causes of these issues.

The percentage of total traffic from organic search

While total traffic from organic search is important to watch for an absolute measure, it can also be misleading due to seasonality and other external factors. Thus, a second metric that is a critical sign of SEO health is the percentage of total traffic that comes from organic search. For example, if you received 1,000 visits last week, and 600 came from organic search, your percentage of organic search traffic is 60 percent.

The percentage of traffic from organic search is a measure that isn't black-and-white or right-or-wrong. This measure should be reason for reflection or questioning. Think of it as the miles per gallon on your car. MPG doesn't dictate how fast you are going or how far you have traveled, but it is important to watch, and having MPG in the right range will yield optimal performance. The same is true with percent of traffic from organic search — too much traffic from organic shows an unhealthy reliance on organic search, while too little shows a missed opportunity to benefit from the free, highly valuable traffic organic search can bring.

In most cases a comfortable range for percent of traffic from organic is 40 to 60 percent. If less than 40 percent of your total site traffic comes from organic search, you are probably missing a significant opportunity to gain additional exposure through investing in SEO. If it is above 60 percent, the site is in a precarious position of dependence on the traffic from SEO efforts, so that if you lost exposure — even through no fault of your own — it could devastate your business.

Keeping an eye on percent of traffic from organic search is best accomplished by looking at the % of Total under the Visits portion of the scorecard area on the Non-paid Search Engines report (see Figure 11.7). Additionally, viewing the trend of changes for percent of traffic from organic will reveal how organic search has grown over time. You can do this by changing the main Graph Mode icons from Single Metric to Compare to Site.

Keyword measurements that matter

The next area of analysis for SEO success and effectiveness involves the analysis of keywords bringing traffic to the site from organic search. The goal of this measurement is to assess how well your

---

FIGURE 11.6

The Search Engines report with Non-paid Traffic selected shows the Total Visits and related metrics from organic search. This report helps understand whether total traffic from SEO efforts is increasing — a sign of success — or decreasing, a sign of declining exposure and failing SEO efforts. Also important, this report provides easy insight into which search engines bring the most traffic.

You can view the percent of traffic from organic search over time by changing the Graph Mode menu of the Search Engines report for Non-paid Traffic to Compare to Site with the Visits metric selected. The graph will show two lines — one for all traffic and one for organic search engine traffic — and calculate the percent of traffic from organic search for each time period shown on the graph (day, week, or month).

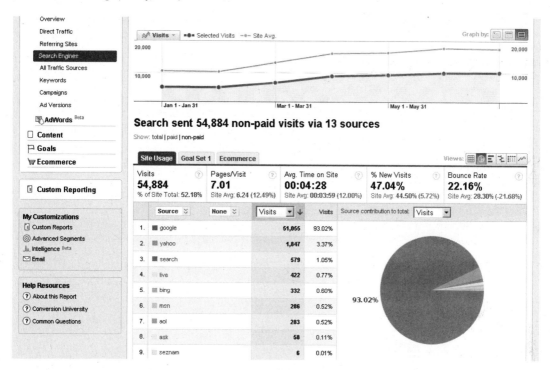

SEO efforts are aligning with the keywords you *want* to receive traffic from versus the keywords that are actually bringing your traffic.

The majority of this analysis can be completed using the Keywords report under the Traffic Sources report section.

In addition to filtering the Keywords report, you can create Advanced Segments that will include traffic from branded or nonbranded keywords. Simply create a new Advanced Segment that includes the Medium `organic` and keywords that match a regular expression encompassing your brand names to create a Branded Search Traffic segment. Copy this segment and change "including keywords that match..." to "excluding keywords that match..." for a nonbranded segment.

Measuring keywords from head to tail

The first area to address when measuring SEO success through keyword analysis begins with measuring the "body" of keywords bringing traffic to your site. The reality for almost all Web sites is that a small number of keywords are searched a vast number of times, while a large number of keywords are searched only a few times. These two types are called the *head* and *tail*, respectively. Figure 11.8 shows head terms and the transition to tail terms.

When measuring head versus tail, watch the total number of unique keywords referring traffic, represented at the bottom-right of the Report Table where the number of rows is listed (for example, "showing 1–10 of 3,232" (see Figure 11.9). The 3,232 number is the total number of unique keywords that referred traffic to the site during the selected time period. You should watch this number and trend it over time — if SEO efforts are working successfully, the number should increase. There is no specific report within Google Analytics to show the trended number of unique keywords — creating such a report is something you will have to do outside of the tool.

Understanding traffic percentage from head versus tail

When it comes to SEO, most people gravitate toward optimizing for head terms. If your Web site sells running shoes, you may be tempted to optimize for a top keyword "shoes" because it receives millions of searches per month, overlooking terms such as "running shoes," "women's hiking boots,"

FIGURE 11.8

This chart illustrates traffic from head terms versus tail terms. Significantly more traffic volume comes from the tail of keywords than from head keywords. Note the total number of keywords is reported in the lower corner of the Data Table.

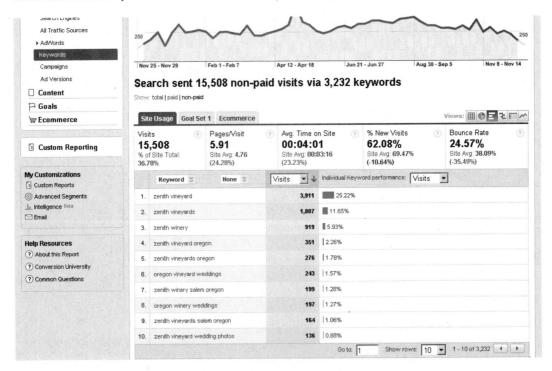

"shoes for toddlers," and hundreds of other related terms. The problem with focusing only on the head terms is that attaining top exposure for these keywords is much harder than for the hundreds, thousands, or tens of thousands of tail keywords. If you could have 10 keywords each bringing 1,000 visits, you would have 10,000 visits. Meanwhile, having a 1,000 keywords each bringing you 100 visits would equate to 100,000 visits, 10 times the total number provided by the head terms.

It is for this reason that good SEO should result in improvements to traffic from *both* head terms and tail terms. Thus, the measure to watch is the percent of traffic coming from the tail by viewing the Keywords report, selecting Non-paid Traffic, and checking the Percentage View, which will show a pie chart. Note the total percentage coming from the gray Other section (the pie chart displays only the top 10 keywords individually, leaving the remaining tail terms in the Other category). Figure 11.10 shows this view.

Another important metric related to the percentage of traffic from head versus tail is to determine the point at which the tail really begins. Look at the top 100 keywords rather than just the top 10 and find the point at which there is a significant drop in traffic coming from each keyword. If the first keyword

---

FIGURE 11.9

This figure shows the percentage view with the Other portion of the pie chart indicating the percentage of traffic from the 11th through *n*th keyword, or the "long tail." The other slices represent the volume of traffic from the top 10, or head, keywords bringing traffic to the site.

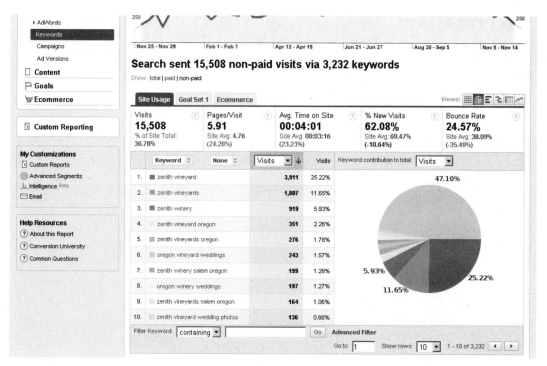

brings 10,000 visits, the 10th keyword brings 1,000, the 20th keyword brings 100, and the 21st keyword brings 9 visits, the "shelf" — where the drop occurs — begins with keyword 21. The longer the head, the better your SEO — ideally you won't see a sharp drop after the top 10 or 20, but rather a smooth decline into the long tail; a gentle slope from head keywords to tail keywords is what you want to see.

FIGURE 11.10

Filtering the Keywords report based on branded keywords (this page) versus nonbranded keywords (opposite page) and comparing the difference in total visits from each will reveal the effectiveness of SEO efforts in defending your brand online and gaining new exposure in the marketplace.

Branded versus nonbranded volume

People use search engines constantly. As a result, much of the time people type a company name or a product name into a search engine rather than navigate directly to a Web site URL. Therefore, it is imperative that you maintain top exposure for keywords containing your company and product brand

FIGURE 11.10 (CONTINUED)

names. Effective SEO efforts should defend brand territory while at the same time expand exposure for nonbranded keywords.

To measure whether SEO is defending brand and increasing nonbranded keyword exposure, you need to watch traffic from branded keywords versus nonbranded keywords. This is best accomplished by creating a filtered version of the Keywords report and adding it to your Dashboard.

The first version should be filtered for keywords that contain brand markers. Use a regular expression to encompass multiple brand name variations, misspellings, and product names. Once the filter is applied, the report will show only those keywords that match the filter criteria — in this case, brand markers.

To measure nonbranded keyword traffic, simply invert the filter used for branded traffic identification by changing "containing" to "excluding" in the Filter Keyword settings.

Once you've created these Keyword reports, note the amount of traffic coming from branded and nonbranded keywords, as well as the number of keywords. You should see increases in both over time; however it's most desirable to see a steady and significant increase from nonbranded traffic, since that increase indicates that you are receiving traffic from people who are not already familiar with your company.

Measuring SEO against goals

While traffic measurement relates to the optimization effectiveness measures, goals relate more to the business effects of SEO. Goal measurement is important because it is entirely possible to increase traffic while hurting your business. Measuring traffic growth alone won't detect this problem until it is too late and you begin to see the damage in the bottom line. Goal measurement will act as an early warning indicator if problems are brewing as well as shine a spotlight on SEO efforts that have a positive effect on your business.

Transactional goals versus engagement goals

Chapter 2 explains the principles of engagement versus transaction-oriented goals in detail. When applied to SEO, both engagement and transactional goals are important. However, search as an inbound marketing channel is inherently more transaction-oriented than engagement-oriented. This is because people who are finding your site through organic search are on the hunt — they are intently seeking information, and if they are looking for something commerce or business-related, the likelihood that they will make a purchase or fill out a form is much higher than if they are casually browsing the Web and click to your site from a display ad.

Measuring SEO value against a goal framework that includes engagement and transactional goals will result in taking both areas into account and rewarding search engines and keywords that drive higher levels of engagement and transaction conversion. Relying solely on transactional goals will deprive your analysis of useful insight into engines and keywords that bring increased engagement, which should be accounted for in the SEO decision-making and management process.

An example of engagement *and* transactional goals for an ecommerce site involves the creation of four goals: Viewing a Category, Viewing a Product's Details, Reaching the Shopping Cart, and

Completing an Order. Which of these goals are Engagement versus Transactional? All goals, except completing an order, should be considered Engagement Goals — even Reaching the Shopping Cart, because achieving this goal does not mean a purchase has been made. By setting these four goals and assigning goal values to each that scale from 1 to 10, you can effectively measure the impact of SEO against visitors who do nothing valuable versus visitors who become slightly engaged and versus those who become customers.

Goal Conversion Rate

Once you've defined Engagement and Transactional Goals, you can begin measuring SEO efforts against these goals. The first measurement to use is Conversion Rate. The Conversion Rate shows the general propensity for traffic from organic search in general, a specific search engine, or a specific keyword to complete a specific goal. Measurement of SEO against Goal Conversion is primarily useful as a means of comparing the value of SEO against other inbound marketing channels and gauging the value to your business of SEO.

If traffic from organic search begins declining in Conversion Rate even as the volume of Visits increases, it is a bad sign because it shows dilution of quality traffic. If SEO efforts result in driving more traffic at lower a Conversion Rate, you could end up focusing on optimization for keywords and search engines that don't drive business success, neglecting attention that should be paid to keywords that do drive business value.

Measuring both the trend of Conversion Rates and the Conversion Rate for specific goals against keywords will reveal SEO efforts that enhance business value overall and the keywords that drive that value. Figure 11.11 shows the Conversion Rate trend for all keywords as well as the keyword-by-keyword Conversion Rates.

Goal Value per Visit

Last but not least in the goal measurement discussion: Goal Value per Visit. Beyond Conversion Rate, Goal Value provides a means of relating SEO efforts to business impact. Goal Value is more important than Conversion Rate because, when configured appropriately, Goal Value takes into account the variation in importance between one goal and another. For instance, to use the previous ecommerce example, viewing a category page in a store is significantly less valuable than completing an order. Using Conversion Rate alone as a measure of value will be misleading, because the same Conversion Rate is not equal to the same value between two goals. (See Chapter 5 for additional information on goal setup.)

The best use for goal values with regard to SEO is the Per Visit Goal Value metric, found on the far right of Traffic Source reports. This metric is built on a calculation that sums all the goal values associated with goal completions for a report. If Goal 1 is worth 1 point of value and has 10 completions and Goal 2 is worth 5 points and has 4 completions, Total Goal Value is 30 ($1 \times 10 + 5 \times 4 = 30$). If there were 20 visits, the Per Visit Goal Value would be 1.50 ($30 \div 20 = 1.50$). The same scenario would report a Conversion Rate of 50 percent for Goal 1 and 20 percent for Goal 2, which would indicate Goal 2 was underperforming, when in fact Goal 2 provided twice the value (20 points) as Goal 1 (10 points).

As with Conversion Rate, trending the Per Visit Goal Value over time and reporting the Per Visit Goal Value metric are two key means of measuring success of SEO efforts at driving business value. The same set of evaluation criteria used for traffic metrics should be applied for branded versus nonbranded keywords, head versus long tail, and similar sets. Groups and keywords that bring a higher Per Visit

FIGURE 11.11

Notice the Conversion Rate trend in the main graph as well as the specific Conversion Rate for individual keywords. Not all keywords are performing well despite bringing plenty of traffic!

Goal Value indicate greater areas of SEO success and should illuminate where further SEO efforts should be focused. Figure 11.12 shows the Per Visit Goal Value trending over time compared to Goal

FIGURE 11.12

The main graph shows the Per Visit Goal Value trending over time compared to Goal Conversion Rate. Notice how Per Visit Goal Value shows a clearer picture of goal value that in some places contradicts the story told by Conversion Rate alone. The Report Table shows the Per Visit Goal Value for keywords displayed in the Comparison View.

Conversion Rate, revealing how goal value provides a clearer picture of performance and sometimes conflicts with what goal conversion alone would indicate.

Measuring ecommerce value

Ecommerce values are based on direct reporting of revenues from your Web site — if you've implemented Ecommerce reporting. This section covers how to analyze Ecommerce metrics in relation to SEO efforts but not the implementation of Ecommerce reporting. (For details on integrating ecommerce reporting into your Web site, see Chapter 5.)

Measuring Revenue versus Conversion Rate

Ecommerce value measurement and goal measurement are similar — the objective of both is to ascertain the business affect of SEO efforts, not just the effect on traffic. Where ecommerce and goals differ is that Ecommerce value reporting is only capable of reporting around transactions — monetary ones, specifically. As explained earlier, goals can be set to a transactional focus or to engagement. In all circumstances you should set up goals and corresponding goal values. If you sell online, then Ecommerce reporting is also critical because it provides finite reporting of tangible value (revenues) from organic search traffic.

Optimizing for gold: How Revenue metrics work together to indicate success

When using Revenue metrics for SEO effectiveness measurement, be careful to avoid the trap of myopic analysis. The propensity is to measure Total Revenue or Ecommerce Conversion Rate alone when considering whether SEO has been effective. While Total Revenue is the bottom-line number to watch, and one that you should see going up, there are other metrics that *influence* Total Revenue that should be used to gauge effectiveness as you manage.

Specifically, the Ecommerce Conversion Rate, Average Value per Transaction, and Revenue per Visit metrics are the "dials" that, when changed, affect Total Revenue even if Total Traffic remains the same. When approaching effectiveness measurement, you must watch these measures as leading indicators of success, just as watching Goal Conversion Rates and Values are leading indicators of SEO success over traffic generation alone.

First, the Average Value per Order influences Total Revenue. If you increase the number of orders by 10 percent but decrease the average value of each by 20 percent, your total revenues fall. Second, the Ecommerce Conversion Rate together with Average Value influence Revenue per Visit, which is the calculation of total revenues divided by total visits.

Revenue per Visit, just like Per Visit Goal Value, is the primary metric to use when assessing SEO work against Ecommerce Value. This is because it is a composite metric — it reflects both the Conversion Rate and the Average Value of each order. But you can't live on Revenue per Visit alone — once you identify with a decline in this metric, you need to reference the Average Value per Order and Ecommerce Conversion Rate to see where the problem lies. Have people been ordering at the same rate and simply ordering fewer items or less expensive ones, or are order values staying the same and fewer people are ordering? Figure 11.13 shows an example of Average Value, Ecommerce Conversion Rate, and Revenue per Visit working together thanks to a motion chart analyzing the three metrics.

Advanced SEO Analysis Techniques

There are so many advanced techniques for SEO analysis that they could probably fill an entire book. However, there are two techniques that are particularly useful in addition to the SEO effectiveness and value analysis described in this chapter: analyzing landing pages and creating special custom reports for SEO analysis.

Understanding landing pages using Advanced Segments

When analyzing traffic from organic search over time, you may find yourself asking, "What pages do these visitors from organic search land on?" If your SEO traffic is declining or increasing, understanding where visitors land on your site when coming from organic search is even more important. The standard Landing Pages report won't readily report landing points for visits from organic search, so this important and valuable analysis may seem impossible.

FIGURE 11.13

This motion chart shows the relationship between total revenue (the Y axis), Ecommerce Conversion Rate, Average Value, and Revenue per Visit. Notice that as the Ecommerce Conversion Rate and Average Value change, the Per Visit Value fluctuates. The Total Revenue reveals the effect these fluctuations have.

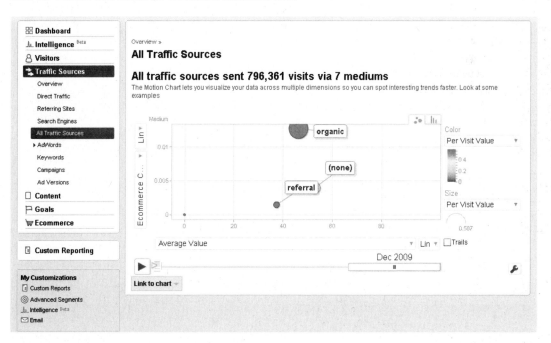

However, there is hope! By combining Advanced Segments and the Landing Pages report, you can easily see from what pages visitors from organic search enter your site. You can do so by selecting the Non-paid Search Traffic segment from the Default Advanced Segments menu, as shown in Figure 11.14. Once applied, this limits the data viewed in the profile to only those visits that came from the Medium `organic`. Once selected, navigate to the Top Landing Pages report under the Content Analysis section to view the top entrance points for people from organic search.

It is important to apply the same concepts of head-versus-tail analysis when considering landing pages. Notice the volume of entrances that occur on the home page and other top-level pages versus other pages deep within the site. If you are experiencing a decline in organic search traffic, pinpointing the pages that were once receiving more entrances from search than they are now is helpful to unraveling the knot of declining organic search traffic.

Run a quick check to determine whether the traffic is declining to your home page or to pages other than your home page by using a report table filter that filters for landing pages containing your home page versus landing pages excluding the home page.

FIGURE 11.14

Select the Non-paid Search Traffic segment from the list of Default Segments in the Advanced Segments menu to see only organic search traffic.

When the filter is applied take note of the main graph — is organic search traffic continuing to decline when considering only the home page? Does traffic decline more steeply for landing pages other than the home page? If the former is occurring, it often correlates with a decline in branded search traffic, while the latter is commonly found alongside a decrease in long-tail nonbranded search traffic. Furthermore, a sharp decline in entrances from organic search to pages deeper within the site is often a strong indicator of a problem with the site being fully indexed or a dilution of content, perhaps for duplication across similar pages or aliased domains.

Creating custom reports for SEO reporting

The value of a custom report is reporting data on one screen that you can't normally access. With SEO analysis, a useful report is one that combines landing page information with traffic and performance metrics. Following the Landing Page scenario earlier, a useful report for assessing the value relationship between landing pages and organic search traffic is one that analyzes organic traffic landing points against Traffic (Entrances) Value (Conversion, Revenue, and Value) metrics.

The report in Figure 11.15 is a custom report that begins with the Medium dimension, allowing drill-down into organic traffic, and has metrics of Entrances, Bounce Rate, Average Time on Site, Pages per Visit, Goal Conversion Rate, Per Visit Value, Transactions, Average Value, and Revenue. After

FIGURE 11.15

This custom report supports analysis of organic traffic landing pages against both traffic and value measures for SEO efforts.

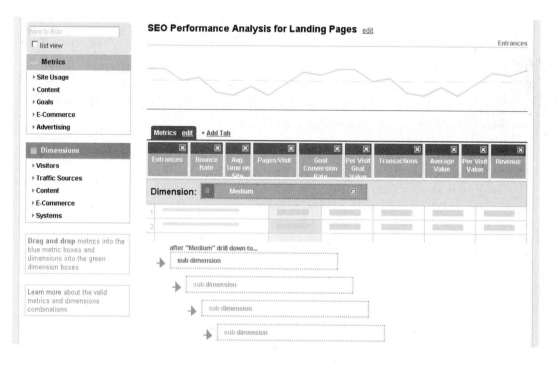

drilling into the `organic` Medium, you can change the dimension from None to Landing Page to see these metrics per landing page.

Validating That Your SEO Metrics Are Accurate

This section covers technical topics for testing and validating whether your metrics reported about SEO are accurate and reliable. Accurate data is paramount to good decision-making — if you base decisions on incorrect data, you will likely make incorrect decisions. This section contains techniques for diagnosing problems and how to remedy them. Note that it is more technical in nature than most of the book.

How Google Analytics tracks organic search traffic

It is probably not a surprise that Google Analytics measures organic (often called "natural" or "unsponsored") traffic from search engines. It does this silently, without any intervention from you, and it tracks *all* major search engines (more than 40, to be exact — who knew there were even 40 search engines out there?). But how is this done?

It's all about cookies — unfortunately, not the edible kind. In Chapter 4, we explain the specifics of Google Analytics cookies and the tracking scripts (GATC). Here we review the practical technicalities of how Google Analytics sets the cookies that identify traffic as organic search. Understanding how cookies and organic search relate is paramount to solving common accuracy problems related to measuring organic search traffic and should broaden your understanding of why you see what you see in the Search Engine and Keyword reports in Google Analytics.

As described in Chapter 4, every visitor and visit session measured by Google Analytics is classified against three categories (dimensions): Source, Medium, and Campaign. Organic search engine traffic is always given the name `organic` for the dimension Medium, and the Source dimension will be set to the search engine's name, for example `google`, `yahoo`, or `bing`. Additionally, search traffic also records a Keyword or Search Term value — the actual keywords or phrases the visitors used in their queries at the search engine.

This classification happens when the Google Analytics tracking tags are executed, usually when the page loads. The tags run through a set of operations to determine what the traffic source cookie values should be. This set of operations is where the Medium dimension value is set to `organic`, Source is set to the name of the search engine, and the search query is captured as the keyword.

The process begins with a simple check: Are there any cookies already in existence? To do this, the GATC first has to determine the *domain* for the cookies. If a customization has been made in the code to define the specific cookie domain setting, the code uses that setting; otherwise it uses the `auto` setting, which sets the cookie domain to the current Web site domain.

Once the cookie domain has been determined, the GATC looks to see if cookies already exist. If no cookies exist, new ones are created. When setting the traffic source information into the cookie, the code first looks to see if there are any manually defined campaign tracking tags (these tags would be used for display ads, e-mail campaigns, sponsored search, and other custom ad campaigns). If tracking parameters are found, the code uses the values found for setting the cookie. If no custom values are found, the code evaluates the `document.referrer` (the specific JavaScript information field that defines the referrer — the page viewed immediately before the current page). If there is no referrer, Source is set to `direct`, Medium is set to `(none)`, and Campaign is set to `direct`.

If a referrer is found, the GATC checks to see if it matches a list of predefined search engines or any custom search engine detection directives that have been defined in GATC custom settings. If the referrer does match, the code sets Medium to `organic`, Source to the name of the detected search engine, Campaign to `(not set)`, and Keyword to the search query used at the search engine. If the referrer does *not* match a known search engine, it is evaluated as a referring site and Medium is set to `referral`, Source to the domain of the Web site, and Campaign to `(not set)`. Referring sites also have the page on the remote site where the visitor came from stored in a special dimension called Referral Path.

FIGURE 11.16

The Hostnames report lists each Web site from which your Google Analytics tags are being run and is useful for detecting aliased domains, caching and translation domains, and even sites that are stealing your content.

321,735 visits came from 171 hostnames

	Hostname	None	Visits ↓	Pages/Visit	Avg. Time on Site	% New Visits	Bounce Rate
1.	www.googlestore.com		320,940	3.67	00:01:15	90.73%	56.49%
2.	translate.googleusercontent.com		283	1.86	00:00:41	60.07%	60.07%
3.	65.55.177.205		102	5.42	00:00:58	85.29%	12.75%
4.	www.mbcpromoshop.com		40	4.30	00:02:36	92.50%	57.50%
5.	checkout.google.com		27	303.89	00:01:54	55.56%	44.44%
6.	youtubeproxy.org		23	1.96	00:00:26	91.30%	65.22%
7.	66.196.80.202		15	1.80	00:00:16	80.00%	60.00%
8.	hide-me-now.com		15	1.47	00:00:18	100.00%	66.67%
9.	cc.bingj.com		14	1.29	00:00:17	64.29%	78.57%
10.	w3.hidemyass.com		12	1.75	00:00:19	75.00%	66.67%
11.	74.125.47.132		9	1.22	00:00:09	77.78%	77.78%
12.	w2.hidemyass.com		9	1.78	00:02:16	55.56%	44.44%
13.	209.85.229.132		8	1.00	00:00:00	62.50%	100.00%
14.	74.125.155.132		8	1.50	00:00:33	50.00%	62.50%
15.	74.125.93.132		8	1.00	00:00:00	50.00%	100.00%

Site Usage / Goal Set 1

Visits **321,735** % of Site Total: 100.00%
Pages/Visit **3.69** Site Avg: 3.69 (0.00%)
Avg. Time on Site **00:01:15** Site Avg: 00:01:15 (0.00%)
% New Visits **90.66%** Site Avg: 90.61% (0.06%)
Bounce Rate **56.49%** Site Avg: 56.49% (0.00%)

Network Location / Hostnames / Connection Speeds / Mobile / User Defined / Custom Variables / Traffic Sources / Content / Goals / Custom Reporting / My Customizations / Custom Reports / Advanced Segments / Intelligence Beta / Email / Help Resources / About this Report / Conversion University / Common Questions

Analytics in Action: Fixing Issues and Finding Opportunities in Search with Catalogs.com

The challenge of managing a catalog Web site that hosts hundreds of merchants ranging from Alloy teen clothing to zZounds musical instruments is that you have to deal with an absolutely enormous number of keywords in your search marketing strategy.

Catalogs.com finds itself in exactly this position, and the advanced features of Google Analytics help the company stay on top of its keywords by focusing efforts on finding and fixing issues, identifying anomalies, and spotting opportunities. With a very heavy investment in and dependence on organic search engines, SEO is a big part of the day-to-day activities at Catalogs.com. One of the most useful reports for an SEO department is the Keywords report, and here is one way to configure it to help you find poor performers and potential areas for improvement.

First, make sure you are looking at the "Non-paid" traffic in the Keyword report, then click on the Ecommerce tab (or one of your Goal tabs if you are not a transactional site) and use a Secondary Dimension of Landing Page. Next pivot by source, showing Visits and Per Visit Value (or Per Visit Goal Value if nontransactional).

Next, use the Advanced filters to zero in. In this example, we are filtering down to *unbranded* keywords that drove at least 50 visitors to a non-informational page and resulted in a per-visit value of less than $0.05.

This report gives a list of all the keywords that attract traffic but are not being effectively monetized. In this single report, you can see the keyword, the page ranking for that keyword, the search engine ranking it, the amount of traffic resulting, and exactly what that traffic is worth to you. This is a fantastic way to do things like:

Why is this so important to understand? Because knowing how the data in your reports gets there is important to understanding what you're analyzing as well as for troubleshooting potential problems.

Checking host names

A quick check to run is analyzing the Hostnames report (choose Visitors ▶ Network Properties), as shown in Figure 11.16. The Hostnames report lists all the domain names from which tracking tags using your Web Property ID (the Google Analytics Account number and Profile Identifier Code) are sending hits. In rare cases the presence of domains other than ones you own may reveal things like content theft, but most of the time you'll simply see your site and content cache and translation domains. In other cases, you'll see lots of domains — domains that you own that are *aliased* to the main site. Aliased domains are a problem both for data accuracy as well as for overall SEO (aliased domains mean that your content can be indexed under different domains, creating duplication of the site's content on multiple domains — something search engines don't like to see).

If you find domains that you own listed, the remedy is to setup 301 redirects for them to consolidate traffic to the main site. Specific steps for setting up a 301 redirect are outside the scope of this book (see

- Find a keyword that you may have thought was worth investing in, but in reality isn't giving you a good return.
- Find a keyword that you are already ranking for but is not providing a quality experience to your user.

Let's take a look at a couple of examples. First, look at these two keywords, both of which are ranking in Google, that are providing traffic but absolutely no return.

Now take a look at the Landing Page dimension. These are /expired/ pages, meaning that someone looking for couch pillows ended up on a page that may have great, relevant content, but essentially says, "Sorry, there's nothing here for you to *do*." Here's a great opportunity to capitalize on traffic that is already coming to the site by improving upon that experience!

Keyword	Landing Page	Total		1. google		2. bing		3. yahoo	
		Visits ↓	Per Visit Value	Visits	Per Visit Value	Visits	Per Visit Value	Visits	Per Visit Value
1. throw pillows for couch	www.catalogs.com/expired/hom...	117	$0.00	117	$0.00	0	$0.00	0	$0.00
2. decorative pillows for couch	www.catalogs.com/expired/hom...	167	$0.00	158	$0.00	0	$0.00	0	$0.00

As a second example, look at the keyword "motivational games." In this case, the keyword is driving traffic on each of the three major search engines, there is a relevant landing page in place, and yet the Per Visit Value is dismal.

Now that you have identified an issue, you can start to ask why. From here, you can take steps to fix it, whether that means optimizing the landing page for conversions or discovering that this keyword just plain doesn't drive revenue.

As you can imagine, there are many insights to be had in this report, and the advanced features of Google Analytics make it extremely easy to turn a list of hundreds of thousands of keywords into a smaller, manageable list of only the keywords that require your immediate attention.

Keyword	Landing Page	Total		1. google		2. bing		3. yahoo	
		Visits ↓	Per Visit Value	Visits	Per Visit Value	Visits	Per Visit Value	Visits	Per Visit Value
1. motivational games	www.catalogs.com/education/m...	93	$0.03	74	$0.02	10	$0.03	5	$0.00

www.analyticsformarketers.com/s/301-redirects for details on this topic). If you find host names that you don't own and that are not external cache and translation sites, you may have someone copying some of your pages, Google Analytics tags included. This copying is more of a legal issue — rather than trying to filter out the extra host names from Google Analytics, you'll need to pursue the copyright infringers who are copying your pages to their sites.

—

CHAPTER 2

Social Media Marketing

Social technologies, ranging from social networks to forums to blogs, have given customers a powerful voice to educate one another directly on the products they buy and the services they use. For marketers, this shift to direct consumer-to-consumer communication has created a new sense of urgency to deliver on promises of satisfaction.

To win in this landscape, businesses must encourage others to spread their message. Through reviews, ratings, and recommendations, past customers inform future ones of what to expect. This chapter explores the basics of how to engage with customers in this channel as well as how to tap into the growing number of conversations to generate customer insight and increase customer satisfaction.

Social Media Defined

In trying to put a label on this nebulous channel, we thought we'd take a page from Dave Evans, author of *Social Media Marketing: An Hour a Day*, who defines social media as "the shift from a broadcast mechanism to a many-to-many model, rooted in conversations between authors, people, and peers … transforming people from content readers into content publishers." Taking this a step further, Evans breaks down social media into three important components: social platforms, social content, and social interactions. These three pillars form the basis of the channel. Table 12.1 shows examples of the major social media platforms as well as some of the social content and social interactions they facilitate.

Looking at this list, you've probably used at least one of these services. To understand the other services, you need to roll up your sleeves and try them out. At its core, social media is about participating in the conversation. You can't participate by just observing, so before moving to the next stage of this chapter, see if you can find a few online communities that interest you and introduce yourself!

TABLE 12.1

Social Media Platforms and the Types of Social Interaction

Social Platforms	Examples	Social Content and Interactions
Personal social networks	Facebook, MySpace, Orkut	Profiles, friends, wall posts, shares, status updates, photos, fans, apps, feeds
Business social networks	LinkedIn, Xing, Sermo, InMobile	Résumés, endorsements, connections, introductions, groups
White-label social networks	Ning, GroupSite, CrowdVine	Similar to personal and business social networks
Photo sharing	Flickr, Smugmug, Webshots	Photos, albums, groups, tags, comments, feeds
Video sharing/Webcasting	YouTube, Vimeo	Videos, ratings, comments, tags
Wikis	Wikipedia, Yahoo Answers, Wikispaces, Google Sites, Mahalo	Wiki pages, modules, backlinks, edits
Podcasting	iTunes, Podcast Alley, Podcast.com	Podcasts, subscribes
Social bookmarking	Digg, Reddit, Delicious, StumbleUpon	Recommendations, votes
Blogging	WordPress, Blogger, MovableType	Blog posts, comments, tags, backlinks, feeds
Microblogging	Twitter, Jaiku, Seesmic, Plurk	Tweets, hash tags, trending topics, follows
Forums	Ubuntu, Google Groups, Big-Boards, PHPBB	Posts, replies, signatures
Review sites	Yelp, Epinions, Travelocity, TripAdvisor, Google Local	Ratings, reviews, recommendations

Social Media Marketing Basics

Looking at the online marketing system we present in Chapter 2's Figure 2.1, it's clear that social media can serve as an important inbound marketing channel. Because social media follows a many-to-many model, connecting consumers directly to one another to share information and experiences, one of

---

FIGURE 12.1

Social media and the online marketing system

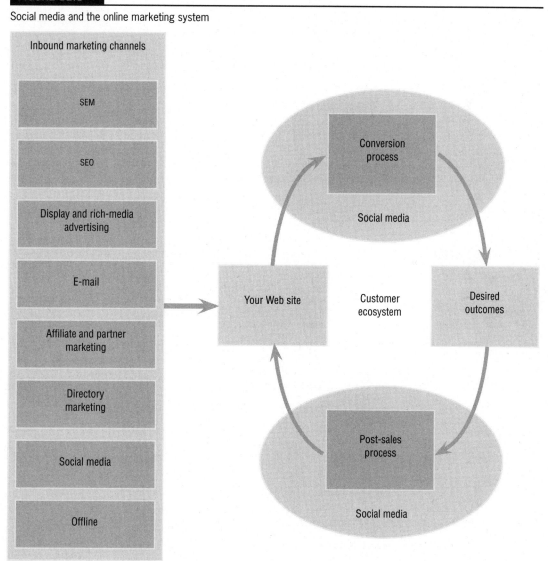

social media's most important roles (from a marketing standpoint) is influencing potential customers in the consideration phase and empowering past customers to share their experiences.

In light of this, we've adjusted the diagram of the marketing system in Figure 2.1 to emphasize this aspect; the revised version is shown in Figure 12.1

As you look at this figure, it is important to recognize a few important things that separate social media from other marketing channels:

- Social media is fundamentally a many-to-many mode of communication, which means you can introduce a topic or add your voice, but you can't control the conversation.
- Many social media sites use the "wisdom of crowds" as the collective voice of the community to decide which content is featured and which gets buried. This means boring or off-topic content gets lost in the noise of the majority.
- Each social media site has its own etiquette and rules. Communities are self-policing and reward contributors with elevated status, while punishing violators with flames and even banishment. The most important rule is to be honest and transparent whenever possible.
- Social media is fundamentally about participation and two-way communication. When designing campaigns in this channel, you need to ensure that they have some element of participation.

Imagine social media as an important factor influencing the purchase and post-purchase evaluation process — except that social media is not something you can control directly. You can fire blog posts, tweets, or videos into the cloud, but you can't control the response you get back. The best ways to put your best foot forward in this area are to work harder to satisfy customers, to be straightforward and transparent about your actions, to apologize when you screw up, to follow the etiquette of each social media platform, and to ensure minimal disconnect between what you tell customers to expect from your product or service and what you actually deliver.

With these guidelines in mind, here are suggestions for activities you can pull together in this channel to form a powerful integrated marketing effort.

- **Listening campaigns and brand management.** The best place to get started with social media is to find out what is already being said about you and your competitors. By using basic tools to monitor the quantity and content of "buzz" around your products, you can uncover valuable insight into the minds of customers. We introduce this concept in Chapter 2 as part of competitive and market research.
- **User education.** Many companies use their blog, Twitter account, or YouTube channel to educate users on their products and services. This education can include distributing tutorials, featuring experiences from past customers, and documenting aspects of the customer experience.
- **Contests and giveaways.** Organizations from Southwest Airlines to Yale University have used Twitter and Facebook to run contests and giveaways that reward users for spreading the marketing message, either by soliciting votes from friends or just rebroadcasting a message to

receive entries. Contest entry can also include submitting photos, videos, designs, or essays that can be a valuable source of collateral.

- **Social CRM/customer support.** Companies such as Starbucks have created moderated forums through tools such as Lithium and Get Satisfaction to actively respond to customer issues and solicit feedback. These communities allow users to help one another; marketers and customer service reps can step in as needed. Companies can also use features and sites such as Yelp to respond directly to customer complaints.

- **Apps and widgets.** Burger King became famous for a campaign where users "sacrificed" five friends on Facebook via a Burger King app to receive a free Whopper. Marketers who can create apps that include a viral component *and* offer valuable functionality can attract new customers even as they give existing ones new ways to interact with a brand.

Measuring Social Media Activities and Campaigns

Social media is a hot area in marketing, so a number of agencies now offer consulting and guidance in how to run social media campaigns. Be aware that no other online channel has more hype surrounding it. The best way to cut through this noise is to get back to basics and identify the key business goals you're trying to impact through your social media activities and ensure you are monitoring them carefully as you proceed.

The best place to get started is to get a strong handle on where your products, competitors, and market are being discussed online and what's being said about you. Fortunately there are several tools, both paid and free, designed to help you. A Google search is always a great place to start, but there are many other options that can help you drill deeper into online conversations.

Putting together a keyword list

With few exceptions, these listening tools are based on *semantic processing*. They attempt to convert unstructured human language into structured data. First, create a list of keywords you can use to find and analyze conversations. This list should include your company name, product, or service names, as well as your competitor's. It should also include keywords related to your industry. You can often find many of these in your AdWords account. For example, we have pulled together the following abridged list of keywords for Google Analytics:

- Company name: Google
- Products and features: Google Analytics, GA, custom reports, motion charts, advanced segmentation, analytics API
- Marketplace: Web analytics, Web metrics, Web site optimization, marketing optimization
- Competitive terms: Omniture, SiteCatalyst, Webtrends, Coremetrics, Yahoo Analytics

Finding relevant conversations online

After you've gone through the obvious step of Googling many of these keywords, there are tools designed to help you understand what's being said in the social media space:

- **HowSociable** (www.howsociable.com): Click an individual item on the results page to be taken to the search page for that channel, highlighting the term you typed. Run the search for your brand and for competing brands.
- **BlogPulse** (www.blogpulse.com): Use basic search to find social media content that references your brand. Be sure to search for competing brands as well.
- **Google Alerts** (www.google.com/alerts): Schedule e-mails to be sent to your mailbox referencing new content that contains your keywords. This is great for monitoring the Web to see if something has leaked.
- **Technorati** (www.technorati.com): Run a basic search across the blogosphere. Pay attention to the *authority* (reach and influence) of the sources returned. Filter results by category or authority level.
- **Twitter Search** (search.twitter.com): Find short messages (tweets) mentioning your company, products, and services.

If you are a small brand and unable to find anything, don't despair. These basic search tools cover many of the major social media platforms, but they don't cover niche communities and forums. For these, turn to Chapter 8 and following the steps listed to analyze your referring sites using the Referring Sites report in the Traffic Sources section of Google Analytics. If you can uncover any forums, you can use the dedicated search on the forum site to dig deeper.

If your brand or product name is generic, or similar to a more visible term, you may have to do some grunt work to separate relevant results. The inability to differentiate generic brand or product names from actual chatter about your brand or product is one of the limitations of semantic processing. For example, if your business is called Acme Plumbing, it might be hard to zero in on relevant conversations.

Quantifying "buzz" with keyword trends

Now that you've identified some of the social media content surrounding your market, another good step is to try and get a baseline measure of the quantity of discussion out there. As you plan a social media effort, it is important to keep your finger on this pulse as a way to establish whether your message is sufficiently interesting to get talked about. You can do this using many of the same free tools previously mentioned. For example, you can use the trend search on BlogPulse to compare mentions of several different keywords over time. Figure 12.2 shows sample results for a few major car brands.

IceRocket, another social media search engine, offers a similar feature with up to five terms. You can also use the e-mail subscribe feature from HowSociable to track buzz around a keyword over time, or use the RSS feature on Twitter Search to subscribe to any tweets mentioning one of your keywords.

There are other helpful tools that make it easy to scan Twitter and other social networks for your brand or product names. TweetDeck is a great tool for tracking multiple search terms in Twitter. If you

FIGURE 12.2

Mentions of major car brands tracked over time

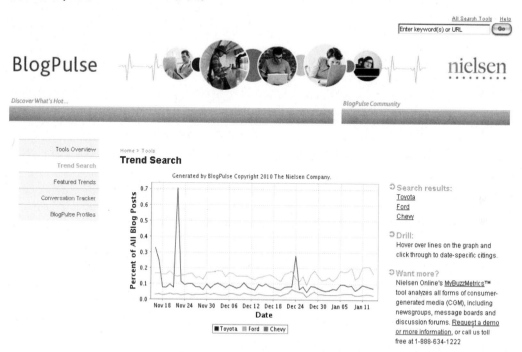

need to track a specific term in multiple social media tools, try SocialSeek: It scans Twitter, YouTube, and Flickr, just to name a few. It also lets you specify a geographic location to search within. At a minimum, these tools allow you to track baseline mentions of the terms you input, which can help you understand whether your efforts to spread a message socially are succeeding.

Understanding content and sentiment

The next stage in analyzing social media activity involves trying to move from a baseline quantitative measure of "buzz" to an understanding of what people are actually saying. This understanding requires either a fair amount of manual work *coding* conversations (turning unstructured responses into quantitative measures) or more advanced semantic processing. There are several services and tools available to help you do this.

- **Scout Labs:** Break down the basic sentiment of social media content into positive, negative, or neutral categories. Monitor topics over time and use collaboration tools to alert team members of trends.
- **Nielsen My BuzzMetrics:** Define your keyword list and get a dedicated analyst to pore through conversations and report back on trends and insights.

- **Radian6:** Monitor conversations over time, decode influencers, and drill into activity on a specific day. Integrate with Salesforce.com and other platforms to connect CRM data with a customer's online identity.
- **Trackur:** Monitor and track basic topics quickly and easily. Includes sentiment tagging and influence measurement.

There are basic techniques you can use to stay focused as you wade into this information. Remember that you want to benchmark your popularity against competitors and gain insight into what your customers want and how they feel about you:

- **Analyze sentiment around product attributes.** See if customers are consistently highlighting one or more aspect of their experience using the same terminology. For example, if you are in the restaurant business and you consistently see reviews on Yelp saying "great food" and "bad service," you have identified an area for improvement. Quantify these mentions to find out what users care about. A simple tag cloud generator, like Wordle, can help visualize the most common terms used.
- **Identify competitive strengths and weaknesses.** Find out what people love and hate about your competitors and use that information to your advantage in crafting persuasive copy. Where possible, use the same terminology used by customers.
- **Solicit testimonials.** If you get a glowing review, ask for permission to reproduce it on your Web site. If you find a strong brand advocate, reach out and show your support. Think of Jared Fogle and Subway.
- **Analyze launches.** Use the discussions you uncover as an early warning system to gauge the response when launching a new product or service. Use this response to predict appropriate inventory levels and decide where to prioritize marketing dollars.

Don't forget to socialize what you find! Send links to RSS feeds and reports for your colleagues to see. Bring feedback from customers to meetings. Use quotes in your presentations. Set a schedule and check in regularly to see what has developed. This will add a whole new dimension of context to the data in Google Analytics.

Analyzing Site Traffic from Social Media

Once your social media campaigns begin to evolve and you move beyond simple listening campaigns, you can start to measure the direct impact social media may have on your Web site and, more important, on your business. Most often the direct impact from a social media campaign is traffic to your Web site and, hopefully, conversions. You must guide traffic to your Web site from the social platform.

When you start to direct traffic back to your Web site using social media, it usually involves posting a link. And more often than not, you don't just post a link, you use a URL shortening service to shrink the URL and save space. You may have noticed that we use shortened URLs throughout this book to link to content on our companion Web site. Shortened URLs do more than save space: Many URL shortening services provide metrics about your URLs, such as how many clicks they get, the types of devices people use when they click your shortened URLs, and where people are located when they click your links.

But URL shortening services cannot tell you what happens to traffic from social media after it lands on your Web site. If we have stressed anything in this book, it is that we want to move beyond measuring traffic and start to measure goals (conversions) and other critical metrics. Therefore, it is critical that you can identify social media traffic sources in Google Analytics. Don't worry, it is fairly easy.

By default, most social media sites will appear as referral traffic in your Google Analytics data. Figure 12.3 shows the All Traffic Sources report. It has been filtered so you can clearly see Twitter and FriendFeed in the list.

Without doing anything, you can see what traffic from Twitter or other social media sites does on the Web site. You can use the Site Usage tab to measure all the standard metrics in Google Analytics, such as Visits, Time on Site, and Pageviews per Visit. Don't forget to put these metrics in context of your Web site and the message you are promoting in social media.

FIGURE 12.3

By default, many social media sites appear as referral traffic in Google Analytics.

If you tweet a link to a blog post, you probably want the person to read the post you are linking to. In this case, the person may click on the link, land on your blog post, read the post, and then leave. When you look at metrics such as Bounce Rate, you may be alarmed to see a high Bounce Rate. Don't be. A high Bounce Rate means that a person landed on your post and left. If that is what you wanted them to do, you achieved your goal. Other metrics such as Pageviews per Visit might also be low because people coming from your links in social media may be leaving after just one page. Again, if this aligns with your objective, don't be surprised.

In addition to basic site usage metrics, you can tie different social media channels directly to outcomes on your Web site using goals. It takes one click on a Goal Set tab for you to evaluate how many conversions were generated by your social media campaign. Remember, a goal can be almost anything in Google Analytics, such as signing up for a newsletter, submitting a contact form, or spending a certain amount of time on the site.

If you are an ecommerce vendor and have configured Google Analytics to track transactions, you can click the Ecommerce tab to view Orders, Revenue, and other metrics that were generated by your social media campaigns. Think of the value! If you use Twitter to tweet about a sale, you can see how many purchases were generated by the link.

But let's dig a bit deeper. We know that social traffic appears as referral traffic, but we want more detailed information about our social media traffic. Using the Referring Websites report under Traffic Sources, you can select a social media site — Twitter, for example — and view which pages contain link back to your site. In the case of Twitter (see Figure 12.4), these pages show a person's Twitter username.

While viewing social media traffic as a referring Web site can be useful, it can often be unreliable. Many people use desktop applications and mobile apps to browse social media. These applications can mask the visitor's true source and cause them to appear as direct traffic. For example, if a person uses TweetDeck to browse Twitter and clicks on a Bit.ly-shortened URL, how will that person appear in Google Analytics data? As direct traffic.

To resolve this issue, you can use campaign tagging, as Chapter 5 explains, to more accurately track the links from social media. The benefit of using the campaign tags is that the tags persist through URL-shortening redirects. Another benefit of using campaign tagging to track social media is the amount of information that you can track. This additional information makes it easier to identify which parts of your social media campaigns work and which do not.

Using campaign tags to track a social media campaign is the same as using campaign tags to track any marketing activity. It begins by defining what you want to track and mapping it to tags that you will add to the links in your social media campaign.

Here is an outline for a simple campaign for a fictional sale. We use Twitter to drive traffic back to the Web site with the intent of generating direct sales from the campaign. We begin by defining how we tag the links in our tweets. We set the Campaign parameter to `spring-sale`, indicating that social media effort is part of a larger marketing effort for the spring sale. We use the Medium parameter to identify that the link appeared in social media and the Source parameter to identify which social media. In this case, the link appears in Twitter, so the Medium is set to `twitter`. Finally, the Content

FIGURE 12.4

By clicking on a referring social media site, you can see which pages people were on when they clicked a link to your site.

parameter is used to record when the tweet was made. That gives us the ability to identify if a tweet at 9 a.m. generates more revenue than a tweet at 3 p.m.

Table 12.2 shows the values used in the Twitter links.

Remember, you are tracking social media, so make sure you adequately represent the different attributes of your messages. After you define the values, it is time to generate the shortened URLs. Place the appropriate campaign parameters in your URL-shortening tool. Figure 12.5 shows a campaign URL added to Bit.ly, a popular URL-shortening tool.

TABLE 12.2

Sample Values for a Fictional Social Media Campaign

Parameter	Query String Variable	Value
Campaign	utm_campaign	spring-sale
Medium	utm_medium	social-media
Source	utm_source	twitter
Content	utm_content	9am-tweet
Campaign	utm_campaign	spring-sale
Medium	utm_medium	social-media
Source	utm_source	twitter
Content	utm_content	3pm-tweet

You can shorten the URL in your social media campaign. This one will go in Twitter.

To analyze the results, view social media alongside your other marketing activities. Social media campaigns, tagged with campaign tracking parameters, appear in the Traffic Sources reports, such as All Traffic Sources, Campaigns, and Ad Versions. Figure 12.6 is the All Traffic Sources report filtered to show the Twitter data from Table 12.2.

The report shows traffic from the different tweet times, which was stored in the content parameter. It's pretty cool how you can segment the traffic to evaluate specific tweets.

Like any marketing activity, you want to align the measurement with the marketing objective. If you are using social media to sell a product, you want to measure sales. If you are using social media to promote Web site content, you may want to measure pages viewed or time on site. You get the idea.

FIGURE 12.5

Enter a tagged URL into a shortening service to track social media campaigns.

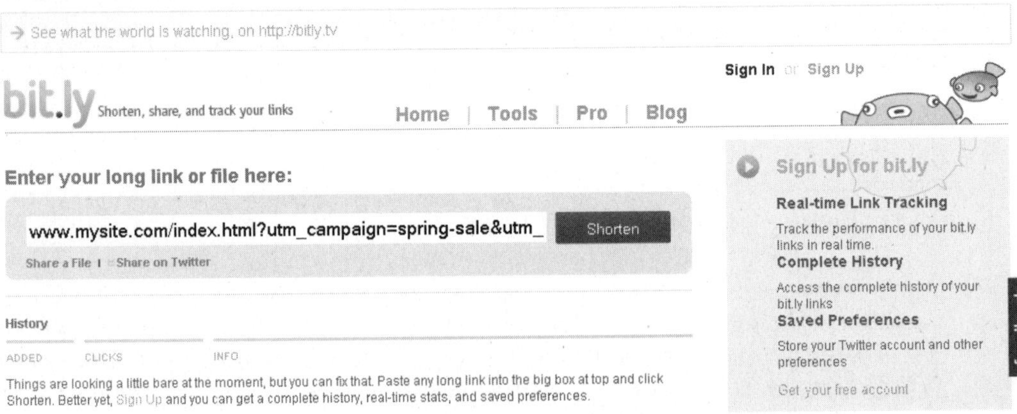

FIGURE 12.6

You can find data from tagged social media links in the Traffic Sources' All Traffic Sources report.

When you connect business outcomes to social media activities, you start to prove the value of your investment in social media. Make sure you have the appropriate Google Analytics features configured correctly. This most often means configuring the appropriate goals to measure your social media campaign. And for all you ecommerce companies, make sure you configure ecommerce tracking to attribute revenue back to social media activities.

Business value measures

The most common uses for social media as a traffic source and specific metrics that can be used to measure the performance are:

- **Listening campaigns and brand management.** Review referral traffic to your site for social Web sites. Even though you are only listening, it is possible that people may be posting links to your site in their social media accounts and driving traffic to your site. Use the Referring Sites report in Traffic Sources to view metrics from these sources. If you find that people are posting links, it may be that you have strong brand evangelists promoting your product or services or people who hate you and are complaining to their social circle.

- **User education campaigns.** Are visitors engaging with the educational information you are promoting? If you are posting content in the form of Web pages, you can use standard metrics — such as which Pages visitors view, Time on Site, and Time on Page — to measure if people are consuming the content. Also important is measuring new traffic to the Web site. Are you reaching a new audience that did not know about your product or service? You can also use features like event tracking to measure how people are interacting with educational videos that you may post to your site.

- **Contest and giveaway campaigns.** Measure the number of contest entries generated by your social media campaign. This number can be easily measured as long as you tag the links you use in the social media and you define a goal for contest entries. Also check the number of repeat visitors who continuously check back for more contests. You can also measure the general buzz generated by your contest using tools like Google Trends and other tools that show the propagation across a social network.

- **Social CRM/customer support.** A majority of social CRM/customer support activities don't take place on the main Web site. They usually exist within a social medium. For example, customers or prospects may interact with a brand on the brand's Facebook fan page. However, customer support may involve using Web site content. Customer support representatives using social media may post links back to content on a support Web site. In this case, it's important to measure which content was promoted and if it was consumed by visitors. For example, if a customer poses a question on Twitter, a customer service rep may respond with a tweet that includes a link to an FAQ page on the company's Web site. In this case, you want to track if the person clicked on the link and if he or she viewed the FAQ content on the site.

- **Sales.** If you're advertising a sale or other special on a social network, you want to measure how effective that social medium is at generating revenue.

Measuring Social Media Tools on Your Site

Up to this point, we have addressed how to measure social media campaigns by using social media to drive traffic back to your site. But what about measuring social media tools that are added to your site? These tools can be an embedded Tweet This link, a video player, a comment feature, a product review feature, or a Facebook Connect application. All these tools help Web site visitors share information about your products and services — it is another type of marketing!

There are many ways to measure social media tools and the implementation and resulting data can vary widely. In fact, configuring Google Analytics to measure certain social tools can be unnecessary work. Let's walk through a few common social media features and see how they can be tracked with, and without, Google Analytics.

Tracking comments

Commenting is an extremely popular feature on blogs and other types of publishing Web sites. From a social perspective, it powers an open dialog between those who publish content and those who consume content. Measuring comments and commenting is critical as it is a direct indicator of how engaging your content is and the interest level of the audience.

Sites that offer a commenting feature should be measuring a number of comment-related metrics. You should minimally be measuring the Number of Comments per Post. This simple number can provide insight into which content is the most engaging to your audience. It does not indicate whether people like or dislike your content, only that the content moved them enough to offer feedback.

You can measure the number of comments with Google Analytics, but this can be complicated. The most logical way to measure comments is by using event tracking. As Chapter 5 mentions, event tracking can measure almost any visitor action. While event tracking allows you to track many attributes of a comment, it also requires a fair amount of configuration.

There are two steps to tracking comments with events. First, define the data you want to collect. While events will let you track basic things, such as the number of comments submitted, you can take it one step further and track additional details about various comments. Events have four attributes: Categories, Actions, Labels, and Values.

For example, you're using a category of Comment for all Web site comments. All the comments on the site are lumped together into one category so you can track them at an aggregate level.

There is a single action associated with the Comment category: Add Comment. Normally, all visitors can only comment.

And finally, for the Label, you use the title of the blog post where the comment was posted. This label helps measure which posts receive comments. Why not use the Value parameter? Remember, Value is just a number that Google Analytics sums and aggregates. It is great for counting the number of seconds that a video plays, but it doesn't have an application when tracking comments on a blog.

The second part of this implementation is adding the event tracking code to the site. Adding the event tracking code is the part where you, or your technical resources, need to program. You need to get under the hood of your site and add JavaScript in the appropriate place, such as when a visitor clicks on the Submit Comment button or when the blog administrator approves a pending comment. Based on the data defined, the code will look like this:

```
pageTracker._trackEvent('Comment','Add Comment','[POST TITLE]');
```

In the line of code, the value *[POST TITLE]* would need to be dynamically replaced with the correct value.

Once all the coding is complete, you can use the basic Event report to view the number of comments left and which posts received the most comments. Use the Category report to view how many total comments have been submitted. Then you can drill down into the Label report to view which posts received the most comments.

Another way you can understand your overall audience is by segmenting the people who leave comments on your site. More often than not, you want people to leave a comment. You can use Google Analytics to bucket the people who leave a comment and then analyze information about them using custom variables.

Creating a custom variable to segment a commenter requires a single line of code. While creating the line of code is simple, placing the code in the appropriate place on your site can be challenging. Remember, the code must be placed when the visitor submits the comment, or you may choose to add the code when the site administrator approves the comment. The code must be generated after someone has submitted a comment:

```
pageTracker._setCustomVar(1,'Visitor-Type','Commenter',2);
```

Note that the code is a visit-scope variable, meaning that it exists only during the visit in which the person leaves a comment. After you have added this code, you can use the Custom Variables report for a basic measure of how many visits were by commenters (see Figure 12.7).

FIGURE 12.7

Use the Custom Variables report to measure visitors who leave comments.

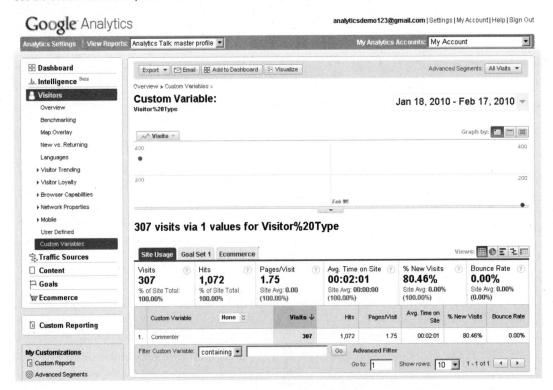

Measuring the number of people who leave a comment gives you an idea of how involved your audience is. Of those that do leave a comment, you can measure how often they participate. By dividing the total number of comments by the number of commenters, you get the metric of Comments per Commenter. This is an effective way to measure how engaged the audience is in your site. And that is the goal: To grow an engaged audience over time.

Tracking subscriptions

Another popular social media tool on many Web sites is a subscription option. You have probably seen this option on blogs and other content Web sites. Understanding how many people subscribe to your content is critical. The subscription identifies the true size of your audience and how many people you can reach with your content.

Remember, not everyone reads the content on your site. For example, people may use a newsreader to consume your information as a *feed*. In these cases, Google Analytics does not provide a lot of insight because readers may never visit your site.

The best tool to measure feed subscribers is FeedBurner. We do not cover how to configure FeedBurner in this book, but if you allow users to subscribe to your content using a feed, you should use FeedBurner.

In addition to tracking the simple number of subscribers, FeedBurner has also been integrated with Google Analytics. FeedBurner automatically adds a Campaign, Medium, Source, and Content Value to all the links in your feed. This makes it incredibly easy to identify traffic from your syndicated feed to your Web site. Each parameter has a default value that you can customize if you choose. The parameter value setting can be found in the Configure Stats section of the Analyze tab, shown in Figure 12.8.

By default, FeedBurner sets the following values for each link tagging parameter:

- **Campaign:** This parameter is set to a combination of information. It starts with the word "Feed" to indicate that the visitor came from your feed. It is followed by the URI (the URL after the domain extension) of your feed and then the name of your feed.
- **Medium:** The channel in which your feed is distributed. This could be `e-mail` for those that choose to get your feed via e-mail or simply `feed` for those who subscribe to the feed using a reader.
- **Source:** This is set to `feedburner` to indicate that the traffic came from FeedBurner.
- **Content:** The application the person used to subscribe to the feed. This could be almost any feed-reading tool, such as Google Reader, Net Vibes, or My Yahoo.

The data appears in your standard Traffic Sources Reports (Campaigns, All Traffic Sources, and so on). Figure 12.9 shows the Campaigns report and that the No. 1 campaign was the RSS feed.

Using FeedBurner does not mean that you can't track the number of subscriptions using Google Analytics. To subscribe to a feed, a person usually needs to click on a Subscribe or RSS link, which normally resides on your Web site. You can use Google Analytics to track the number of people who click the Subscribe link. However, you won't get an exact number of people subscribing to the feed because there are additional steps that must occur after the visitor clicks the Subscribe link. Specifically,

FIGURE 12.8

You can change the values FeedBurner uses for the link tagging parameters in the Configure Stats section.

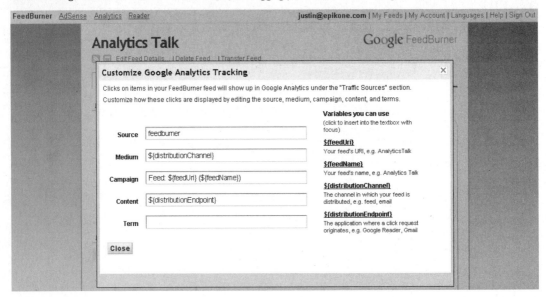

visitors can often choose how they want to subscribe. But tracking the clicks on the Subscribe link is a good proxy and provides a rough number of subscribers.

In this example, you're using events to track clicks on an RSS link. You could use Virtual Pageviews, but without setting up additional profiles and applying filters across your account, it may pollute the Pageview data. All you need to do is define the data for the event (a category and an action) and add the code to the Subscribe link.

Note that you are defining only a category and an action. You only want to get an idea of how many subscriptions you are getting; that is, basically a count of how many people are clicking the link. Once you have the event-tracking code, you can add it to your link, like this:

```
<a href="http://www.feeds.com" onClick="pageTracker._trackEvent('rss
    Subscription','Subscribe to feed');">Subscribe to Feed</a>
```

Remember, when adding JavaScript to a link, it is best to create a custom function that ensures that the Google Analytics code executes before the browser redirects the visitor to the value in the anchor tag.

You can use a standard event report, such as the Category report in Figure 12.10, to identify how many people are clicking on the subscribe link.

In addition to counting the number of subscribers, you can use analysis tools, such as Secondary Dimensions, to identify which traffic sources are generating the most RSS subscriptions such as a particular campaign or a random referral. Figure 12.10 shows the Secondary Dimension set to Source. The key to the analysis is that by using a Secondary Dimension, you can evaluate planned activities by

FIGURE 12.9

The Campaigns report shows that a feed is the number one source of traffic for this site.

looking for planned sources of traffic. Or you can discover unplanned sources of conversion by identifying unexpected sources in the Secondary Dimension column.

Remember, this data is just a proxy — you are measuring how many people clicked on the link with *the intent* of subscribing to your feed, but you are not measuring how many actually completed the signup. But using an event should give you a general idea of the number of subscriptions and maybe — just as important in some analysis scenarios — the *intent* of people to subscribe. Again, that is the point: Subscribers are people who are engaged. And you want to engage your audience and grow the size of your engaged audience over time.

FIGURE 12.10

You can view feed subscribers by choosing Content ▶ Event Tracking ▶ Categories.

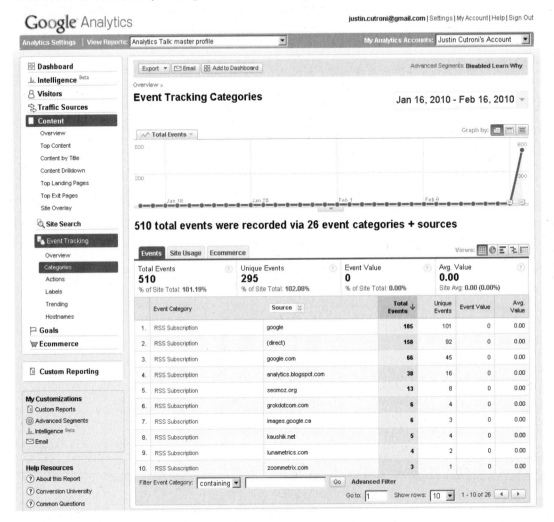

Tracking content-sharing tools

Another common social feature on many sites, not just blogs, is the ability to share content over a social network, such as Facebook and Twitter.

This example focuses on L.L. Bean and sharing products. How the product appears in the social network depends on the social medium. If you choose to share an item using Twitter, the Web site creates a shortened URL using Bit.ly and opens a new window for `twitter.com` where you can log in and write your own tweet that includes the shortened URL. If you use Facebook, an actual widget showing the product, a description, and a link to the product appears in your profile.

The Measurement Goal is to track how many times visitors share and if the sharing ultimately has an impact on your business. This is a two-part process, measuring the act of sharing and measuring the traffic to your site from shared content.

Tracking content-sharing usage

There are multiple tools you can use to track sharing tools. One way to use Google Analytics to track *share usage* is to simply track the clicks on the sharing links. In this example, we use event tracking to track how many times people click on the various sharing options. This solution is almost identical to how you can track comments and RSS subscriptions.

To use event tracking, begin by defining the data. You need to identify the different values for the Category, Action, and Labels. In this example, you use a value of `Product Sharing` for the Category. Next you define a few values for the action. You need multiple actions to differentiate the various ways that people can share the product. L.L. Bean offers visitors five ways to share a product: Facebook, Digg, Delicious, StumbleUpon, and Twitter.

You need a separate action for each medium the visitor might choose to share the item. So for Facebook, you create a value of `Share on Facebook`. For StumbleUpon, you create a value of `Share on StumbleUpon`, and so on. By creating different actions for each social medium, you can measure where your audience tends to hang out online.

Finally, you need to define Labels. Because you're sharing products, use the name of the product, such as `Bean Boots by L.L. Bean, 10-inch Thinsulate`. Now put it all together. A generic version of the code might look like this:

```
<a href="http://www.site.com" onClick="pageTracker._trackEvent('Share
    Product'),'Share on [MEDIUM NAME]', '[PRODUCT NAME]'">
```

The items in brackets should be replaced with specific values. So `[MEDIUM NAME]` is replaced with the social networks where people can share the products. And `[PRODUCT NAME]` is replaced with the actual name of the product that was shared. Don't forget to format the `[MEDIUM NAME]` and `[PRODUCT NAME]` values with script-friendly characters (only alphanumeric characters). Strip out any special characters such as quotation marks. You can see that the implementation could take significant work, but the data is useful. You can use the Event Tracking reports to view what products people share and where they share them.

Knowing where people share your products can help determine which social mediums you, as a company, want to participate in. If you know that a majority of your site visitors are sharing products on Twitter and Facebook, you may choose to carefully monitor and participate in those networks. You might also discover that you wasted a lot of money by building a Facebook Connect app that no one uses. Or you could discover that most people choose to share using a different option, like StumbleUpon, and thus choose to make that logo larger. There are lots of things to learn!

Likewise, knowing which products are being shared the most can help identify trends in popularity, and thus which products you should feature on your home page or in your marketing . You can even use the information to determine the order of products for your site search results.

Tracking traffic from content-sharing tools

Another way you can integrate Google Analytics with sharing is through campaign tracking. This option depends on where you are sharing the information and the technology that provides the sharing. Most sharing mechanisms embed some kind of link back to the product page.

If visitors click on that link, they will likely appear as a referral in your Google Analytics data. However, if you want to get a bit more detail, you can add campaign tags to the link that appears in social media. You could use a simple link-tagging strategy to identify that this link originated via the Share a Product feature. You could set the `utm_campaign` parameter to `product-sharing`, the `utm_medium` parameter to `social-media`, and the `utm_source` parameter to the name of the social network where the link was located.

Note that some links in Facebook apps can be finicky when it comes to campaign tagging. It is often better to take the tagging out of the Facebook app and have the server add the link-tagging

Tracking Social Media at Lollapalooza.com

Here's an example that brings together tracking social media tools on your site and driving traffic to your site. When C3 Presents, the folks behind music festivals such as Lollapalooza and Austin City Limits, decided to incorporate social media into the event Web sites, they went all out.

From custom Facebook Connect applications to Twitter updates, a MySpace blog, a bulletin, and site postings to e-mail

sharing and AddThis, it was not hard for visitors to use some kind of social media on the site. As you can imagine, this investment in social media was substantial, and at the end of the day, the only question that mattered was "Did it work?"

To answer this question, C3 engaged with WebShare, a Google Analytics authorized consultant. The first step was to define what "work" meant. The defined goals of social media, in the case of concert promotion, ultimately revolved around ticket sales, but understanding how the various social media applications were being used was the foundation. Generally, C3 wanted to know:

• Are people interacting with the social media features? Which ones? Are they buying tickets as a result?

• Do the sharing applications drive additional visitors to the site? Which ones? Are they buying tickets?

To answer these questions, two Google Analytics features were used: event tracking and campaign tagging.

Using event tracking (see Chapter 5 for more details), a hierarchy of Categories, Actions, and Labels defined different social media interactions. For example, if a visitor used Facebook

parameters. So the Facebook link will be something like `http://www.llbean.com/
fblanding/123412341234`, which on the L.L. Bean server redirects to the tagged link:

```
http://www.llbean.com/products/items.aspx?item=123412341234&utm_
    source=facebook &utm_campaign=product-sharing&utm_
    medium=social-media
```

Once a tagged link has been published to a social medium, you can use the standard Traffic Sources reports (such as Campaigns, All Traffic Sources, and Ad Versions) to evaluate whether Traffic — and, more important, Revenue and Conversions — resulted from sharing the product.

Social media is a rapidly evolving medium. We hope that this section has given you a few ideas on how you can use Google Analytics to track site traffic coming from social media sources and social media tools on your site.

Connect to share a custom lineup, an event was recorded of the Category `share`, an Action of `facebook`, and a Label of `custom schedule`.

Once this data was collected, the Event Tracking reports were used to measure the impact of social media on the bottom line. And by using Pivot Tables and Secondary Dimensions, it was easy to answer questions such as "How many tickets and how much revenue resulted from people in Chicago who used Facebook Connect and found the site on the keyword 'lollapalooza 2009'?"

Understanding how many visitors arrived at the site as a result of social sharing was equally important, and the ticket sales and revenue resulting from these visitors was again the ultimate measure of success or failure. Campaign tagging, along with URL shortening, was used to accomplish this.

For example, when visitors clicked on the Twitter icon to share the content they're viewing, the tweet text is pre-filled with something like "Check out the Lollapalooza Lineup at `http://bit.ly/XHmA1`."

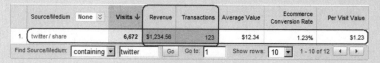

When the visitors clicked on the link, they were taken to the full URL, which included the campaign parameters necessary to source the visit to a Medium of `share` via the Source `twitter`, and now C3 could see just how many tickets were sold from Twitter sharing.

Measuring E-mail Marketing

E-mail has long been a favorite tool of marketers. It is an extremely effective way to target highly qualified individuals with a well-crafted and creative message. E-mail can be used a number of ways by marketers. In addition to generating sales, it can be used to retain customers, build communities, and test brand messages.

Regardless of how your e-mail marketing is used, the measurement and optimization are fairly straightforward: You want to define what makes a successful e-mail campaign, measure your campaign, and then segment your data to understand why it did, or did not, succeed. The key is tracking what your e-mail visitors do on the site after coming from an e-mail.

E-mail: What's It Good For?

Before we dive into metrics and tracking, let's take a step back and explain at a high level how you can use e-mail. After all, it is difficult to define and explain how to measure e-mail if we don't define how to use e-mail first.

Marketers use e-mail for many reasons. One of the most common uses is to acquire new customers. Many organizations place a high priority on building their e-mail lists through online and offline interactions with people. For example, many sites have an e-mail newsletter sign-up prominently placed on the site. The newsletter e-mail addresses gathered can then be used in different kinds of acquisition campaigns to generate new customers.

E-mail is also a wonderful retention tool. Most people know that it costs less to get a previous customer to convert than to win a new customer. And e-mail is an extremely effective way to reach out to those who have previously purchased and entice them to purchase again.

Using e-mail as a retention tool can be exciting. Very rarely do marketers send a generic message to individuals who have purchased before. Marketers usually mine the customer list, segmenting on various pieces of information (such as demographic information or purchase history) to send a specific message to a specific group. This ability to segment and target increases the chances of getting a previous customer to convert again.

The challenge is to accurately track whom to send messages to, which segments they belong to, and which messages are sent. If you don't know which segments convert, you are not doing your job as an analyst.

E-mail is also used for some of the most mundane business activities. Order confirmations, shipping notifications, newsletters, and so on are all done by e-mail today. But these communications are important. Every communication with a customer or potential customer represents your brand and could make or break the relationship.

Regardless of how you choose to use e-mail, you must clearly define the intended purpose. Defining the desired results provides critical context to gauging the success of e-mail, or any marketing activity for that matter. For example, if you are running a new customer acquisition campaign, the goal may be to generate 100 new customers. If you are trying to make your e-mail marketing more effective, your goal may be to increase the number of people who open your e-mail. Again, you need to define what success is so the measurement can align with the desired outcome.

Defining E-mail Measurement

E-mail metrics can be divided into two categories: pre-click data and post-click data. Both offer different insights into the process of e-mail marketing. Think about it: Like any marketing activity, e-mail is a process that you try to push people through. This process has clearly defined steps. There are metrics that help provide insight into each step, helping you gauge where you may have problems.

Pre-click data

Pre-click data describes everything that happens before a person clicks a link in an e-mail. These metrics describe the upper end of the process. Pre-click metrics help you understand if there is a problem with the deliverability, creative, or message in your e-mail. Pre-click data includes metrics such as:

- **Number of E-mails Sent.** As the name implies, this is the number of e-mails sent during the campaign. If you don't know how many e-mails were sent, you have no idea of the size of the audience you can reach with your e-mail. This metrics helps put all other metrics into context. Is 500 visits from an e-mail campaign good or bad? If you sent 1,000 e-mails, it's good; if you sent 100,000, it's bad!
- **Number of E-mails Bounced.** A bounced e-mail is an e-mail that is returned by the receiving address. Measuring the number of bounces helps you understand the quality of your list. You obviously want to reduce the number of bounces as much as possible.

- **Number of E-mails Opened (open rate).** This is the number of e-mails opened. There is a debate about "opens" due to how this metric is tracked. Normally an "open" is tracked when an image loads in the recipient's inbox. However, most modern e-mail tools, like Microsoft Outlook and Google Gmail, block images, which dramatically reduces the accuracy of this metric. Does that mean that you should not use this metric? That is up to you. We believe that trending a metric over time helps establish a baseline and negates many of the issues caused by tracking problems. We also believe that educating stakeholders about the potential problems with metrics can help everyone determine how much weight should be placed on certain numbers. The number of e-mails opened can help you understand how persuasive your subject line is. Remember, if recipients do not open your e-mail, there is no way they will ever take action on your e-mail, regardless of its purpose. This metric is often reported as a percentage, making it easy to understand what percentage of your e-mails were opened. Obviously you want to increase this percentage over time.
- **Clicks.** This is the number of clicks the e-mail receives. Clicks are a great proxy to gauge whether your message and creative are persuading recipients to take action. If you are not getting clicks, your e-mail is not persuading the recipient, and that is a problem.

All these metrics assist in the optimization of your e-mail content.

You have probably figured out that pre-click data does not come from Google Analytics. Google Analytics can track only what happens on your site. It cannot track what happens in a person's e-mail inbox. Pre-click data comes from the tool you use to send your e-mail. There are many tools on the market today that provide e-mail services, and almost all of them provide pre-click metrics. Figure 13.1 shows MailChimp, a popular e-mail tool.

Post-click data

Post-click data is e-mail related data collected after the user clicks the e-mail and arrives on your site. This is where the integration of e-mail marketing and Google Analytics comes into play. If pre-click data tells you how effective your e-mail is at attracting attention, post-click data tells you how good you are at closing the deal.

Post-click data include many of the usual metrics in Google Analytics:

- **Bounce Rate.** The Bounce Rate for an e-mail helps you understand how relevant the landing experience is to the message included in the e-mail. E-mail campaigns with a high Bounce Rate warrant investigation. If you are taking the time to craft a well-thought-out message and send it to a specific part of your e-mail list, you should be able to place the recipient on a landing page that relates to the content of the e-mail. As is normally the case, if people do not move beyond your landing page, they probably can't do what you want them to do.
- **Pageviews and Time on Site.** These classic engagement metrics can help you understand if e-mail traffic is engaging with the content on your site. Depending on the purpose of your e-mail, these metrics may be critical. If your e-mail is part of a product education campaign,

FIGURE 13.1

Almost every e-mail tool, such as the MailChimp tool shown here, has some kind of reporting for pre-click data.

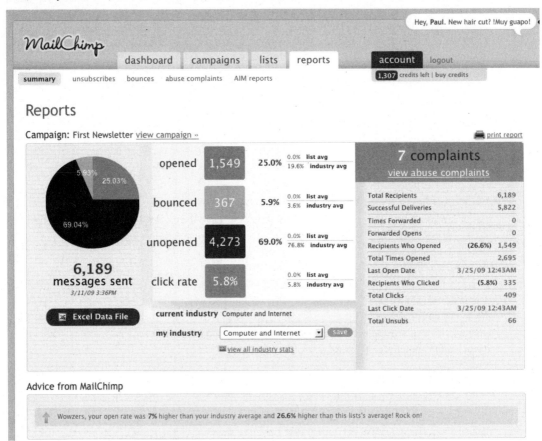

you want to measure whether people are looking at the correct content and how much time they spend on those pages.

- **Conversion Rate.** No matter what your business, you have conversions, and you probably use e-mail marketing to generate those conversions. Tracking the number of conversions from e-mail is how you truly measure success for e-mail marketing. In addition to your standard business conversions, you may have specific conversions for an e-mail campaign. For example, if you are an ecommerce site, you may send an e-mail to your existing customers asking them to create an account on your site. In this case, the goal of the e-mail, or conversion, is about how many accounts were created rather than sales generated.

- **Revenue.** If you are an ecommerce business, and the goal of your e-mail is to generate revenue, it is important to measure exactly how much revenue each e-mail campaign generates. When you know the revenue an e-mail campaign generates, you can calculate other metrics like E-mail ROI, Revenue per E-mail, and so on.

Post-click data does not magically appear in Google Analytics. You must configure Google Analytics to accurately separate e-mail data from other marketing activities. We explain how to track an e-mail in Google Analytics and do the analysis in the next main section.

Continuously improving your e-mail campaigns

All the data must lead to a continuous improvement process. Every time you discover something new during your analysis, make note of it and apply what you learn to your next e-mail campaign. For example, if you learn that a specific segment of your e-mail list responds well to a specific message, you may want to test variations of that message during your next e-mail campaign. At the end of this chapter, we look at a case study that demonstrates how segmenting data and continuous testing can improve the performance of e-mail.

Tracking E-mail with Google Analytics

You integrate e-mail tracking with Google Analytics using campaign tracking and link tagging. (If you are unfamiliar with campaign tracking and link tagging, refer to Chapter 5 for an overview.)

Your job is to define values for all the link-tagging parameters. The values you use represent the different attributes of your e-mail campaign. Remember: An e-mail campaign can be broken into many smaller parts. You may be segmenting your e-mail list into small groups and then sending variations of the creative to each group. You may also be sending different segments of your e-mail list to different landing pages. When you combine these segments, you have a many-to-many relationship that can complicate the campaign-tagging process.

Let's walk through a simple ecommerce-based campaign. This campaign is a promotional sale sent to existing customers, and you want to segment the list by gender and purchase history. You'll also send different creative versions to each group and send them to different landing pages. You need to capture all this information in Google Analytics and be able to determine what combinations generate conversions.

Start with the Campaign parameter. There is one campaign, and all recipients are in the same campaign, named `2009fall-sale`. Adding the date to the Campaign parameter name makes it easy to compare campaigns across years.

But you can use the campaign for more than simply the campaign name. You could also add information to describe what type of e-mail campaign you're sending. You can add information to the Campaign parameter to describe what kind of e-mail campaign you are sending. For example, you could add `[retention]` or `[acquisition]` to the campaign name. By adding the type of e-mail, you can easily gauge the type of campaign by looking at the campaign name; for example, `2009fall-sale[retention]`.

TABLE 13.1

Sample Campaign Tracking Parameters for an E-mail Campaign

Parameter	Query String Variable	Values
Campaign	utm_campaign	2009-fall-sale[retention]
Medium	utm_medium	email
Source	utm_source	male-last30days male-last60days male-60daysplus female-last30days female-last60days female-60daysplus
Content	utm_content	male-ver-1 male-ver-2 female-ver-1 female-ver-2 und-ver-1 und-ver-2

TABLE 13.2

E-mail Metrics and Common Insights

Metric	Type	Insights
E-mails Sent	Preclick	How big of an audience are you reaching with e-mail? This metric should increase over time.
E-mails Bounced	Preclick	How good is the quality of your e-mail list? Was there a high percentage of bounced e-mails? This metric should decrease over time.
E-mails Opened	Preclick	Did the recipient find my e-mail subject enticing enough to open the e-mail? If recipients do not open your e-mail, it is impossible for them to take action.
Clicks	Preclick	Was the e-mail persuasive enough to generate a click? Over time, are you getting more and more people to click your e-mails?
Bounce Rate	Postclick	Did your landing page meet the expectations and the needs of the e-mail recipient? Normally if the recipient does not move past your landing page, they can't convert.
Pageviews/Time on Site	Postclick	Did the e-mail recipient engage with the Web site after clicking the e-mail? Did they view more than one page and spend a significant amount of time on the site?
Conversion Rate (or Revenue)	Postclick	Did your e-mail achieve the goals that you defined? Did the recipient buy your product, engage your content, or otherwise meet your objectives?

Next, you need to define a Medium for your e-mail. The Medium helps you compare the different methods for marketing to people. It may seem silly, but email is the Medium for e-mail. By using the value of email for *all* e-mail you send, you can identify the impact that e-mail has on your business. Remember, consistency matters when it comes to campaign tracking. A simple discrepancy such using e-mail instead of email as the Medium value can cause trouble when analyzing your data.

Now, you need to define values for the utm_source parameter. Remember, Source helps you understand more about the e-mail the visitor received. This value can be as simple as newsletter, special offer, or another value that indicates which e-mail you sent to the recipient.

But you can do even more with Source. We suggest you use Source to track more additional information about who receives the e-mail. In this example, you are going to segment the list by gender and last purchase date. You need to include this information if you want to measure which segments performed well and which did not.

Next, you are going to format the Source parameter as gender-purchase history. You could have any of three values for gender: female, male, and unknown. You could also have multiple values for purchase history; last30days, last60days, or 60daysplus. When you combine the gender with the purchase history, you get a huge number of combinations. Tagging e-mail can get complicated! But it is also extremely useful.

The final parameter is the Content parameter, utm_content. Use this parameter to track the version of the e-mail you send to the recipient. By adding this parameter, you can measure the creative versions that you send to the different segments of your list.

Now, you need to put this all together and tag the links in your e-mails. Some of the parameters could have a huge number of values, specifically the Source and Content parameters. And when you combine all the parameters, the number of combinations can really start to grow. Just look at all the values in Table 13.1. You absolutely must be organized. As we have mentioned, you should use a spreadsheet to help manage all this information.

Every link in every e-mail must now be tagged. So an e-mail going to a female who bought a product in the last 30 days and is receiving e-mail version 2 would have a link that looks like this:

```
http://www.mysite.com/landing.html?utm_campaign=2009fall-sale
    [retnesion]&utm_medium=email&utm_source=female-last30
    &utm_content=female-ver-2
```

For the most part, there is no additional configuration necessary to track e-mail. However, be sure you have the goals configured in Google Analytics. If the goals of your e-mail align with the goals you have already configured in Google Analytics, you are set. But if the goal of your e-mail does not match one of your configured goals, you may need to add another goal to Google Analytics.

Some e-mail tools automatically integrate with Google Analytics. You're probably thinking, "Now they tell us!" Most of these integrations involve the automatic tagging of the links in your e-mails using default data from your campaign. More sophisticated e-mail tools provide the option to override the default values with custom values. Take the time to evaluate and understand whether your e-mail tool integrates with Google Analytics, and if it does, *how* it integrates. Poor integration won't help you, even if it is automated.

Data and Analysis

Analyzing both pre-click and post-click data can help you identify where you are having trouble in your e-mail marketing campaign. Remember: The different data types tell you about the entire process of e-mail marketing. Table 13.2 shows pre-click and post-click metrics mentioned earlier in the chapter and what the metrics can tell you about the performance of your e-mail campaign.

FIGURE 13.2

Use the Campaigns report to find your e-mail campaigns and evaluate performance.

Now let's focus on post-click data, which is data about Web site traffic from e-mail campaigns. Remember: All post-click data comes from the information in your link tags.

Use the Campaign report shown in Figure 13.2 to get a general idea of how your campaign performed.

The Campaign report is a good way to evaluate the big-picture performance of your e-mail campaign. This report is useful but can often be too general to explain why the campaign was successful. Simple metrics like Visits, Bounce Rate, and Conversion Rate can provide good insight. For example, if you sent 100,000 e-mails and had just 1,000 visits, there was an issue with getting people to click in the e-mail. If your campaign had a 65 percent Bounce Rate, you know there was an issue with the landing experience. While this information is useful, much of the juicy data comes when you start to segment the data using the Source and Content parameters.

You begin the segment analysis by clicking the name of the campaign, then segmenting the campaign by Source using the Dimension pop-up menu. Because you know you are looking at a specific

FIGURE 13.3

Segmenting the e-mail campaign by Source helps you understand which segments are performing well.

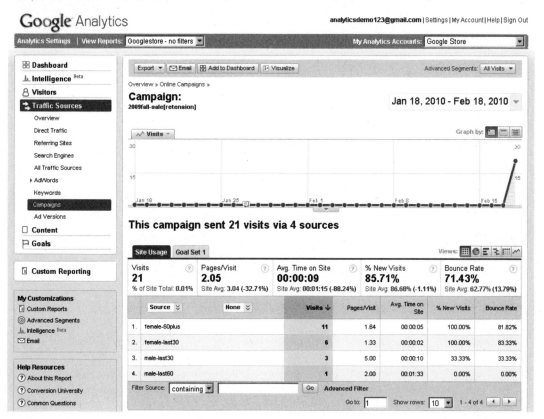

e-mail campaign, you don't need to segment by Medium. But segmenting by Source should provide more insight because of the data in your link tags. As Figure 13.3 shows, you can now see which sources in your e-mail campaign are performing well.

But you want to dig further. Remember, you used Source and Medium to add more information to Google Analytics. Now let's look at the Content information, which identifies which e-mail variation the visitor clicked. Using the Secondary Dimensions feature in the report, choose Ad Content; Google Analytics adds this information to the report. Now, not only do you see the different segments (in the Source column) but also the different ad variations in the Ad Content column (as shown in Figure 13.4).

FIGURE 13.4

Segmenting by the Ad Content dimension provides more insight into which recipients prefer which ad versions.

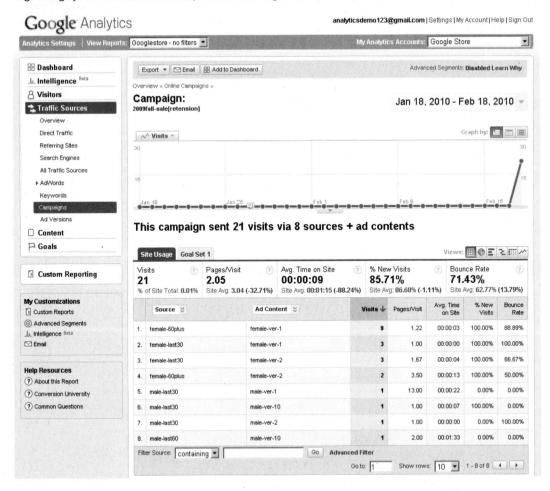

It is also important to analyze the landing page experience. Remember: You can send e-mail to different landing pages. Some e-mail campaigns have custom landing pages while others use existing content on your site. Does one work better than the other? It depends! This is a critical piece of post-click information that you can use to identify which landing page works best at converting visitors.

The entire goal is to see how the Bounce Rate changes for different Source/Content/Landing Page combinations. You added a lot of information to the Source parameter. Matching that information with the Landing Page Bounce Rate and then evaluating the entire experience is critical.

FIGURE 13.5

Pivoting the data to view the Source, Ad Content, and Landing Page dimensions of an e-mail campaign.

The easiest way to view the Bounce Rate for different Source and Ad Content combinations is by using a Pivot Table, a data visualization option available in most Google Analytics reports.

To create a Pivot Table, click the Pivot icon in the top-right corner of the Data Table (see Figure 13.5). Once you have the Pivot Table display, you can pivot the data by almost any dimension. In this case, use the Landing Page to see which pages work best for the various e-mail versions. Next, pivot the data by the Ad Content: Notice that you now can view each e-mail variation (the Ad Content parameter) as a column. You can choose two metrics to view at a time, as shown in Figure 13.5.

Using Segmentation and Testing to Improve an E-mail Newsletter Program

The AARP is one of the largest membership organizations in the nation, and it's well known for supporting issues important to the Baby Boomer generation. What is not as well known is that the AARP has a leading Web site, AARP.org, that publishes content focused on the health and well-being of people of any age.

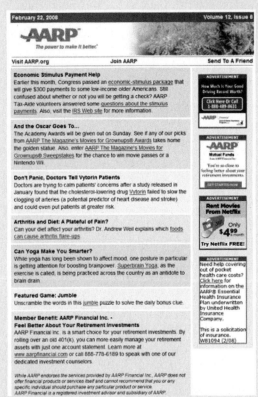

The AARP's Online Marketing group is responsible for generating awareness of the site and driving traffic to it. While it uses several classic online marketing channels such as SEO, PPC, and paid media to accomplish this, the group is also responsible for publishing a weekly e-mail newsletter called the Webletter.

The Webletter is sent each week to millions of people who signed up at AARP.org to receive the Webletter or are current AARP members. It features several articles from AARP.org and is designed, written, and sent out by the AARP's Online Marketing group.

When the AARP's Online Marketing department took over the management of the Webletter, the e-mail newsletter had industry-standard open and click-through rates — but overall a poorly engaged audience. While this wasn't a cause for panic, it did point to an opportunity to improve the program.

The AARP's Online Marketing group decided to address this, and within 18 months, the Webletter emerged as AARP.org's No. 1 driver of traffic, with three-digit lifts in open rate, click-through rate, and weekly click volume. In addition, a much higher percentage of the audience was actively engaged, opening the Webletter, reading the articles, and clicking through to the site regularly. While several factors contributed to the success, there were two primary drivers, both of which we mention in this chapter.

In addition to analyzing a single campaign, you can look at e-mail in the context of all your marketing activities. Using the All Traffic Sources report and viewing the Medium dimension gives you a good view of each Medium regardless of performance (see Figure 13.6).

This Medium view of the data is particularly effective when you are trying to gauge the ROI of your various marketing activities. While you cannot calculate ROI for e-mail marketing in Google Analytics (there is no metric for e-mail investment in Google Analytics), you can easily extract conversions or revenue from Google Analytics and perform the necessary calculations in Excel.

One was list segmentation. The first thing the AARP did to improve the Webletter performance was to segment the list into three groups based on click and open behavior. This divide-and-conquer approach allowed the AARP to tailor the subject line and newsletter layout to consider each user's level of engagement, therefore increasing the relevancy of the message. The segments were:

- **Active:** The most engaged subscribers who were reading and responding almost every week.

- **Passive:** Subscribers who had potential. They were opening the Webletter, but weren't clicking through to AARP.org yet.

- **Inactive:** Subscribers who were not opening *or* clicking. These were likely people who had lost interest in the newsletter and needed to either be re-engaged or removed from the list.

The second driver was testing. Once the segments were identified, the AARP collaborated with one of its agency partners, Brooks Bell Interactive, to create a weekly "A/B test" of the Webletter. This meant that the AARP did not send a single version of the Webletter; it sent up to 10 versions *every* week. Each version of the e-mail was tagged differently to measure how it performed. The AARP tested subject lines, tweaks to the layout, imagery, length, and URL text. The AARP always included a control group to compare tests to, and it rolled out changes to the newsletter only once the tested version outperformed the control group. Some of the winning elements that the AARP discovered were layouts with a table of contents, personalized subject lines, benefit-focused headlines, and "Click to Continue" URLs.

The key is that A/B testing became a systematic and consistent process at the AARP. Once the AARP Online Marketing group ran the first test, it was easy to adopt a testing rhythm that allowed the team to stay focused, gather learnings, and increase the effectiveness of the program one week at a time. Before the team knew it, the Webletter program was delivering outstanding results.

The success of the AARP's Webletter program demonstrates the powerful effect of segmentation and e-mail testing. While testing requires more time, resources, strategy, and analysis, it's the best way to tailor your program to what your customers *want*. This is clearly a win-win: a better e-mail experience for customers and more results for the organization.

FIGURE 13.6

View the Medium dimension in the Traffic Sources report to review the overall performance of e-mail marketing in the context of all mediums.

If you're not tracking e-mail with Google Analytics, you are only getting half the picture. And when you do track e-mail with Google Analytics, the key is to track as much information about your e-mail marketing as possible. Knowing which e-mails were delivered to which people helps drive your ability to segment e-mail lists and send the right message to the right person.

Extending Google Analytics

Tracking Offline Marketing

The world of marketing has undergone a major change over the last decade. With the mass adoption of the Internet, marketers have new ways to reach huge numbers of people. And as consumers spend more and more time online, rather than engaging with offline media, marketers have started to shift their ad spend from offline mediums to online.

But offline marketing is not going away, at least not any time soon. Instead we're seeing a complex marketing environment in which consumers are exposed to many different messages in many different media. In fact, it's becoming more and more complicated to identify which marketing activities drive business success.

In this chapter, we want to simplify the world of tracking offline marketing activities with Google Analytics. We look at common offline marketing activities, such as print, direct mail, radio, and television, and address what we can do with Google Analytics to measure the effectiveness of your offline efforts, from tracking Web site traffic from offline marketing activities to revenue and conversions

Tracking TV and Radio

TV and radio have long been marketer's tools to reach a broad audience. But the direct measurement of the impact of these media can be difficult to measure. Offline marketing has focused on building brand awareness and consumer education. Television, radio, and a majority of the print ads are used for a number of reasons, such as telling the general public why a product or service is great. Companies have spent ungodly amounts of money on television and radio ads to push their message. Just look at Super Bowl ads in the U.S.

Tracking ads without an online component

At first glance, it would appear that offline marketing have little to do with the online world. But consumers who are constantly bombarded with offline messages from a specific brand may begin to engage that brand in the online world by visiting its Web site or searching for information about the brand. Your goal is to figure out how these people engage online and whether they convert at your business goals.

The challenge with measuring TV and radio campaigns that don't contain a direct online component is isolating the offline material that generates an online action. For example, if Sue sees an ad on CNN, searches Google for "fidelity investments," and visits the Fidelity Web site, how do you connect those actions and tie them to the original ad on CNN? Remember, there was nothing in the ad that directly asked Sue to go online: Sue decided to check online on her own.

The best chance to measure the impact of TV and radio ads that don't contain a Web component is to try to measure Web traffic based on the offline marketing decisions. Specifically, align the measurement technique with the attributes of the ads.

Most TV and radio media is purchased based on geographic location, called a *designated market area* or DMA. In addition, offline marketing usually appears or runs at a specific time. This is called *day-parting*. So you have two pieces of information — time and location — for segmenting Web site data and looking for trends.

Using the Map Overlay report in the Visitors section, you can compare data for cities where offline marketing campaigns exist versus cities where marketing activities do not exist, and look for any correlations. Is there a difference between the two? If so, it may be caused by the offline marketing activity.

But take this technique one step further. Rather than just measuring traffic from a geographic area, segment that traffic based on the traffic source. Specifically, look at direct traffic from different geographic locations. The reason to look at this segment is that if they see a brand-based message, most people will try to type the URL for the brand into the browser. This traffic would appear as direct traffic in Google Analytics. There are many ways to view direct traffic in Google Analytics, but perhaps the easiest is to apply the default Advanced Segment for direct traffic.

Now review the Map Overlay report and view it by city, as shown in Figure 14.1. You want to compare the direct traffic in the locations you're targeting with your offline marketing versus direct traffic in locations that do not have offline marketing. If there is a difference in the data, you can make a general assumption that your offline activity is having some type of effect. If the cities that have offline marketing are outperforming those that do not have offline marketing, you could make the general assumption that the offline marketing is having a positive effect.

In addition to direct traffic, you should also review organic branded traffic in the geographic areas where there is an offline marketing effort. It may be that a person remembers your brand and then searches using your brand as a keyword (or part of a keyword phrase) at a later time. You can measure branded organic searches for a geographic area and compare that information to other geographic areas

FIGURE 14.1

The Map Overlay report segmented by direct traffic.

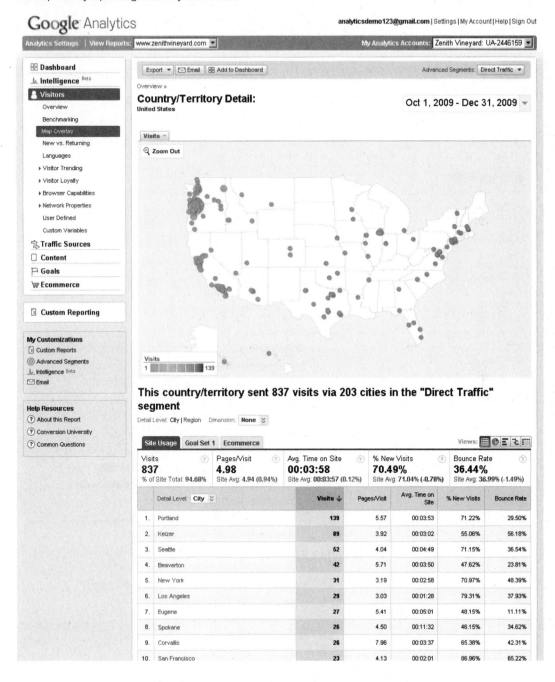

FIGURE 14.2

The Visits report, found in the Visitor Trending section, can be configured to show traffic by the hour of day.

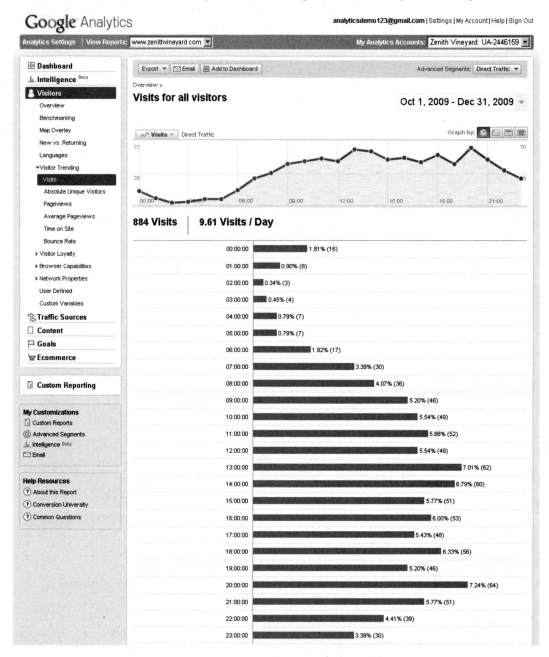

that do not have offline campaigns to determine if there is a difference. Again, this is best done using an Advanced Segment.

Yet another way to gauge the effect of offline advertising on your online traffic is to take advantage of day-parting. Certain types of offline marketing, such as TV and radio advertising, can be run at specific times of the day. You can view data in Google Analytics based on the hour of the day using the Visitor Trending section's Visits report, shown in Figure 14.2.

Using the Graph By option below the Date Selector changes the data based on the hour of the day you select. While day-parting can be helpful, remember that visitor behavior may not always be reflected in this data. Some people may not react directly after exposure to an offline ad. For example, a person may hear a radio ad for a specific product during the commute to work, but may not respond to the ad until later in the day or even at night. It obviously depends on each individual. But it's still a good idea to analyze time-based traffic to your site and understand the traffic in the context of your offline marketing.

And don't forget that you can apply a direct traffic Advanced Segment to view direct traffic by hour of day or a branded organic Advanced Segment. You can even go one step further by modifying the Advanced Segment to include a geographic location, one where you invest in offline marketing. Again, your goal is to compare how direct and branded organic traffic in a geographic region where you buy offline advertising performs against other areas.

Obviously you can see that measuring offline advertising is not an exact science. It's difficult to accurately attribute the performance of offline marketing when there is no direct online component. But if your offline activities contain some direct connection to online, such as a URL, your measurement and analysis capabilities become greater.

Tracking ads with an online component

TV and radio marketing that contain an online call to action are much easier to track and can generate interesting data. This tracking is based on a simple concept: using a dedicated, unique URL in your TV or radio advertisements and then tracking the traffic to that URL. Not only is this a simple concept, it can be used to make offline campaign impact measurable. Like all things Google Analytics, the exact solution you use depends on your situation.

Using a redirect for tracking

Most companies trying to track a TV or radio spot and its online impact use a custom or unique URL in the ad, often called a *vanity URL*. A vanity URL appears only in your TV or radio ad and forwards all traffic to an existing Web site. For example, Fidelity Investments may use the URL www. InvestSmarter.com in an offline ad even though the URL does not represent a real Web site (the visitor is redirected to the appropriate content on the main Fidelity site). The goal is to measure how often that URL is used.

The key to measuring a vanity URL in Google Analytics is to use campaign tracking and link tagging. However, you need to do it differently when working in the offline world. In online analysis, link tagging involves the addition of query string parameters to the URL used in the marketing campaign. However, you can't add the parameters to a URL used in a TV or radio ad: All those parameters will make the URL too long, too hard to remember, and too prone to entry errors, so nobody will bother to type them into a browser.

The solution is to use a URL redirect that manipulates the landing page URL. When a person types www.InvestSmarter.com into a Web browser, you would redirect him or her to www.fidelity.com/?utm_campaign=2010campaign&utm_source=cnn&utm_medium=tv. The link-tagging parameters added during the redirect identify that the visitor originally came from a TV ad on CNN. How do you know? Because the person entered a vanity URL only used in that specific ad.

The actual implementation is different for each Web site due to the technologies used; there is no one-size-fits-all implementation. You could use a programmatic redirect or a server-side redirect. Some hosting companies like GoDaddy and some domain registrars like Hover let you create a redirect in a domain control panel. Regardless of the implementation, the experience for the visitor is the same: Someone types in a URL used only in a specific offline ad. The URL then redirects the person to an existing page, and during the redirect, campaign parameters are added to the URL to identify the person as originating from that offline source.

Like any campaign, it's critical to define useful values for the campaign tags. The values will depend on your business and the medium you're working in; for example, a URL for an ad appearing in print will be different from an ad appearing on TV. Still, here are some general guidelines:

- **Campaign:** Use the name of the campaign. If it's a specific campaign, such as a fall sale, you might use a value of `fallsale2009`. If you're running a brand campaign over a longer time period, you could use a more general name like `brand-education`. It all depends on the type of campaign you're running.
- **Medium:** Normally, you can use a value of `tv` or `radio` for Medium. This value provides enough information to make it easy to identify how television or radio campaigns perform against other marketing mediums.
- **Source:** If possible, try to use the network carrying the ad as the Source. Different networks have different audiences, and different audiences respond to a marketing message differently, so identifying which network audiences perform best is critical. If you know which networks drive the best traffic to your site, you can focus advertising dollars on those networks.
- **Content:** The Swiss Army knife of campaign parameters, this parameter can be used for many things. When creating a value for the Content parameter, think about the attributes of the ad and medium you are working in. If your ad is based on the day of the week, you could use the Content parameter to identify weekday ads versus weekend ads. You can also use it to identify different creative versions of the ad.

Once the custom URL has been placed in an ad, the redirect has been created, and your ad is running, you should start to see data in Google Analytics. If you're analyzing a specific campaign, the Campaigns report in the Traffic Sources section is a great place to start. You can easily spot your TV or radio campaign and review all sorts of information, from general Traffic data to Conversion and Ecommerce data.

FIGURE 14.3

The All Traffic Sources report is a good way to identify how well offline marketing channels are performing compared to online marketing channels. Choose Medium from the Show pop-up menu to view the different mediums driving traffic to your site.

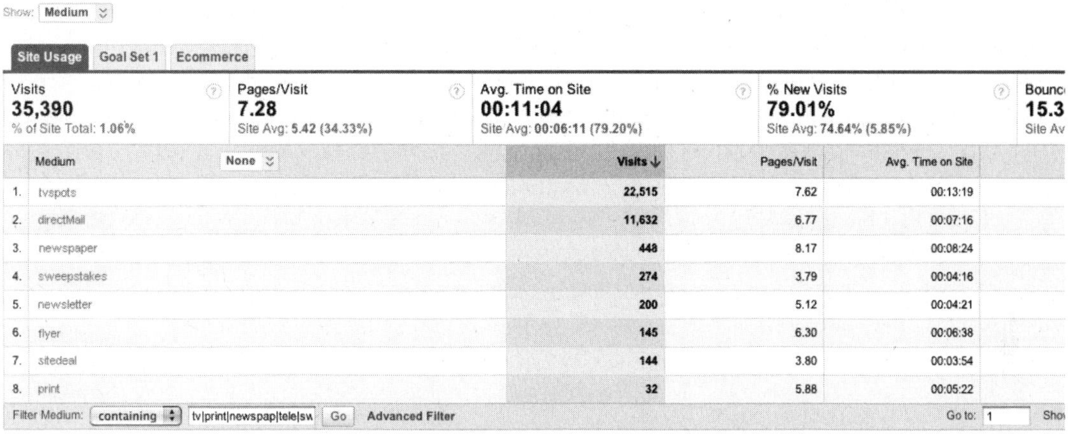

Show: Medium ▾

| Site Usage | Goal Set 1 | Ecommerce |

| Visits
35,390
% of Site Total: 1.06% | Pages/Visit
7.28
Site Avg: 5.42 (34.33%) | Avg. Time on Site
00:11:04
Site Avg: 00:06:11 (79.20%) | % New Visits
79.01%
Site Avg: 74.64% (5.85%) | Bounc
15.3
Site Av |

	Medium	None ▾	Visits ↓	Pages/Visit	Avg. Time on Site
1.	tvspots		22,515	7.62	00:13:19
2.	directMail		11,632	6.77	00:07:16
3.	newspaper		448	8.17	00:08:24
4.	sweepstakes		274	3.79	00:04:16
5.	newsletter		200	5.12	00:04:21
6.	flyer		145	6.30	00:06:38
7.	sitedeal		144	3.80	00:03:54
8.	print		32	5.88	00:05:22

Filter Medium: [containing ▾] [tv|print|newspap|tele|sw] [Go] Advanced Filter   Go to: 1   Sho

If your offline campaign is part of a larger campaign, you may want to start with the All Traffic Sources report. You can easily identify the different Source/Medium combinations used in the offline marketing. Figure 14.3 is the All Traffic Sources report showing different mediums, including many print mediums.

Remember that as you analyze the data, it's important to know the goal of the marketing activity. Was the campaign focused on selling a product or services? If so, is the campaign generating a lot of revenue or leads? If so, does this traffic segment differ from one geographic location to another? Or does it change based on the time of day?

It is critical to use this data to assist in TV and radio spending decisions. If you learn that TV ads that are run in the morning generate a lift in engaged traffic that converts well, you will probably want to keep running those ads.

If you use Google AdWords to run your TV ads, you can use a specific report in Google Analytics to analyze your campaign. The TV reports include metrics about how often your TV ads are played and how many impressions are created. This data is graphed with traffic to the Web site to help you look for a connection between measurements such as TV Impressions and Website Visits. Or more important, Revenue!

Remember, correlation does not necessarily mean causation but is instead an indicator that you should dig deeper into the data using segmentation. A more reliable way to measure the performance is to always use a vanity URL when your offline ad has an online component.

Tracking microsites

So far, we've talked about tracking offline activities that contain a Web component, specifically a URL. Another way organizations integrate offline and online campaigns is by using a microsite. Microsites are small Web sites designed to match the offline marketing creative and message.

When a microsite is used, it's important to capture not only the traffic coming to the microsite but also what that traffic does on the site. The microsite must have clearly defined business objectives, and those objectives must be tracked with Google Analytics. You may need to configure goals, funnels, or other settings to truly understand the performance of the microsite and behavior of the visitors.

Regardless of the goal of the microsite, it's still critical to use vanity URLs and redirects in all offline marketing activities that drive traffic to the microsite.

One situation that can complicate a microsite setup occurs when a microsite is used to drive traffic to a secondary site, where a conversion may occur. For example, a print ad may be used to drive traffic to a microsite. Then the microsite is used to drive traffic to a third-party site where the conversion occurs. This situation is called a *cross-domain setup*, and it can change your implementation.

Cross-domain situations, introduced in Chapter 5, can be difficult to configure. In the case of a microsite, you must decide if it's important to track the marketing activity to the microsite and then from the microsite to the third-party site. If so, then you must implement cross-domain tracking between the microsite and the third-party site.

If it is not important to track the marketing activity through the microsite and all the way to the third-party site, you don't have to implement cross-domain tracking. If cross-domain tracking is not implemented, all conversions on the third-party site are attributed as referral conversions from the microsite. Is this bad? It depends on your organization and your needs. If you know all traffic to the microsite comes from a specific campaign, you can probably conclude that most microsite referral conversions originated from that campaign.

However, if there are multiple marketing activities driving traffic to the microsite, and you do not implement cross-domain tracking, it will be difficult to gauge the performance of each individual marketing campaign based on conversions on the third-party site. In this case, it's best to use cross-domain tracking.

Tracking Print Ads

Tracking print ads is similar to tracking TV or radio ads: Use a vanity URL in your print ads and attach campaign-tracking information using a type of redirect. Make sure you're adding as much information to the campaign tags as possible so you can get a granular view of which parts of the print campaign are working and which are not.

When deciding on your link-tagging strategy, remember that a print campaign can run in different kinds of print (newspaper, magazines, and so on) and can contain different kinds of creative. You want to capture all the information you need to differentiate your various initiatives, so let's review each campaign parameter and how you might populate it for a print campaign:

- **Campaign:** As always, which marketing activity does this activity belong to? Is it a brand awareness campaign or is the campaign focusing on a specific product? The key to creating a value is to use something you can identify and understand when you look at the Google Analytics reports.
- **Medium:** We suggest using something to define what kind of print ad you are working with. This could be `magazine`, `newspaper`, `brochure`, or anything to describe the printed material used in the campaign.
- **Source:** Use the Source parameter to store more information about the print ad. For example, if the ad appears in *Time* magazine, you could use the Medium `time`. Or, if the ad appears in the *Boston Globe* newspaper, you could use the Source `bostonglobe`. The benefit is that if the ad appears in multiple newspapers or magazines, the Source parameter will identify which newspaper or magazine generates the most traffic.
- **Content:** The Content parameter can be used to track a number of things. It is most commonly used to identify different ad creatives used in different publications. But the `print` Content parameter can also be used to track insertion and run dates, making it easier to analyze whether there was a date impact on the data.

The trick with print advertising is to create a separate vanity URL for each combination of link-tagging parameters. If an ad runs in three magazines, and there are two versions of each ad, there need to be six unique vanity URLs. Table 14.1 shows the combinations for this example.

The more ads or the more ad variations, the more vanity URLs needed for the campaign. Rather than using a vanity URL for each combination, you could use a separate subdirectory on the site. For example, `url.com/offer`, `url.com/offer2`, `url.com/offer3`, and so on. You still need a redirect, but it's usually easier to create a subdirectory or virtual directory than a completely new domain.

Although it's easier to set up a redirect on a subdirectory, it's often harder to get people to remember the subdirectory name. Most people will remember the main Web site domain in the ad, but they will forget the subdirectory. If you want to increase the chances they will remember the

TABLE 14.1

Sample Campaign Parameters for a Magazine Campaign

Vanity URL	utm_campaign	utm_medium	utm_source	utm_content
url1.com	fall-sale	magazine	time	ad1
url2.com	fall-sale	magazine	newsweek	ad1
url3.com	fall-sale	magazine	economist	ad1
url4.com	fall-sale	magazine	time	ad2
url5.com	fall-sale	magazine	newsweek	ad2
url6.com	fall-sale	magazine	economist	ad2

subdirectory, you could offer some type of incentive. For example, you might offer those using the subdirectory a discount or some type of coupon.

Tracking Direct Mail

Tracking a direct-mail campaign is similar to tracking a print campaign. Today, many direct-mail campaigns are structured to drive traffic to a Web site to complete a type of action. The key is to capture as much information about the direct-mail campaign in your campaign tags as possible.

The following ideas will help you tag your links for a direct-mail campaign:

- **Campaign:** Use the name of the marketing campaign running. If this is a singular campaign, you can put a date in the campaign name for future comparisons. However, if the direct-mail

Analytics in Action: Breezes.com

Although Breezes, a family of Caribbean and Latin American all-inclusive resorts, certainly knows the value of online advertising, its marketing team hasn't forgotten about offline advertising media like television and newspapers. After working with WebShare, a Google Analytics authorized consultant, Google Analytics has become an integral part of measuring the impact of Breezes' marketing dollars, including these offline initiatives.

Consider two examples — one involving television, the other involving newspapers — that demonstrate how Breezes tracks the online response from television campaigns and newspaper advertisements using vanity URLs and server-side redirects.

Take a look at a still shot of the final frames of a 30-second TV spot at left. While Breezes could have used its actual Web site address and looked at reports for the time period during which the campaign was running, by geography, and with an Advanced Segment of direct traffic to try to *guess* the impact, a much more accurate measurement is to use a vanity URL and a redirect.

By using a different domain for TV ads that is *only* used for TV ads (in this case, breezesresorts.com), the marketers at Breezes know that people who type this URL into their browser are doing so as a result of seeing this TV ad. The last step is to set up a redirect that takes the users from the vanity domain to a URL like the following:

```
http://www.breezes.com/tvLanding/?utm_source=Turner&utm_medium=TV&utm_
    term=TV-EBB103-BZ&utm_campaign=winter2009
```

Now, any visitors who found the Web site as a result of the television campaign are tracked!

campaign is part of a larger marketing initiative, you can place the date in the Content parameter to avoid confusion when looking at the Campaigns report.

- **Medium:** Direct mail can be identified using a Medium of `direct-mail`. This Medium makes it easy to compare all the different traffic channels driving visitors to your Web site.
- **Source:** In the past, direct mail relied on list segmentation to send different messages to different people. This is similar to segmenting an e-mail list. In the same way that you track the different segments that receive e-mail campaigns, you can capture the recipient segment for direct mail using the Source parameter. For example, if you're sending e-mail to different genders, you may want to include the gender information and perform an analysis based on recipient gender.

Below is an example of an ad that ran in the *New York Times*. In this case, a special subdirectory was used instead of a vanity domain, and when the visitors type `breezes.com/nyc` into their browser, they're automatically redirected to a URL like:

```
http://www.breezes.com/nycLanding/
    ?utm_campaign=BreezesPanama&utm_
    source=NewYorkTimes&utm_medium=
    newspaper&utm_content=weekend
```

Voilà! The online impact of that particular *New York Times* ad is now being tracked in Google Analytics, and swapping out the `utm_source` value for another newspaper provides the data to make decisions around how to allocate and divide marketing budgets on advertising media and specific opportunities.

The danger in using subdirectories rather than vanity domains is that users might not actually type in the `/nyc`, and if they don't, they won't be redirected to a tagged URL and so will appear as direct traffic. To help reduce this risk, it's often helpful to provide an incentive for typing in the extra characters, and in this case a special offer was used.

An important point to remember is that offline ads aren't going to get 100 percent of their audience to break out a laptop and head to the Web — in large part, you're engaging in offline advertising to reach an audience that's *not* online. A good practice to help you measure the full impact of your offline ads is to use dedicated tracking phone numbers along with these other techniques.

TABLE 14.2

Sample Campaign Parameters for a Direct Mail Campaign

URL	utm_campaign	utm_medium	utm_source	utm_content
url.com/landing1	2010ffall-sale	directMail	segment1	ver1
url.com/landing1	2010ffall-sale	directMail	segment1	ver2
url.com/landing1	2010fall-sale	directMail	segment1	ver3
url.com/landing1	2010fall-sale	directMail	segment1	ver4
url.com/landing1	2010fall-sale	directMail	segment1	ver5
url.com/landing1	2010fall-sale	directMail	segment1	ver6
url.com/landing2	2010ffall-sale	directMail	segment1	ver1
url.com/landing2	2010ffall-sale	directMail	segment1	ver2
url.com/landing2	2010fall-sale	directMail	segment1	ver3
url.com/landing2	2010fall-sale	directMail	segment1	ver4
url.com/landing2	2010fall-sale	directMail	segment1	ver5
url.com/landing2	2010fall-sale	directMail	segment1	ver6

- **Content:** Capture the version of the direct-mail piece you send. You could also include the drop date (the date the mail is sent) to track the performance of different drop dates.

For example, you want to send direct mail as part of the 2010 fall sale. This mail will go to people who are not customers but are in a CRM system and part of a mailing list. There will be six versions of the mail, and there will also be two different landing pages. Table 14.2 shows a basic matrix of how the campaign tagging parameters might look.

With such a large number of combinations, you might consider using a subdirectory or virtual directory rather than a vanity URL. A virtual directory is often easier to set up but is still as memorable to the recipient. As we explained in the "Tracking Print Ads" section of this chapter, it can be difficult to get people to type in the subdirectory part of the URl. There needs to be some kind of incentive, like a coupon, to make the subdirectory stick in their memory.

Offline marketing is not going away any time soon. Marketers are creating new ways to use offline marketing to push traffic online and ultimately generate more conversions and revenue.

—

Using the Data Export API, Community Additions, and Other Tools

If you've used any Google products other than Google Analytics, or if you follow Google in the news, you probably know that Google likes to involve the online community as much as possible. The same is true for Google Analytics. Google invited marketers, developers, and general users to contribute to the development of Google Analytics in a number of ways.

In the end, we believe the involvement of the Google Analytics user community will drive much of the innovation in the Web analytics industry. Consider for a moment products like Google Maps that started out as features solely on Google's Web site. Yet, after creating the ability for others to develop tools and features and to tie into the Google Maps platform through an API, there has been an explosion of new and creative uses of Google Maps that would otherwise never have come into existence. Google Analytics supports a similar level of openness for creating new ideas, tools, and products that are based on or related to the Google Analytics platform.

This openness has resulted in many Google Analytics tools and hacks becoming available. In this chapter, we will discuss the Data Export API in further detail, as well as some of our favorite tools and hacks that can help you get more out of Google Analytics.

Hello Data! Understanding and Using the Google Analytics Data Export API

The Google Analytics Data Export API is an extension to Google Analytics allowing direct querying of the data within a given Google Analytics Profile. Using the API, you can build applications and tools that extract, analyze, and report on the data contained within a Google Analytics Profile. The API supports refinement of the data extracted through use of dimension and metric combinations, filters, and Advanced Segments.

Common uses for the Data Export API include:

- Direct, manual access to large sets of data with specific criteria and ready for import into another analysis tool.
- Creating custom Dashboard applications.
- Extracting data for analysis with data visualization tools.
- Merging Google Analytics data into other data analysis or business intelligence applications.
- Integrating Web site usage data from Google Analytics into content management systems.
- Importing data into Excel or other spreadsheet applications.
- Building specialized data integrations or analysis tools for internal systems.

NOTE

The Data Export API is still a Labs product at the time of this writing. A Labs product from Google is still in constant development and thus may change frequently and significantly. You can learn more about Labs products from `http://code.google.com/labs`. We recommend referencing the latest documentation on the Data Export API when planning and building API applications.

Many of the tools reviewed later in this chapter use the Data Export API. Without the API, getting data out of Google Analytics and into other tools required a manual process of accessing reports within the Web-based interface; exporting reports to CSV, TSV, or XML formats; and importing the exported data into tools of choice. Automated importing was simply not feasible, though a few hacks were developed to create unofficial APIs. However, such unsupported approaches to extracting data are risky because changes to Google Analytics can easily render them unusable. With the release of the official API, these worries have all but vanished, leaving a solid, supported, and actively improved means of gaining access to your data within Google Analytics.

Learning the Data Export API

The best way to learn how to use the Data Export API is to experiment with it. Google has provided a wealth of technical documentation for the API as well as sample code and an interactive, fully functional Data Explorer tool that allows you to easily create real API queries against your data and see real results from the API. The Data Explorer is an effective mechanism for trying queries and experimenting to see what kind of results you can expect. The Client Library documentation includes sample code that demonstrates some fairly simple queries you can run against the API. These provide a good basis for developing an introductory application of the API. We've created a resources page with links to additional resources from Google for the Data Export API at www. analyticsformarketers.com/s/api.

Where to start building useful applications

Building an API-based application must begin with identifying the questions you want answered and problems you want solved by the application, not just the tactical set of data you want retrieved. Will you need to repeat the query? What are date-related requirements — do you need daily, weekly, monthly, quarterly, or yearly data? Will needs for analysis change over time? What kind of flexibility for changing analysis needs should the application support?

The second step in building an API application begins with outlining the procedures needed to convert raw data into business intelligence. The data that comes from the API will be straightforward data. How will that data be handled, processed, analyzed, merged, or otherwise dealt with to produce the needed insights?

Third, we recommend using the Data Explorer tool to generate and test queries and expose the required raw data for your application. Using the Data Explorer early in the application development process will provide you with a rich understanding of how data from the API will look once exported. Another great resource to consider is the Java example library, which includes code to export query data to Google Docs spreadsheets, providing a means to simplify the prototyping of business logic and analysis processes for your application.

NOTE

The Google Analytics Data Export API doesn't provide any ready-made data presentation or visualization tools. When you call the API, you get back data — numbers — no graphs, explanations of the numbers, or the like. If your application needs a chart, you'll have to build the chart based on the data that comes back from the API.

Finally, we can't stress enough the value of creating a prototype of the application on one of the directly supported languages.

Recommendations and other considerations for working with the API

Google maintains libraries for Java, JavaScript, and Python. These libraries will likely reduce the maintenance burden on your organization by minimizing development requirements when the Data Export API is changed. While virtually any programming language can use the Data Export API protocol, Google has created a number of libraries and code samples that are ready to use for building applications. The advantage of developing on one of these libraries is that Google keeps them updated as the Data Export API is updated. If you build your own custom library, you will need to make changes to it as the Data Export API is developed and changes further.

Data from the Export API comes formatted in XML, so you can use any language supporting an XML parser to interpret the exported data. However, as the data structures (in XML) evolve, your application may require updates. Planning in the initial application design stage will save headaches later.

Additionally, keep in mind that some environments are better suited to high-volume processing. JavaScript (in a Web browser) is decent for analyzing smaller data sets, but as data complexity increases, we recommend using a dedicated environment (such as Python or Java), typically hosted on another server as a Web application.

All Data Export API queries require authentication with a Google Account that has access to the Google Analytics Profiles you want to analyze with the API. Applications that run only on user-initiated requests can use the session-based Google authentication model. Automating server-side processing typically requires a dedicated Google Account for the application because the credentials for the account need to be stored within the application.

Technical and Diagnostic Tools

When it comes to Google Analytics, everything starts with the tracking code. No tracking code, no data! And no data means no insights. As an analyst, it's your job to validate that your tools are configured correctly, and a big part of that job is checking the tags and ensuring that the settings in your accounts stay up to date with current business and analytic needs.

There are two types of tasks involved: detection of problems when they arise and diagnostic troubleshooting work. Detection tasks are mundane at best and should be automated whenever possible. Diagnostic troubleshooting tasks are for the most part not something that can be automated, and they require specialized knowledge and tools.

NOTE

We have created a page with further details and links to download these and other tools useful for Google Analytics technical analysis and diagnostics at www.analyticsformarketers.com/s/technical-tools.

The technical tools in this section help Google Analytics users better manage their tags and diagnose configuration issues. These tools are oriented to diagnostic work as opposed to applications that can be used for more in-depth analysis of your data.

Browser-based troubleshooting and diagnostic tools

These are tools that run within your Web browser and can be used to troubleshoot and diagnose problems with Google Analytics implementation, JavaScript, tracking calls, cookies, and data-reporting hits. These are tools we use daily in delivering technical consulting and support to companies, and we hope you will find them useful resources as well.

Firefox browser and Firefox tools

Firefox is, or should be, your new best friend. The number of tools available for Firefox that can be used for technical debugging, diagnostics, and troubleshooting is astounding. We found a few of these tools indispensable for Google Analytics work. (To get Firefox, go to www. analyticsformarketers.com/s/getfirefox.)

Here are the key Firefox tools you should get:

- **Firebug:** This tool allows you to dissect a page, modify code, run JavaScript calls through an integrated console, and analyze every aspect of the page, including running scripts, tracking hit requests, and more. Using Firebug, you can verify that page tags are present, tracking scripts are executing, cookies are being set, and tracking hits are going through to Google Analytics or your Urchin server. Additionally, Firebug is a critical tool for doing on-the-fly tag customization testing using its JavaScript console. Download it from www. analyticsformarketers.com/s/getfirebug.

- **Firecookie:** The Firecookie extension is a powerful cookie analysis tool built to integrate with Firebug. Firecookie provides a complete cookie analysis and debugging tool. You can see when cookies are created or modified within the Firebug console, view cookie contents, modify cookies on the fly, delete or block cookies, and much more. Download it from www. analyticsformarketers.com/s/firecookie.

- **Live HTTP Headers:** This traffic-monitoring tool runs within Firefox as a browser extension. Using this tool allows you to see requests for data between your Firefox browser and remote servers, Google Analytics included. Live HTTP Headers is best used to detect the presence and contents of utm.gif tracking hits. If you're trying to diagnose a tracking problem, verifying that the tracking hits are actually happening is the first step, and verifying what the contents of those hits are is the second step. Look for the __utm.gif hits and inspect them to ensure the parameters contain the expected values. Download it from www.analyticsformarketers.com/s/liveheaders.

TIP

When using Live HTTP Headers, you can streamline data analysis by filtering to include only requests related to Google Analytics. This saves you from picking through the dozens, sometimes hundreds, of other requests for files that your browser makes on a routine page load. To add the filter, open Live HTTP Headers, click the Config tab, and under the Filter URLS with RegExp option enter google-analytics. Select the checkbox to activate the filter (deselecting the checkbox deactivates the filter if you need to see all data requests). The result allows requests for Google Analytics tracking scripts and tracking hits to be displayed, but blocks requests for other files and pagers within Live HTTP Headers.

- **Web Developer Toolbar:** This is a power-user tool designed for Web site developers to easily analyze page contents. Among its many features, the cookie viewer is probably the most useful. The cookie tools allow deletion of all session cookies and domain cookies, as well as the ability to view cookies at any given point in time through a new browser tab. The ability to open and view the cookie contents in a new tab after a page has loaded is superior to the capabilities of Firecookie in that it allows you to essentially save the state of cookies. If you are trying to diagnose cookie integrity problems with Google Analytics, viewing cookies first on one page, then on another, and comparing the two sets of cookies is critical. Web Developer Toolbar also provides one-click options to disable JavaScript and `meta` redirects — useful when trying to detect and diagnose cookie problems related to script-based or `meta-refresh` redirects. Download it from `www.analyticsformarketers.com/s/webdevtoolbar`.

- **Web Analytics Solution Profiler:** Commonly known as WASP, this debugging tool helps identify issues with many Web analytics tools, not just Google Analytics. WASP was originally created by Stéphane Hamel (a respected ebusiness strategist and Web analytics consultant and principal of Immeria.net) and is now owned by iPerceptions. WASP provides a Firefox extension that views the tracking cookies and the image requests used to send data to Google Analytics, enabling the Web analyst to ensure that the tracking code is functioning correctly. WASP also includes a powerful crawler that can scan a Web site and check that all pages have been tagged, similar to SiteScan GA. There are three versions of WASP, each with slightly different functionality. The free version of WASP limits the use of the Firefox extension to 30 minutes per day and limits crawler use to 20 pages per crawl. The analyst version of WASP costs $69 and includes the same Firefox extension and crawler. However, the usage limits for both are greater. The analyst version provides unlimited use of the Firefox extension and 50 pages per crawl. The corporate/market research version costs $699 and offers unlimited use of all features. If you're commonly checking the page tags on a site, you should take a serious look at the analyst version of WASP. It makes it easy to debug issues with the cookies or the image request. If you're a large organization, take some time to evaluate the corporate version. Download it from `www.analyticsformarketers.com/s/wasp`.

Chrome browser

Chrome is the Web browser from Google. A new entrant to the browser marketplace compared to Internet Explorer and Firefox, Chrome has quickly grown in popularity due largely to its stability as a browser. It was designed to enhance the speed of resource-intensive Web applications. Chrome also boasts some fantastic development and debugging tools. Download it from `www.analyticsformarketers.com/s/chrome`.

Here are the key Chrome tools you should get:

- **JavaScript Console:** This tool delivers a rich diagnostic interface similar to Firebug for Firefox, but it is more full-featured. This tool is most useful for analyzing the order in which events occur on a page, as in when the Google Analytics tags are loaded and tracking hits are sent through, thanks to the console's Timing feature. Like Firebug, you can issue direct JavaScript commands through the console and analyze existing script activities. This tool is built into Chrome.

- **Speed Tracer:** This extension for Chrome enables advanced script analysis. Using Speed Tracer, you can quickly dig into each and every JavaScript execution on a page and see how long it takes to process, see the order in which it occurs, and detect scripting problems. This is useful for identifying conflicts between Google Analytics tags and other JavaScript running on the page. Download it from `www.analyticsformarketers.com/s/speed-tracer`.

Other tools and browsers

While we love Firefox and Chrome for their tools, we recognize there are other browsers out there. If you're still using Internet Explorer as your primary browser, we suggest switching to Firefox or Chrome for the ease of use, security, and the tools listed above. If you decide to stick with Internet Explorer, there are useful tools for it, as well as for non-browser-dependent testing and diagnostic work:

- **Fiddler:** This is a powerful traffic-monitoring tool. Like Live HTTP Headers for Firefox, it detects requests for data between your Web browser (Internet Explorer, Safari, Chrome, or Firefox, though "listening" to Firefox requires that a Firefox extension be installed) and Web servers. However, because it is an independent program that basically runs between your browser and your computer's Internet connection, it isn't subject to missing data requests as Live HTTP Headers is sometimes prone to do. Fiddler2 has features for analyzing requests at a more detailed level — even binary contents. One of the most useful features is the WebForms view under the Inspectors tab that makes it easy to analyze the components of the utm.gif hit. Download it from www.analyticsformarketers.com/s/fiddler.
- **DebugBar:** This is an Internet Explorer extension for Web development and debugging work. It is as powerful as Firebug in the Firefox browser and a must-have for troubleshooting and working with Internet Explorer. DebugBar includes a DOM inspector, HTTP listener (like Live HTTP Headers or Fiddler), JavaScript inspector, and Console (like Firebug), HTML Validator, and many more features. Note that DebugBar is not free for professional use. Download it from www.analyticsformarketers.com/s/debugbar.
- **IECookiesView:** This tool allows you to easily inspect, edit, and delete cookies for Internet Explorer in an easy-to-use graphical interface. It allows you to view the contents of your Windows-based cookies folder, showing each cookie and enabling selective deletion of cookies for a single domain (rather than using the Delete Cookies option in Internet Explorer), inspecting individual cookie contents, and even manually modifying a cookie's contents. Download it from www.analyticsformarketers.com/s/ie-cookies.

Web-based technical and diagnostic services

Because Google Analytics runs *client-side* (that is, in the browser), technical debugging and diagnostic work relating to page tags and Google Analytics scripts must be done within the browser, using a browser-based or add-on tool. However, there are limitations to what you can do with a browser-based tool. For example, validating tag presence on all pages of your site is tedious with a browser-based tool, so a service-based tool can be more efficient. Here are three you should consider:

- **SiteScan GA:** SiteScan is a tag-monitoring tool provided by EpikOne, a Google Analytics authorized consultant. It scans the pages on your site and checks for the Google Analytics Tracking Code (GATC). When it checks for the tracking code, it ensures that the tracking code has a Google Analytics Account number and that it includes a call to _trackPageview (). SiteScan can check your site for the standard ga.js version of the tracking code or the previous version of the tracking code called `urchin.js`. There are two versions of SiteScan: free and premium. The free version scans the first 100 pages of a Web site and can be run only three times per day. The premium version scans 30,000 pages per scan and can be run an unlimited number of times per day. SiteScan Premium is part of an EpikOne tool called AnalyticsViews, which we cover later. For most organizations, the free version of SiteScan will suffice. Regardless of the version, SiteScan generates an Excel file with all the pages scanned and reporting whether the pages contain the Google Analytics page tag. You can quickly identify which pages on your site have been tagged and which pages have not. Remember: No page tags, no data! In addition to scanning your pages, SiteScan also identifies common Web site configurations that normally cause configuration issues, including subdomains, non-HTML files, and query string parameters. Note that SiteScan uses the Google index for detection of pages to test and doesn't directly crawl your site, so if you have pages that are not indexed, SiteScan won't check them. Download it from `www.analyticsformarketers.com/s/sitescanga`.

- **Analytics Healthcheck:** This diagnostic tool (provided by Analytics Pros, another Google Analytics authorized consultant) checks for common implementation problems. However, it operates differently from other tools on the market. Analytics Healthcheck analyzes data from Google Analytics using the Data Export API, checking for statistical anomalies produced when certain implementation issues are present. Upon detection of problems, Analytics Healthcheck details the issues found and presents resources for solving the problems. Download it from `www.analyticsformarketers.com/s/healthcheck`.

- **Analytics Checkup:** This suite of tools built by an Australian-based Google Analytics authorized consultant, Mangold Sengers, looks for misconfigured or nonconfigured settings in your Google Analytics profile and provides recommendations on what to change. Analytics Checkup also provides additional tools for custom Dashboard creation, auditing tracking code implementation, and building properly tagged campaign URLs. Download it from `www.analyticsformarketers.com/s/analytics-checkup`.

Reporting Tools and Analysis Tools

Let's face it, reporting is, and always will be, part of Web analytics. As much as you try to focus on analysis, you'll always need to provide standard reports to the stakeholders. The key with reporting is to minimize the time spent on the reports.

With the launch of the Google Analytics API, a number of companies created reporting tools to help Google Analytics users present data in new and different ways. These tools don't necessarily help draw more insights, but instead reformat the data to meet your internal analysis needs.

Tools for integrating data into Excel

Microsoft Excel has long been a Web analyst's favorite tool for conducting custom analysis, create dashboards and reports, and modify and re-present data from Google Analytics. One of the biggest challenges to working with Excel is getting data from Google Analytics into Excel and then updating that data once you've built a report or dashboard based on the data. Thanks to the Google Analytics Data Export API and the hard work of several companies, there are a handful of tools available that streamline the process of accessing data within Google Analytics and getting it into Excel, as Table 15.1 lists.

Other analysis tools

There is a world of opportunity beyond Excel-based tools. While spreadsheet programs provide complete control of data analysis and presentation, working with them can be cumbersome. There are a growing number of analysis tools built specifically for analyzing and reporting data from Google Analytics.

TABLE 15.1

Google Analytics Tools for Excel

Name and URL	Pros	Cons
Excellent Analytics www.analyticsformarketers.com/s/excellent Cost: free	• Simple installation • Easy to use • Open-source-developed • Limited only by API dimension/metric compatibility	• Limited support • No automation for updating dates when refreshing queries • No errors when invalid dimension/metric combination is used
Tatvic GA Excel Plug-in www.analyticsformarketers.com/s/tatvic Cost: $199 (personal), $499 (agency)	• Commercial product with professional support included • Guided user interface for creating queries • Supports dynamic date changes when refreshing queries • Queries can be based on values from cells such as profile name, which makes updating queries easy	• Limited to three dimensions per query • No multiuser support • Not a free product
ShufflePoint www.analyticsformarketers.com/s/shufflepoint Cost: $29 to $199 per month Note: ShufflePoint also works with PowerPoint and Google Gadgets.	• No macros or add-ins required for Excel • Creates PowerPoint presentations with data driven text, chart, and table placeholders • Uses a single query to display results for all your Google Analytics profiles at once	• Cost is ongoing, recurring monthly • Not a true Excel plug-in, it requires interacting in a Web interface for some functions • Uses custom querying language that is more powerful but harder to learn

- **Analytics Views:** This advanced reporting tool offered by EpikOne — the same team that created SiteScan GA — is based on the Google Analytics API and offers a number of template and custom reporting options. Analytics Views groups reports by type: SEO, visitor engagement, ecommerce, and many others. If Analytics Views lacks a ready-to-go report you need, you can build your own report using its drag-and-drop interface. We like Analytics Views for the large number of templates and the ability to customize the metrics in a report. We also like the ability to rebrand the report with your logo. Analytics Views offers both free and paid versions. Download it from www.analyticsformarketers.com/s/analytics-view.

- **Concentrate:** From Juice Analytics, this is one of our favorite analysis tools. It helps you understand the long tail of keywords on your Web site. If you've ever done keyword analysis, you know there can be thousands of keywords that drive traffic to a site. Sorting through all that data is — let's face it — almost impossible. Concentrate categorizes your Web site keywords to help you understand which keywords work and which do not. Using the Google Analytics API, Concentrate extracts your keywords directly from Google Analytics and applies an algorithm. The algorithm categorizes the keywords and creates different visualizations to help you understand keyword performance. There are multiple versions of Concentrate. Each has limits on data processing. The free version allows you to connect one Google Analytics account to Concentrate and process a maximum of 1,000 keywords. Paid versions (starting at $39 per month) provide higher limits on the number of keywords you can process. At the very least, you should try the free version, since this tool is a huge asset for keyword analysis. Download it from www.analyticsformarketers.com/s/concentrate.

- **Enhanced Google Analytics (EGA):** Another tool from the team at Juice Analytics, EGA is a script for the Greasemonkey Firefox extension that adds a What's Changed button to the Referring Websites page in Traffic Sources and provides various Keyword reports in Google Analytics. When you click the What's Changed button, the extension filters the data in the report and shows you the data that has changed the most over the last week. This is extremely useful! Think about it: How often do you scan a list of referring Web sites or keywords and see the same data week in and week out? You're really interested in the data that has changed. But this information can often be buried in the mass of data. EGA does all the hard work of identifying what's changed for you. With one simple click, EGA creates a table in your report showing which data has changed the most in the last seven days. Download it from www.analyticsformarketers.com/s/enhanced-ga.

- **Trakkboard:** Made by Trakken, a Google Analytics authorized consultant based in Germany, this is a desktop dashboard tool built using Adobe AIR technology. It is a free tool that allows creation of multiple customized dashboards, each with the ability to add many dashboard tiles containing various metrics and charts including visits, visitors, goal funnels, top keywords, and traffic source trends. Download it from www.analyticsformarketers.com/s/trakkboard.

- **Treemap Visualizer:** This is another open-source project for data analysis using the Google Analytics Data Export API, and it is free. Treemap is built by the team at Google and can be used through an interactive example on the code site, or downloaded and installed or modified as you see fit (thanks to its open-source license). Treemap analyzes multiple data points using the "treemap" visual data display method of nested, colored boxes. Treemap Visualizer makes identifying winners and losers among large sets of data easy and fun. Download it from www.analyticsformarketers.com/s/treemap.

Other Tools and Hacks

These tools, scripts, and plug-ins are designed not for a specific analysis or debugging, but to extend page tagging and data collection, modify how the Google Analytics scripts or cookies work, or add functionality to the Google Analytics administrative or reporting interfaces. Google Analytics authorized consultants and others have built these hacks and tools.

You can access links to all these tools at www.analyticsformarketers.com/s/more-tools.

- **Google Analytics Report Enhancer (GARE):** Built by ROI Revolution, GARE is a Greasemonkey script for Firefox. It modifies the Google Analytics reporting interface by adding additional dimensions to the Dimension menu, creating additional columns in the Report Data Table, and creating custom metrics not normally available in Google Analytics.
- **Analytics Pros Engine (APE):** This platform from Analytics Pros includes tag management for controlling Google Analytics tags implemented on your site without modifying page-level or template code. In addition, APE uses a custom JavaScript library to extend data collection to track outbound link clicks, file downloads, e-mail link clicks, and form field interactions, as well as track interactions (such as mouse-over and focus) on *any* in-page element based on a powerful rules-configuration engine. Last, APE can back up raw Google Analytics tracking hits into a private data warehouse service, allowing Google Analytics users to retain a copy of raw, unprocessed data and reprocess it at will with Urchin software.
- **Conversion Works campaign history utmz hack:** This hack uses custom code developed by Conversion Works to create a user-defined segment cookie that contains the campaign history of each visitor. Standard Google Analytics campaign conversion attribution uses a last-in method — this hack extends Google Analytics to report all the campaigns a visitor has responded to.
- **Actual Metrics LinkTagger script:** This script extends data collection for Google Analytics to include outbound links, clicks to download files, e-mail link clicks, and automatically add cross-domain linker() methods to links and forms, if needed.
- **Dimensionator bookmarklet:** A simple yet powerful tool by Analytics Pros allows access to dozens of "unlisted" dimensions. DMA, Second Page, Exit Page, and Day of Week are all extremely useful dimensions that are available but not accessible through the standard Google Analytics interface. Dimensionator makes access to and use of these invaluable dimensions a breeze. It works in any Web browser and requires no plug-ins — just a simple bookmarklet link.

- **Better GA Plugin:** A full-fledged extension for Firefox that compiles a number of Greasemonkey Userscripts into one easy-to-install tool. It includes more than 18 of the most popular scripts, including See All Rows, links from Keywords reports to Google Insights for Search, integrated social media metrics for Content reports, and easier selection of data ranges for year versus previous year comparisons.
- **Goal Copy plug-in from LunaMetrics:** This Firefox extension enables copying goal settings between goals within a profile or across profiles, making a once-tedious and time-consuming task something that can be accomplished in minutes rather than hours when you're dealing with a large number of complex goals. This is an indispensable tool for any Google Analytics Account administrator.

—

PART

VI

Appendixes

Other Resources

The Web analytics industry changes fast. Almost as fast as Google Analytics! While books can provide a foundation for learning, blogs can help keep you up to date with changes to products and analysis techniques. Here are a few of our favorite sources for industry news and information.

Blogs

Occam's Razor by Avinash Kaushik

`http://kaushik.net/avinash`

If we may be so bold, this might be the greatest Web analytics blog on the Internet. Avinash has a knack for making complex subjects easy to understand and even easier to apply. If you read one Web analytics blog, read this one.

Analytics for Marketers by us

`http://analyticsformarketers.com`

Analytics for Marketers is the companion blog for this book. Here you'll find timely information about Google Analytics and the Web analytics industry in general. You'll also find updates to the book content as well as many resources referenced in the book.

Analytics Talk by Justin Cutroni

`http://cutroni.com/blog`

As one of the first bloggers to cover Google Analytics and Web analytics, Justin has a talent for describing how Google Analytics works, how to configure it, and how to analyze the data for business success.

Analytics Prose by Caleb Whitmore

`www.analyticspros.com/blog.html`

Caleb has been cranking out great content for almost two years. This blog includes technical tips, tricks, hacks, industry knowledge, product announcements, and posts by guest bloggers.

Official Google Analytics Blog

`http://analytics.blogspot.com`

The official Google Analytics blog provides valuable information about updates and changes to the product as well as tips on how to use Google Analytics. This is a must-read to stay up to date on Google Analytics.

Advanced Web Metrics by Brian Clifton

`http://advanced-web-metrics.com`

Brian Clifton is a former Google Analytics employee and author (you'll find his book listed later). On his blog, Brian offers interesting insights about Google Analytics and Web analytics in general.

VKI Studios Blog

`http://blog.vkistudios.com`

VKI Studios is a Google Analytics partner in Vancouver. Its blog covers not only Google Analytics, but online marketing, testing, and Web site usability. If you're just starting to move beyond qualitative data, this is a good blog to read.

WebShare Blog

`www.websharedesign.com/blog`

Here you'll find posts on the topics of Web design and traffic acquisition, paid and organic search strategies, analytics and business intelligence, conversion testing, interviews, videos, and more. Could they possibly cover anything else!

Grok Dot Com

`www.grokdotcom.com`

Published by the team at Future Now, this blog focuses on understanding human reactions to marketing, sales, PR, and evolving media. While that may seem to have very little to do with Web analytics and Google Analytics, it uses data to pull everything together.

LunaMetrics

`www.lunametrics.com/blog`

The team at LunaMetrics does a great job of really digging into topics. It goes beyond regurgitating what's in the Google Analytics support section and takes the time to dissect a topic.

ROI **Revolution**

`http://roirevolution.com/blog`

The ROI Revolution blog features tips, tricks, and hacks related to Google Analytics as well as a plethora of useful Google AdWords information.

E-marketer

`www.emarketer.com/blog`

Another blog that covers all aspects of marketing. E-marketer publishes loads of consumer research to help businesses better understand where to take their marketing activities.

Econsultancy

`http://econsultancy.com/blog`

A blog about digital marketing that covers everything from strategy to analytics to technology. It provides a broad view of online marketing and how to measure it.

ClickZ

`www.clickz.com`

Clickz offers a number of different blog feeds covering everything, including social media, e-mail marketing, paid search, and analytics. You can't go wrong with any of its content; it's always fresh and thought-provoking.

Books

While some books become irrelevant due to fast pace of change in the world of online marketing, these books will always be useful. They all deserve a place on the marketer's bookshelf.

The Search by John Batelle

The Search is one of the defining books on the Internet. It provides an entertaining background on where the search industry came from and where it's going.

Web Analytics an Hour a Day by Avinash Kaushik

Avinash's first book lays the foundation for how to conceive and implement a Web analytics strategy at your company. This is an invaluable reference that you'll pick up and use once a week.

Web Analytics 2.0: The Art of Online Accountability and Science of Customer Centricity by Avinash Kaushik

Avinash's second book continues his ever-evolving thought process on how to measure an online business and use that data to be more successful.

Web Analytics Demystified **by Eric T. Petersen**

One of the first Web analytics books to market, this classic is still applicable today. Eric covers all things analytics from measurement tools, to KPIs, to how to perform analysis.

Big Book of Key Performance Indicators **by Eric T. Peterson**

A follow-up to Eric's first book, the *Big Book of Key Performance Indicators* is an e-book full of KPIs and how to define them. If you need to define success metrics for your Web site, you should use this book as a reference.

Marketing in the Age of Google **by Vanessa Fox**

This book, authored by ex-Google employee Vanessa Fox, is a business person's view of search and why it's a critical part of every company's online strategy. If you're having trouble understanding why you should be focusing on search engine optimization this is the book for you.

Don't Make Me Think **by Steve Krug**

A classic in the Web site usability world, this book will help the beginner understand why usability is important and explain how to get started in five minutes.

Advanced Web Metrics **by Brian Clifton**

Brian Clifton dives into the technical aspects of Google Analytics, covering advanced topics and configurations.

Made to Stick: Why Some Ideas Survive and Others Die **by Chip Heath**

At its core, *Made to Stick* is about telling stories. Digging deeper, Chip Heath explains that every good story has simplicity, unexpectedness, concreteness, credibility, emotions, and stories. As analysts we're always telling stories, and this is a good guide.

Landing Page Optimization **by Tim Ash**

Landing Page Optimization is a how-to guide for landing page testing. It goes into great depth and describes how to identify what page to test, different tools to use to test with, and how to interpret the result.

Always Be Testing: The Complete Guide to Google Website Optimizer **by Bryan Eisenberg and John Quarto-vonTivadar**

ABT is truly the complete guide to Google's Website Optimizer. From describing how the product works to how to implement a test, Bryan and John help you shift your Web site testing program into high gear.

Cult of Analytics: Driving Online Marketing Strategies Using Web Analytics **by Steve Jackson**

Steve helps you lay out and develop a plan to tackle Web analytics in your company. From defining metrics to creating the necessary processes, this book will help beginners and experienced Web analysts implement a winning Web analytics strategy.

Six Pixels of Separation **by Mitch Joel**

Mitch does a great job breaking social media down to what it actually is: a way for companies to engage with their customers and potential customers. Using real-life examples, this book will help you craft your use of social media.

Social Media Marketing: An Hour a Day

Like all books in the Hour a Day series, *Social Media Marketing* lays out a methodical, well-thought-out process for you to follow when developing and deploying a social media strategy. This is the place to start when learning about social media and how to develop a social media strategy.

SEO an Hour a Day **by Jennifer Grappone and Gradiva Couzin**

In this book, we spend a lot of time defining how to measure search engine optimization efforts. But if you've never done SEO before, or are looking to brush up on your skills, this book offers step-by-step instructions on how to implement SEO for your company.

—

Glossary

CPC, PPC, bounce rate, SEM, CPM, unique pageviews, unique visitors, impressions, … What do all these things mean? This glossary, and this book, will lift the mist that veils a thorough understanding of Google Analytics, the Web, and performance marketing.

Many of the definitions in this glossary are taken directly from the official Google Analytics glossary (with permission, of course), with some additional explanations of our own. The other terms we've defined ourselves, taking care to align with industry and global standards but also integrate further explanation that is consistent with use of these terms in this book.

You'll also find additional glossary resource links in this appendix for bookmarking in your browser.

Common Google Analytics Terms

There are many common terms used in Google Analytics. Rather than trying to define all these terms here and reinvent the wheel, we recommend you visit the official Google Analytics glossary at www.analyticsformarketers.com/s/ga-glossary.

Absolute Unique Visitors   The count of unique visitor cookie IDs in a given time period. Note that a common mistake with this metric is to sum several time periods rather than measuring the time period at once. For example, reporting the absolute unique visitors per month and adding up the totals will not produce an accurate number of absolute unique visitors — measuring the year as a whole will produce a lower, and accurate, number.

Advanced Segment   A customizable subset of data that can be defined by the Google Analytics user through configurable sets of criteria applied at the session/visit level. An advanced segment that includes all visits where the page matched `product1.html` will include all data from visits that viewed the `product1.html` page at any point during their session.

AdWords   Google's advertising platform.

anchor string   The anchor is the portion of the URL that comes after a hash symbol (#). For example, in `http://www.site.com/store.php?categoryid=1#top`, the `#top` portion is the anchor string.

Bounce Rate   The percentage of visits that contained only one page view or interaction. For example: a visit that loads just the home page and leaves would have only one interaction recorded, and thus be considered a bounce. A visit that loads the home page *and* interacts with an element that triggers an Event Tracking call would not be considered to have bounced.

Campaign   A dimension for traffic source measurement. The Campaign dimension can be defined manually through a campaign tracking tag. If not defined manually, Campaign is set to a predefined value of `(not set)`, `(organic)`, or `(referral)`.

conversion   A completion of a defined goal or transaction.

Conversion Rate   Conversion rate is the percentage of all visits in a sample that completed a defined goal or transaction.

cookie   A cookie is a small text file created by a Web browser on a user's computer. Cookies are intended to contain minimal information needed by the Web site and browser in order to deliver the functionality of a page. Cookies are required for such activities as logging into a Web site (because a means of identifying the remote computer to the Web server is required). Google Analytics requires cookies for its visitor, visit, and campaign-tracking identification functions. Google Analytics cannot work without use of the first-party cookies it creates. *Also see first-party cookie.*

Cost Data   Data about advertising spend imported from AdWords.

custom metric   A customized calculation based on a set of metrics and mathematic operators. Google Analytics doesn't (as of when this book was written) support custom metrics.

custom report   Custom reports are a feature in Google Analytics allowing users to create reports with their own selection of dimensions and metrics. Custom reports can support up to 10 metrics, five dimensions per report, and multiple tabs of metrics per report.

Dimension   A category for classifying information about a visit or visitor. The City, Campaign, Medium, and Landing Page Dimensions all describe information about a visit — where the visit came from geographically, the campaign and medium they came through, and the page the visitor entered on.

domain name   A domain name, such as `site.com`, is part of the Domain Name System (DNS), a fundamental component of the Internet that connects the numerical Internet Protocol (IP) address (for example, `192.168.2.1`) that is the basis for communication between servers and computers on the Internet. A domain name consists of the top-level domain (TLD) such as `.com` or `.co.uk`, the primary domain (such as the `site` in `site.com`), and possibly subdomains (such as the `www` in `www.site.com` or `secure` in `secure.site.com`). In the context of Google Analytics, a domain name is most relevant in relation to the cookies that are used by Google Analytics. Google Analytics cookies are specific to a domain. Cookies defined for a primary domain can be accessed by pages and scripts running on the primary and any of its subdomains. Cookies set to a subdomain cannot be accessed by the primary domain or "sibling" subdomains, while child subdomains (such as `secure1` in `secure1.checkout.site.com`) can access such cookies. *Also see cookie; first-party cookie; and third-party cookie for more about cookies and domains.*

exit page   The last page of a visit — every visit has an exit page.

Exit Rate   The exit rate is the percentage of time a page is the last page viewed in a visit in relation to the number of times the page was viewed (page views). The exit rate equals exits divided by page views.

filter   A filter is a set of criteria against which each `utm.gif` tracking hit sent into a Google Analytics Profile is evaluated. Filters can dictate that only certain conditions allow a hit to be included (resulting in all nonmatching hits being ignored), excluded (resulting in all hits that match the exclude criteria being ignored), or modified (such as through a search/replace, changing the case, or having values moved or changed based on advanced criteria). Filters are applied to profiles within a Google Analytics Account and, when applied, all tracking hits sent to that profile are evaluated against all filters applied to the profile.

Filter field   Fields are categories for raw tracking data as they come in from the `utm.gif` tracking hit. Filters work by applying a filter pattern against data in a Filter field. *See `utm.gif` request parameters.*

Filter Pattern   A Filter Pattern is a regular expression that defines how data in a Filter field should be evaluated.

first-party cookie   A first-party cookie is a cookie that can only be written to and read from the domain name or host name where it is being set. First-party cookies are considered more secure because they cannot be used to track a user from one Web site to another Web site that is not part of the same domain. Google Analytics exclusively uses first-party cookies. One of the most common data accuracy issues with Google Analytics comes from this fact and is a result of not configuring the Google Analytics Tracking Code (GATC) on a site appropriately for the domain name architecture of that site. *See also cookie; third-party cookie.*

GATC (Google Analytics Tracking Code)   The JavaScript code that is placed into a Web page's HTML source code and includes the function definitions and methods used to collect and report information to Google Analytics.

Gmail Account   Gmail is Google's e-mail service, and a Gmail Account is inherently a Google Account. Many people erroneously believe that a Gmail Account is required for using Google Analytics; what actually is required is a Google Account. *See Google Account.*

goal   A goal is a defined point of interaction that can be reaching a particular page or set of pages as defined by a regular expression, or reaching a threshold of interaction (either time spent on the site or a number of pages viewed).

Google Account   A Google Account is Google's universal, individual sign-on used for all Google services a person wants to access. A Google Account can be associated to one or more e-mail addresses. A Gmail Account is inherently a Google Account, although any e-mail address can be used to create a Google Account. We prefer to think of a Google Account in the sense of a "Google ID" — a unique sign-on that is specific to the individual and transportable, rather than specific to a particular service from Google or other company.

Google Analytics Account   A Google Analytics Account is the account with the Google Analytics service. Each account has an account number and account-level settings, such as data sharing and privacy controls, a friendly account name, links to AdWords and other Google services, users, filters, and profiles. A Google Analytics Account is signified by an account number, such as UA-30247.

hit   A hit is a commonly used term typically used to refer to a visit or a pageview. For example, "The Web site had 50,000 hits last month" or "The home page was hit 100,000 times yesterday." Technically, a hit is neither a visit nor a pageview, but rather simply an entry of data in a log file that indicates there was a file requested from a Web server. Practically speaking, a hit is best equated to an impression or a single instance of something occurring. The term hit should not be used to refer to session or visitor-level data.

host name   The technical term for the domain name portion of a Web site URL as well as a dimension (called *hostname*) in Google Analytics. For example, in `http://www.site.com/store.php?categoryid=1`, the host name is `www.site.com`.

HTML   The Hypertext Markup Language, the foundational computer markup language of the Internet, is designed to convey the layout of information communicated as part of the HTTP communications standard. See the W3C standards and definitions link in this glossary for further definition and history of HTML.

JavaScript   An object-oriented scripting language used within both Web-based and non-Web-based applications. It is primarily used in the form of client-side JavaScript, implemented within a Web browser to allow the development of enhanced user interfaces and dynamic Web sites. Google Analytics relies on JavaScript for its standard data collection and tracking functions.

Keyword   A dimension designed to record the search query used by visitors entering the Web site from an external search engine.

Landing Page   A dimension defining the first page viewed during a visit.

Log file   A text file containing lines of information. In the Web analytics sense, a log file is most commonly created by a Web server that receives and responds to server requests. Each request to the server is a hit and contains information about what was requested. *See hit.*

Medium   A Dimension intended to contain information about the high-level channel, or "medium," through which a visitor came to the site. Examples of mediums include organic search, radio ads, and e-mail marketing, which might be named `organic`, `radio`, and `email`, respectively.

metric   A fixed number or a calculated number including a percentage ratio, amount of time, or monetary or other numerical value. Examples of metrics include Visits, Visitors, Page Views, Revenue, and Transactions.

Page   A dimension intended to contain information defining the URI or other custom descriptor such as a virtual pageview or other string describing a tracked interaction of a Web site page measured in Google Analytics. For example, `/download/case-study.pdf` would be a virtual pageview recorded with an `onclick` tracking call.

Page Title   A dimension intended to record the contents of the HTML title (the string between the `<title></title>` tag) on the page from which the GATC was run and the tracking hit was reported. *See GATC.*

Pageviews   A metric reporting the number of times a given page was viewed, regardless of the number of visits or visitors that viewed that page.

profile   A profile is a collection of data based on a Web Property ID after it has been received from tracking hits and processed into profile report databases. Data within a profile is accessed through the Google Analytics reporting interface or Data Export API.

query parameters   Web addresses can contain text, called a string, after the ? that is used as a way to convey codes and other information. These codes are called query parameters. If you have multiple parameters, you separate them with &. Each query parameter contains a parameter name and value. For example, in `/store.php?categoryid=1`, the query parameter is `categoryid` and here has a value of 1.

referrer   The URL of the Web page viewed immediately prior to the current page being viewed.

regular expression   A pseudo programming language designed for easy human-to-computer pattern matching definitions.

report profile   *See profile.*

request stem   The part of a Web page address that comes after the hostname but before the ?. For example, in `/store.php?categoryid=1`, the portion before the ? (here, `/store.php`) is the request stem.

request URI   URI stands for Uniform Resource Identifier and refers to the part of a Web page address (URL) that comes after the host name, including the request stem and any query parameters.

session   A session is a defined period of interaction from an identified visitor or user. *Session* is synonymous with *visit*. Sessions in Google Analytics are defined as a continuous period of interaction with the Web site until a browser is closed or there is 30 minutes of inactivity. (You can adjust the timeframe of 30 minutes through tracking tag customizations.) Session identification is based on session and visitor cookies and is prone to being skewed when tracking tags are not configured properly for a Web site's domain name architecture.

Source   The name of a dimension in Google Analytics intended to record information about the origination place (such as `twitter.com`) that a visit accessing a Web site came from.

third-party cookie   A third-party cookie is a cookie that can be set and read from a domain other than the current domain. For example, if a user is browsing `www.site.com` and an image from `www.trackingsite.com` is loaded, the trackingsite.com server could try to send a cookie along with the image. That cookie would be considered a third-party cookie to `www.site.com`, because it originated from `www.trackingsite.com`. *See also first-party cookie.*

tracking hit   In Google Analytics, synonymous with a request for `utm.gif`. Generally, a tracking hit refers to any means of reported information sent via a server request and recorded into a log file.

Unique Pageview   A metric that, in the context of a single page, reports the number of visits that viewed that page. Compare this term to *Pageviews*, a metric that reports the number of times a page was loaded regardless of the number of visits or sessions during which it was viewed.

Unique Visitor   *See Visitor.*

URL   URL stands for Uniform Resource Locator and refers to the entire string that appears in a Web address. It includes the protocol (`http://` or `https://`), the host name or domain (`www.site.com`), the request URI (which contains the request stem and query parameters), as well as the anchor string.

`__utm.gif`   The technical name of the image pixel that is requested by the Google Analytics Tracking Code (GATC) and used to report information collected by the tracking code to the Google servers for processing into report profiles.

Visit   *See session.*

Visitor   A Visitor is intended to be a unique person, but the constraints of browser and cookie technology make it impossible to always identify a person uniquely. Therefore, a Visitor is most precisely defined in Google Analytics as the Unique Visitor ID value of the `__utma` cookie. The `__utma` cookie is persistent by default, meaning the same set of cookies unique to a specific browser on a specific computer — thus, Visitor is usually a specific browser on a specific computer and will remain as long as they are not deleted or the site is visited within the cookie expiration period. (The expiration period can be defined in a tracking tag customization.)

Web Property ID   The unique Google Account and Profile ID number that `utm.gif` tracking hits are recorded against and from which Profile reports are built. A Web Property ID forms the foundation of a data stream coming from the page tags where that Web Property ID has been used. An example Web Property ID is `UA-30247-2`, where `UA-30247` relates to the Google Analytics Account and `-2` related to the Profile ID.

Common Marketing Terms

ad click   A click on an online advertisement as measured by the platform serving the ad. Not to be confused with a *visit*, which is measured on the Web site by the Web analytics tool. Clicks and visits rarely align.

B2B (business-to-business)   Marketing that is intended to promote the products or services of one business to other businesses.

B2C (business-to-consumer)   Marketing that is intended to promote the products or services of one business to consumers (people, not business entities).

banner ad   Visual ads common to many Web sites that are horizontal or vertical rectangular ads.

CPA (cost per action)   Paying for media and advertising exposure based on a fixed fee paid when a certain action is performed, such as completing a purchase or registering for a download.

CPC (cost per click)   Paying for advertising and media exposure on the basis of ad clicks received, as recorded by the ad-serving platform.

CPM (**cost per thousand impressions**)   A means of paying for online media based on the impressions or number of times an ad is present on a Web page. CPM literally means *cost per mille*, where *mille* is the Latin word for *thousand*, so CPM refers to buying impressions in lots of 1,000. A $10 CPM means spending $10 for 1,000 impressions of your ad. Note that the word impression is commonly assumed to mean that a person saw the ad, when in reality many online ads are never actually looked at by the user even though they were present on the page.

CTR (**click-through rate**)   The percentage of time an ad is clicked on in relation to the number of times it is displayed (impressions).

display ad   A larger set of online advertising wherein the advertising is visual in nature. Examples include banner ads, interstitial ads, and rich media ads with interactivity.

e-mail marketing   Using e-mail communications for explicit marketing purposes.

e-marketing   E-marketing is the same as e-mail marketing in most countries. But in some cultures, it is used to refer to the entire realm of online or electronic marketing.

impression   An advertisement being recorded as present on a page. It is often thought to be an advertisement being viewed by a person, but many online ad impressions are not actually seen by Web site visitors.

natural search   *See organic search.*

organic search   The main body of result listings on a search engine. Organic listings are not paid for and cannot be influenced directly by paying a fee to a search engine. Organic listings are ordered by a search engine's algorithm based on the keyword entered and the contents of the search engine's index. The algorithm tries to perceive what the searcher wants to find and orders the results from the index with the most relevant pages for that search at the top of the list.

performance marketing   The philosophy of marketing that is driven by data and strives to gain higher and higher levels of business performance and value through the application of measurement, testing, learning, and measurement cycles.

PPC (**pay per click**)   *Same as CPC (cost per click).*

SEM (**search engine marketing**)   Paying for traffic by buying ads in search engine results. *Also called sponsored search.*

SEO (**search engine optimization**)   Adjusting the use of terms in your Web pages to better match the terms that users use, to increase the chances of getting a high rank in search results.

search marketing   The general field of marketing and advertising that occurs on search engines. Includes organic search and paid or sponsored search.

social media   Media that is highly social in nature. Examples include blogs with comments and user feedback, Facebook, Twitter, MySpace, social bookmarking sites, and user-driven product review sites.

sponsored search   The paid placements of advertising that occur on search engine result pages to the side and top of the organic results. *Also called SEM.*

viral marketing   Marketing efforts that drive the rapid spread of a product, offer, Web site, piece of content, and so on by one person to another through word of mouth (talking, sharing, in social media, and so on). Viral marketing spreads like a virus — spreading from person to person as they view and share the marketing materials.

Google Analytics Dimension Definitions

The following dimension definitions are based on the Google Analytics Data Export API documentation. These definitions apply both to data within the Google Analytics reports as well as the Data Export API. (You can see these definitions at `www.analyticsformarketers.com/s/ ga-dimensions`.)

Visitor dimensions

`ga:browser`   The names of browsers used by visitors to your Web site. For example, `Internet Explorer` and `Firefox`.

`ga:browserVersion`   The browser versions used by visitors to your Web site. For example, `2.0.0.14`.

`ga:city`   The cities of Web site visitors, derived from their IP addresses. The City field falls in a hierarchy of geographical groupings used in Google Analytics, which proceeds in the following order: Continent, Subcontinent, Country, Region, Subregion, and City.

`ga:connectionSpeed`   The qualitative network connection speeds of Web site visitors. For example, `T1`, `DSL`, `Cable`, and `Dialup`.

`ga:continent`   The continents of Web site visitors, derived from IP addresses.

`ga:country`   The countries of Web site visitors, derived from IP addresses.

`ga:date`   The date of the visit. An integer in the form *yyyymmdd*.

`ga:day`   The day of the month from 01 to 31.

`ga:daysSinceLastVisit`   The number of days elapsed since visitors last visited your Web site. It is used to calculate visitor loyalty.

`ga:flashVersion`   The versions of Flash supported by visitors' browsers, including minor versions.

`ga:hostname`   The hostnames that visitors used to reach your Web site. In other words, if some visitors use `www.googlestore.com` to reach your Web site, this string appears as one of the hostnames used to reach your Web site. However, if other visitors also come to your Web site via `googlestore.com` or via an IP redirect from a search engine result (`66.102.9.104`), those values will also be present in this field.

`ga:hour`   A two-digit hour of the day ranging from 00 to 23 in the time zone configured for the account. This value is also corrected for daylight savings time, adhering to all local rules for daylight savings time. If your time zone follows daylight savings time, there will be an apparent bump in the number of visits during the change-over hour for the day per year when that hour repeats. A corresponding hour with zero visits will occur at the opposite changeover. (Google Analytics does not track visitor time more precisely than hours.)

ga:javaEnabled   Indicates Java support for visitors' browsers. The possible values are Yes and No.

ga:language   The language provided by the HTTP request for the browser. Values are given as an ISO-639 code (for example, en-gb for British English).

ga:latitude   The approximate latitude of the visitor's city. Locations north of the equator are represented by positive values and locations south of the equator by negative values.

ga:longitude   The approximate longitude of the visitor's city. Locations east of the meridian are represented by positive values and locations west of the meridian by negative values.

ga:month   The month of the visit. A two-digit integer from 01 to 12.

ga:networkDomain   The domain name of the ISPs used by visitors to your Web site.

ga:networkLocation   The name of service providers used to reach your Web site. For example, if most visitors to your Web site come via the major service providers for cable Internet, you will see the names of those cable service providers in this element.

ga:operatingSystem   The operating system used by your visitors. For example, Windows, Linux, Macintosh, iPhone, and iPod.

ga:operatingSystemVersion   The version of the operating system used by your visitors, such as xp for Windows XP and ppc for PowerPC-based Macintosh.

ga:pageDepth   The number of pages visited by visitors during a session (visit). The value is a histogram that counts pageviews across a range of possible values. In this calculation, all visits will have at least one pageview, and some percentage of visits will have more.

ga:region   The region of Web site visitors, derived from IP addresses. In the U.S., a region is a state, such as New York.

ga:screenColors   The color depth of visitors' monitors, as retrieved from the visitor's browser. For example 4-bit, 8-bit, 24-bit, and undefined-bit.

ga:screenResolution   The screen resolution of visitors' monitors, as retrieved from the visitor's browser. For example: 1024x738.

ga:subContinent   The subcontinent of Web site visitors, derived from IP addresses. For example, Polynesia and Northern Europe.

ga:userDefinedValue   The value provided when you define custom visitor segments for your Web site. For more information, see http://code.google.com/apis/analytics/docs/tracking/gaTrackingVisitors.html#customVisitors.

ga:visitCount   Number of visits to your Web site. This is calculated by determining the number of visitor sessions.

ga:visitLength   The length of a visit to your Web site measured in seconds and reported in second increments. The value returned is a string. To replicate the Length of Visit report in the user interface, after requesting the data, you can convert the string value to a number and sum the visits for a group of visit durations.

ga:visitorType   A value indicating if visitors are new or returning. The possible values are New Visitor and Returning Visitor.

ga:week   The week of the visit. A two-digit number from 01 to 52.

`ga:year`   The year of the visit. A four-digit year from 2005 to the current year.

Campaign dimensions

`ga:adContent`   The first line of the text for your online ad campaign. If you are using mad libs for your AdWords content, this field displays the keywords you provided for the mad libs keyword match.

`ga:adGroup`   The ad groups that you have identified for your campaign keywords.

`ga:adSlot`   The position of the advertisement as it appears on the host page. For example, the online advertising position might be side or top.

`ga:adSlotPosition`   The order of the online advertisement as it appears along with other ads in the position on the page. For example, the ad might appear on the right side of the page and be the third ad from the top.

`ga:campaign`   The names of the online ad campaign you use for your Web site.

`ga:keyword`   The keywords used by visitors to reach your Web site, via both paid ads and through search engine results.

`ga:medium`   The type of referral to your Web site. For example, when referring sources to your Web site are search engines, there are a number of possible mediums that can be used from a search engine referral: from a search result (organic) and from an online ad on the search results page (cpc, ppc, cpa, cpm, cpv, and cpp).

`ga:referralPath`   The path of the referring URL. If someone places a link to your Web site on his or her Web site, this element contains the path of the page that contains the referring link.

`ga:source`   The domain (such as google.com) of the source referring the visitor to your Web site. The value for this dimension sometimes contains a port address as well.

Content dimensions

`ga:exitPagePath`   The last page of the session (the *exit page*) for your visitors.

`ga:landingPagePath`   The path component of the first page in a user's session (the *landing page*).

`ga:pagePath`   A page on your Web site specified by path and/or query parameters.

`ga:pageTitle`   The title for a page, as specified in the `<title></title>` element of the HTML document.

`ga:secondPagePath`   The path component of the second page in a user's session.

Ecommerce dimensions

`ga:affiliation`   Typically used to designate a supplying company, brick-and-mortar location, or other product affiliation.

`ga:daysToTransaction`   The number of days between users' purchases and the related campaigns that led to the purchases.

`ga:productCategory`   Any product variations (such as size and color) for purchased items as supplied by your ecommerce application.

ga:productName   The product name for purchased items as supplied by your ecommerce tracking method.

ga:productSku   The product codes for purchased items as you have defined them in your ecommerce tracking application.

ga:transactionId   The transaction ID for the shopping cart purchase as supplied by your ecommerce tracking method.

ga:visitsToTransaction   The number of visits between users' purchases and the related campaigns that led to the purchases.

Internal search dimensions

ga:searchCategory   The categories used for the internal search if you have this enabled for your profile. For example, you might have product categories such as electronics, furniture, and clothing.

ga:searchDestinationPage   A page that the user visited after performing an internal Web site search.

ga:searchKeyword   Search terms used by Web site visitors on your internal site search.

ga:searchKeywordRefinement   Subsequent keyword search terms or strings entered by users after a given initial string search.

ga:searchStartPage   A page where the user initiated an internal site search.

ga:searchUsed   A value that separates visitor activity depending upon whether internal search activity occurred or did not occur. Values are Visits With Site Search and Visits Without Site Search.

Navigation dimensions

ga:nextPagePath   A page on your Web site that was visited *after* another page on your Web site.

ga:previousPagePath   A page on your Web site that was visited *before* another page on your Web site.

Event dimensions

ga:eventCategory   A string containing the category of the event.

ga:eventAction   A string containing the action of the event.

ga:eventLabel   A string containing the label of the event.

Custom variable dimensions

There are five custom variables available in the API. You can request a custom variable value by using its corresponding number (from 1 to 5). For example, to get the value for the custom variable set to 2, use ga:customVarValue2.

ga:customVarName(n)   A string containing the name for the requested custom variable.

ga:customVarValue(n)   A string containing the value for the requested custom variable number.

Google Analytics Metric Definitions

The following metrics definitions are based on the Google Analytics Data Export API documentation. These definitions apply both to data within the Google Analytics reports as well as to the Data Export API. (You can see these definitions at www.analyticsformarketers.com/s/ga-metrics.)

Visitor metrics

ga:bounces   The total number of single-page visits to your Web site.

ga:entrances   The number of entrances to your Web site. The value is always equal to the number of visits when aggregated over your entire Web site. Thus, this metric is most useful when combined with dimensions such as ga:landingPagePath, at which point entrances as a metric indicates the number of times a particular page served as an entrance to your Web site.

ga:exits   The number of exits from your Web site. As with entrances, it is always equal to the number of visits when aggregated over your entire Web site.

ga:newVisits   The number of visitors whose visit to your Web site was marked as a first-time visit.

ga:pageviews   The total number of pageviews for your Web site when aggregated over the selected dimension. For example, if you select this metric with ga:pagePath, it returns the number of pageviews for each page.

ga:timeOnPage   How long a visitor spent on a particular page or set of pages. Calculated by subtracting the initial view time for a particular page from the initial view time for a subsequent page. Thus, this metric does not apply to exit pages for your Web site. The value from this metric is returned in the XML traffic log as a string, with the value represented in total seconds. Different client libraries have various ways of representing this value, such as a double, float, long, and string.

ga:timeOnSite   The total duration of visitor sessions over the selected dimension. For example, suppose you combine this field with a particular ad campaign. In this case, the metric displays the total duration of all visitor sessions for those visitors who came to your Web site via a particular ad campaign. The value from this metric is returned in the XML traffic log as a string, with the value represented in total seconds. Different client libraries have various ways of representing this value, such as a double, float, long, and string.

ga:visitors   Total number of visitors to your Web site for the requested time period.

ga:visits   The total number of visits over the selected dimension. A visit consists of a single user session.

Campaign metrics

ga:adClicks   The total number of times users have clicked on an ad to reach your Web site.

ga:adCost   Derived cost for the advertising campaign. The currency for this value is based on the currency that you set in your AdWords account.

ga:cpc   Cost to advertiser per click.

ga:cpm   Cost per thousand impressions.

ga:ctr   The click-through rate for your ad. This is equal to the number of clicks divided by the number of impressions for your ad (that is, how many times users clicked on one of your ads in pages where that ad appeared).

ga:impressions   The total number of campaign impressions.

ga:uniquePageviews   The number of different (unique) pages within a visit, summed across all visits

Content metrics

ga:uniquePageviews   The number of different (unique) pages within a visit, summed across all visits

Ecommerce metrics

The currency value for all revenue-based metrics adhere to the guidelines described in the Google ecommerce guidelines (see `http://code.google.com/apis/analytics/docs/tracking/gaTrackingEcommerce.html` for the `ga.js` API).

ga:itemRevenue   Total revenue from purchased product items on your Web site. See the tracking API reference at `http://code.google.com/apis/analytics/docs/gaJS/gaJSApi.html` for `_addItem()` for additional information.

ga:itemQuantity   The total number of items purchased. For example, if users purchase two Frisbees and five tennis balls, they have purchased seven items total.

ga:transactions   The total number of transactions.

ga:transactionRevenue   The total sale revenue, including shipping and tax, if provided in the transaction. See the documentation for `_addTrans()` in the tracking API reference at `http://code.google.com/apis/analytics/docs/gaJS/gaJSApi.html` for additional information.

ga:transactionShipping   The total cost of shipping.

ga:transactionTax   The total amount of tax.

ga:uniquePurchases   The number of product sets purchased. For example, if users purchase two Frisbees and five tennis balls from your site, they purchased two product sets.

Internal search metrics

ga:searchDepth   The average number of subsequent pageviews made on your site after a use of your internal search feature.

ga:searchDuration   The visit duration to your site where a use of your internal search feature occurred.

ga:searchExits   The number of exits on your site that occurred following a search result from your internal search feature.

ga:searchRefinements   The number of refinements made on an internal search.

ga:searchUniques   The number of visitors to your site who used your internal search feature.

ga:searchVisits The total number of visits to your site where a use of your internal search feature occurred.

Goal metrics

There are 20 goals available in the API. You can request a goal value by using its corresponding number (from 1 to 20). For example, if you want the number of goal starts for goal 13, you would use ga:goal13Starts.

ga:goal(n)Completions The total number of completions for the requested goal number.

TABLE B.1

utm.gif Request Parameters

Variable	Description	Example value
utmac	The account string. It appears on all requests.	utmac=UA-2202604-2
utmcc	The cookie values. This request parameter sends all the cookies requested from the page.	utmcc=__utma%3D117243.1695285.22%3B%2B __utmz%3D117945243.1202416366.21.10. utmcsr%3Db%7C utmccn%3D(referral)%7C utmcmd%3D referral%7C utmcct%3D%252Fissue%3B%2B
utmcn	This starts a new campaign session. Either utmcn or utmcr is present on any given request. It changes the campaign tracking data; but does not start a new session	utmcn=1
utmcr	This indicates a repeat campaign visit. It is set when any subsequent clicks occur on the same link. Either utmcn or utmcr is present on any given request.	utmcr=1
utmcs	The language encoding for the browser. Some browsers don't set this, in which case it is set to –.	utmcs=ISO-8859-1
utmdt	The page title, which is a URL-encoded string.	utmdt=analytics%20page%20test
utme	The event tracking data parameter.	The value is encoded.
utmfl	The Flash version	utmfl=9.0%20r48&
utmhn	The host name, which is a URL-encoded string.	utmhn=x343.gmodules.com
utmipc	The product code. This is the SKU code for a given product.	utmipc=989898ajssi
utmipn	The product name, which is a URL-encoded string.	utmipn=tee%20shirt
utmipr	The unit price. It is set at the item level, and its value is set to numbers only in U.S. currency format.	utmipr=17100.32
utmiqt	The quantity.	utmiqt=4

`ga:goalCompletionsAll`   The total number of completions for all goals defined for your profile.

`ga:goal(n)Starts`   The total number of starts for the requested goal number.

`ga:goalStartsAll`   The total number of starts for all goals defined for your profile.

`ga:goal(n)Value`   The total numeric value for the requested goal number.

`ga:goalValueAll`   The total numeric value for all goals defined for your profile.

TABLE B.1 (CONTINUED)

`utm.gif` Request Parameters

Variable	Description	Example value
utmiva	The variations of an item, such as `large`, `medium`, `small`, `pink`, `white`, `black`, or `green`. The string is URL-encoded.	`utmiva=red;`
utmje	This indicates if browser is Java-enabled. `1` is true.	`utmje=1`
utmn	The unique ID generated for each `utm.gif` request to prevent caching of the `utm.gif` image.	`utmn=1142651215`
utmp	The page request of the current page.	`utmp=/testDirectory/myPage.html`
utmr	The referral, a complete URL.	`utmr=http://www.example.com/aboutUs/index.php?var=selected`
utmsc	The screen color depth	`utmsc=24-bit`
utmsr	The screen resolution	`utmsr=2400x1920&`
utmt	A special type variable applied to events, transactions, items, and user-defined variables.	`utmt=Dog%20Owner`
utmtci	The billing city.	`utmtci=San%20Diego`
utmtco	The billing country.	`utmtco=United%20Kingdom`
utmtid	The order ID, a URL-encoded string.	`utmtid=a2343898`
utmtrg	The billing region, a URL-encoded string.	`utmtrg=New%20Brunswick`
utmtsp	The shipping cost, in values such as for unit and price.	`utmtsp=23.95`
utmtst	The affiliation. It is typically used for brick-and-mortar applications in e-commerce.	`utmtst=google%20mtv%20store`
utmtto	The total, in values such as for unit and price.	`utmtto=334.56`
utmttx	The tax, in values such as for unit and price.	`utmttx=29.16`
utmul	The browser language.	`utmul=pt-br`
utmwv	The tracking code version.	`utmwv=1`

Events metrics

`ga:totalEvents`   The total number of events for the profile, across all categories.

`ga:uniqueEvents`   The total number of unique events for the profile, across all categories.

`ga:eventValue`   The total value of events for the profile.

`utm.gif` request parameters

Table B.1 contains the full listing of the possible parameters passed in via the `utm.gif` request. Not all parameters are passed in with every execution of the tracking code, because some apply only to certain conditions, such as campaign referrals or shopping carts. When using this reference, keep in mind that you are looking for those variables that most commonly apply to the page or request you are investigating. (You can see these definitions at `www.analyticsformarketers.com/s/utm-gif-parameters.`)

Additional Glossary Resources

Ask Apache Web development glossary: `www.analyticsformarketers.com/s/ask-apache.`

E-consultancy Web analytics and optimization resources: `www.analyticsformarketers.com/s/e-consultancy.`

SEMPO (Search Engine Marketing Professionals Organization) search engine marketing glossary: `www.analyticsformarketers.com/s/sempo.`

SEO Book Glossary of SEO Terms: `www.analyticsformarketers.com/s/seobook.`

SEOmoz Complete Glossary of Essential SEO Jargon: `www.analyticsformarketers.com/s/seomoz-jargon.`

The W3C Consortium glossaries: `www.analyticsformarketers.com/s/w3c.`

W3 Schools Web glossary: `www.analyticsformarketers.com/s/w3-schools.`

Web Analytics Association standards: `www.analyticsformarketers.com/s/waa-standard.`

—

Index

W

X

Y

Z

Google Analytics Individual Qualification Test Coupon

The Google Analytics Individual Qualification Test (GA IQ) allows individuals to demonstrate proficiency in Google Analytics.

The curriculum was developed by Google Analytics experts and is continually updated by Google to ensure that it is in synch with the latest Google Analytics features.

Free online training and access to the GA IQ test can be accessed at www.conversionuniversity.com. Agencies, Certified Partners, and other organizations can point their staff to the GA IQ training and the GA IQ exam to verify their proficiency. Students can also benefit from the free training and then prove their proficiency by taking the test.

We hope that readers of this book will want to further their knowledge of Google Analytics by accessing the online training materials at www.conversionuniversity.com. We are happy to offer a 50 percent coupon to the first 10,000 people who wish to take the GA IQ test afterwards. Just enter **PerformanceMarketing** in the Promotional Code box when purchasing the Google Analytics Individual Qualification Test.

Happy Testing!

—*Eva Woo, Product Marketing Manager, Google Global Certified Partners*